Management, Uncertainty, and Accounting

Akira Nishimura

Management, Uncertainty, and Accounting

Case Studies, Theoretical Models, and Useful Strategies

palgrave
macmillan

Akira Nishimura
Beppu University
Oita-City, Oita, Japan

ISBN 978-981-10-8988-6 ISBN 978-981-10-8989-3 (eBook)
https://doi.org/10.1007/978-981-10-8989-3

Library of Congress Control Number: 2018944442

Cover illustration: © Johannes Hulsch / EyeEm
Cover design by Ran Shauli

Printed on acid-free paper

This Palgrave Macmillan imprint is published by the registered company Springer Nature Singapore Pte Ltd.
The registered company address is: 152 Beach Road, #21-01/04 Gateway East, Singapore 189721, Singapore

Preface and Acknowledgments

"What is accounting?" has been my research theme for a long time, ever since Professor T. Okabe, my dissertation advisor, posed this question to me at the graduate school of Kyoto University. This question has extended to an inquiry into the essential nature of management accounting and management since I made management accounting research my career. As part of this inquiry, I wrote *Management Accounting: Feed-Forward and Asian Perspectives* (Palgrave Macmillan, 2003), in which, based on the practical connection between the creative control function of management and the cognitive control function of accounting, I defined the function of management accounting as cognitive control for business value creation. From this, I analyzed new management accounting practices and theories in the 1970s and their future directions from a feed-forward viewpoint and through comparative studies of Western and Asian management accounting, after clarifying the fundamental development of traditional management accounting. Coinciding with major global changes in the political economy over the 14 years since this publication, business management and accounting systems have undergone great changes and become more complicated. As the essential natures of these systems become more intangible and incomprehensible with greater uncertainty, it is increasingly necessary to examine them in relation to uncertainty and risks from the well-honed feed-forward viewpoint. The present book examines the relationship of management and management accounting with uncertainty and explains the contemporary situation and structure of management accounting based on this examination.

This book thus aims to clarify this relationship fundamentally through a historical and global examination of contemporary management accounting and to understand both their positive features (harmony and social creativity) and negative applications (discord and private manipulation).

To clarify the thesis of this book, it is desirable to sketch the position and point of each chapter briefly in the context of the overall conceptual framework of the book. In reference to the relationship of management and management accounting with uncertainty, Chap. 1 introduces basic concepts such as workmanship, emulation, control, scientific management, and standard costing through the advanced early twentieth-century theories of Taylor, Harrison, Veblen, and Knight. Following these theories, this book presupposes uncertainty as an unavoidable phenomenon in human society, while remaining convinced of the human intelligence and power to control it. Neither firms nor human beings can escape uncertainty because the human instinct for workmanship and a propensity for emulating each other in efficiency easily become negative work habits ("irksomeness of labor" in *Veblen*) and wasteful and inefficient competition in a competitive ownership society. Firms cannot avoid uncertainty as long as their subsistence relies on competitive production. However, they also have instinctive intelligence and power to control risk and uncertainty through workmanship and emulation for efficiency. Management and management accounting take the form of measurement, evaluation, and control to transform conflict and discord into harmony and stability, and their development represents the process by which humans and society have endeavored to cope with risk and uncertainty to secure reasonable production and distribution for their existence.

However, emulation for efficiency has become the emulation for the perpetual ownership of wealth beyond harmony and stability, causing intensified uncertainty. This also results from human propensities. Management and accounting are abused in this case, and accounting in particular is improperly used to deceive society in the form of window dressing accounting. These behaviors degrade business value. Society thus asks accountants to secure business value through harmony between management accounting and financial accounting and to make trustworthy disclosures of the corporate financial situation. Enterprises must organically manage opportunity and risk, and managers should equip themselves with virtuous ethics through regulation, which plays an important role in controlling the enterprise's risks and uncertainty.

Accordingly, Chap. 2 examines the contemporary situation of enterprise governance and internal control systems and their meanings, with reference to enterprise risk management. This examination is closely related to the contemporary function of management and accounting—transforming conflict and discord into harmony and stability. In this case, how does the special cognitive control function of profit relate to uncertainty? When management and accounting must plan for and control opportunity, risk, and uncertainty for strategic management, profit management becomes more significant; even if profit is measured by a feedback method, its planning must be practically founded on the feed-forward recognition of opportunity and risk that is finally incarnated as accounting income. Under present global and forward-looking business strategies, enterprises must forecast and control profit opportunities and risk or invisible value that is transformed into profit or loss. If managers cannot recognize this transformation of business value from opportunity and risk to accounting income, they cannot properly make strategic decisions to create business value. Regarding this, Chap. 3 discusses the concept of business value. Simultaneously, opportunity is qualified as profit opportunity in terms of business strategy from the same viewpoint of probability as risk. Both profit opportunity and risk hold important positions in strategic profit management. I thus adopt business value as a concept that connects profit opportunity and risk with accounting profits in business management. This examination raises the next subject: the meaning of accounting (cognitive control function) that plans, measures, analyzes, and evaluates their intricate relations.

To address this, Chap. 4 first defines the concept of uncertainty, and then profit opportunity and enterprise risk, referring to representative scholars in the fields of business management and accounting. This clarifies how management and accounting recognize and control uncertainty in business planning, implementation, and evaluation. This discussion obtains the important meanings of Demski's ex post programming model in accounting control of uncertainty, in which the senior managers' forecast ability and the control ability of middle and lower management can be measured and evaluated through forecast profit (or opportunity) variance and opportunity cost variance by using linear programming and profit variance analysis. This model is forward-looking in controlling uncertainty and enterprise risk, even though it is structured on feedback control. This book considers the epoch-making idea of this model on risk management in comparison with traditional management accounting and, with continual reference to this model, analyzes the features and structures of contemporary enterprise risk management.

Chapter 5 practically examines profit opportunity and risk management in connection with the strategic innovation and organizational structure (i.e., resources and organizational capability) of an enterprise that innovates, because the probability of profit opportunity and enterprise risk cannot be predicted, regardless of innovation and organizational structure. This book thus pays special attention to Simon's "opportunity space" and to Haynie's concept, which considers the relation between opportunity and resources. This chapter examines the exploitation of profit opportunity and the elimination of enterprise risk in the three latest innovations in production and management: the lean production method, agile supply chain systems, and global innovation. The chapter simultaneously elucidates the function of management accounting and profit design systems as an expansive form of cost design, linking these with innovations and continuous improvements (Kaizen in Japanese), in terms of profit opportunity/risk-based variance analysis and feed-forward control. This examination leads to a strategic management control model that copes with uncertainty through opportunity/risk variance analysis and innovation or improvement under a cycle of feed-forward and feedback control.

Moreover, the present meaning of comprehensive opportunity/risk management must be studied from the perspective of the strategic management accounting model. The strategic management accounting model plays an important role in preparing proactive information and providing managers with variance information to exploit profit opportunities, transform risk into profit opportunity, and minimize risk. Previously, some accounting scholars have described the gap between strategic and organizational requirements and financial accounting information as a defect in traditional management accounting. From this, they have developed activity-based costing (ABC) and balanced scorecard (BSC) based on nonfinancial information. However, even if an accounting system measures nonfinancial information, as long as it depends on feedback control, there will be a critical gap between information and forward-looking strategies, and the system will be useless for strategic and forward-looking organizational management. Considering these gaps, strategic management accounting must be forward-looking, globally cognitive, and comprehensively control oriented (Chap. 6). Thus, Chaps. 5 and 6 clarify the direction and problems of contemporary management accounting.

Chapter 7 examines cost design as a recent strategic management accounting method from a forward-looking, global viewpoint. As consciousness of environmental protection and health and safety deepens, some Japanese companies spatially and temporally introduce risk management into cost design, for example, transforming it into an environmentally conscious cost design system that includes supply chain and product life cycle costing. This transformation aims at reducing risk in the production process from suppliers to their own factories and exploiting profit opportunity through synthetic risk management, based on the integration of high quality and low cost. This chapter introduces an environmentally conscious type of cost design seen in Japanese enterprises and examines the situation of Japanese enterprises in supply chains and environmental protection from the viewpoint of cost and risk management.

Chapter 8 touches upon a comprehensive profit opportunity and lost opportunity control (COLC) model into which profit opportunity/risk management and feed-forward control are integrated, after summarizing the cognitive control of uncertainty in existing management accounting and reevaluating and extending the meaning and structure of cost design with reference to the theoretical and practical development of management and accounting. This COLC model, as well as unified management of profit opportunity and risk, represents a framework of contemporary management accounting that copes with uncertainty in pursuit of sustainable business growth. The chapter examines the risk recognition of Japanese firms and suggests the application of the model to risk management and its disclosure (accountability). Chapter 9 applies this model to foreign exchange risk management, which uses the COLC model to plan for profit opportunity and risk, encourage proactive measures (i.e., *Kaizen*, continuous improvement) against financial risks, and provide protection against unmeasurable change in derivatives and hedge accounting. Integration of the COLC model with a profit design system allows wider application of management accounting as a result of its strong strategic direction and proactive cognitive control function.

In the next chapter, before turning to the examination of Chinese business management and enterprise risk management, it is helpful for further development of management and management accounting to describe the synthetic relationship between value, environment, risk, cost design, and profit design as its extended figure to which this book refers in connection with uncertainty.

As described above, this book clarifies the meanings of strategic management accounting under strong economic uncertainty by shifting the examination process from enterprise governance through the relation between uncertainty and management accounting to the COLC model and the unified management of profit opportunity and risk. The remaining two chapters describe changes in management accounting and contemporary enterprise risk management in Chinese enterprises, because no planned economy or state-controlled society can be immune to uncertainty or risk, as long as there are negative labor habits ("irksomeness of labor" in *Veblen*) and wasteful, inefficient competition. Chapter 11 depicts changing management and accounting systems in Chinese firms. It describes expanding strategic businesses in the global economy, progressing from Chinese domestic markets to Asian, African, and Western markets by means of governmental support and price strategies, as well as modular production and cheap labor costs. In relation to these businesses, I refer to the reorganization of state-owned enterprises through absorbing social capital and private enterprises. Correspondingly, as competitive Chinese enterprises have grown in the international market, a gap has also expanded between these global state-managed enterprises and small- to medium-sized enterprises. The business model of global enterprises using cheap labor, modular production, and agile supply chains to increase competitive power internationally has overtaken the Japanese style of self-developed technology and management in the international market in terms of short-term price strategies. However, this method cannot also escape risks and uncertainty.

Thus, Chap. 12 investigates characteristics and structures of government-based enterprise risk management in contrast to the COLC model. As governmental strategy in China shifts from 'absorbing foreign power' to 'going global', enterprise risk intermingles deeply with political risk, and it becomes more difficult to recognize and control enterprise profit opportunities and enterprise risk proactively by using accounting information and methods. Governmental support and the evasion policy of bankruptcy in the securities market obscure the relation between profit opportunity and risk, simultaneously expanding, for example, bank profit opportunities and steel company risks. The steel company can exist under heavy obligations while continuing to pay rent and the bank regards this as a profit opportunity. Even so, social risk and uncertainty substantially increase. As it is increasingly difficult to recognize and control true enterprise risk while strongly integrating enterprise strategies with governmental policy, the COLC model has become increasingly ineffective in China. Thus, a completely different model from the COLC model will be needed in the future.

It follows from the above mentioned that uncertainty had profoundly influenced management and management accounting in their structures and development, while these systems have grappled with uncertainty and risk as the object of control for a long time. Moreover, as far as the Western and Japanese enterprises are concerned, the COLC model and the unified management of profit opportunity and risk exactly express the latest development in enterprise risk management and the control of uncertainty.

Lastly, I would like to express my own devotion to this research and my gratitude to many researchers and friends for their heartfelt support. Honestly, I do not yet completely understand the essential nature of bookkeeping and accounting, despite having continually studied them for over 60 years, since I first encountered them in high school. Even so, I am convinced that we can logically understand them only by gaining a clearer conception of workmanship and control, emulation and management, uncertainty, harmony, and cooperation. This book was motivated by this conviction. Although the bookkeeping that forms the foundations of accounting is such an intelligible method as to be able to keep accounts after studying a simple entry method based on the two rules of addition and subtraction, questioning the fundamental truths of its procedures leads one into a labyrinth. No calculation system is better at simultaneously recognizing and controlling stocks (balance sheet) and flows (income statement) and synthesizing economic activities at a given point of time into periodical accounting than double-entry bookkeeping of debit and credit accounts. This system allows bookkeepers, accountants, and managers to recognize and control economic activities simultaneously. Considering the unsuccessful history of resistance to attempts to replace 'debtor and creditor' accounts with 'increase and decrease' or 'revenue and expenditure' accounts, the double-entry bookkeeping with 'debtor and creditor' accounts is a historical crystallization of human instinct and propensities. Still, over the course of its historical development, the bookkeeping has taken such multifarious and complicated forms that it is difficult to grasp its substance. In particular, when the bookkeeping takes the modern forms of financial and management accounting systems to discharge accountability through disclosure and controllability, its substance becomes invisible because of the capital and management relationships in an organization.

Contemporary bookkeeping and accounting are so complicated that human beings can be strongly influenced by their application. We should discern the substance of bookkeeping and accounting scientifically and apply it to human well-being and social harmony. However, we are apt to make light of scientific and historical examinations of this substance, owing to the simplicity and lucidity of the system and the convenience of profitability recognition. This book is a clue in the mystery, a scientific approach to the complexity of simplicity.

I end this preface by expressing my heartfelt gratitude to some people who were key to the fruition of this book. When I wrote the papers comprising the first half of the book, Professor Ibrahim Kamal Abdul Rahman (Kuala Lumpur business school, Malaysia), Professor Normah Omar and Associate Professor Wee Shu Hui (MARA University of Technology, Malaysia), Professor Chan Yoke Kai (the Singapore University of Social Science University), Professor Maliah Sulaiman (International Islamic University, Malaysia), and Professor Roger Willett (Victoria University of Wellington, New Zealand) actively supported my research and the establishment of the Asia-Pacific Management Accounting Association. In relation to the papers comprising the latter half of the book, I gratefully acknowledge helpful discussions I had with Professor Emeritus Masayasu Tanaka (Tokyo University of Science, Japan), Professor Noriyuki Imai (Meijo University, Japan), and Professor Johei Oshita (Kyushu University, Japan) on cost design, risk management, and the contemporary structures of management accounting. My special thanks are due to Professor Yoshihiro Ito (Waseda University) for permission to use diagrams regarding ECCD. I also thank Professor Shinsuke Wada (Osaka University of Commerce, Japan) and Associate Professor Shunsuke Adachi (Shimonoseki City University, Japan) for their valuable comments on my papers. I am indebted to Professor Okihiro Maruta (Kyushu University, Japan) and Associate Professor Nobuhiko Nakaya (Nagoya University, Japan) for his assistance in collecting the material. Particularly to Professor J. Oshita, I express the highest gratitude for his long academic support and friendship.

I am most grateful to Kyushu University Library and Beppu University Library for their permission to use and consult their materials, literature, and electronic journals, without which I could not have finalized the papers comprising this book. I am also thankful to the editors and reviewers at the *Asia-Pacific Management Accounting Journal*, the *Journal of Management Control*, and the *International Journal of Business and Management* for giving me opportunity to publish my papers and for their useful comments and suggestions for improving them. This book was based on the papers published in these journals. The extensive research needed to complete this book was made possible through Grants-in-Aid for Science Research from the Japan Society for the Promotion of Science, which generously supported my research many times. I thus acknowledge here the generosity of that organization.

I am most grateful to various copyright holders for their permission to use the materials in this book. Every effort has been made to contact all copyright holders for usage permissions, but some may have been inadvertently omitted. If this is the case, the publishers will be pleased to make the necessary arrangements at the first opportunity.

Finally, this book was made possible largely by the support and devotion of my wife, Junko.

Oita-City, Japan Akira Nishimura

Contents

List of Abbreviations

CO_2	Carbon dioxide
COLC	Comprehensive Opportunity and Lost Opportunity Control
COSO	Committee of Sponsoring Organizations of the Treadway Commission
DFE	Design for environment
ECCD	Environmentally conscious cost design
ECM	Environmentally conscious manufacturing
ECP	Environmentally conscious product
EDINET	Electronic Disclosure for Investors, 'NET work'
GPS	Global Positioning System
IFRS	International Financial Reporting Standards
JAMS	Japan Association of Management System Researchers
LCA	Life cycle assessment
LCC	Life cycle costing
METI	Japanese Ministry of Economy, Trade and Industry
MOE	Japanese Ministry of the Environment
NLI Research Institute	Nippon Life Insurance Research Institute
PAIB	Professional Accountants in Business Committee
RFID	Radio-frequency identifierfication
ROM	Return on management
RPR	Ratio of Net Profit to Revenue

SASAC	State-owned Assets Supervision Administration Committee
TRC	Tokyo Marine & Nichido Risk Consulting, Co. Ltd.
UHF	Ultra high frequency
VBM	Value-based management
VBMA	Value-based management accounting

List of Figures

List of Tables

CHAPTER 1

Introduction

1.1 Fundamental Issues of This Book

This book aims to examine the relationship of management and management accounting with uncertainty and to clarify the changing forms that management and management accounting have taken as different types and situations of uncertainty arise. This chapter begins by sketching the basic contents of the book and the fundamental concepts on which they are based. The overview in this chapter is done through the lens of the leading theories of business and management at the beginning of the twentieth century; other chapters go into additional detail about the specific phases in management accounting that emerged in this conceptual framework.

In a capitalist society, management and management accounting have mainly been considered either *methods for business enterprises* to create and capture profits or merely *calculation techniques* that are not inherently linked with capitalism or *profit creation*. Although the social and technical aspects of these two views of management and management accounting are connected in a practical business enterprise, it is still important for theoretical research to ask whether management and management accounting fundamentally contribute to making a profitable business, or whether they are simply a general technique used by any organization rather than a fundamental characteristic of a profitable business. To start, we should first clarify the essential characteristics of management and management accounting, as well as their relation to social problems. This

A. Nishimura, *Management, Uncertainty, and Accounting*,
https://doi.org/10.1007/978-981-10-8989-3_1

may not be such a simple task, given that management and bookkeeping as a basis of accounting existed before the formation of capitalist society; scientific management, modern accounting, and management accounting developed as the development of the capitalist economy; and now management and management accounting are also used in socialist or state-controlled economies. Further, in capitalist economies they are closely linked with social problems such as risk management, supply chain management, and product life cycle costing. The key to understanding the essential characteristics of management accounting may be to look back over the basic theories of business enterprise and entrepreneurship from the beginning of the twentieth century when management accounting was established. This allows us to examine the relationship of management and management accounting with uncertainty, because uncertainty, which consists of unforeseeable events and foreseeable events to a certain extent in decision-making process, has exerted critical influence on the situations in which they are used and how their uses have changed over the years.

Unlike other animals, humans intentionally choose when and how to labor and, as Veblen (1898) indicates clearly, man is "in an eminent sense an intelligent agent" (p. 188) who not only acts in response to environmental stimuli but also mentally makes note of these habits and the propensity of these acts, appreciates their trends, and then puts the environmental forces around him to use in his life. This makes up the most important concept in Veblen's theory that "workmanship" is a human instinct (see Taka 2005). As long as humans undertake mental and physical work, the behavior of management and accounting also serves as a self-control function for efficiency (Nishimura 2003). Even before the advent of scientific management, workers demonstrated self-control and self-responsibility, that is, they planned work procedures and controlled their processes to achieve the desired goals. This self-control function was present in humans even with no formal supervision or wage system (Taylor 1911, p. 16). However, as the scientific management system developed historically, what was previously self-controlled has been divided into the work of labor and the work of planning and control, namely labor and management. Moreover, accounting also developed simultaneously to keep up with this evolution in management functions. Personal memory and basic record-keeping were replaced with accounting systems for measurement and evaluation. Even though it took different forms in each age, management accounting also originated from these accounting functions.

At the beginning of the twentieth century, Taylor systemized the principles of scientific management, which replaced the rules of thumb and self-taught methods previously used by workers. According to these principles, workers could be more efficient by working in cooperation with managers who planned for and controlled the work process. At the same time, standard costs were developed based on the exact amount of time of a task required and workers could accomplish their tasks efficiently and earn wages proportionate to their efficiency. Moreover, this also laid the foundation for the management accounting system. As management and management accounting are derived from 'workmanship', their methods and techniques are primarily human-centered. However, they were actually affected by social situation (labor slowdown and labor disputes), and at present they strongly show their social color. Therefore, there is a further point that needs to be clarified: how and why does such a fundamental characteristic as workmanship connect with contemporary subjects such as risk management, environmental protection, and sustainable growth? For this clarification, in next sections, management and management accounting are first analyzed from the viewpoint of uncertainty related to profit opportunity and enterprise risk (which later leads to profit/loss), and then are connected to the concepts of the entrepreneur and the businessman. Then, the historical development of management and management accounting is examined in terms of uncertainty and the control of uncertainty.

1.2 Management and Management Accounting

Scientific Management

To elucidate the fundamental characteristics of management and management accounting, it is advisable to examine them retroactively from the beginning of the twentieth century when these concepts were established, as their primitive and fundamental nature in their early days reveal characteristics that are harder to deduce from their complicated form in the contemporarily global economy. First, it may be useful to look specifically at the early conception of management. Taylor, a founder of scientific management, proposed a way to harmonize conflicts between employees and employers, and in turn to heighten social welfare by increasing wages and profits and by replacing workers' own way of informal rules of thumb and self-control with the principles of scientific management. These changes would then lead to improved product quality and increased productivity from increasing workers' efficiency and the support of management in terms of time and job management (e.g., standardization, education, and training) (Taylor 1911). He summarized the components of scientific management in the following five points:

> ***Science***, not rule of thumb;
> ***Harmony***, not discord;
> ***Cooperation***, not individualism;
> ***Maximum output***, in place of restricted output;
> ***The development of each person to his or her greatest efficiency and prosperity***. (Taylor 1911, p. 74: emphasis added)

With scientific management, a standard for one task can be developed by using time and motion studies, the most suitable workers can be selected for the task required, the most efficient standards can be established, and shared goals for all workers in an organization can be developed. Therefore, workers must continually be educated, trained, and enlightened by professional managers, and responsibilities and functions must be impartially divided between workmen and managers who cooperate with each other. As a result, workers can earn higher wages than previously and employers can also obtain the benefits of higher productivity and efficiency. At the same time, strikes and 'soldiering' are avoided and harmony is formed within the organization. (Taylor uses the term 'soldiering' to describe workers working in a slow and unmotivated manner, just as conscripted soldiers with no motivation to do more than the minimum required to obey an order.) This results in prosperity for individual businesses and society more broadly. In those days, labor dispute and 'soldiering' (slow working) might be unforeseeable or risk events in managers' decision-making process. Taylor tried to use scientific management based on 'science' and 'impartiality' to switch this discord to harmony (coordination and balance). This was surely the first step toward uncertainty control in management system.

Science, harmony, and impartiality, as well as *efficient* management, are key points on which to focus when looking at Taylor's principles of scientific management. Although Taylor placed much significance on the reduction of labor cost and the creation of the highest possible productivity, he also had a strong emphasis on science, harmony, and impartiality. His goal was to find principles for reforming workers' habits and eliminating soldiering and other irksome habits of labor ("the irksomeness of labor" in Veblen's phrase: see Veblen 1898). His main goal was not to simply develop a few management techniques, but to identify the *principles* of *scientific* management that are universally applicable to every organization (Taylor 1911, p. 11).

Management and Recording

Another point that Taylor emphasizes is the importance of *recording* (p. 62). The critical difference between scientific management and the old system based on informal rules of thumb is that the former includes establishing scientific standards for work, recording the actual performance, and comparing workers' performance with the standards. Scientific management can fulfill its function only when actual performance is objectively recorded and evaluated using scientific norms, and workers accept remuneration in line with this performance. When the recording of performance is connected with an accounting system, the sustainability of the management system is secured because all of the managed work is recorded monetarily, measured, classified by account items, and periodically analyzed and evaluated. Furthermore, in management accounting (standard cost accounting and budgetary control), all standardized times are converted into standard costs and these standard costs are compared with actual costs in variance accounts, and efficient and inefficient operations are identified through cost variance analysis. This accounting information is fed back to management control (Nishimura 2003). Harrison (1918b), who systemized standard cost accounting, emphasizes the connection between the accounting of standard time and the process of scientific management. He describes this connection as follows: "With standards and no records we are in the position of a traveler with a time table and no watch, while conversely with records and no standards we are in the position [of a traveler…] with a watch but no time table" (p. 392). In regards to standard costs, he points out that "in a concern where standard costs are used, every member of the organization will be provided with definite incentives, responsibilities and records of accomplishment" (p. 392). Thus, management accounting is related not only to efficiency but also to organizational harmony (common goals and cooperation). Budgetary controls also lead to organizational direction and harmony, particularly between production departments and sales departments through the use of targets for profits, expenses, and costs.

McKinsey (1922) also established a budgetary control system with a strong focus on organizational balance. Concerning serious situations such as unbalanced production and sales and the strategic importance of planning balance, he points out the following: "Many firms lost prestige by such actions during the years 1918 and 1919. It is necessary, therefore, to consider production or purchasing possibilities in planning the sales campaign. In other words, the sales function and the production or purchasing function are so closely interrelated and interdependent that they must be considered jointly in planning executive policies" (p. 15). Budgetary management has also been used in the present era of strong uncertainty to harmonize organizational conflicts, particularly imbalances between the strategic targets of senior managers and the practical goals of middle managers, lower-level managers, and workers on the production and sales floors.

As described above, the combination of scientific management and cost accounting made progress in the field of management accounting possible and strengthened the durability, stability, and synthetic power of business management. Thus, management accounting played a useful role in organizational harmony, balance, and cooperation, as well as efficient management. However, it must be noted that this is only one side of modern management, since more serious conflicts, confusion, and discord are often caused in society from the unscientific and conspiratorial use of this management and accounting system (see also Taylor 1911, p. 67).

1.3 Scientific Management and Concepts of "Entrepreneur"/"Businessman"

Similarities and Differences Between Veblen and Taylor

Systematic theories of business enterprise and management were developed at the beginning of the twentieth century, when economists began to reappraise the economic theories that presupposed the rational *economic man* and the rationality and objectivity of economic rule. These theories focused not only on the separation of ownership and management but also on the subjective functions and roles of the entrepreneur and the businessman from the institutional and ethical viewpoints (see Kurogi 2001, 2002). Because this book is mainly interested in understanding the essential functions of management and management accounting in business enterprises, this author must look back to the starting point of management and management accounting at the beginning of the twentieth century and clearly reexamine Taylor's principles of scientific management closely from the viewpoint of Veblen's theory of *business* enterprise and F. H. Knight's concept of the entrepreneur (1921) since they paid needed attention to uncertainty and risk. This approach will get to the core of the issues examined in the book and provide insight into the essence of management and management accounting.

Veblen focuses primarily on business enterprises and businessmen and, at the same time, shares profound insights into their positive and negative roles in directing large machinery and industrial processes that constituted the physical bases of their profitable businesses and the nature of economic fluctuation (i.e., the boom-and-bust economic cycle). Ahead of this discussion, he presents two key concepts, namely the instinct of workmanship and the proclivity in human society for emulation. He then elucidates the forms they take in peacetime and in times of war interdependently and what habits and thoughts are established in these periods. To summarize, in peacetime, they take the forms of economic and industrial efficiency, and those who develop the highest efficiency are treated with the greatest respect; in times of pillage and war, workmanship is not emphasized and those who have power or force (e.g., property and ownership at that time), as well as the leisure class, tend to form habits and propensities that promote the irksome actions of labor (Taka 2005; Kuita 2009). Regarding this issue, Veblen points out that "[u]nder the canon of conduct imposed by the instinct of workmanship, efficiency, serviceability commends itself, and inefficiency or futility is odious. Man contemplates his own conduct and that of his neighbors, and passes judgment of complacency or of dispraise. The degree of effectiveness with which he lives up to the accepted standard of efficiency in great measure determines his contentment with himself and his situation. A wider or persistent discrepancy in this respect is a source of abounding spiritual discomfort" (Veblen 1898, p. 196). According to him, business enterprises pursuing profit do not run on the axis of industrial efficiency that leads to social welfare because these enterprises do not seek a durable efficiency for overall welfare, but only exploit workmanship for monetary transactions or differential benefits. Thus, the habits and proclivities that create "the irksomeness of labor" also develop in a war-time or profit-oriented society (see Taka 2005; Kurogi 2001, 2002).

According to Veblen, businessmen who control investment for profit purposes mainly aspire for property and monetary gain, or profit through credit and stock ownership, rather than to directly gain from industrial processes and efficiency. However, management and accounting related to industrial efficiency are matters of interest to them in terms of standardization and integration because of cost reductions. In particular, the more prominent management and accounting become in purchasing and sales in the development of a business, the more necessary standardization and professionalization become. For this purpose, some managers are hired for and engage in profitable business. As a result, businessmen depend strongly upon an ownership and credit system in which members of the leisure class find the habits and proclivities of labor irksome and view workmanship and emulation for efficiency in a negative light.

As for management itself, business management is distinguished from pecuniary business. Veblen stated, "The management of the various industrial plants and processes in due correlation with all the rest, and the supervision of the interstitial adjustments of the system, are commonly conceived to be a work of greater consequence to the community's well-being than any of the detail work involved in carrying on a given process of production" (Veblen 1904, p. 15). This contribution to well-being differs more from the profitable contribution of the business than from the detailed work in the production process since "business management has a chance to proceed on a temperate and sagacious calculation of profit and loss, untroubled by sentimental considerations of human kindness or irritation or of honesty" (Veblen 1904, p. 31). In the twentieth century, business management, including accounting, focused on the control and recording of impersonal contracts, invisible relationships between sellers and buyers and monetary transactions. This stands in marked contrast with the prior periods, such as the era of bartering (when workmen strived to visibly show their high skill and workmanship for consumers) and the industrial age. Under joint-stock company system and the modern credit system and in relation to 'its employees and other companies', business management adjusted interstitial industrial processes through the combination and selection of actions, from a pecuniary perspective, that have given rise to economic fluctuation and conflict.

It is noteworthy that salaried managers engage in the business management. Pecuniary business is not completely separated from industrial processes and efficiency, but the former places the latter under restrain in its own way. Thus, despite the habitual and routine work of managers in production and efficiency management, the selected managers begin to associate with the *profitable* works of business management. In contrast with Veblen, Taylor addresses the principles of *scientific management*, not only for efficiency management specifically and the fundamental functions and roles of management generally but also for social well-being. Thanks to Taylor, management accounting became closer to efficiency management in production processes, rather than closer to the approach of financial accounting to *profitable business* management. Moreover, his method converted 'the irksomeness of labor' (systematic soldiering, labor disputes) into workmanship (scientific efficiency) by means of standardization. These scientific principles led workmen and businessmen to prosperity. The important point to note is that he overcame the irksome habit of labor by means of the principles of scientific management. To borrow Veblen's terms, Taylor looked for the balance between *profitable business* and *industrial efficiency*, or, in other words, a way toward community well-being from the viewpoint of *efficient management (industrial processes and workmanship)* rather than profit management for business enterprise or *the emulation for unproductive actions.*

Knight's Theory of Uncertainty and Scientific Management

By analyzing the structure of enterprise and the features of entrepreneurs in connection with *uncertainty*, Knight took a different approach than Veblen, despite their common interest in the concepts of profit and entrepreneurs ('businessmen' in Veblen's terminology) (see Kurogi 2002). According to Knight, in business life there are two types of uncertainty: unmeasurable uncertainty and measurable uncertainty. The latter, that is, risk, can be measured by empirical, statistical, or mathematical probability, whereas the former is only recognizable by estimation and judgment, not these probabilities (Sakai 2012; Kurogi 2001). It is the unmeasurable uncertainty that gives rise to differential benefits or profit. This is because the uncertainty can be controlled only by an entrepreneur who has the ability to estimate and judge this uncertainty and to use other knowledge and experience in their decision-making. This special ability to control unmeasurable uncertainty gives rise to differential profit compared with the average business enterprise, whereas controlling for risks or measurable uncertainty through the use of routine management cannot produce such profit. At the same time, the entrepreneur must bear responsibility for the risks of wrong decisions; routine managers do not face such risks.

However, some selected managers or higher level executives must act as entrepreneurs because they share some of the same special abilities as entrepreneurs to account for control of uncertainty. The entrepreneurial aspect of their work grows in importance as broad and complicated business uncertainty increases. Therefore, these managers can share in *profit* by assuming an entrepreneurial function. This situation is quite different from Veblen's case in which the salaried *managers* work in business management on behalf of businessmen. In Knight's case, management is divided into senior managers who are concerned with unmeasurable uncertainty and the middle managers and lower-level managers who engage in work involving routine risks (Kurogi 2002). (Regarding Knight's theory of uncertainty, this chapter only refers to the general framework of the theory and it is discussed in more detail in Chap. 4.)

It is worth noting that in both theories, management accepts a share of remuneration not only for the routine adjustment of risk but also for profitable and uncertain business; in Knight's conception, senior managers actively function as entrepreneurs, whereas, in Veblen's model, managers seek to build a profitable business through the use of other salaried employees. The commonality in their theories is the superiority of profitable business management over routine management in the sense that the former strongly affected the latter's situation. In contrast, Taylor emphasizes the harmony of work and organizational units from the angle of routine management in a different manner than the concepts of Veblen's businessman and Knight's entrepreneur.

Uncertainty, Profit, and Management

Table 1.1 shows the abovementioned points in a simple chart in which Veblen's and Knight's fundamental arguments are compared, keeping Taylor's thoughts in mind.

Table 1.1 Comparison of key concepts of Veblen and Knight

Items	*Veblen*	*Knight*
Profit	Cause of economic fluctuation/ economic crisis Profit, and credit and stock systems	Result of unmeasurable uncertainty Differential benefit
Pursuer of profit	Business enterprises and businessmen Salaried managers (business management)	Entrepreneur (through estimation and judgment) Senior managers (share in profits)
Management	Profitable business management **Efficient management (routine)**	Management of unmeasurable uncertainty **Risk management (routine)**
Other key concepts	**Workmanship (workmen)** **Emulation for efficiency** Leisure class	**Mathematical or a priori probability and statistical probabilities to evaluate risk** Estimate and judgment: unmeasurable *uncertainty*

Note: Bold letters denote a connection with Taylor's theory

Fundamentally, Veblen and Knight discuss their main themes (business enterprise and businessmen for Veblen and uncertainty and entrepreneur for Knight) with the concept of profit as the central point. In Veblen, profit urges business enterprises and businessmen to adjust interstitial industry, but this approach results in large business fluctuation (crises) and uncertainty. Alternatively, in Knight, entrepreneurs can use his or her ability to judge and estimate uncertainty to manage unmeasurable uncertainty and capture differential profit. In contrast with their thoughts that profit has a causal relationship with confusion or uncertainty (Kurogi 2002), Taylor advocates a meaning of efficient management that harmonizes conflicts and confusion in work and organizations. Management accountants also absorbed Taylor's philosophy to systemize its function of efficiency and harmony as standard cost accounting and budgetary control. These thoughts shed more light on important aspects of business enterprises, although they must be grasped jointly.

As this book is interested in clarifying the relationship of uncertainty with management and management accounting, it should clarify how management and management accounting have been influenced by the concept of profit in capitalist society and how their unique functions of harmony are related to uncertainty and confusion. At the same time, this book pays greater attention to the fact that management that plays a role in moderating conflicts between employers and workers in business enterprises now have more control than ownership in terms of their power and share of profit remuneration. At present, senior managers in big businesses use their position of management control to gain enormous monetary remuneration and stock dividends. Although this seems to be fair and proper in terms of their contribution to efficiency and harmony, it may bring about serious social confusion and uncertainty when unfair, dishonest, or illegal manipulation or fraud are used to maintain and strengthen their power and benefit. Apart from this question, we must now return to our main subject. In following sections, we examine the actual situations of management and management accounting from a historical perspective in regards to uncertainty.

Establishment of Modern Business Management and Management Accounting: The Fusion of Scientific Management and Standard Cost Accounting

G. Charter Harrison (1918a, b, c, 1919a, b; 1920), who was aware of business uncertainty, points out the necessity of comprehensive scientific management and the elevation of cost accounting from empiricism to science to cope with uncertainty. According to him, it is very difficult in the industrial world to forecast with certainty what tomorrow will bring. This situation obscures accountants' vision as to the fundamental principles of cost accounting, in particular those accountants who hold fast to the retrospective thought and methods of traditional accounting. Thus, accountants should start a widespread revolution in cost accounting methods (1919b, p. 485). Harrison notes the need for "a complete revolution in accounting thought and techniques" and "a drastic readjustment of ideas on part of accountants as to the fundamental principles of accounting" (1919b, p. 484).

He tried to carry out such a revolution in cost accounting methods from a prospective or forward-looking viewpoint in terms of the comprehensive development of Taylor's scientific management and the fusion of this comprehensive management and standard cost accounting. First, he tried to apply the principles of scientific management not only to shop management but also to the "phases of human activity" (1919a, p. 314).

His scientific method called for the recognition and control of efficiency and inefficiency from the perspectives of not only standardized time but also standard cost and enterprise profit. Further, given a standard cost in a shop, he called for the cost to be used for the improvement of enterprise profit through coordination of sales departments and production departments and the development of flexible sales policies. Harrison did not confine the function of the accounting department to recording and inspecting past events, but expanded it into coordinating and harmonizing activities across departments. According to Harrison, the accounting department is the only department that can harmonize all activities across the whole enterprise by expressing them in terms of dollars and units. Time and motion studies, standard practice instructions, and planning and coordination belong to the province of scientific management, while accounting is related to "showing the extent to which the results actually obtained conform to the standards set up" through the maintenance of records (1918b, p. 392).

In those days, accountants mainly focused on recording actual results and standards, ascertaining 'variations' between them, revising standards and plans, and providing managers with these records in order to eliminate inefficiency and meet standards and established plans. They were more inclined to use cost planning rather than cost control through detailed variance analysis and the succession of management through the variance account system connected with the profit and loss statement (Nishimura 2000). For example, Harrison's "parallel statement" (1918c,

p. 461) of actual results and standards, expressed their variance as percentages, could provide efficient engineers with information on time efficiency, but was too intricate to build up variance accounts in connection with income accounts. However, standard cost accounting opened the way to management accounting and accounting control of cost and profit. McKinsey (1924), after the study of budgetary control (1922), made a fresh development in standard cost accounting and budgetary control as management accounting by focusing on synthetically harmonizing total activities in an enterprise with sales budget as the main axis.

At the same time, Harrison advocated the continual revision of standard costs to cope with a complexly changing business environment because he favored continually giving efficient engineers, managers, and entrepreneurs concrete information on where the firm currently stands, how the present position differs from the targeted direction, and what methods they must adopt to meet their goals. For this purpose, he advocated the constant revision of standard costs according to changing conditions.

The combination of scientific management and standard cost accounting was a direct precursor to the establishment of management accounting. We should further inquire into the subsequent development of management accounting in relation to uncertainty and risk.

1.4 Uncertainty and the Development of Management and Management Accounting Models

Historical Development of Management and Management Accounting

This section examines the historical development of management and management accounting on the basis of the discussion above. Regarding this development, scientific management and standard cost accounting in the 1920s was followed by management science and the profit variance analysis model in the 1960s, which then led to integrated management and cost design (target costing) in the present age. These stages represent key steps in the development of management accounting. These three stages indicate a changing process from feedback (reflective) to feedforward (proactive) control, with the second stage being the transition between the two forms of control (see Chaps. 4 and 5 of this book, as well as Demski 1967, 1969; Nishimura 2003). More concretely, scientific management and standard cost accounting were a complete planning and control system based on a feedback control system. In the age of management science and *A Statement of Basic Accounting Theory* (ASOBAT) in the 1960s and 1970s, management accounting was integrated with mathematics, information theory, and behavioral science for optimal management and its control system shifted from feedback control to feed-forward control. Relative truth took the place of absolute truth in these planning processes for business value, and optimum value (profit) was planned for the given condition as a result of scientific decision-making among many alternatives. In this case, decision-makers were conscious of uncertainty beforehand and worked to select feasible alternatives, which stands in contrast with the case of scientific management in which uncertainty was recognized after the fact through variance analysis between the planned values and actual results. This cognition of uncertainty in advance made it possible to cope with risks in the control process and clarify lost opportunity (opportunity cost) through variance analysis after the fact, which led to more suitable planning for business in future periods. Unusual phenomena or unmeasurable uncertainties that were previously captured only in the estimation and judgment of entrepreneurs became recognized and controlled, even if not completely, in the management system through the use of advanced mathematics, information science, and behavioral science. Measuring unmeasurable uncertainty became a new challenge for management science and its related accounting system, which aimed to establish a more efficient and effective management system.

In the 1980s and 1990s, the concept of management, beyond the planning and control system in a closed organization (company), began to take a newer form that was related to the integration of not only organizational management among top managers, middle- and lower-level managers, and general workers in an enterprise group but also interindustry management (including supply chains and physical distribution), which was needed to establish sustainable growth under balanced business conditions. For example, Japanese companies established an integrated management system, commonly referred to as the 'Toyota-style management system', to integrate cost reduction with the best quality through broad-based and long-term practices and the sharing of experiences. This style of management controlled two factors that formed a trade-off relationship with each other (e.g., cost vs. quality or function) and worked simultaneously to make the best use of production factors in terms of both cost and function. Specifically, management systems such as concurrent engineering, just-in-time production, zero inventory, pull production method, supply chain management, and visible management (Andon, Kanban, etc.) embodied the synthetic reorganization of production and work organizations and methods, and revolutionized management thought. These methods, though based on Taylor's scientific ideas of planning and control, changed time and motion studies into the synthetic studies of time, cost, and function in the production, physical distribution, inventory, and training systems. At the same time, these studies were based on more practical, mathematical, and experienced research and represented a more global judgment than entrepreneur's judgment and the optimum decision in management science.

Based on the above management methods and ideas, management accounting has developed simultaneously. In the same way that standard cost accounting and budgetary controls were established based on scientific management, Demski's ex post programming system developed as a new management accounting model that corresponded with developments in management science in terms of fundamental evolution of the entire framework for planning and control processes. This system measured ex post optimum profit (the optimum profit based on actual observed profit) by using linear programming methods, evaluated ex ante optimum profit from the angle of the ex post profit, clarified the forecast ability of senior managers, and identified incorrect planning methods. Further, this system used the ex post profit to evaluate problems in operation processes through its comparison with the actually observed performance from the viewpoint of opportunity cost variance. In this system, senior managers choose the best alternative and plan the ex ante optimum profit after synthetically examining external conditions and internal problematic factors and taking them into account as the constraints in linear programming. They then evaluate certain uncertainties and risks and potential countermeasures against them as much as possible beforehand. At the evaluation stage, unmeasurable uncertainties, as well as senior managers' inability to estimate uncertainties and operations-level managers' mismanagement of activity, can clearly be recognized through the comparison of ex post profit and actual profit after the fact, and countermeasures against unmeasurable uncertainties could be reexamined for planning ex ante optimum profit in the next period. Although Demski did not show this planning and control process in the system of accounts, Nishimura and Hirai (1983) gave an accounting expression to this system and clarified the meaning of profit variance analysis from the accounting angle. This ex post programming model may be more clearly expressed by the system of accounts and may be transformed into a synthetic and sustainable management system by its combination with accounting methods and thoughts.

In contrast with the above standard cost accounting and Demski's ex post programming system, cost design created by Japanese manufacturing companies is a thorough feed-forward system in which ex ante planning values and target costs are optimized in light of actual conditions through the comparison of long-term strategy (sustainable growth) with short-term strategy (present competitive strategy). Preparatory improvements and target costs fulfill their functions as a control standard for continuous improvement in the production process from the angle of integrating low cost with high quality and function. Finally, as a result of variance analysis between target costs and actual costs, information on lost profit opportunity and potential future improvements is given for planning ex ante profit in the next period. In this case, the planned improvements in cost and function are scientifically backed with industrial engineering, total quality control, concurrent engineering, value engineering, and cost tables (see Tanaka, M. 1985, 2002).

Furthermore, concerning the relation of uncertainty to management and management accounting, uncertainties are proactively forecasted in the ex ante planning process and the preventive improvement process, and extensive and fine-grained improvements and countermeasures against risks are uninterruptedly developed in the process of implementing target cost. Such success results from effective planning, thorough improvement activities, and the focus of organizational members being placed on innovation and improvement throughout the whole organization. This *cost* accounting system can also be applied to *strategic profit* planning and control. Therefore, uncertainty seems to be mitigated more effectively by properly implementing an integrated management system. The contemporary ability of the cost design model to control uncertainty is far superior to the ability of standard cost accounting model connected with scientific management and Demski's ex post programming model with management science. This ability will be still more enhanced by the innovative profit design model.

Chapters 7, 8, and 9 depict the extensive application of this cost design system in relation to supply chain management, life cycle costing, and foreign exchange risk management. This cost design and its principles are applicable in the global context and keep step with the socialization and understanding of integrated management.

Logical Analysis of Management and Management Accounting Systems

When management and management accounting are surveyed from the historical and international viewpoints, the uncertainty of business enterprises has continued to increase as complex and rapid changes in the society and the marketplace occur, and management accounting has also continuously strengthened the functions of stability and harmony by enhancing its inherent informational ability for efficiency, effectiveness, and value creation. The rapidly increasing uncertainty mainly results from the widening and intensifying competition in globalized markets.

Figure 1.1 summarizes the historical development of management principles and management accounting systems and their status in the three stages of development. At the same time, some representative management accounting methods in each stage are presented in this figure along with the primary management accounting models. Moreover, to clarify how these management accounting models have coped with uncertainty, the general characteristics of management and management accounting and the differing aspects between them should first be examined in the three stages. To make the characteristics and differences clear,

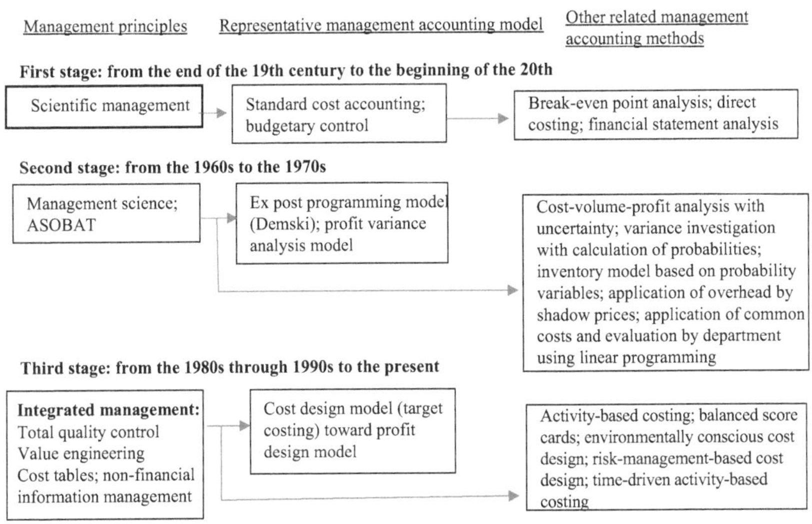

Fig. 1.1 Development of management and management accounting

Fig. 1.2 shows planning (left side) and control (right side) on the horizontal axis, and ex ante action on the upper side and ex post action on the lower side on the vertical axis. This classification clarifies the proactive and preventive or reactive and reflective planning and control processes of each system through the combination of these four factors: planning, control, ex ante action, and ex post action.

In the first stage, the A (planning)-B (control) process in Fig. 1.2 represents the basic nature of traditional management accounting, including standard cost accounting, in which production and management processes are directed, coordinated, and supervised using ex ante planned values and actual performance is compared with the ex ante planned values, analyzed, and evaluated, and accounting information related to this management process (profit and cost) is fed back to the management in the next period. The ex ante value is an absolutely true value based on time and motion studies and past experience, but does not take future uncertainty into consideration. Thus, this uncertainty is measured after the fact by comparing

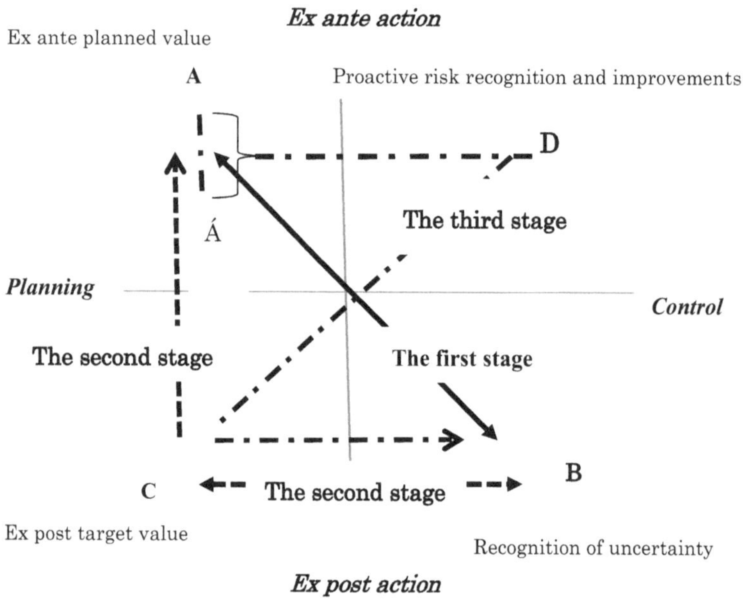

Fig. 1.2 Recognition and control of uncertainty under the three management accounting systems

the ex ante value with actual results. This management accounting model is a feedback system in terms of recognizing and controlling uncertainty after the fact. Its harmonization function is limited to such foreseeable conflicts as organizational soldiering by workers. This model represents a single feedback control loop.

In the second stage, although it is the same as the first stage or the traditional management accounting that the production and management processes from planning (A) to its result (B) is controlled by ex ante value (A), the content and meaning of evaluation is completely different from that in the first stage where the result (B) is evaluated by ex ante value (A) as an absolute true value. Here, not only the result (B) but also planning process (A) is simultaneously evaluated by ex post value (C) as practically optimum value, which is calculated based on the result (B) by linear programming model. There are just two evaluation processes: evaluating ex ante value (A) and the actual performance (B). Thus, the process of A – B – C – "(C – A) · (C – B)" marks the second stage. The second and the first from the right in the row, or (C – A) and (C – B) represent senior manager's cognitive ability of uncertainty and managers' and workers' controllability level of uncertainty on the shop floors. The step C – B corresponds to the basic form of A – B in traditional management accounting. However, this management accounting model based on quantitative and mathematical application is completely different from the traditional one in terms of the use of the ex post optimum value that is calculated under the same condition as the actual result using the linear programming method. This difference exerts influence on the evaluation of the ex ante planned value and the actual observed value, which is related to the ability of senior managers to plan for uncertainty and risks, and middle- and lower-level managers' ability to control risks in operational processes. Profit variance between C and A is analyzed to evaluate the forecast and judgment ability of senior managers, while the variance between C and B is used to evaluate the middle- and lower-level managers' ability to coordinate and supervise production factors against risks.

A (ex ante planned value based on long-term strategy);

- Á (ex ante planned value based on short-term competitive strategy), followed by comparison and analysis between A and Á;
- D (proactive improvements);
- C (ex post planned value or profit based on the most realistic strategy, or target cost in cost design with control and improvements);
- B (actual result), followed by evaluation and continuous improvements.

The variance between C and A is profit forecast variance, whereas the variance between C and B is opportunity cost variance. This management system accounts for feed-forward control over a long-term process, notwithstanding its fundamental structure of feedback recognition and control in terms of calculating ex post optimum profit after the fact. This management accounting model includes a dual feedback control loop.

As management has shifted from feedback control through proactive control based on feedback to an integrated loop of feed-forward and feedback controls, the management accounting model similarly shifted. The third management accounting model takes the form of 'the third stage' in Fig. 1.2.

In this case, step C has a completely different meaning from step C in Demski's model and is not calculated based on the observed value after the fact. In this case, step C, or target cost, is decided through variance analysis between A (allowable cost: long-term strategic cost) and Á (estimated cost: presently competitive strategic cost) and proactively implemented realistic improvements during the process. Planning and control processes are carried out both proactively and preventively, and variance analysis is continuously connected with proactive and reactive improvements. The variance between target cost and actual cost clarifies lost opportunity and future necessary improvements, and feeds back into the planning process in the next period. In this model, uncertainty is forecasted and controlled beforehand in the process of ex ante planning and through proactive improvements. Managers and accountants can also recognize and respond to this uncertainty after the fact through variance analysis between steps C and B and make improvements. This fundamental framework of cost design model is also applicable to the profit design model. A profit design system may allow for more adequate control of uncertainty and lessen the influence of uncertainty on the planning process in the next period because it creates a more immediate and objective (proactive) recognition and control of uncertainty related to profit (the whole target of business). This design system of cost or profit is founded by an integrated loop of feed-forward control and feedback control.

1.5 New Synthesis of Information, Management, and Management Accounting at the Present Stage

Regarding the shift from a cost design model to a profit design model, it may be useful to look more closely at its relationship with the measurement of profit opportunity and enterprise risk, which has been studied in relation to a comprehensive opportunity and lost opportunity control (COLC) model and the unified management of profit opportunity and enterprise risk discussed in Chaps. 7, 8, and 9. This inquiry is also related to clarifying the contemporary characteristic of management accounting and its future development.

These chapters introduce a model in which profit opportunity and enterprise risk are forecast and controlled through increasing the cognitive level of their probabilities from both a long-term and a short-term viewpoint, or, in other words, from both the angles of sustainable growth strategy and present competitive strategy. With their two planned values compared beforehand, and the present optimum value planned through variance analysis and proactive improvements, it is possible to decrease the variance. Such a value in practice may include yearly target profit, which captures the fundamental direction of the whole organizational management. Alternatively, there is the possibility of another method according to which target profit is planned through analyzing variances and implementing proactive improvements for their reduction after deciding the expected (or allowable) profit on the basis of long-term profit opportunity and enterprise risk on the one hand and estimated profit on the basis of current competitive profit opportunity and enterprise risk on the other hand, which are then compared,.

However, in both models there is a serious problem for decision-makers who must estimate reliable probabilities of profit opportunity and enterprise risk to precisely plan accounting profits. Without a reliable estimate of these probabilities, managers and accountants cannot build trustworthy business or profit targets in practice. Although, according to Knight, entrepreneurs can rely on their special ability for estimating and judging this unmeasurable uncertainty and can acquire the differential profit in comparison with average entrepreneurs, at present all enterprises face "unprecedented changes" (Klovienė and Gimžauskienė 2014, p. 60) and must cope with them using more objective and informative methods rather than subjective estimation and judgment to achieve sustainable growth.

In management accounting in the present day and in the future, profit opportunity and enterprise risk must be objectively measured by using globally developed databases and cloud computing, rather than subjective estimation. Thanks to advances in contemporary information technology, management accounting can also evolve in a more modern direction (see Murthy 2016; Brecht and Martin 1996). The application of information technology to business management fortunately tends to focus on strategic decision-making and profitability. As Molloy and Schwenk (1995) states, some firms use information technology to "clearly identify both a strategic problem and crisis decision" and "the use of information technology should be able to expand these limits [of human information processing and communication] by improving the quantity, quality, and efficiency of data collection and storage processing and communication" (p. 285) (see also Baldwin 2015; Sakata 2016; Kelly 2013; Drnevich and Croson 2013). Big data, cloud computing, and other socialized information resources make it possible for chief executive officers (CEOs) and chief financial officers (CFOs) to plan for and control profit and cost based on profit opportunity and enterprise risk more definitely than ever before. However, data must be collected, selected, and analyzed by strategic information technologists. Particularly, the target for selecting data and their analysis are so important in determining the probabilities of the future occurrence of profit opportunity and enterprise risk that the chief information officer (CIO), as a strategic information analyst, should cooperate with the CEO as the strategic decision-maker and with the CFO as the planner of financial strategy and accounting information system. The CIO can make the best of big data and global information resources to determine the reliable probability of profit opportunity and enterprise risk involving the creation of enterprise value under the CEO's strategic decision-making and the CFO's financial and accounting (profitability) strategy.

As a result, the accounting department can develop profit and cost designs and the CEO can also build a comprehensive management system in which information circulates among feed-forward and feedback controls for exploiting and creating new value. In the case of Toyota, which has developed a cost design model, it may be possible in the near future to apply data mining techniques to business strategy and profit design model since this automobile company already uses data to manage vehicles on the road and develop new models (Toyota 2016). Under the connection between medium- and long-term business strategy and profit design, production and sales are also planned for and controlled from a global and long-term viewpoint. The circle from feed-forward to feedback information and control makes possible the flexible and durable improvements and innovations across the whole organization with the cooperation of the CEO, CIO, and CFO. Therefore, profit and cost designs may play a critical role in developing the timing and location of the processes needed to secure the continuity of the comprehensive management system.

Figure 1.3 seeks to schematize the relationship between the COLC model and profit design in the continual cycle of feed-forward and feed-back information and controls. In this figure, business strategy is not limited only to the short-term profitability, but must extend to the overall well-being of society in areas such as environmental protection, energy conservation, and health and safety considerations.

Maybe enterprises must adopt environmentally conscious profit design in the near future to achieve sustainable business growth. The model in Fig. 1.3 represents a challenge for enterprises to measure 'the unmeasurable uncertainty' as certainly as possible through the cooperation of the CEO, CIO, and CFO. In this cooperation, the information technology revolution and digitally connected organizational capabilities and the investment in these areas "fundamentally alter the set of business-level strategic alternatives and value-creation opportunities that firms may pursue, as well as change the relative attractiveness of pursuing those options on a risk and reward basis" (Drnevich and Croson 2013, p. 484).

It is important to note from the discussion above that managers and management accountants should transform the present model of manage-

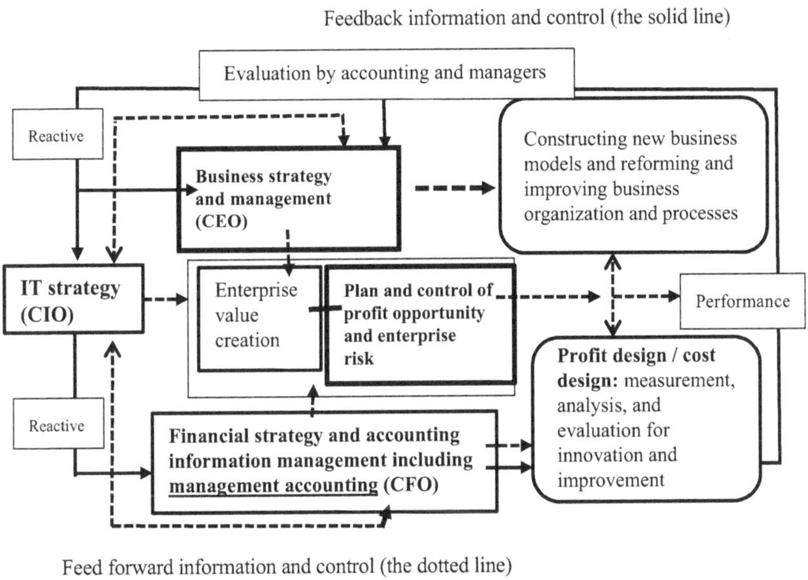

Fig. 1.3 Enterprise strategies and the COLC model

ment and management accounting into more evolutionary models and systems to harmonize conflicts and disorders and to fulfill their key functions (i.e., scientific planning and control, and the measurement and reporting of financial information) and to realize their objectives (i.e., efficiency and effectiveness, and profit calculation). The fulfillment of functions and the meeting of objectives are inseparable in management and management accounting from the control of uncertainty. Previously, entrepreneurs and senior managers confronted uncertainty using only their own ability to estimate and judge. At present, unmeasurable uncertainty can be dealt with using routine planning, control systems, and continuous improvements supported by evolutionary information technology, and the uncertainty can be partly transformed into measurable and controllable uncertainty or risk. At the same time, all members of an organization (not only senior managers but also middle- and lower-level managers and workers) should always be conscious of risks and proactively and preventively cope with them. This management accounting model can be applied globally for whole organizations, industries, the environment, and social services, from the factory to the product life cycle, and from short-term to long-term management. As a result, the ability of entrepreneurs and senior managers to estimate and judge unmeasurable uncertainty can be used for other purposes such as the establishment of new management systems that lead to innovation, business improvement, and increased social welfare.

In regard to the function of harmony in management and management accounting, the last point to note is their dysfunction in the global society. In the twenty-first century, many investors, stakeholders, and even citizens have suffered serious damage from financial manipulations and accounting scandals. Even though these events ultimately caused corporate governance, internal controls, and risk management to achieve greater stability and harmony, it leaves room for doubt as to why management and management accounting could not stop financial and accounting manipulation from occurring in the first place. This may be affected by the fact that senior managers now assume the tremendous power and have decisive control over company's decision-making and management, taking the place of stockholders and entrepreneurs/businessmen. Moreover, those who have long trusted *scientific* management and *true and fair* systems of accounting may not have kept strict watch for antisocial, unscientific, and self-centered behavior. The function of harmony in management and management accounting is also strongly influenced by social consciousness and corporate structures, not only by innovated methods. Therefore, in the present era of rapidly increasing uncertainty, even with the necessary and highly scientific and harmonized methods of management and accounting, citizens should more deeply understand businesses and their machinations, and equip themselves with stronger understanding and ethics against the uncertainty that has developed in the marketplace and may lead to negative behavior by businesses. The book discusses the relationship of management and accounting with uncertainty from such a perspective.

Lastly, it is time for this author to summarize his own thoughts in reference to the concepts of Taylor, Harrison, Veblen, and Knight, since the relationship of management and management accounting with uncertainty has been examined on the basis of their theories, which represented new innovation in business management and accounting in relation to conflict, crisis, risk, and uncertainty at the beginning of the twentieth century. Even though human beings naturally have the instinct of workmanship and the propensity for emulation, they always transform workmanship and emulation into another form under different social systems and thinking patterns. Under all sorts of ownership systems, emulation for industrial efficiency is easy to change into competition for parasitic gains when such gains can be valued over workmanship ability, which then leads to pillage or exploitation. At the same time, a superabundance of unearned income changes workmanship in a way that brings about the negative habits (irksomeness) of labor. Conflict and discordance in various economic activities have been caused by the human shift from workmanship to the negative habits of labor, and from the emulation of efficiency to competition for parasitic gain, which can lead to social discord and conflict for possessions, profit, and financial benefits. Human beings are confronted through such social conflicts and through natural disasters with risks and unmeasurable uncertainty. However, human beings naturally also have intelligence and the power to control their situation in order to change discord back to stability and 'the irksomeness of labor' back to workmanship. Management and management accounting represent just part of this control function toward harmony beyond conflict, even though their misapplication gives rise to more serious uncertainty. Therefore, they must be scientific and workmanship oriented when seeking to control uncertainty. Viewed in this light, scientific management and accounting is a human wisdom for coping with conflict and discordance under uncertain business circumstance. Early in the twentieth century, human beings, on the basis of their instincts of 'workmanship' and 'emulation for efficiency', established the scientific systems through which they can recognize economic activities and results from both the stock and flow sides and use this information to direct, coordinate, and supervise business processes. At the same time, the COLC model and profit design in this book are developed as an important question of the day from the above theoretical framework.

1.6 Conclusion on Contemporary Management and Management Accounting in Uncertainty

Although management and management accounting have been affected by the various conditions of political economy in each era, uncertainty has fundamentally exerted critical influence on them. In this sense, their development is a history of how they have grappled with uncertainty. At present, given the rapid increase in uncertainty, in the three development stages of management and management accounting that were discussed above, the last stage is now taking a new form of profit design based on the COLC model and the integrated management of profit opportunity and enterprise risk. In the three stages, uncertainties had been recognized and controlled by changing the management model from feedback and retrospective standpoint to feed-forward and prospective standpoint, while also shifting the foundation of accounting system from subjective judgment through mathematical measurement to the integrated science of value engineering, cost engineering, and behavioral science. Accordingly, accounting models have changed from standard cost accounting through ex post optimum programming and profit variance analysis to cost design. Furthermore, the third stage is now moving to a new stage in which profit design, including cost design, proactively recognizes and controls for uncertainty in cooperation with the COLC model, the integrated management of profit opportunity and enterprise risk, and global information strategies. Management and management accounting in this stage is positioned in the cycle of feed-forward and feedback controls in which the three strategies of information, business management, and finance/accounting synthetically decide profit and cost targets based on profit opportunity and enterprise risk information, and plan for and control proactive improvements and innovations sustainably from not only the angle of profitability but also the broader social viewpoints of environmental protection, health and safety, and harmonious human relationships.

This book arrives at the conclusion that the control functions and science of management and management accounting advocated at the beginning of the twentieth century continue to play a role in managing uncertainties and responding to changes and complexities in the global finance-oriented economy and an era of intensified competition. Historical and logical research on the functions and the science of management and management accounting clarifies their unique and universal aspects. This book tries to shed new light on these topics, even if only a little.

As for Veblen's concepts of workmanship and 'the irksomeness of labor', the more these concerns have magnified, the greater the need for improvements in management. Therefore, it remains an unsettled question how profit design and cost design models will develop in the more complicated and changeable economy with greater levels of uncertainty and what form they may take in the future. It may safely be assumed that uncertainty and stability in business are strongly influenced by the intelligence and ethics of senior managers who shift between *workmanship* and *the negative habits (irksomeness) of labor*. Therefore, scientific management and management accounting that are based on *workmanship* and harmony are necessary for the development of socially oriented business.

Chapters 10 and 11 also refer to the relationship of management and management accounting with uncertainty in China. When we consider a 'socialist market economy' in line with Veblen's concepts, orthodox 'socialist planned economy' is fundamentally established by the idea of workmanship and the emulation for industrial efficiency and a 'closed policy', while socialist *market economy* allows enterprises to emulate for profit, stock ownership, and finance in international markets. Even though either of the two cannot avoid uncertainty, the latter is confronted by wider and longer uncertainties or risks because of global competition and international economic cycles than the former that is distressed by risks caused by difficulty to plan national supply and demand and stagnant science and technology behind international standard. Thus, Chap. 11 inquires into contemporary Chinese enterprise risk management. As a result, we profoundly recognize the general and peculiar relationships of management and management accounting with uncertainty in human societies.

My passion for writing this book gushes out from the desire to highlight a path toward workmanship, scientific management, and emulation for social well-being and peace against the irksomeness of labor, rules of thumb for management, and emulation for pillage and war. My aspiration is to find a path toward harmony beyond conflict and confusion.

Bibliography

Baldwin, H. (2015, June 9–15). The Rapidly Changing Role of the CIO, *Computer Weekly*, pp. 15–16.

Brecht, H. D., & Martin, M. P. (1996). Accounting Information Systems: The Challenge of Extending Their Scope to Business and Information Strategy. *Accounting Horizons, 10*(4), 16–22.

Demski, J. S. (1967, October). An Accounting System Structures on a Linear Programming Model. *Accounting Review, 42*(4), 701–712.

Demski, J. S. (1969, October). Decision-Performance Control. *Accounting Review, 44*(4), 669–713.

Drnevich, P. L., & Croson, D. C. (2013). Information Technology and Business-level Strategy: Toward an Integrated Theoretical Perspective. *MIS Quarterly, 37*(2), 483–509.

Harrison, G. C. (1918a, October). Cost Accounting to Aid Production-1, Application of Scientific Management Principles. *Industrial Management, 56*(4), 278–281.

Harrison, G. C. (1918b, October). Cost Accounting to Aid Production-II, Standards and Standard Costs. *Industrial Management, 56*(4), 391–398.

Harrison, G. C. (1918c, December). Cost Accounting to Aid Production-III, The Universal Law of System. *Industrial Management, 56*(5), 456–464.

Harrison, G. C. (1919a, April). Cost Accounting to Aid Production-VII, Extension of Application of Scientific Management Principles. *Industrial Management, 57*(4), 314–321.

Harrison, G. C. (1919b, June). Cost Accounting to Aid Production-IX, Conclusion and the Future of Cost Accounting. *Industrial Management, 57*(6), 314–321.

Harrison, G. C. (1920, March). Scientific Basis for Cost Accounting. *Industrial Management, 59*, 237–242.

Kelly, L. (2013). CIOs Should Be Prepared for Broader Role in the Future, *Computer Weekly,* 30 July–5 August, pp. 22–25.

Klovienė, L., & Gimžauskienė, E. (2014). Development of Accounting System According to the Information Technology. *Review Of Economic Studies and Research Virgil Madgearu, 2*, 59–74.

Knight, F. H. (1921). *Risk, Uncertainty and Profit*. Chicago: University of Chicago Press. Reprint version: Cosimo Classic, New York, 2005.

Kuita, T. (2009, June). 'Business Enterprise' and 'Businessmen's Viewpoint' in Veblen's Theory of Business Enterprise. *Artes Liberales, 84*, 103–125. Iwate University.

Kurogi, Ryo. (2001). Frank Knight's Conception of Entrepreneur and the Competitive Economic Order: The Significance of Risk, Uncertainty, and Profit (Japanese), *Annals of the Society for the History of Economic Thought*, The Japanese Society for the History of Economic Thought, *40*(November), 43–55.

Kurogi, Ryo. (2002). Homogeneities and Divergences between Veblen and Knight: On Their Theories of the Entrepreneur, *Annals of the Society for the*

History of Economic Though, The Japanese Society for the History of Economic Thought, *42*(November), 71–83.

McKinsey, J. O. (1922). *Budgetary Control.* New York: The Ronald Press Company.

McKinsey, J. O. (1924). *Managerial Accounting.* Chicago: University of Chicago Press.

Molloy, S., & Schwenk, G. (1995). The Effects of Information Technology on Strategic Decision Making. *Journal of Management Studies, 32*(3), 284–311.

Murthy, U. S. (2016). Researching at the Intersection of Accounting and Information Technology: A Call for Action. *Journal of Information Systems, 30*(2), 159–167.

Nishimura, A. (2000). *Accounting Control and Management Accounting.* Tokyo: Doubunkan.

Nishimura, A. (2003). *Management Accounting in Asia: feed forward and Asian perspectives.* Hampshire: Palgrave Macmillan.

Nishimura, A., & Hirai, K. (1983, December). New Development of Profit Variance Analysis on a Linear Programming Model. *Business Accounting, 35*(3), 113–127.

Sakai, Y. (2012). The Economic Thought of Frank Knight: With Special Reference to Risk and Uncertainty, *CRR Discussion Paper*, Shiga University, No. J-19, 1–26. http://hdl.handle.net/10441/9743.

Sakata, J. (2016). Analytical Study on Strategic Use of Information System and the Depth of Chief Information Officer's Competence. *The Journal of J.F. Oberlin University Business Management Review, 7*, 23–47.

Taka, T. (2005). Veblen's Theory of Evolution and the Instinct of Workmanship: An Ethological and Biological Reinterpretation. *The History of Economic Thought, 47*(2), 32–44. The Society for the History of Economic Thought, Japan.

Tanaka, M. (1985, July/August). New Approach to the Function Evaluation System in Value Engineering, *International Journal of Production Research, 23*(4), 625–638.

Tanaka, M. (2002). *Profit Strategy and Value Engineering: How to Implement Practical Cost Design.* Tokyo: Sangyo Noritu University Publisher.

Taylor, F. W. (1911). *The Principles of Scientific Management.* New York/London: Harper & Brothers Publishers. (Reprinted version: Martino Publishing, Mansfield Centre, CT, 2014).

Toyota Motor Co. (2016). Toyota, Acceleration of "Connected Technologies", *Toyota Global News*, 4 January, http://newsroom.toyota.co.jp/jp/detail/10140379/.

Veblen, T. (1898, September). The Instinct of Workmanship and the Irksomeness of Labor. *American Journal of Sociology, 4*(2), 187–201.

Veblen, T. (1904). *The Theory of Business Enterprise.* New York: Charles Scribner's Sons. (Reprinted Version: Martino Publishing, Mansfield Centre, CT, 2013).

CHAPTER 2

Enterprise Governance and Management Accounting from the Viewpoint of Feed-Forward Control

2.1 Introduction

This chapter aims to clarify the role and function of contemporary management accounting and the management accountant in relation to *enterprise governance*, in the sense proposed by the Professional Accountants in Business (PAIB) Committee of the International Federation of Accountants (IFAC) (PAIB 2004; Connell 2004). The chapter also relates enterprise governance to management accounting through the concept of feed-forward control.

Enterprise governance integrates conformance or *corporate governance* with performance or *business governance*. Corporate governance includes the protection of stakeholders from unfair and fraudulent behavior by the management. Business governance, which seeks to securely create value and attain strategic goals, ensures good corporate governance. However, it cannot be dissociated from conformance. Conformance and performance depend upon the social and economic behavior of management. This matter is discussed from the viewpoint of a globally changing management environment.

The management environment has become more unstable and uncertain in the presence of greater competition and as a result of developments in information technology and quickly changing consumer trends. Crises can quickly arise, even in previously profitable enterprises, either caused by or causing poor governance practices. As a result, the social responsibility of directors and management to stakeholders has become a focus of

A. Nishimura, *Management, Uncertainty, and Accounting*,
https://doi.org/10.1007/978-981-10-8989-3_2

attention. Enhanced disclosure, accountability, and auditing standards have been widely canvassed issues in relation to corporate governance. However, little discussion of the role of management accounting and the management accountant in enterprise governance has taken place in this context.

In the next section, I first sketch the international development of corporate governance and its structural characteristics in different countries. Second, I review the relationship between business failure and corporate governance in Japan after 1990. Third, the importance of risk management, especially internal control, to business governance is discussed. Fourth, I address the meanings of feed-forward control in the context of enterprise governance. In the conclusion, for the effective application of risk management to enterprise governance, I advocate more disclosure of information on strategy and risk, based upon the viewpoint of feed-forward control.

2.2 Institutional and Capital Structural Aspects of Corporate Governance

A spate of recent scandals such as WorldCom and Enron illustrate how unethical practices involved in the use and disclosure of accounting information can defraud the stakeholders of enterprises, including employees, creditors, and the government and shareholders (Stuart and Stuart 2004). It is evident in such cases that oversight procedures adopted by boards of directors are often inadequate, chief executives and senior managers are capable of dishonest behavior, and auditors are often not independent. As a result, collusion between various parties can occur. This experience has led to institutional reforms in corporate governance.

Tables 2.1 and 2.2 summarize some of the measures that have been taken by Western and Asian nations, respectively, in dealing with legal issues in corporate governance. In the West, countries mainly tackle internal control problems in which matters of governance such as the independence of directors, independent oversight procedures, internal auditing and disclosure, and accountability practices are legally enhanced. Internal control is increasingly integrated with the broader concept of risk management. International organizations such as OECD and IFAC play an important role in building legal and institutional systems for good corporate governance.

A common feature in Asian countries is that legal changes in corporate governance are associated with the inflow of capital from Western coun-

Table 2.1 Requirement of corporate governance law and regulation in the West

International organization, nation, and area	*Requirement of law and regulation*	*Comment*
European Union	A High Level Group of Company Law Expert (November 2002)	A modern regulatory framework for company law in Europe
	An Action Plan (May 2003)	Modernizing company law and enhancing corporate governance in the European Union—a plan to move forward
	Federation des Experts Comptables Europeens (September 2003)	A discussion paper: the financial reporting and auditing experts of corporate governance
International Federation of Accountants	A Task Force on Rebuilding Confidence in Financial Reporting (July 2003)	Rebuilding public confidence in financial reporting: an international perspective
Organisation for Economic Co-operation and Development	The OECD Principles of Corporate Governance (1999)	
	The Revised Draft Principles (January 2004)	
Australia (MM)	Corporate Governance Council; The Australian Stock Exchange	Principles of good corporate governance and best practice recommendation (March 2003)
	Corporate Law Economic Reform Program: 9 Bill (July 2004)	Audit reform, corporate disclosure, and executive remuneration and the outcome and consultation
Canada (MM)	The Joint Committee on Corporate Governance (the Saucier Committee)	Beyond compliance: building a governance culture (November 2001)
France (RM)	Vienet Report (1995 and 1999)	
	Bouton Report (2002)	
	Combined report of the three reports (October 2003)	The corporate governance of listed corporations
Italy (RM)	The Preda Report (October 1999)	Under the sponsorship of the Italian Stock Exchange
	Its Revised version (July 2002)	

(*continued*)

Table 2.1 (continued)

International organization, nation, and area	*Requirement of law and regulation*	*Comment*
Netherlands (RM)	The Dutch Code of the Best Practice (2003) The Tabaksblat Committee (December 2003)	The 40 recommendations of the Peters report The two-tier board structure (management and supervisory board)
United Kingdom (MM)	Cadbury Report (1992) Combined Code on Corporate Governance (1998) A Revised Combined Code (July 2003)	
United States (MM)	Sarbanes-Oxley Act (2002) Breeden Report on the Future Corporate Governance of MC (formerly World Com) (August 2003)	

Note: (MM) shows the Market Model, while (RM) the Relationship Model

Sources: PAIB 2004, 49–52; Solomon and Solomon 2004, 161ff; Banks 2004, 26

tries and their economic influences. Consequently, many countries follow the example of American and English codes and requirements. For example, Japan followed the American Committee of Sponsoring Organizations of the Treadway Commission's (COSO) *Internal Control-Integrated Framework* to establish oversight management and remuneration committees and to appoint independent, nonexecutive directors to boards of directors to improve corporate governance (The Society for the Study of Risk Management and Internal Control 2003). Similar influences can be seen in Korea, Malaysia, and elsewhere. Legal and institutional interference with the processes of the corporate governance is a consequence of the international change in the business environment and of widespread distrust with the management of large multinational enterprises. The present situation has parallels with that of the 1930s.

Capital market structure is considered important in determining the strength of corporate governance. There are two main models of corporate governance, which reflect cultural and capital structure differences: the capital

Table 2.2 Requirement of corporate governance law and regulation in Asia

Nation and area	*Requirement*	*Content*
China	Ministry of Finance: Standards of Internal Accounting Control: Fundamental Standard, and Money Funds, for Trail Implementation (Jun 2001)	Enhancing internal checking system
Hong Kong	The Standing Committee on Company Law Reform (June 2003)	Concerning corporate governance reform
Japan (RM)	Amendment of Auditing Standard (January 2002)	Enhancing internal control and risk approach
	Ministry of Economy and Industry: Internal Control in the New Risky Age (June 2003)	Guidelines for internal control functioned together with risk management
	Amendment of Commercial Code (from 2001 to 2002)	Enhancing corporate governance
Korea (HM)	Committee on Corporate Governance: Code of Best Practice for Corporate Governance (February 2003)	
Malaysia (HM)	Financial Committee on Corporate Governance: Code on Corporate Governance (March 2000)	
Singapore	Amendment to the Companies Act (July 2002)	
	The Council on Corporate Disclosure and Governance (August 2002): Corporate Governance and Disclosure Requirements	To review and enhance the existing framework on corporate governance and promote good corporate governance in Singapore, taking into account international best practices
Thailand (HM)	The Stock Exchange of Thailand The SET Code of Best Practice for Directions of Listed Companies (Corporate Disclosure Standards) 19 January 1998	
	Best Practice Guidelines for Audit Committee 23 June 1999	
	Regulations of the Stock Exchange, 22 January 2001	

(continued)

Table 2.2 (continued)

Nation and area	*Requirement*	*Content*
Taiwan	Amendment of the Corporate Law (November 2001) Corporate Governance Best-Practice Principles for the Taiwan Stock Exchange Corporation and GreTai Securities Market Jointly (October 2002)	

Note: HM shows the mixed model of MM (market model) and RM (relationship model)

Sources: PAIB 2004, 49–52; Solomon and Solomon 2004, 161ff; Banks 2004, 26–7

market or 'neo-classical' model (Banks 2004; Dietl 1998) and the relationship model. The neo-classical model focuses on the strengths of competition, forcing transparency and independent auditors on capital markets. The relationship model focuses on the enhancement of corporate governance through the close relationship of enterprises with governments, banks, workers, and other interested parties. As indicated in Tables 2.1 and 2.2, the former is Anglo-American while the latter is Continental European in origin.

Many Asian countries follow a hybrid of the two models. The Anglo-American type provides openness and contractual control in enterprise management, and the application of the agency principle based on market principle reduces dependence on bureaucracy (bureaucratic control). Close relationships between banks, companies, and other organizations, in contrast, have also been considered to provide advantages in good corporate governance in Japan because they encourage long-term stability. Both types of regime have been found wanting in recent times, however. The Enron and WorldCom scandals in the United States have brought into question the effectiveness of the neo-classical model. The changed global political and economic circumstances that weakened banking sector in Japan have reduced the effectiveness of its network of governance and many Japanese companies have failed.

Germany originated a representative type of the relationship model, still followed by many Japanese enterprises. Under this approach, it is the function of a supervisory board (Aufsichtsrat) to represent social interests made up of shareholders and workplace representatives (Niyama 2001; Itami 2000). However, this has also not prevented "corporate scandals and other problems arising" (Appleyard and Pallet 2004). Evidently, application of neither the market nor relationship model can guarantee a solution to the problems besetting corporate governance.

Management of self-interest and arrogance is a feature of unfair and fraudulent practices in corporate governance. Another feature, not so frequently noted, is that failures of corporate governance are closely related to weak and unchecked strategies and risk management. Without good business governance, good enterprise governance cannot be achieved in an unstable and rapidly changing world economy. Legal requirements and structural models only touch upon the apparent adjustment issues arising between management and stakeholders and cannot alone solve the fundamental problems of enterprise governance. Successful corporate governance fundamentally originates from the implementation of successful strategy and risk management. Enterprises must now shift their standpoint from avoiding risks to managing them, "since risk is essential for growth" (Prickett 2004).

These problems are more difficult to overcome in Asia than the West. In most Asian countries, few top managers are comfortable with the 'philosophy of corporate governance'. Furthermore, their understanding of the principles of corporate governance is weak, since the separation between ownership and management, or between the directors and chief manager, is less pronounced than in Western countries. It is common for the chairman of an enterprise to be closely connected with the owners and managers of the same enterprise through family relationships. Also, auditors and directors are not appointed independently (Solomon and Solomon 2004; Kim 1995).

2.3 Bankruptcy and Corporate Governance in Japan

Now the structural roots of unfair and fraudulent behavior by management should be examined. This analysis is illustrated by Japanese cases. Effective corporate governance is a necessary but not sufficient condition for the sustainable creation of business value in the long run. The present, imperfect systems of enterprise governance do not cope with structural changes in the economic and business environment. Therefore, to build effective enterprise governance systems, we must recognize such structural change and provide strategic countermeasures to deal with its impact. The current Japanese experience serves as an example of this principle.

Table 2.3 One hundred large-scale bankruptcies in Japan after the Second World War: Its trend (money unit = million yen)

Period	*Number of companies*	*Average liabilities per bankrupted company*
1975	1	150,000
The 1980s	4	286,400
The 1990s	70	394,021
The 2000s (Until January 2001)	25	642,963

One company which is private ownership and no capital account is omitted from the list

Sources: Nikkei Venture 2001, 264–7. (See also Enterprise Bankruptcy in Japan: http://www.tdb.co.jp/tosan/syukei/03nen.html)

Table 2.3, in chronological order, shows the average liabilities per company of the top 100 large-scale bankruptcies in Japan since 1975. After the collapse of the bubble economy, both the number of bankruptcies and the amount of liabilities per company continued to increase over the next ten years, decreasing slightly in 2003. Profitable enterprises continue to face risks in the aftermath of these failures. The industrial sectors that most strongly impact upon the prosperity of others in this respect are banking, securitized loans, resort development, hotel, and golf course management (see Table 2.4). Their average ratio of liabilities to capital stock per company is higher than other sectors. There is no complete means for ensuring the safety of creditors. The buffer to defend stakeholder from risks becomes much smaller in the presence of bank and insurance company failures. Life insurance and construction companies, although their average liabilities to capital stock are less than the above sectors, have also had a strong influence on other sectors in the aftermath of the period of firm failures. Although average liabilities per company and the ratio of liabilities to capital stock in the manufacturing sector are the lowest of all the sectors, this sector is also still threatened by the earlier series of bankruptcies.

The data in Table 2.4 shows the high ratio of liabilities to capital stock among failed companies in a number of sectors. Enterprises with high-liability profiles provoke unease among the business community. From Table 2.5, the ratio of liabilities to capital stock was 7794.8 million yen in bankrupt companies with 10 to 50 million yen of capital stock. This pattern continues extends over a long period of time, though somewhat diminished. In 2003, the number of bankrupted companies was 16,624 with lia-

Table 2.4 Average liabilities per bankrupted company and the ratio of liabilities to capital stock by industry (money unit = million yen)

Industry (number of company)	*Average liabilities per bankrupted company*	*Ratio of liabilities to capital stock*
Life insurance (3)	2,815,497	48.6
Banking, lease, and securities business (44)	395,523	983.8
Real estate dealer (26)	262,739	4093.4
Department store and supermarket (6)	347,247	1317
General merchant and trading company (2)	446,263	17.2
Construction (6)	939,799	141.7
Shipping agent and transportation (2)	342,150	58.6
Venture capital (1)	500,000	113.6
Resort development, hotel, and golf course management (7)	240,802	1078.5
Manufacturing (2)	177,839	42.3

One company which is private ownership and no capital account is omitted from the list

Sources: Nikkei Venture 2001, 264–7. (See also Enterprise Bankruptcy in Japan: http://www.tdb.co.jp/tosan/syukei/03nen.html)

bilities of 11.78 billion yen, down about 14% in comparison with the previous year's figures of 19,458 and 13.8 billion yen, respectively (Fig. 2.1).

Under these circumstances, what does the accounting concept of capital stock mean? According to Marple (1936), the funds contributed by the stockholders are a buffer giving a margin of safety to creditors. However, the function of capital stock as 'a buffer for the creditors', common in many code law countries of Asia following the Continental European tradition, appears to have diminished. Capital stock has been transformed to a concept that does not take into account the effect of feedback control on creditors' protection.

Imperfect corporate governance has obscured facts about the business environment. Risky business practices have been stimulated with 'a check-free empire' of corporate management in Japan, since management is not accountable to the board in any useful sense (Mochizuki 1995). The perceived view that Japanese business has a long-term stable perspective in its approach to investment has contributed to ignorance regarding the need for management accountability. All enterprises should take precautions not only to protect their own business from risks but also to posi-

Table 2.5 Average capital stock by capital size in one hundred large-scale bankrupted companies and the ratio of liabilities to capital stock by capital size (money unit = million yen)

Capital size (Number of company)	*Average liabilities per bankrupted company*	*Average liabilities to capital stock of the company*
L.10–50 (11)	190,628.7	7794.8
K.60–90 (8)	315,950	4119.2
J.100 (10)	264,320	2643.2
I.160–400 (10)	216,871	889.5
H.460–587 (11)	284,048	554.6
G.610–900 (3)	258,180	377.4
F.1000–1565 (7)	334,965	268.8
E.2000–2816 (8)	477,190	200
D.3112–6916 (13)	345,215	72.1
C.11787–17680 (9)	827,779	57.5
B.20262–39763 (6)	866,884	53.1
A.57598–85000 (3)	2,662,098	40.3

One company which is private ownership and no capital account is omitted from the list

Sources: Nikkei Venture 2001, 264–7. (See also Enterprise Bankruptcy in Japan: http://www.tdb.co.jp/tosan/syukei/03nen.html)

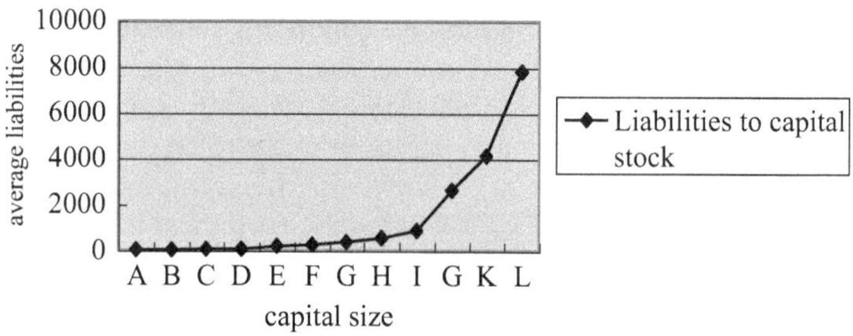

Fig. 2.1 Trend of average liabilities to capital stock by size. (A=3 companies from 57,598 to 85,000 in capital size (unit: million Japanese yen); B=6 companies from 20,262 to 39,763; C=9 companies from 11,787 to 17,680; D=13 companies from 3112 to 6916; E=8 companies from 2000 to 2816; F=7 companies from 1000 to 1565; G=3 companies from 610 to 900; H=11 companies from 460 to 587; I=10 companies from 160 to 400; J=10 companies in 100; K=8 companies from 60 to 90; L= 11 companies from 10 to 50. The figure is drawn based on Table 2.5)

tively manage the risks caused by supply chains, buyers, and suppliers of finance. Risk repercussions on enterprises, including the manufacturing sector, from the increasing interconnectedness of business in the information economy, is a new challenge for enterprise governance. Therefore, for sustainable success in business, management must embrace a strategic focus and implement risk management, in addition to institutionally and structurally established corporate governance.

2.4 Risk Management and Business Governance

In Japan, many enterprises have lost public confidence due to unfair or fraudulent practices since the early 1990s. Window dressing, through misleading disclosure practices, has exacerbated the social and financial consequences of bankruptcy. A corporate culture in which chief executives make arbitrary or self-interested decisions and ignore the inconvenient recommendations of independent managers continues to be a barrier to reform. For example, in the large supermarket chain Daiei Inc., the chairman failed to change his firm's unsuccessful strategies due to the placing of too much importance on family management interests and to the giving of insufficient weight to independent advice from professional subordinates (Imoto 1999).

Poor business governance practices can occur at any level of an organization and negatively impact on public confidence. In the Yukizirushi (Snow Brand) Dairy Manufacturing Company, the top producer of dairy products in Japan, senior managers were unaware of low-quality control standards that caused basic hygiene in cleaning equipment to be compromised, inevitably leading to consumer anger when the matter entered the public domain (Special Article 2000). When bureaucratic governance procedures in the Mitsubishi Motor Corporation concealed consumer complaints of vehicle defects, its profit sharply dipped as a result of lost social confidence. According to one shop manager, "during peak times, about 20 customers would visit the shop each day, but since last scandal, the number has dropped to two" (*Japan Times*, 22 August 2004). These examples show that large companies, which neglect good business governance, perhaps in the pursuit of short-term financial gain, run the risk of negatively impacting their longer-term interests.

In Japan, as elsewhere, internal control in the 1950s was defined as an internal check system. It was viewed as a means to preserve company assets, secure the accuracy and reliability of accounting data, and facilitate business efficiency and effectiveness. Internal control is now more closely related to corporate governance. The relationship between internal control and governance, however, now needs to be examined from the viewpoint of strategy and business governance, that is, value creation and performance.

Most failures of business in Japan in the 1990s were connected with deficiencies in strategy and risk management. The immaturity of strategy management, senior managers' desire to expand their businesses without consideration to changes in the global economic environment, led to accounting manipulation, window dressing, and unfair and fraudulent behavior. Poor corporate governance practices, involving secrecy, rule-breaking, and criminal activity, accelerated imprudent *strategic* management and the acceptance of risky or low rate of return projects. It is evident that bad enterprise governance results from defective strategy and business risk control. The basic principle of finance, that risk has to be balanced against return (opportunity), is forgotten or ignored.

Therefore, a company that devotes itself only to corporate governance, particularly the conformance to the requirements of law and regulation, overlooking the need for good business governance with respect to strategy and risk management, will likely fail to achieve its objectives in the long run. In a competitive and rapidly changing economic environment, sound business governance is necessary for sustainable business growth. The view that this argument supports the position that "good corporate governance is a necessary, but not sufficient, foundation for success" (PAIB 2004, p. 5) is becoming more widely accepted. As COSO states: "while internal control can help an entity achieve its objectives, it is not a panacea".

Financial and management accounting have the same origins, since disclosure cannot realize accountability without controllability (Nishimura 2003). Disclosure without controllability is an empty ceremony (Nishimura 2003, Preface). To integrate social confidence with the sustainable creation of value, disclosure with controllability based on accountability is required. Corporate governance without business governance is only a formal compromise between management and stakeholders. It must tie up with the oversight of value creation activities to management. The idea that 'enterprise governance' referred to in this chapter is a possible solution to current problems in corporate governance originates in an idea proposed by the PAIB.

'Enterprise governance' is a comprehensive term encompassing corporate governance, conformance, and business governance and value creation (PAIB 2004, p. 10). Corporate governance is related to accountability and assurance, while business governance is related to value creation and resource utilization. The PAIB (2004) summarized the relationships of the two governances as follows:

> Enterprise governance is an emerging term, which describes a framework covering both the corporate and the business governances of an organiza tion. Achieving a panacea of good corporate governance that is linked strategically with performance management will enable companies to focus on the key drivers that move their business forward. This is both a challenge and an opportunity.

The distinguishing feature of business governance is its assessment of risk from the two angles of internal control and strategic management. A *Strategic Scorecard*, but not *the Balanced Scorecard*, fills the strategic oversight gap. The Strategic Scorecard is not a planning tool, but it is an oversight tool to help the board of directors grasp all aspects of the strategic process. It is made up of four basic elements: strategic position, strategic options, strategic implementation, and strategic risks. By using the scorecard, the governing board of an enterprise can identify the key points in, and timing of, effective strategic decision-making and recognize "milestones in strategic implementation together with the identification and mitigation of strategic risk" (PAIB 2004, p. 6). Such a scorecard thus attaches importance to filling the strategic oversight gap in transformational changes such as mergers, acquisitions and bankruptcies, which the balanced scorecard does not address (PAIB, p. 24). While the balanced scorecard is operational and reactive with respect to a given strategy, the Strategic Scorecard fulfills its function with respect to transformation and abrupt change. Prickett (2004, p. 15) argues that the Strategic Scorecard forces boards to consider where the company is now, what its options are, and how it will manage risks.

Table 2.6 Differences between feedback and feed-forward control systems

Control system	*Planned value*	*Object of sensor*	*Assessor*	*Effective device*	*Result*
Feedback	Absolute truth	Actual action	Variance between plan and actual action	Reflective, reactive control	Actual performance close to plan in next period through ex post variance
Feed-forward	Relative truth	Virtual action	Variance between plan and virtual action	Proactive, preventive control	Preparatory performance close to plan through ex ante variance

The author believes that the Strategic Scorecard is founded on the recognition of the need for feed-forward control. The conceptual distinction between feedback and feed-forward control is described in the above table. Generally, feedback control begins where feed-forward control ends. Feedback control must correct the imperfect achievement of goals that feed-forward cannot realize. In this case, the imperfect feed-forward is only the forecast part of feedback control. However, by nature, feedback control is not necessary for perfect feed-forward control. Theoretically and practically, both the concepts are independent. Feed-forward control is critical to effective enterprise governance and the implementation of a Strategic Scorecard, not because of the necessity to forecast and estimate, but because it supports the realization of the goal of sustainable progress through proactive and preventive control of enterprise resources. In contrast, feedback control is reactive and reflective and alone does not thoroughly serve the needs of a Strategic Scorecard.

2.5 Enterprise Governance and Feed-Forward Control

Contemporary enterprises in a world afflicted by scandals are usually large, composed of thousands of employees whose activities are diverse and complex. Individuals in such enterprises deal with issues of strategy and risk on a daily basis. The corporate culture of obedience to a chief executive's directions is not well suited to the challenges of sustainable growth and best corporate governance (Special Report 2003). Risk management can be proactively and preventively implemented only where all individuals are conscious of strategy and risks.

Most advocates of corporate governance tend to fill oversight gaps in the constitution of boards and auditing committees by suggesting the enlargement of the feedback functions of accountability, disclosure, and internal control. However, in order to root out the causes of unfair and fraudulent behavior, senior managers should not only strengthen the accountability and disclosure of the implementation process of strategy and risk management but also assess strategy and its related risks as accurately as possible by collecting environmental information, preventively and proactively. In the case of operational risk, a proactive and preventive approach depends upon networking with suppliers chains through electronic communication and quick transportation systems (Collier and

Berry 2002). The manner in which the Strategic Scorecard could be used as part of feed-forward control and connected with accountability and disclosure processes is shown in Fig. 2.2.

Accountability is a basic requirement for large enterprises to be socially tolerated. Disclosure and controllability would be pointless in present-day society without accountability. Contemporary enterprises should therefore integrate accountability with disclosure and controllability. The three basic elements of enterprise governance should be based on feed-forward and feedback control systems. Strategic management is often transformational and unstable because it confronts the risks of such events as mergers and acquisitions. However, risk-taking provides opportunities for profit. In a competitive and changing world economy, enterprises must take unavoidable risks in order to pursue a sustainable value-creative strategy. Furthermore, large enterprises have to be proactively sensitive to environmental protection and preservation interests, since their size makes it impractical to reactively and reflectively control the potentially harmful wider impact of their activities. As roundtable discussion participants pointed out in the *Journal of Strategy + business* (2003, p. 57):

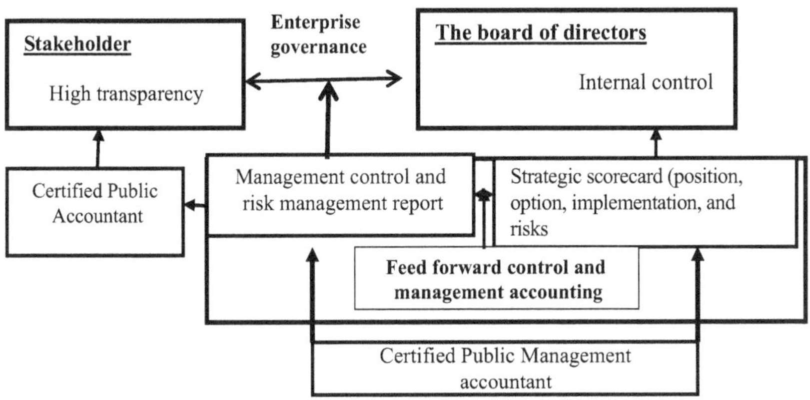

Fig. 2.2 Enterprise governance and feed-forward control. (Note: All the risks of an enterprise cannot be disclosed. Only the assessment and proactive control of the risks related to the selected strategies are illustrated in the report. The report is composed of the progress of strategy and its prospect, the possibility of risks related to it and the preventive actions to make them minimum, and the present situation of the strategy and risks. Source: PAIB 2004, 20)

> The day of Charisma is over, challenging uncertainty by which growth opportunity is created becomes more and more important, and faith must be integrated with information and certainty.

Khurana (Special Report 2003, p. 57) notes that trust takes a long time to build but can be lost overnight. Many Japanese bankruptcies among large businesses originate in distrust. Due to self-interest, arrogance, and ignorance, senior managers continue to disregard the advices of junior management and employees, thereby losing social trust.

Management accounting should emphasize the need for feed-forward control, linking this with enterprise governance and performance. Risk management is sometimes claimed to be essentially proactive and strategy is really a "living thing" (Prickett 2004, pp. 14–15). Japanese enterprises have historically succeeded in penetrating international markets with goods of high quality and low cost. I have argued elsewhere that part of this success is due to the adoption of feed-forward control systems (Nishimura 2003). Feed-forward control *has* contributed to Japanese strategic management but it now needs to be integrated with risk management. The role of feed-forward control is not only to forecast risks but also to assess risks as objectively as possible, through collecting business environment information, using preventive and proactive methods to alter the risks associated with strategic goals and to achieve planned goals. Feedback control is insufficient for such a realization.

Senior management are responsible for the processes of feed-forward and feedback controls but it is also necessary for these to be reported to the board of directors and stakeholders to attain effective governance. Accountability is closely connected to information on feed-forward and feedback controls. The board or independent committee should review and check the process of feed-forward control: assessing risks and checking management control. Accountability depends upon information about the processes of feedback and feed-forward controls (see Fig. 2.3). Good enterprise governance is built by the integration of accountability, disclosure, and controllability from the viewpoints of both feed-forward and feedback controls. The oversight gap and the value creation under risky business environment must be resolved on the basis of feed-forward control and information.

A question pertaining to the relationship between business governance and feed-forward control is: "Who can assess risks and check managers' strategy-implementation process and risk management from the viewpoint of feed forward control?" This question is related to a generic

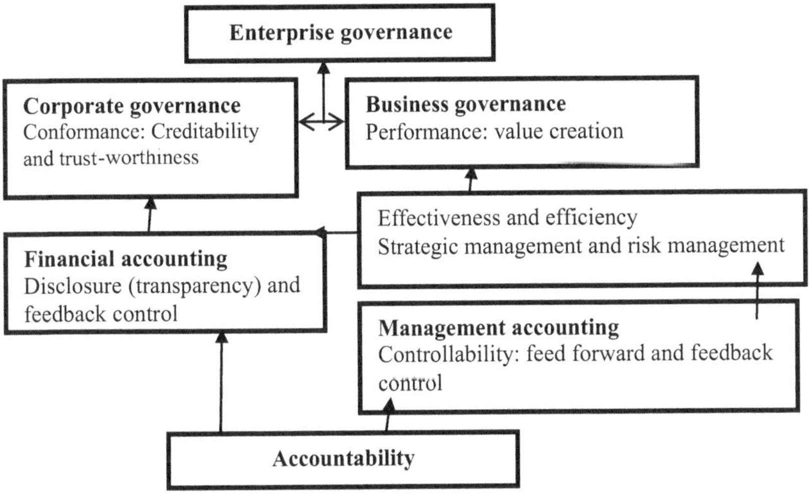

Fig. 2.3 Business governance and management accounting. (Source: PAIB 2004, 20)

reporting problem. When laypersons are given information relating to feed-forward control by management, it cannot be readily interpreted and checked. Therefore, internal professional accountants and, in particular, certificated public management accountants (CPMA) need to play the same role in auditing management control process as external public accountants do in the financial accounting arena. Proper disclosure and accountability practices relating to management control processes should be assessed and checked by CPMAs or their equivalents. In countries such as Japan where the management accounting profession is as yet relatively undeveloped, this calls for reforms of the education system and the establishment of a system of qualification and certification for public management accountant.

The board of directors is ultimately responsible for business strategy. Therefore, with the support of public management accountants and oversight committees, the board should review the process of strategy implementation by the chief executive and senior managers as well as make strategy (PAIB, p. 12). Enterprise governance would be enhanced if information on strategy and its related risks were given to stakeholders in a management control report or a strategy and risks report closely connected to Strategic Scorecard. Figure 2.2 illustrates the suggested relationships between business governance and CPMA's role. In the Mitsubishi Trading Company today, data numerically grading projects and estimating the market value of their related assets and the probability of bankruptcy and failure are incorporated with every investment project risk management system (Abe et al. 2000). If these data were included in publicly accessible concise management control reports, transparency and social confidence in enterprise would be heightened.

2.6 Conclusion

Financial reporting, based on international standards, is quite uniform in large companies in most nations. Substantial resources have been invested in recent years in improving the impact of financial reporting on effective corporate governance. Management accounting reporting practices are, in contrast, widely different between countries. Far fewer resources have been devoted to improving enterprise governance by implementing better management accounting practices. Consequently, more effort should be made to increase the role of management accounting and management control systems in order to integrate corporate governance with successful value creation or effective business governance. The inclusion of nonfinancial information in management accounting and its organic connection with financial reporting, which have long been advocated (e.g., Dressler 2002; Kaplan 1984), surely becomes the first step to development of good enterprise governance. However, it is more important for comprehensive risk management and business value management as the key of good enterprise governance to reexamine management accounting information and financial reporting from the global and proactive (i.e., feed-forward) perspective. Countries that have underdeveloped certified public management accounting practices should examine the role of professional management accounting bodies such as the CPMA in relation to strategic risk management in order to establish good *enterprise governance*. A feed-forward approach to management control is central to this reformative process of management accounting structure and profession. To support these endeavors, accounting education must be reformed into the synthetic structure of financial and management accounting from the forward-looking perspective.

Bibliography

Abe, T., Yoshikawa, K., & Hasegawa, H. (2000). Risk Management in IT Business Age. Nikkei Information Strategy, December (monthly), 37, Tokyo: Nikkei Business Publication.

Appleyard, T., & Pallet, S. (2001). *Successful Foreign Acquisitions* (pp. 16–17). Burlington: CIMA publishing.

Banks, E. (2004). *Corporate Governance: Financial Responsibility, Controls and Ethics* (pp. 26–27). Basingstoke: Palgrave Macmillan.

Collier, P. M., & Berry, A. J. (2002). Risk in the Process of Budgeting. *Management Accounting Research, 13*, 273–297.

Connell, B. (2004, April). Perspective on Enterprise Governance, Presented to the *CMAC Management Accounting Conference*, Kuala Lumpur.

Dietl, H. M. (1998). *Capital Markets and Corporate Governance in Japan, Germany, and the United States* (pp. 23–44). London: Routledge.

Dressler, S. (2002). Management Accounting Master: Closing the Gap Between Managerial Accounting and External Reporting. *Journal of Cost Management, 16*(January/February), 18–29.

Imoto, S. (1999, June). What Distinguishes Nakauchi (Chairman of Daiei) from Ito (Honor Chairman of Ito Yokado Co. Ltd.)? *Nikkei Venture*, 82–86.

Itami, H. (2000). *Japanese Corporate Governance*. Tokyo: Nihon Kezai Sinbun.

Japan Times. (2004). Scandal-wracked Mitsubishi Motors Struggling to Survive, *Japan Times*, August 22.

Kaplan, R. S. (1984). The Evolution of Management Accounting. *The Accounting Review, 59*(3), 390–418.

Kim, K. S. (1995). *Chaebol and Corporate Governance in Korea* (pp. 47–49). Arbor: UMI Dissertation Services, a Bell & Howell Company.

Marple, R. P. (1936). *Capital Surplus and Corporate Net Worth* (p. 7). New York: The Ronald Press.

Mochizuki, K. (1995). Preface: Project Objective, In David H. Kaufman (Ed.), *Japanese Corporate Governance: A Comparative Study of Systems in Japan and the United States* (pp. ix, 15). New York: The Asian Institute.

Nikkei Venture. (2001). *Study on Bankruptcy*. Tokyo: Nikkei BP.

Nishimura, A. (2003). *Management Accounting in Asia: feed forward and Asian perspectives*. Hampshire: Palgrave Macmillan.

Niyama, Y. (2001). *Dispute on Corporate Governance. Study Meeting of Business and Law Affairs*. Japan: Tokyo.

PAIB. (2004). *Enterprise Governance: Getting the Balance Rights*. New York/London: IFAC/CIMA.

Prickett, R. (2004, March). Up the Right Tree. *Financial Management, 33*(1), 12.

Society for Study of Risk Management and Internal Control. (2003). *Internal Control in the New Age of Risks*. Tokyo: The Japanese Ministry of Economy and Industry.

Solomon, J., & Solomon, A. (2004). *Corporate Governance and Accountability* (pp. 169, 177, 179 and 181). West Sussex: John Wileys and Sons.
Special Article. (2000, December). Risk Management in the New Day of Information Technology. *Nikkei Strategy*, 26–46.
Special Report. (2003). The Leadership: Challenge 2003, *Strategys+Business*, pp. 49–50.
Stuart, I., & Stuart, B. (2004). *Ethics in the Post-Enron Age*. Cincinnati: Thomson South-Western College Pub.

CHAPTER 3

Conceptual Analysis of Value-Based Management and Accounting: With Reference to Japanese Practices

3.1 Introduction

As the globalization of the finance-oriented economy and the global development of financial enterprises accelerate, manufacturing firms are also shifting toward becoming strongly financially oriented. In addition, many large enterprises are tending toward the enlargement of their organizations and driving their rivals out of the markets in order to sustain their dominant positions. Multinational enterprises may be too big and selfish and lie beyond social control. Some companies tend to adopt financial means and to manipulate their positions to earn wealth in the global business arena and to conceal these true financial situations despite the social entreaty for enhanced accountability and disclosure. Many financial instruments may have been developed through fabricated accounting techniques (e.g., accounting for derivatives) that promote financial activities and which prevent investors from realizing the concealment of their unfair and dishonest transactions. On the other hand, however, accounting manipulation has actually been enhanced in order to conceal earnings connected with financial instruments. Thus, financial businesses have become vast not only through complex financial transactions but also via the repeated purchase and absorption of other operating businesses: takeover bid or merger. At the same time, all operating businesses are facing keen competition in the international markets under the rapid development of information and transportation technologies. Every day they should compete with their rivals in the development of new types of product.

A. Nishimura, *Management, Uncertainty, and Accounting*,
https://doi.org/10.1007/978-981-10-8989-3_3

Under such an extremely financially structured economy, the severe competition in the international markets, short-lived consumer sentiment, and rapid change in technology force all operating enterprises to continually improve the quality of their products while at the same time endeavor to minimize their costs in order to gain competitive advantages. This is because the enterprises that fail to do so would be taken over and merged by worldwide financial firms. Consequently, all enterprises expose themselves to the risk of being purchased or forsaken by financial firms and shareholders whenever they cannot create better and higher value-added products relative to their rivals. Given such a situation, they should also recognize themselves not just as going concerns, but as commodities which are unstably traded in the markets, just like their products. Therefore, each enterprise has a double character: it is a manufacturer, selling a product, hence has a product value (i.e., generates sales revenue); and it is an entity, exchangeable as a commodity, hence has a commodity value (i.e., the value of what is worth). It will be quite uncorroborated to survive perpetually as a going concern in the competitive markets even if the enterprise exerts its utmost.

Presently, no firm can survive without withstanding risks and uncertainty under severe competition. Such a stern reality prescribes the functions and roles of contemporary management accounting. This chapter aims to examine the relationships between value-based management (VBM) and accounting in Japan and clarify the basic framework of VBM accounting (VBMA). Therefore, the chapter begins by investigating the relationship between value and management, but, before doing so, provides existing literature on VBMA to clarify its subject of controversy. It then goes on to clarify the basic characteristics of contemporary management accounting based on VBM with reference to Japanese practices. Finally, the chapter attempts to construct variance-analytic models for VBMA, utilizing Demski's model and Cost Design (Nishimura 2003).

In conclusion it is summarized that VBMA as a provider of proactive and reactive information serves VBM, which adopts reliable feed-forward and quick feedback controls to make a decision and evaluate performance for the enhancement of value creation, and it shifts away from partial and financial measurement to proactive and integrated one including nonfinancial. At the same time, both VBM and VBM put emphasis on visualization and virtualization to prevent enterprises from irrevocable loss and deteriorative value creation.

3.2 Existing Literature and Accounting Cognition

Business enterprises have been assessed from the viewpoint of the capital markets, since they have been perceived in terms of their value as exchangeable properties. In the earlier stages, the concept of value was symbolized as shareholder value in management (Malmi and Ikäheimo 2003). Financial accounting first restructured its valuation and measurement methods in accordance with this concept which had also an effect on management accounting. Recently, however, with the growth of the knowledge economy and economic networks, management should be paying more attention to EVA_{TM}, residual profit, and cash flow discount, especially where their social and synergic ability can result in higher value relative to the total for each factor of production. Thus, a great deal of thought has been exerted on the relationship between value creation and cultural and communal communication (Cant 2006). Consequently, management researchers and accountants have begun to examine the management process from the perspective of knowledge, human resources, business networks, and value chain, or value added. Their perspective has shifted away from the short-term shareholder toward the long-term shareholder value management, and the stakeholder value management as well as sustainable growth (Rappaport 2006; Porter and Kramer 2006; Cant 2006). Actually, some companies in Japan and Germany reconsider 'Anglo-Saxon capitalism', which has caused investment funds to exhaustively cross over border, the intensification of jungle M&A, and the stronger voice of stockholders and group for the 'Third Way' differently from the Rhein or Japanese one based on social joint decision (Ishiyama, et al. 2006; Geissler et al. 2006).

Möller and Svahm (2006) depict three stages in the development process of business networks: the current business nets, the business renewal nets, and the emerging new business nets. They also clarify today's characteristics of value creation management, particularly pointing out that for them it is important to stress the complex collaborative learning models and the uncertainty and ambiguity related to value activities as a result of radical changes in old value activities.

Recent management accounting discussions and practices have resulted in some fruitful outcomes: cost design, in which cost management is combined with functions and quality (value); balanced scorecard (BSC), in which financial and nonfinancial measurements are connected, strategy is permeated into the total membership of an organization, and social synthetic power is generated; and activity-based costing (ABC), which distinguishes between value added and nonvalue added and strengthens the former. However, only scant literature has studied the general framework of VBMA, which refers to the new relationship between value management and accounting, and the exchangeable value's effect on management accounting, with the latter's transfiguration into a new type. It is extremely vital to make clear how management accounting has changed and how it ought to change to support VBM.

Hilton (2005) discussed management accounting from the angle of value creation at an early time. He is interested in 'value to [the enterprises'] shareholders by leveraging the strength of [the enterprises'] brand'. Therefore, ABC related to activities and value added, and value chain became his subject of discussion. With regard to the Japanese literature, Japanese scholars have energetically studied cost management with relation to value (function) in terms of cost design, and, here, Tanaka (1995, 2002) is the most enthusiastic; he has recently studied management accounting from the viewpoint of value concepts. Tanaka et al. (2006) characterize contemporary management accounting as multivalue management and point out that since the activities of the enterprises should be various, they need to be evaluated likewise, with aspects tackling environmental value, economic value (fair market value, investment value, stock value, etc.), social value, and brand value. Basically, they emphasize that there exist plural values in business management and these should be harmonized at the core of stockholder value (Tanaka et al. 2006). Monden (2006) barely examines accounting issues in VBM, although he describes the functions of human assets from the viewpoint of shareholder value. Ueno (2007) rightly describes VBMA management accounting in the development process from cost- through profit- to value-based management accounting. Although these researchers have made some important contributions to the development of management accounting, it is however yet to be made clear how management accounting is related to the value concepts and how accounting measures and controls these values.

3.3 Value and Management

Basic Concepts

Profits and costs have for a long time been mainly used as fundamental concepts in management accounting, since they could monetarily and directly measure and evaluate the planning process and performance and hence help managers plan and control the business process. Why do accounting students, who, as Bell (1925) formerly averted the usage of value, conceive of measurement as the most important function of accounting, keep on debating the concept of value in management accounting in the face of its inability to directly measure economic activities? Before elucidating the reasons for this, we should clarify the relationship between value and management.

Generally speaking, value is an extremely abstract and general concept related to human judgment or utility, but it needs to take a concrete form for measurement and evaluation in accounting. Therefore, when we examine the relationship between value and management, we should study more deeply the contradiction between the abstract and concrete, or the general and individual.

In economics, value has been used as utility, usefulness, or effect, since in a general sense it is related to the individual's psychological and preference conditions, but otherwise it takes the concrete form of price or capital, which can be measured in terms of money. Smith (1776) pointed out two different meanings for the word value: the utility of some particular object (value in use) and the power of purchasing other goods (value in exchange).[1] Marx (1867) also elucidated the relationship between abstraction and concreteness of value, according to whose theory the individual and concrete value of usefulness takes the most abstract form of exchangeable value in its exchange process and gradually develops toward such more concrete concepts as goods, money, price, and capital, although the concrete concept of working hour is common to all value concepts. Anyway, value is surely contradictory in terms of utility and exchangeability and takes various different forms in different stages of exchange process.

It must be confirmed that the double aspect of utility and exchangeability for a product to take as value also applies to a company. A company has also the double aspect of value in use and value in exchange. It is utility for a company to create profit through product (value) production: to efficiently and effectively produce products of high quality and at lower cost for competitive advantage. However, assets value to guarantee the value production is not always consistent with the whole value of a company (enterprise value), since the financial markets would evaluate it from the viewpoint of exchangeability and future ability for profitability. It is of importance to clarify that value in production differs from value in the market, which reflects future profitability and exchangeability. Therefore, a company should integrate value management in production with value management in the market. Management must not only control the production process based on market demand but also enhance the market value of the company by strengthening brand value or social reliability. Incidentally, this chapter also regards 'value' as 'functions divided by cost' as well as 'exchangeable enterprise value'.

As the double aspect of a company as a value producer and an exchangeable value in market regulates the characteristics of VBM, management must proactively and preventively control value production in step with enterprise value due to risky and uncertain environment, while management accounting must provide synthetic and proactive information and analytical results to management, which deals with risks and uncertainty. Today, therefore, management accounting must basically focus on value production from the wider aspect of organization and culture (Olsen 2002).

Double Aspect of Management

In today's world, senior managers should assess and control the value production processes within the context of their relation to the market value of enterprise. In other words, they should develop competitive products of high value, concurrently enhancing the social value of their enterprise through offering attractive brands with high reliability. Nobody could launch into a significant argument with contemporary management and accounting without the recognition of common value concepts.

In contrast to the traditional methods, contemporary management must enhance not only the individual value of their products but also the entire worth of their companies. Each value of product is produced and controlled in one factory, that is, value production in the company, while the whole value of the company is created with the cooperation of the market-conscious employees under value-based leadership, that is, value formation inside the markets. Thus, because value creation consists of value production and value formation, managers should pay attention not only to efficient and effective production but also to social responsibility and reliability of their company.

However, value production does not easily translate into value formation nor always lead to value creation. At present, business enterprises would not succeed in VBM without the strategic integration of these two aspects. Acquisition as tool for simple business expansion (value formation), if it proves to be in conflict with 'a new growth platform' (Laurie et al. 2006), would lead in the long run to value destruction, not value creation.

Sometimes, the short-term view of market share (short-term request for dividends by shareholders) often means the sacrifice of the long-term nature of value production, since senior managers operate earnings in accounting and undermine value creation (Rappaport 2006). Even a minor defect in these aspects of management may lead to a complete ruin of the business enterprise, so the balance between the production and formation of value is of critical importance to good value creation. Indeed, we have a typical example where the fiendish leadership for value resulted in hollowed value creation. This occurred during the 1990s when Kenneth Lay and three other top executives, namely Fastow, Skilling, and Causey, orchestrated 'one of the largest cases of corporate fraud in the United States history', making Enron 'Houston's most benevolent financial donor' and the company that 'actively encouraged employees to embrace these professed values by involving themselves with local charities' (Glynn and Jamerson 2006). Thus, value-creative management must keep in step with the long-term strategy and enterprise governance (Nishimura 2006a, b, c: see also Chap. 1).

3.4 Structure of Value-Based Management

Leadership and Uncertainty

As mentioned above, partial and individual management must connect with the whole management of business value. More concretely, all members of an enterprise should understand its mission and strategy, which senior executives decide based on various competitive conditions and social responsibility, while the ideas and feelings of employees should be absorbed in the senior executives' strategic decision-making, since they always work at the place closest to strategic markets (customers) and advanced technologies. Value-based leadership plays the most important role in translating strategy into action and managing value (culture) creation. Culture is a value common to an organization and enterprise culture is always carried out under value-based leadership (Worline and Boik 2006; Bouch 2006). Powely and Taylor (2006) point out that "leadership is not a position but rather a relationship (p. 194)", and "at the collective level, healing refers to coordinated activity by several individuals who aim to restore harmony, security, and integrity to individuals in their care. The role of leaders, then, is to help organizational units return to health by being attuned to and concerned for the social relationships of their organizations" (p. 197).

Value-based leadership and cooperation for value creation become more important in the contemporary world of high risk and strong strategic competition, because risk must be preventively and proactively managed and changed into profit opportunity in order to enhance the prospects for profitability. Weick (2006) also states that the "role of values in high risk organizations is to provide a direction for people who are thrown into the middle of unknowable, unpredictable events that don't play by the rules" (p. 65). According to him, high-risk organizations must devalue misspecification, wrong estimation, and misunderstanding, while they must be careful of people who pay too much attention to success, simplicity, strategy, and anticipation. Today's operational and financial risks would not be lessened without the proactive cooperation of all members of an organization.

Visible and Virtual Management

VBM is value-creative management built on the value-based leadership and cooperation: risk and strategy management for value creation within the context of social reliability. It must be both preventive and proactive in order to avoid decisive failure, since financial markets and value formation regulate value production and value creation, which are both very unstable and subject to uncertainty. Under these circumstances, senior managers must perceive risks and try to transform them into profit opportunities. For this purpose, therefore, quick feedback and reliable feed-forward controls assume vital importance. The former quickly enables revision of errors, hence the avoidance of critical defects and failures, while the latter facilitates the prediction of outbreaks of errors, and the exercise of preventive and proactive risks control. Thus, contemporary management needs to integrate visual management with virtual management: quick feedback with reliable feed-forward control (Nishimura 2005).

The integration of virtual and visual management plays an important role in minimizing opportunity cost and maximizing profit opportunities. In order to establish an effective VBM system, control should be visual in relation to quick feedback control and concurrently virtual in relation to reliable feed-forward control. Therefore, with the strong cooperation of and harmony with all employees, sensitive monitors, precise observers, and mobile controllers should be prepared for the fulfillment of quick feedback and reliable feed-forward controls. When these control systems fulfill their functions perfectly, the enterprise would be able to gain a competitive advantage in the value creation.

Visualized management has been adopted by the Japanese enterprises in the form of the *Kanban* and *Andon*[2] systems where all employees at the workshops can use them to find defects and failures through warning lights as soon as they occur and cooperatively immediately correct them. This, together with quick feedback control, makes it possible to perfectly realize high-quality products at low cost as a result of cooperative multiskills and the saving of high repair costs which add up in loose and slow feedback control systems. Recently, the Kanban system has become electronic in some Japanese companies called *Kanban system* with ultra high frequency (UHF) and radio-frequency identification (RFID).[3] When materials move from storage to a factory, electronic *Kanbans* with RFID give the control center information on the changed amount of material inventory and the flow of each material, and each worker operates his/her job according to the *Kanban*. Some Japanese companies that have adopted the *Kanban system* have set many cameras and sensors at the ceiling of the shop to concentrically and individually monitor the flow of work and control stoppage or problematic places in the production process (see optical transmission equipment in Fujitsu[4]). This is an example of quick feedback management.

Virtual management has also been introduced in some Japanese companies for preventive and proactive management. *Shiseido*, a cosmetics company, uses computer and picture technologies to help customers buy the most suitable goods, since before purchase they can visually make up their faces on the computer display by freely arranging the imitative cosmetics, which simulate the actual goods of the company (see Development of Virtual Make-Up Picture System[5]). Once, Nissan Motor Company also planned to design order-made cars together with the customers on computer displays before production when agreement is reached between the two (Tanaka 1991). These are examples of reliable feed-forward management.

These quick feedback and reliable feed-forward management systems would create the opportunities for cost minimization and profit maximization through interviews between the suppliers and demanders. The organic connections between quick feedback and reliable feed-forward controls and between visual and virtual management systems play more important roles in actualizing value creation than in the past (reduction of opportunity cost related to sales and inventory risk). The more important the maximization of opportunity and the minimization of risk are, the quicker feedback control and the more reliable feed-forward control must be.

According to the above content, we can picture the framework of VBM in Fig. 3.1. Fundamentally, VBM consists of reliable feed-forward and quick feedback controls. The former aims at estimating reliable and realizable target and certainly transforming risks into profit opportunities before performance.

The latter quickly uses some new methods to amend wrong performance and change profit opportunities into profits and actualize its maximum. Eventually, VBM is a management system that tries to change uncertainty into profit opportunity and risk with some probability. At the same time, as shown in Fig. 3.2, through VBM, big risk is reduced to small loss and transformed into opportunity which then is turned into big profit.

Some Practices of VBM in Japan

With regard to Japanese VBM, Olympus Corporation, a manufacturer of precision machines and instruments, considers the enterprise value not as shareholder value but as stakeholder value. The company focuses on 'the involvement with society, the joint ownership of value with society, and the offer of value to society', of which every employee is conscious as well as whomever it does business with. At the same time, Canon Electronics

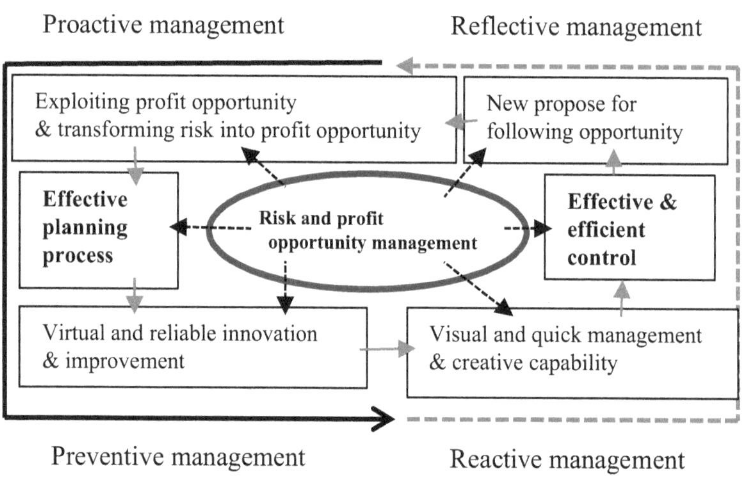

Fig. 3.1 Framework of VBM

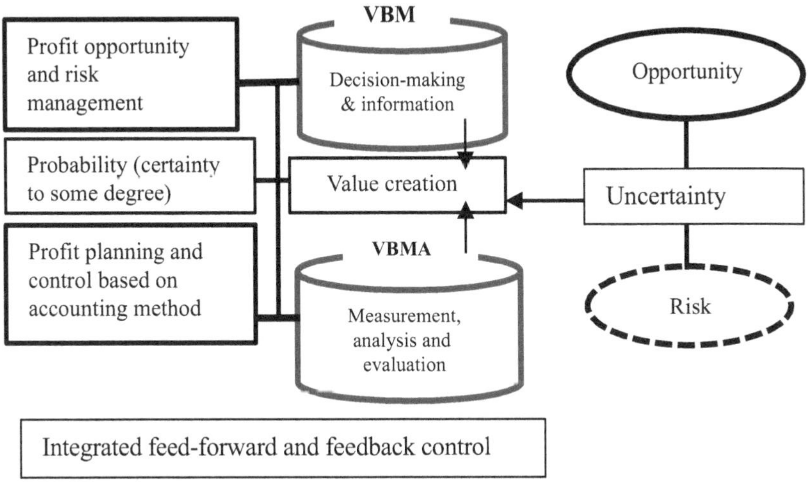

Fig. 3.2 Structure of VBM and VBMA

Inc. stresses leadership with value, which fully taps every employee's talents for the development of new technology and products (Sakamaki, 2007).

It is also noteworthy that many Japanese companies have aggressively researched on and developed new visual and virtual management systems in order to connect the efficient and effective production with risk and strategic management. NTT Data Corporation applies the Andon system to the area of system development for Kaizen (continual improvement) (Special Issue 2007). NEC has pursued real-time, lifecycle, and risk management systems based on the IT system. The company uses vendor-managed inventory (VMI: virtual inventory) to minimize inventory risk at the stages of production and materials' procurement, which are related to international business across borders. At the same time, NEC has adopted production order-attached RFID in the Yonezawa factory to realize a 10% increase in productivity. The whole process (from assembly and inspection to packaging and shipment) is unified in terms of management through this visible system. RFID enables the company to avoid waste in the assembling process and improve quality through the standardization of the working process. An example of this shows the reduction of 100,000 barcode reading works, which is due to replacing the manual barcode reading with RFID automation resulting in the standardization of operations based on online monitoring. This real-time management makes it possible to connect every workshop directly with the nerve center of decision-making. Futaba Industrial Company, which produces automobile components, has also aimed at becoming the 'No. One Factory' in the world through global production and management: facilities and production systems which anybody can use to produce the same product at the same input and quality in any of the company's factories anywhere in the world. The company has tried to fundamentally realize this goal by means of a visual, recognizable, and usable system.

Some Japanese companies have adopted virtual and visual management to visualize opportunities and risks and have proactively and quickly reactively used various methods to transform risks into profit opportunities. Accordingly, management accounting must be more visual and virtual management accounting than the traditional one, in order to support this management.

3.5 Value-Based Management Accounting and Analytical Model of Variance

Some Rudimentary Experiences

We have experienced the rudimentary connection of quick feedback control and reliable feed-forward control systems in Japanese and American management accounting. Cost design gave an earliest concrete form to VBMA in Japan, relying on value engineering and value analysis, in which the cost of a product is virtually and visually estimated and controlled at the product design stage from the viewpoint of a long-term profit plan and a competitive strategy. The allowable cost is estimated by subtracting the target profit from target sales, while, in accordance with the competitive strategy, estimated cost is calculated through a cost table or reverse engineering, which is more competitive relative to its rivals in terms of price and functions (quality). After variance between these two costs are analyzed and rectified through proactive improvements and new innovations, target cost is decided upon at the design and development stages for a new product. If the target cost is achieved, the company will be able to acquire a larger market share relative to its rivals. Consequently many Japanese motor companies have enhanced not only their sales revenues but their own business value.

We can count on ABC and BSC as successful examples of business strategy management based on quick feedback control. ABC is a cost measurement and management system connected with strategic value creation: cost is calculated on the basis of activities, a distinction is made between profitable (value-added) and nonprofitable (nonvalue-added) activities, and effective and efficient information is given to managers. The direct connection between cost and activity reduces the gap between VBM and strategic cost management.

On the other hand, BSC galvanizes the strategic mission into action. In order for the strategy and mission to penetrate the entire organization, BSC focuses on four stages relating to finance, customers, learning/growth, and the internal business process, even though the financial target is most important. Every member of the company should have a common value for the achievement of the mission (Kaplan and Norton 1996). Thus, the financial information must be integrated with the nonfinancial in strategic decision-making (Bhimani and Langfield-Smith 2007). For management accounting, the realization of its function becomes more distant from the financial measure and much closer to nonfinancial value (functions and satisfaction).

Despite such progress in management accounting, presently however world-class companies should pursue the more organic integrated system of quick feedback and reliable feed-forward controls than prevalent Cost Design, BSC, or ABC.

Structure of Variance Analysis

According to changing management viewpoints, as stated about Cost Design, ABC, and BSC, contemporary management accounting has also shifted from the cost- and profit-based management accounting systems to VBMA. We can make a picture of VBMA in Table 3.1, in contrast with the cost- and profit-based ones. As I have discussed the characteristics of each process of management accounting development in other papers (Nishimura 2003, 2005), traditional management accounting is based on cost-based one, which is distinguished by standard costing related to efficiency and waste control and feedback control. The quantitative and mathematical management accounting is mainly connected with profit-based one, of which opportunity costing and the transformation into feed-forward control are typical for decision-making.

Table 3.1 Development process of management accounting

Management accounting	*Management*	*Control*
Drifting management accounting	Management through financial accounting	Management Control in a haphazard way
Traditional management accounting	Management through optimum scientific time study and cost accounting	Feedback control through variance analysis
Quantitative management accounting	Management through decision-making among alternatives	Feed-forward-oriented feedback control
Integrated management accounting	Management through value engineering and cost design	Virtual (reliable) feed-forward control and visual (quick) feedback

Table 3.2 Surrogate for forecast profit variances (the case of new investment)

	Strategic (long-term) perspective	–	Competitive (short-term) perspective	=	Index for control
Forecast capital cost	Expected cost	–	Estimated cost	=	Forecast risk variance
Forecast revenue	Expected revenue	–	Estimated revenue	=	Forecast opportunity variance
Indicated control	Minimization of forecast risk variance and transforming risk into opportunity				

At present, this focus on value not only is a phenomenon confined to management accounting but also applies to financial accounting. Management accounting is much more strongly based on the relationship with stakeholder value (business value) than financial accounting oriented toward shareholders, so let us turn to an examination of why value has become a key concept in management accounting.

Firstly, it is quite obvious that the traditional viewpoints and methods of management accounting, based only on financial information like cost, have not coincided with the recent changing environment due to the development of the financially structured industry and the intensely competitive international markets. We would not be able to recognize and manage the whole value creation and value chain of companies using the cost or profit concept, since the whole value chain of interconnected companies is inconsistent with the total sum of their partial values. The chained value of management resources, social reputation and brand, and the skill of the engineers depict the whole value of a company. Each company is also always evaluated as an exchangeable commodity in the financial markets. Such partial concepts as cost or profit are not pertinent for measuring and managing the integrated value process.

Secondly, cost or profit cannot directly measure the value creation process, since the process is more comprehensive and abstract as well as concrete than cost. Therefore, we cannot also directly calculate its process by means of value, since, unlike cost or profit, it is not a concept for measurement. Although value is a key concept in contemporary management and accounting, it is not an accounting concept for evaluation and measurement. We should however use accounting concepts such as profit or cost indirectly in order to recognize and measure the value creation process, since the category of value is not instrumental in measuring it, although the category plays an important role in grasping and managing the factual structure of the contemporary enterprise. Because the accounting concepts cannot be directly used, they must be metamorphosed in another form.

Traditional thought of management accounting measured the business process directly by means of accounting concept like profit or loss, and tried to achieve profit as much as possible without perceiving that something might be hidden behind loss or profit. What is presently most important, however, is to find and realize the largest profit opportunity and create the opportunity for cost minimization. For this purpose, the world-class companies should adopt the visual (quick feedback) and virtual (reliable feed-forward) management system to bring out in the open what is hidden. Contemporary management accounting should more strongly look forward due to the increased uncertainty of value creation caused by radical changes in the value drivers (Möller and Svahn 2006, p. 989; Scapens 2006). COSO properly refers to the relationship between uncertainty and value:

> All entities face uncertainty, and the challenge for management is to determine how much uncertainty the entity is prepared to accept as it strives to grow stakeholder value. Uncertainty presents both risk and opportunity, with the potential to erode or enhance value. Enterprise risk management enables management to efficiently deal with uncertainty and associated risk and opportunity and hereby enhance the entity's capacity to build value. (COSO 2004)

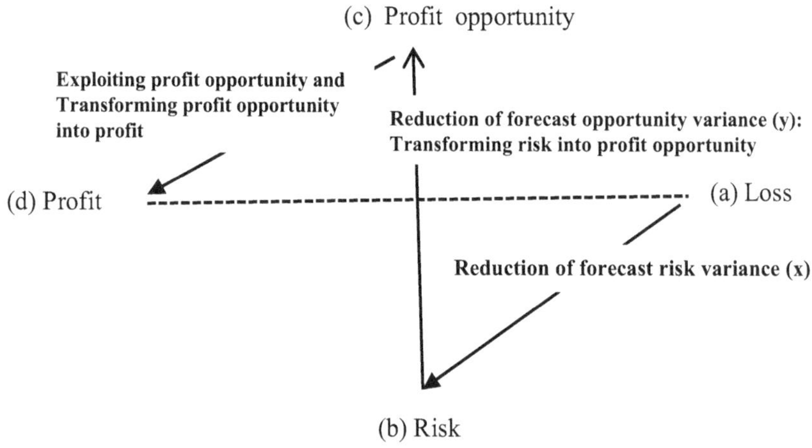

Fig. 3.3 Proactive profit management

The relationship between profit opportunity and risk is managed as depicted in Fig. 3.3. The solid line in this figure shows how to manage the profit opportunity and risk which hide behind the visible profit and loss. In order to support the strategic decision-making, management accounting should first collect information on profit opportunity and risk and measure their numerical values. The long-term and strategic amounts of opportunity and risk, measured on the sustainable growth of business and dividend policy, are compared with their short-term and competitive amount based on competitive strategy.

As a result of the two numerical comparisons, the target profit opportunity and risk are decided. All units and employees should do their best to proactively and preventively diminish these variances and achieve the target of profit opportunity and risk. This calculation is an ex ante process carried out at the decision-making stage. Senior managers use the information (a-b-c-d) to maximize profit opportunities and minimize risks:

$$\text{Long-term opportunity} - \text{short-term}\left(\text{virtual}\right)\text{opportunity}$$
$$= \text{forecast opportunity variance}\left(\text{y}\right)$$

$$\text{Long-term risk} - \text{short-term}\left(\text{virtual}\right)\text{risk} = \text{forecast risk variance}\left(\text{x}\right)$$

In order to facilitate easy understanding, we use estimated cost and estimated revenue as a surrogate for profit opportunity and risk to explain the above equations in Table 3.2, because investment in a value-creative project may be made looking on both the expected revenue and the capital cost (expected risk)[6]:

What is most important is to preventively and proactively interweave them with the target values in order to erase these variances by collecting strategic and competitive information and adopting pertinent effective improvements. This target calculation is made in order to secure the general strategy for a company, but it also indicates the individual targets for each organization. Thus, reliable feed-forward management should be carried out in this process.

Moreover, the two target values should be compared with the actual values (profit and loss) after performance. It is certain that the targets will never be consistent with the actual values. Managers should recognize these variances as opportunity cost variance or avoidable risk variance and utilize them to adopt various methods and minimize variances in the following period. This is quick feedback control.

$$\text{Target opportunity} - \text{actual profit} = \text{opportunity cost variance}$$

$$\text{Actual loss} - \text{target risk}\left(\text{expected loss}\right) = \text{avoidable risk variance}$$

This calculation process is ex post and is feedback control. We summarize the above equations in Fig. 3.4.

These variance analyses can give managers information on profit opportunities and risks and help them preventively and reflectively to control the production process from the viewpoint of value creation. For the implementation of VBM, "a project leader who can measure value creation through accounting and finance, and who has the capacity to change the corporate landscape" is strongly required in the contemporary business enterprise (Karame 2004). At the same time, management accountants should use feed-forward databases to build models in order to create value (Calderon et al. 2003).

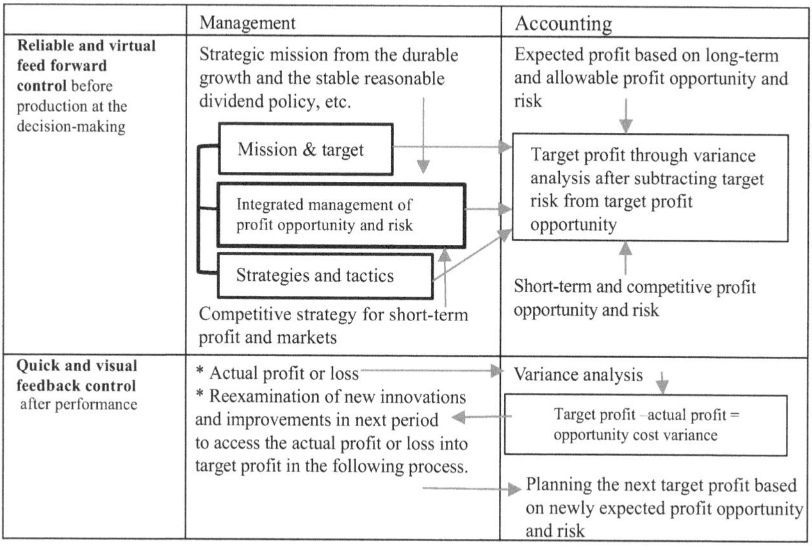

Fig. 3.4 VBM and variance analysis

3.6 Conclusion

The analytical model of accounting, as described above, helps management make a decision and evaluate performance for value creation by providing information on profit opportunities/risks and its analytical results. The ex ante and ex post analyses give proactive and reflective information to managers who carry out reliable feed-forward and quick feedback controls under uncertain and risky business environment. Under the keen competition in international market, continuous advance in technology and short-lived consumer sentiment, all enterprises always face risks and uncertainty and try to keep away from crucial risks or take risks for bigger opportunities (see Fig. 3.4).

Therefore, from the angle of risk management, management should not only effectively and efficiently control production process but also enhance enterprise value. At the same time, it should also combine the former with the latter for value creation. All members of an enterprise must look more forward and be more proactive and quickly reactive. In addition, the organic cooperation of organizational members must tie up with the leadership with value in order to establish reliable feed-forward and quick feedback management system. After all, VBM and VBMA should be virtual and visual, since VBM is proactively and reactively carried out in relation with risks and uncertainty by the proactive and reactive support of accounting information.

This chapter has endeavored to clarify some pertinent aspects of VBM and VBMA by highlighting certain Japanese VBM practices and to examine the framework of VBM and VBMA by means of conceptual approach. This goes a long way toward developing the practically applicable model of VBMA and theoretically formulating an outline of management accounting history in connection with the previous researches, since this work may lead to clarifying fundamental factors which have historically accelerated management accounting development.

However, much still remains to be done in this chapter. First, by using some empirical evidences, it must be made clear how to concretely transform risks into profit opportunities, since the relationships between risks and profit opportunities are so intricately bilateral as to be incomprehensible. Secondly, the conceptual framework of VBM and VBMA should be more deeply testified by empirical study in order to be more persuasive. Lastly, because the variance analyses were only theoretically and abstractly inquired in this chapter, they should be further expanded into actually applicable models. As a result, these empirical studies would give a power of persuasion to the conceptual approach in this chapter, which laid the foundation to the formation of practical and applicable VBM and VBMA. The relationship between VBM and enterprise governance has not been touched on in this chapter despite its importance, since it was observed in the previous chapters (see also Nishimura 2006a, b, c).

Notes

1. Adam Smith also pointed out that "The word VALUE, it is to be observed, has two different meanings, and sometimes expresses the utility of some particular object, and sometimes the power of purchasing other goods which the possession of that object conveys. The one may be called 'value in use'; the other, 'value in exchange'" (Smith, Adam, Inquiry into the Nature and Causes of the Wealth of Nations, 1776 (Modern Library: New York, 1937, p. 28)).
2. Andon is a lamp that lets other workers know the need for the cooperative resolution of a problem when it occurs on an assembly line. When a worker

at the problematic line draws the switch cord, Andon goes on and off, and other workers know the problem and cooperatively resolve it with hm.

3. "Radio-frequency identification (RFID) is an automatic identification method, relying on storing and remotely retrieving data using devices called RFID tags or transponders. An RFID tag is an object that can be attached to or incorporated into a product, animal, or person for the purposes of identification using radio waves. All RFID tags contain at least two parts, one is an integrated circuit for storing and processing information, modulating and demodulating a radio frequency (RF) signal and perhaps other specialized functions. The second is an antenna for receiving and transmitting the signal" (Wikipedia, http://en.wikipedia.org/wiki/RFID). "Ultra High Frequency (UHF) offers a greater communications range than other frequency bands. As a result, the use of the UHF RFID system for full traceability of products has been growing in the retail and logistic industries, UHF tags, however, are subject to multi-path interference, an inherent problem for electromagnetic signals, which can make a RFID tag unreadable even if it is within the range of the reader" (NE Asia Online 2006 March 30, http://neasia.nikkeibp.com/dailynewsdetail/003799?ST=English).
4. Seehttp://enterprise.watch.impress.co.jp/cda/topic/2005/12/09/6810.html.
5. See Shiseido, 'Development of Virtual Make-Up Picture System': http://www.sankei.co.jp/enak/2007/jam/kiji/29lifemake.html.
6. See Chopp and Paglia, 'Build a Culture of Value Creation': http://gbr.pepperdine.edu/021/print_vbm.html.

Bibliography

Bell, H. W. (1925). *Accountants' Report* (2nd ed.). New York: The Ronald Press.

Bhimani, A., & Langfield-Smith, K. (2007). Structure, Formality and the Importance of Financial and Non-financial Information in Strategy Development and Implementation. *Management Accounting Research, 18*(1), 3–31.

Bouch, W. G. (2006). FedEx Freight-Putting: People First. In H. D. Edward & K. K. Cameron (Eds.), *Leading with Values: Positivity, Virtue and High Performance* (pp. 29–54). Cambridge/New York: Cambridge University Press.

Calderon, G. T., Cheh, J. J., & Kim, I. (2003). How Large Corporations Use Data Mining to Create Value. *Management Accounting Quarterly, 4*(2), 1–11.

Cant, S. (2006, April). Value-based Management. *Financial Management*, pp. 33–34.

COSO. (2004, September). *Enterprise Risk Management-Integrated Framework: Executive Summary Framework,* The Committee of Sponsoring Organizations of the Treadway, NJ (US).

Geissler, C., Ikeda, R., & Cook, A. (2006, July). Corporate Germany Must Change? *Diamond Harvard Business Review* (Japanese version), pp. 44–56.

Glynn, M., & Jamerson, H. (2006). Principled Leadership: A Framework for Action. In D. E. Hess & S. K. Cameron (Eds.), *Leadership with Values: Positivity, Virtue, and High Performance.* Cambridge, NY: Cambridge University Press.

Hilton, W. R. (2005). *Managerial Accounting: Creating Value in a Dynamic Business Environment* (6th ed.). New York: McGraw-Hill.

Ishiyama, S., Kimura, Y., & Kumagaya, T. (2006, July). German Business Report. *Diamond Harvard Business Review* (Japanese version), pp. 68–174.

Kaplan, R. S., & Norton, D. P. (1996). *The Balanced Scorecard: Translating Strategy into Action.* Boston: Harvard Business School Press.

Karame, M. (2004, May). Leading a Value-Based Management Implementation. *The Trusted Professional, 7*(8). http://www.nysscpa.org/trustedprof/504/tp15.htm.

Laurie, L. D., Doz, Y. L., & Sheer, C. P. (2006, May). Creating New Growth Platform. *Harvard Business Review,* pp. 80–90.

Malmi, T., & Ikäheimo, S. (2003). Value Based Management Practices – Some Evidence from the Field. *Management Accounting Research, 14*(3), 235–254.

Marx, K. (1867). *Capital: A Critical Analysis of Capitalist Production, Volume 1.* Moscow: Foreign Language Publishing House.

Möller, K., & Svahm, S. (2006, July). Role of Knowledge in Value Creation in Business Nets. *Journal Management Studies, 43*(5), 994–989.

Monden, Y. (2006). Business Value, Human Assets and Organizational Restructuring. In Y. Monden, K. Miyamoto, K. Hamad, G. Lee, & T. Asada (Eds.), *Value-Based Management of the Rising Sun* (pp. 3–4). Singapore: World Scientific Publishing.

Nishimura, A. (2003). *Management Accounting in Asia: feed forward and Asian perspectives.* Hampshire: Palgrave Macmillan.

Nishimura, A. (2005). Strategic Management and Contemporary Management Accounting. In A. Nishimura & R. Willett (Eds.), *Management Accounting in Asia* (pp. 1–8). Singapore: Thomson Learning. (A division of Thomson Asia Pte Ltd.).

Nishimura, A. (2006a). Enterprise Governance and Management Accounting from the Viewpoint of Feed Forward Control. *Asian-Pacific Management Accounting Journal, 1*(1), 1–17. Public Knowledge Project (Open Journal System). http://arionline.uitm.edu.my/ojs/index.php/APMAJ/issue/view/20.

Nishimura, A. (2006b). Analysis of Industrial Structure and Profitable Structure in China; Recent Development and Problems Chinese State-owned Enterprises: Structures of Industry and Deficit. *Business Administration and Management Accounting in Asia* (pp. 257–279 and 311–334), Tokyo: Chuou Keizai Publisher.

Nishimura, A. (2006c). *Business Management and Management Accounting in Asia (Japanese)*. Tokyo: Chuokeizai Publisher.

Olsen, E. (2002). Rethinking Value-Based Management. *Handbook of Business Strategy*. http://w.w.w.bcg.com/publications/files/Rethinking-Value-Based-Mgmt-Sept-02pdf.

Porter, M. E., & Kramer, R. M. (2006). Strategy & Society: The Link Between Competitive Advantage and Corporate Social Responsibility. *Harvard Business Review*, January, *84*(12), 78–92.

Powely, H. E., & Taylor, N. S. (2006). Values and Leadership in Organizational Crisis. In H. D. Edward & K. S. Cameron (Eds.), *Leading with Values*. New York: Cambridge University Press.

Rappaport, A. (2006, September). Ways to Create Shareholder Value. *Harvard Business Review*, pp. 67–77.

Sakamaki, H. (2007). Digging Out Profit Through Elimination of Waste. *Business Research, 1*, 33–40.

Scapens, W. R. (2006). Changing Times: Management Accounting Research and Practices from a UK Perspective. In A. Bhimani (Ed.), *Contemporary Issues in Management Accounting* (pp. 329–354). Oxford: Oxford University Press.

Special Issue. (2007). Work Visualization and Workshop Improvement. *Nikkei Research, 4*, 19–47.

Tanaka, T. (Ed.). (1991). *Contemporary Management Accounting System*. Japan: Chuou-keizaisha.

Tanaka, M. (1995). *Theory and Practices of Cost Design*. Tokyo: Chuo-keizaisha Publisher, Co.

Tanaka, M. (2002). *Profit Strategy and Value Engineering: How to Implement Practical Cost Design*. Tokyo: Sangyo Noritu University Publisher.

Tanaka, M., Ishizaki, T., & Harada, N., eds. (2006). *Accounting for Performance Evaluation: The Development of Plural and Various Evaluations*, Chou-Keizaisha, 22–29.

Ueno, S. (2007). *Management Accounting for Value Creation*, 3rd ed. Zeimukeirikyoukai.

Weick, E. K. (2006). The Role of Values in High-Risk Organization. In H. D. Edward & K. S. Cameron (Eds.), *Leading with Values: Positivity, Virtue and High Performance* (pp. 55–67). Cambridge/New York: Cambridge University Press.

Worline, M., & Boik, S. (2006). Leadership Lessons from Sarah: Values-Based Leadership as Everyday Practice. In D. Edward & K. S. Cameron (Eds.) (ibid., 108–131).

CHAPTER 4

Uncertainty and Management Accounting: Opportunity, Profit Opportunity, and Profit

4.1 Introduction

Management accounting is generally defined as a control method based on accounting information, in which business process is planned, analyzed, and evaluated by using the concepts of profit and cost. In other words, management accounting constitutes the methods and knowledge of accounting that serve business management. However, in the present period of high uncertainty, is profit information useful for future-oriented business management? Can an enterprise, relying on profit information from past performance, plan for and control its business in an unforeseeable future? If this is not the case, we must consider information on profit opportunity and enterprise risk (in the strict sense that this risk has a specific probability in relation to business organization and environments) in the present that may lead to the actualization of profit or loss in the future (Kumarasinghe and Willett 2010; Nishimura 2006a, b, c). Furthermore, the methods for measuring and controlling profit opportunity and enterprise risk in management accounting must be considered and developed. In an examination of the literature, past research has not clarified the proactive meaning of accounting information and the concept of profit opportunity, which are closely related to business management under serious uncertainty. Some view accounting information as financial value, while others view it as having more general value beyond financial purposes (i.e., the information on the amount of resources and economical value). It is also debatable whether profit in today's management accounting means

A. Nishimura, *Management, Uncertainty, and Accounting*,
https://doi.org/10.1007/978-981-10-8989-3_4

accounting profit or opportunity (i.e., identifying the best of many alternatives) (Nishimura 2003) that reflects future business direction under uncertainty.

We should, therefore, inquire into the relationship between uncertainty and business management and reconsider the concept of profit in management accounting in relation to uncertainty, since management accounting is carried out through forecasting and controlling uncertain economic activities and connecting this information within the existing organizational structure. For this purpose, this chapter will first examine how management theories have dealt with uncertainty and, secondly, examine what effect uncertainty has on the concept of profit. Thirdly, it will examine a theoretical framework for opportunity, profit opportunity, and profit in reference to real-world business practices, as some insight can be gained from the recent bankruptcies of large companies that have resulted from uncertainty and their countermeasures.

4.2 Uncertainty and Controllability in Business Management

Until now, uncertainty has been debated in business management from the viewpoint of controllability. According to economists, balancing production and consumption was originally too uncertain and unforeseeable to be resolved by human hands alone. Marx (1867, reprinted 1965) stated that consistency in this area was as "the leap taken by value from the body of the commodity into the body of the gold" (*Salto mortale der Ware*).[1] Smith (1776, reprinted 1937) pointed out that an individual who intended only his own gain through production of the greatest value also was led by an 'invisible hand'. No manufacturer can forecast changes in markets and business environments with complete certainty, which ultimately influence the sale of the products manufactured. A manufacturer must rely solely on the confidence in his or her calculations of the probability of revenue realization. Putting much faith in one's probabilities is precarious and pointless if technology and markets change suddenly and dramatically and become increasingly complicated. Although Smith dutifully acknowledged the difficulty of maintaining balance between production and consumption and entrusted its settlement to the 'invisible hand' (i.e., to the market itself), management scholars have long believed that management can maintain the balance in production and demand by using management knowledge, models, and information systems. Recently, some researchers have started to incorporate *unforeseeable* uncertainty into their research, although they also believe that it can be controlled through such a method as trial and error or selection-ism (Sommer et al. 2004, 2009; see Table 4.1). However, in the last decade, several large American manufacturing companies and banks have collapsed. In Japan, the 2011 earthquake, tsunami, and nuclear accident seriously damaged production lines, which have negatively impacted some large manufacturing companies. These events are truly unforeseeable and are those from which recovery is very difficult. In order to specifically define the relationship between uncertainty and profit, we should reexamine the decision-making process through which managers have thought to be able to transform uncertainty

Table 4.1 Uncertainty and management

Authors	*Background and causes of uncertainty*	*Attitudes toward uncertainty*	*Main player*
Smith, Adam (1776, reprinted 1937)	Dissociation of production and market arose from the division of labor and competition	***Invisible hand*** guides market and price	Middleman
Knight, Frank H (1921)	Uneven distribution and imbalance of knowledge related to the changes of markets and technologies	Management organization acts as a quantitative system of knowledge; responsible management	***Entrepreneur***
Chandler, Alfred Jr. (1977)	Dissociation between markets and production arose from large-scale industry (large-scale fixed facilities; large-scale fixed costs)	***Visible hand*** controls markets through vertical integration of management and concentrated organization	Hierarchy of management; managerial revolution; managerial capitalism
Langlois, Richard N (2003)	Complexity of market networks originated from the dissolution of value chain and the modular production system	***Vanishing hand***: reentrance of market on the stage; vertical nonintegrated system of management	Decentralized organization and units; market
Sommer, Svenja C and Christoph, Loch H (2004)	Dynamic environments: ***unforeseeable uncertainty*** and high complexity	Unknown unknowns	Selection-ism and trial and error

into a certain condition, as has been stressed under the banner of the 'managerial revolution' and 'managerial capitalism' (Chandler 1977, p. 11). Further, the chapter considers profit management under uncertainty, which should be the focus of the study of management accounting.

We survey the views of management researchers who have referred to the dissociation between production and market and have proposed some countermeasures to control uncertainty. Table 4.1 shows how various management theories have grappled with uncertainty, such as Smith positing the existence of the 'invisible hand'.

Interestingly, in strong contrast to Smith (1776, reprinted 1937), Knight (1921, reprinted 2005), Chandler (1977), Sommer et al. (2004), and Langlois (2003) share a common viewpoint in which they trust the power of humans (or management organization and methods of management) to control uncertainty. However, the logical process of each is different from the others: Knight focuses on the *entrepreneur*; Chandler on the *vertical hierarchy of management*; and Langlois on *modular production systems and vertical non-integrated organizations*. Langlois, whose ideas on the vanishing hand follow directly from the invisible hand of Smith and the visible hand of Chandler, does not emphasize the deepened uncertainty and unmanageable chaos that frustrates business managers. He focuses on the contemporary, new characteristics of modular manufacturing systems and the functions of vertical nonintegrated organizations in relation to the controllability of uncertainty.

Although they surely considered uncertainty an important and troublesome problem, Knight, Chandler, and Langlois all have a strong confidence in the ability of management to control uncertainty through information, organizational system, and models. Certainly, their ideas, which were socially complemented by Berle and Means's (1932) ideas on the division of ownership and concentrated management and the independence of manager control in private corporations and by Burnham's 'Managerial Revolution' (1941), have dominated the field of management. Thus, management accounting, in keeping step with these ideas, has also moved forward under the prevailing belief that uncertainty can be controlled. The debate on the relationship between uncertainty and profit, which will be examined in this chapter, is also a result of this field of thought, since, according to these scholars, uncertainty brings forth profit and controllability over uncertainty allows for the management of profit. Management and accounting have tried to find opportunity and profit in the uncertain world and to plan for and control profit opportunity under the strong belief that uncertainty can be controlled. The next section examines the relationship between uncertainty and profit in detail under Knight's theory.

4.3 Knight's Theory on Uncertainty and Profit

Uncertainty and Knowledge

According to Knight, perfect knowledge gives rise to profits, in contrast to imperfect knowledge, which does not. Knight states that "profit arises from the fact that entrepreneurs contract for productive services in advance at fixed rates, and realize upon their use by the sale of the product in the market after it is made", even though profit is indirectly connected with changes in economic conditions (Knight, pp. 197–8). Entrepreneurs who rely only on known rules and experiences cannot forecast future changes in environment and the rise of severe competition and fulfill contracts made in advance. Therefore, quantitative knowledge that leads to the accurate knowledge of the future plays an important role in determining "the possibility of every possible outcome" (Knight, pp. 198–9). Profit is deeply related to future knowledge, judgment, vision, foresight, probability, and reaction before the materialization of a situation. Accurate, quantitative knowledge leads to "the reduction of uncertainty" (Knight, p. 293) and the magnification of certainty.

On the basis of the thoughts above, the ownership in a joint-stock company, where ownership is diffused and control concentrated, comes together to elect directors who exercise control over general policies and choose the officials to carry out its business. Stockholders must depend on the knowledge of others to obtain accurate information on the situation in the business and its problems, and rely on others to determine the means for affecting change (Knight, p. 292). Executives chosen by directors generally oversee business policy and selects subordinates who make most of the actual decisions involved in control of the company. According to Knight, the "fundamental principle underlying organized activity is therefore the reduction of the uncertainty in individual judgments and decisions by grouping the decisions of particular individual and estimating the proportion of successes and failures, or the average quality of his judgments as a group" (Knight, p. 293). As a result, officials who are free from responsibility can be distinguished from stockholders who must bear the risk of error in decision-making. While the person who makes routine decisions and deals with 'uncertainty as a matter of routine' or who seeks to eliminate foreseeable uncertainty (no risk-taking) receives a fixed salary, the stockholders, who take part in unforeseeable decision-making or do not exercise routine management, are the ones who are exposed to risks and receive any profit earned. Executives who are chosen by stockholders to oversee business policy and select subordinates also receive profits, since they use their judgment together with the quantitative knowledge of subordinates to produce profits by controlling future changes in economic conditions. We must point out Knight's 'revolutionary' conversion of function from a senior manager to *entrepreneur.* According to Knight (1921), this conversion occurs when the manager exercises judgment involving "liability to error" and gets the other members of the group to submit to his direction on the condition that he takes responsibility for the disappointed results of his choices. At this point, "the nature of the function is revolutionized: the manager becomes an entrepreneur". As a result of his responsible decision-making, such an entrepreneur produces "profit" and receives a part of profit.

Knight elaborates on the role of the executive by stating that the "fundamental fact of organized activity is the tendency to transform the uncertainties of human opinion and action into measurable probabilities by forming an approximate evaluation of the judgment and capacity of the man. The ability to judge men in relation to the problems they are to deal with, and the power to 'inspire' them to efficiency in judging other men and things, are the essential characteristics of the executive" (Knight, p. 311). We find "a complicated division or diffusion of entrepreneurship, distributed in the typical modern business organization by a hierarchy of security issues carrying every conceivable graduation and combination of rights to control and to freedom from uncertainty as to income and vested capital" (Knight, p. 300).

Entrepreneur's Connection with Profit or Risk

According to Knight, in contrast to determining the value of the contribution of workers and equipment to physical production,

> the facts upon which the working-out of the organizations depends can no longer be objectively determined with accuracy by experiment; all the data in the case must be *estimated,* subject to a larger or smaller margin of error, and this fact causes differences more fundamental than the resemblances in

> the two situations. The function of making these estimates and of 'guaranteeing' their value to the other participating members of the group falls to ***the responsible entrepreneur*** in each establishment, producing a new type of activity and a new type of incomes entirely unknown in a society where uncertainty is absent. (Knight, p. 276)

An entrepreneur of an organization must always face uncertainty and must estimate and guarantee the value produced in uncertain conditions, subject to some margin of error. A person cannot enjoy profits without taking risk. In the modern corporation, the managerial functions of dealing with uncertainty fall to the responsible entrepreneur, while routine controllers and persons working with some higher degree of certainty have no such responsibility.

Regarding entrepreneurship, one may say from the above that it has the dual aspect of organization activity: ownership, which is related to responsible decision-making of business strategy and risk-taking, and management control, which is related to the strategy. However, as the division between ownership and management and of management function becomes evident, apart from the ordinary management control under certainty, entrepreneur in a company takes a definite form as an executive who promotes a new enterprise or creates new business value and is responsible for its outcome and the inherent risks. Because uncertainty has such a strong influence on certain functions in a business organization, the division of organizational activity becomes important. Knight points out that "in the first place, occupations differ in respect to the kind and amount of knowledge and judgment required for their successful direction as well as in the kind of abilities and tastes adapted to the routine operations. Productive groups or establishments now compete for managerial capacity as well as skill, and a considerable rearrangement of personnel is the natural result. The final adjustment will place each producer in the place where his particular combination of the two kinds of attributes seems to be most effective" (Knight, p. 269). After all, "the organization of industry depends on the fundamental fact that the intelligence of one person can be made to direct in general way the routine manual and mental operations of others". Although uncertainty is primarily controlled by selecting personnel and specializing in one of the following four functions (knowledge and judgment, foresight, specialization, and risk-taking), ultimately their functions are personalized in *entrepreneurs*, who responsibly direct economic activity and are rewarded with a part of 'profit' and persons who furnish them with productive services in the wage system (Knight, p. 270).

Regarding profit, Knight states that the only "risk" that leads to profit is a unique uncertainty resulting from an exercise of ultimate responsibility.

> Profit arises out of the inherent, absolute unpredictability of things, out of the sheer brute fact that the results of human activity cannot be anticipated and then only in so far as even a probability calculation in regard to them is impossible and meaningless. The receipt of profit in a particular case may be argued to be the result of superior judgment. (Knight, pp. 310–11)

According to him, management organizations consist of risk-taking entrepreneurs, who tackle uncertainty, and hired managers, who do routine control services under comparative certainty, with the goal of creating a system that produces superior judgments on profit.

Knight gives us some important points for our argument as follows: profits are closely combined with *uncertainty*, profits are realized as a result of increased *probability* through perfect knowledge, and *entrepreneurs* play a critical part in systematically generating quantitative knowledge and accurately grasping future changes in economic conditions. These issues involving the concept of profit will be examined later.

Langlois (2003) examines how merchants protect against uncertainty and seek profit opportunities in the period before the American Civil War, as well as how management systems are handled within a corporate structure adapted to "the needs of new technology and of new profit opportunities" (Langlois, p. 357 and p. 353). He takes profit opportunity for granted when uncertainty and protections against it are called into question. Chandler (1977, p. 449) also points out that forecasted information and the variance in the actual results increase the "possibilities for rational choices between alternative investments and alternative methods of financing them".

These arguments about the relationship between uncertainty and opportunity (or profit opportunity) opened a new path for executives' strategic decision-making and the organizational structures, in which management and production structures carry out strategic decisions with the goal of transforming strong uncertainty into enhanced certainty. At the same time, opportunity and profit management has been systematically discussed in the literature in connection with decision-making problems, which are the foundation of the management accounting structure pertaining to uncertainty.

4.4 Uncertainty and Decision-Making

The Works of Simon and Anthony, and Nonprogrammed Decision

The work of Simon (1969, pp. 5–6) elucidated decision-making problems and deepened executives' desire to mitigate uncertainty. He divides decisions into repetitive and programmed decisions and nonprogrammed decisions. While the programmed decisions need not be treated de novo each time they occur since there is a defined procedure for handling them, the nonprogrammed decisions cannot adopt "cut and dried method for handling problems since they are novel, unstructured, and consequential". As for nonprogrammed decisions, "the problem hasn't arisen before, or their precise nature and structure are elusive or complex" (p. 6). The techniques for nonprogrammed decision-making shift from the three traditional methods of (1) judgment, intuition, and creativity, (2) rules of thumb, and (3) selection and training of executives to more modern solutions such as the heuristic problem-solving techniques applied to training human decision-makers and the construction of heuristic computer programs (p. 9). Simon focuses on increased heuristic problem-solving processes through the human-initiated usage of computers. Because human thinking is governed by programs in which myriads of simple information processes are organized, "programs can be written to describe human symbol manipulation, and these programs can be used to induce a computer to simulate the human process" (p. 26). He argues that computer simulation has the important effects of explaining heuristic processes used by people "in their non-programmed problem-solving and decision-making activity" (p. 32). He also holds the belief that uncertainty can be controlled by heuristic problem-solving processes supported by computers.[2]

Simon has exerted a strong influence on business management and management accounting. To further understand decision-making problem in profit management, we must examine two representative thoughts that could be subject to Simon's influence in the mid-1960s. First is Anthony (1965), who discussed the framework of strategic planning, management control, and operational control. In parallel with Simon, he divides planning into strategic planning that seeks to optimize, not suboptimize, the effectiveness of the whole organization in unexpected scenarios (p. 35) and planning for the control of regular processes. In strategic planning, to which we pay particular interest, "problems, opportunities, and bright ideas do not arise according to some time timetable" (p. 38).

Strategic planning combines with "what happens over a considerable period in the future" (p. 53) and long-term consequences (p. 68) to create such complexity that one is unable to think of "a complete specification of alternatives courses of action" (p. 57).

A person making strategic decisions who has a choice among several alternatives may view strategic planning in relation to opportunity as follows: "Strategic planning should be done whenever an opportunity is foreseen or a problem arises, and it should be done according to whatever type of analysis is most suitable for the proposal or problem" (p. 66). Concretely, "strategic decision is made effective not only by its own fitness to evolving circumstance but by the commitment of individuals and groups inspired always by their own needs and sometimes by uniquely appropriate leadership" (p. 62).

A person can have confidence in transforming uncertainty into certain conditions by using effective strategic planning, although at the same time, he or she must perceive the unknowable uncertainties of the future.[3] Under such conditions, after strategic planning decisions have been made, management control and operational control can be carried out efficiently and effectively. In such cases, we should pay attention to the idea of connecting strategic planning with opportunity. In the strategic planning process, opportunity under uncertainty takes the shape of a choice among various alternatives, each with a given probability. According to Anthony, "strategic planning should be done whenever opportunity is foreseen or a problem arises". This leads to new issues: What is opportunity? How are opportunities and uncertainties transformed into alternatives or items with a certain probability? These questions may be the most critical issue in contemporary management accounting.

ASOBAT's Thought and Decision-Making Process

A Statement of Basic Accounting Theory (*ASOBAT*) from the American Accounting Association (AAA) (1966) follows the same path as Anthony, based on Simon, and gives management accounting a concrete structure for decision-making involving nonprogrammed activity. *ASOBAT* depicts the four dimensions of management in a matrix of unprogrammed (equivalent to nonprogrammed) and programmed activities and planning and control functions: top-level planning (unprogrammed planning), control of factory operations (programmed control), the implementation function (planning programmed activities), and the control of unprogrammed activities (AAA, p. 44). These dimensions are particularly related to the first two of the following four objectives of accounting: (1) making decisions concerning the use of limited resources, including the identification of crucial decision areas, and determination of objectives and goals, (2) effectively directing and controlling an organization's human and material resources, (3) maintaining and reporting on the custodianship of resources, and (4) facilitating social functions and controls (p. 4). In *ASOBAT*, unprogrammed planning is thought of as a decision-making activity involving the selection of alternatives, which is closely connected with accounting information received beyond both the conventional model and historically valued transaction data. Relevant information is derived from cost behavior analysis, use of time-adjusted cash flow projections, the reporting of projected alternatives using ranges and probability distributions, the development and manipulation of inventory, and other management models and simulation techniques (p. 38).

Moreover, *ASOBAT* discusses the decision-making process at length and puts forth four key steps: (1) recognizing and defining the problem, (2) searching for alternatives solutions, (3) evaluating the alternative solutions, and (4) selecting an alternative based on the results of evaluation (p. 45). An important problem about controlling unprogrammed activities is identified as follows:

> For un-programmed activities control is more difficult. Here, the methods are often unspecified, or unknown in advance, and it is difficult, if not impossible, to assess intermediate methods or results on the way toward achievement of the specified plan. The problem is exemplified in the control of research and development where there are few guides for methodology and the nature of the goal is often relatively unknown. Indeed, management is in the position of having to control such an activity without knowing exactly what the activity should be doing. (p. 46)

For decision-making in such situations, data besides traditional models and economic data are used in addition to traditional accounting information to select the best alternative since a decision cannot be made without the reduction of uncertainty and the enhancement of probability (p. 60). Knight, Simon, and Anthony share the strong conviction that by using information, models, and simulation, management can overcome uncertainty that cannot be known and specified.

Demski's Model and Profit Management

We recognize that Simon, Anthony, and *ASOBAT* share a common stance on uncertainty in management, namely that uncertainty can be controlled through stable and systemized decision-making and expanded information and models (see Fig. 4.1). Along this stream of thought, we need to examine the model that Demski (1967, 1969) designed and developed to forecast future profit and control the decision-making process using the concept of opportunity cost. This model is the first valuable method for accounting researchers to examine an uncertain world. Demski (1967) proposed an ex post system related to profit variance analysis, where the forecast variance of profit is calculated as a result of variance between ex ante profit and ex post profit, and opportunity cost variance is recognized as the variance between ex post profit that should be realized under proper

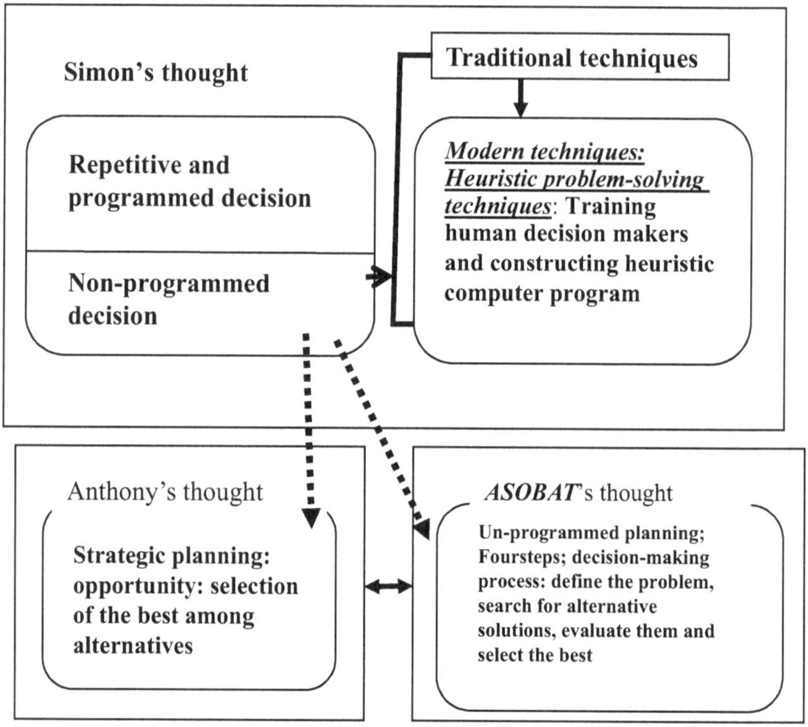

Fig. 4.1 Uncertainty and decision-making

execution and control and the actual profit. Of course, the same business conditions as actually observed profit must be assumed when ex post profit is calculated. Demski clarifies the relativity and uncertainty of estimated profit and the relative authenticity or objectivity of ex post profit. As a result, opportunity cost variance is calculated on the basis of actual profit in comparison with ex post profit. The concept of opportunity cost indicates how much practical planning and control performance varied from the authenticated and *accurate* profit under a changeable environment, as calculated using a linear programming method. Although his model contributed to the progress of management accounting science, he unfortunately analyzed opportunity cost from the angle of actual profit, or reality, since ex post profit is calculated after the measurement of actual profit, assuming the same conditions as in actuality. Thus, because he insisted on feedback control, the model represents *post-opportunity cost*. Instead, the variance of forecast profit would relate to the forecast ability of opportunity in uncertainty (Nishimura 2003).

Under the wide fluctuation and complexity of the contemporary global economy, actual management should make decisions on ex ante and ex post profits in advance, before the actual profit is measured. It is problematic how management forecasts opportunity and profit opportunity in advance before the materialization of actual profit, as long as profit is based on opportunity. Although Demski proposed a model that uses opportunity cost to control the process of decision-making and performance evaluation using feedback control, top managers might have to search for better opportunities beforehand in actual business management. At this stage, the relationship between profit opportunity under weaker certainty and another profit opportunity under stronger certainty and the opportunity cost and risk must also be forecasted and controlled in advance using a feed-forward control. This variance represents the distance of profit opportunity from uncertainty, or *prior-opportunity cost*, while the variance between optimum profit opportunity and actual profit shows *post-opportunity cost*. Such a feed-forward system displays the relationship between optimum profit opportunity and risks and facilitates risk management. In addition, when profit opportunity is specified in the form of two different types of profits: for example, market-competitive profit and long-term strategic profit (growth-durable profit), their variance also shows the way toward optimum profit opportunity in an accounting-measurable form. The target calculated as its result of their comparison plays a role in implementing feed-forward profit controls, such as finding new innovate methods proactively to reduce variance beforehand and improving existing working behaviors and structures. When the estimated optimum profit or optimum profit opportunity is compared with actual profit, the variance is calculated as true opportunity cost.

The idea of cost design, invented by Japanese car companies, has taken the concept of feed-forward control over cost management and led to the development of cost variance analysis. Cost variance analysis uses the comparison of two ex ante costs (long-term target and short-term competitive costs) and their variance to forecast and control the optimum cost within certain bounds of probability. Then, the variance between the optimum cost (target cost) and actual cost shows lost opportunities for cost reduction. Cost design variance analysis is much closer to the idea of controlling opportunity or profit opportunity and profit from a feed-forward accounting angle than the Demski model. However, in Japanese corporate management, target cost as ex ante costs may also be estimated under stronger certainty.

4.5 Some Cases of Lost Profit Opportunity in Large Business

Unfortunately, we cannot yet clarify what relationship exists between uncertainty and opportunity, or between opportunity and profit, although the aforementioned authors used methods such as models, decision-making process, computer-based heuristic problem-solving processes, and extended information to transform uncertainty into profit under real conditions. As they point out, because uncertainty is elusive and intangible, opportunity related to uncertainty is also vague and difficult to grasp. However, management researchers have tried to directly forecast an opportunity as a profit opportunity by means of selecting alternatives. To repeat, opportunity does not always exist under definite probability. Opportunity is uncertain and is not completely foreseeable and each opportunity provides decision-makers only one chance to act on what is expected to be realized in the future.

Is it possible to objectively control uncertainty? Until now, management researchers have dealt with unforeseeable uncertainty as controllable, but recently some have started to discuss *unforeseeable* uncertainty itself, as shown in Table 4.1. Actually, managers have selected opportunities suitable to their purpose or desire, which has a certain subjective or objective probability. Therefore, at the same time, risks also take shape and those who take advantage of an opportunity should be responsible for the risk. Risk arises based on the probability of an opportunity and no one would take risks without the expectation of having a good chance to succeed. In this chapter, profit opportunity refers to an opportunity with some subjective or objective probability that may transform into profit in the near future. Although profit opportunity is more specifically forecasted as budgetary or estimated profit in accounting, when profit can be estimated with higher probability, the concept of profit opportunity is completely different from that of budgetary or estimated profit. This difference is because profit opportunity is still uncertain and is only estimated with weaker probability than budgetary profit, which is estimated under higher probability, since the profit could not consummate control function in an organization, if not so. Profit opportunity is selected from many possible opportunities on the basis of business goals, in connection with the organizational structure; equally risk is also more accurately expressed as enterprise risk under the same specific conditions (business organization and environments) as profit opportunity. By looking at lost profit opportunities in actual business experiences that have occurred recently, we can contribute greatly to the study of this problem.

We now live in the time when we encounter things that nobody has previously experienced. As Ingrassia describes in his book, *Crash Course* (2011), older generations could not even image the bankruptcy of General Motors (GM), or "America's banks going broke". Did GM have no opportunity at all? It may not matter whether there was opportunity or not, but whether or not executives could perceive opportunities and transform them into profit opportunity.

According to Ingrassia (2011), Honda's sales of small subcompacts increased from 20,000 in 1972 to 220,000 in 1977 by exporting from Japan to America, and at that time Ford was interested in buying four-cylinder engines from Honda to use in Ford small cars. However, Henry Ford II declared: "No car with my name on the hood is going to have a Jap engine inside." After that, the Big Three likely felt dismayed by the fact that Honda's Ohio motorcycle plants and car factory started to topple the Big Three and UAW dominance when Honda brought successful management and motivation to American workers (p. 64). The power to turn opportunity into profit opportunity requires looking squarely at the objective facts of a changeable business environment and the existing organizational structure, including all the employees' morale and motive, whereas the dominant factor in turning opportunity into risk or missed opportunity is arrogance and sycophancy. As a result of having expended its energies on financial policy and diversifying its businesses early in the twentieth century on what the company viewed as a golden opportunities for profit, GM had "far too many U.S. brands, too many dealers, too many factories, and too many workers, all of which added huge layers of unnecessary costs". Moreover, GM CEO Rick Wagoner rejected the recommendations of an internal "deep dive" analysis report to cut the excess production capacity (p. 155). In the end, the excess production capacity and shortage of credit that resulted from "high-paid and low skilled jobs" and "high-rebate to dealers" ultimately led to the bankruptcy.

We can learn about lost profit opportunity from GM management, particularly from its bankruptcy, just as we learned about advanced and standard management models in a university business administration course. The bankruptcy was not caused by the management model or information system but by management people, including the CEO, managers, dealers, and UAW workers. Ingrassia (pp. 273, 277) interestingly states:

> General Motors had virtually invented the modern corporation with professional managers, as opposed to family founders, presiding over decentralized operations that were governed by central financial control. It had pioneered modern marketing, public relations, and the hierarchy of brands that made automobiles vehicles for social as well as physical mobility. It had set standards for everything from style and design to corporate healthcare plans.

We had another important lesson.

> Another broad lesson applicable far beyond the car business was that judgment trumps structure almost every time. On paper, pre-bankruptcy GM had the right structure for corporate oversight. The board of directors consisted of almost entirely of outsiders, not members of management, who were led by a 'lead independent directors.' That was the good news. That bad news was that CEO was Rick Wagoner and lead director was George Fisher, who piled mistake upon miscalculation upon misjudgment while the rest of the board simply watched. (Ingrassia, p. 277)

"Complacency, arrogance, and hubris" bred by great successes that extended over a long time held all the persons concerned in GM from looking directly and objectively at real facts, and made them miss a chance to transform opportunity into profit opportunity and make a timely transformation of the company. Even excellent management system and governance structure are not given full play by arrogant leadership and dispirited employees. At the same time, we should not forget that the active ability of people and organizational power can change risks into profit opportunities.

Arrogance and hubris are by no means special characteristics of US automobile companies. Toyota in Japan, the competitive counterpart to GM, whose management systems such as the JIT and Kanban systems are world famous, was also bogged down by arrogance and hubris, this despite the fact that Nissan had also already been tormented by its bureaucratic organization in 1980s. Toyota grew the sales of its cars from 1.6 million in 2000 to 2.6 million in 2007 in the United States. It continued to invest in the construction of new plants in the United States and Canada on a large scale, setting its sight on the goal of being 'the Greatest in the World'. The expansion included the San Antonio Plant for manufacturing full-sized pickup trucks in 2005, a new plant for manufacturing sport cars and RAV4s in Ontario, Canada, and a construction program for an SUV plant at the State of Mississippi, United States, in 2008, despite the fact that the company was confronted with serious quality problems. Specifically, 2.38 million cars were recalled for anticipatable safety defects in 2005. The new president of Toyota Corporation, Akio Toyoda, told a news conference in Beijing that the quality problem was mainly a result of the company giving too much priority given to growing market share and earnings (*Wall Street Journal*, Japanese version, 2 March 2010). He criticized previous top auto managers in the corporation because no other employees in the company were empowered to make decisions except them. Collins (2009) points out as follows:

> We will encounter multiple forms of hubris in our journey through the stages of decline. We will see hubris in undisciplined leaps into areas where a company cannot become the best. We will see hubris in a company's pursuit of growth beyond what it can deliver with excellence. We will see hubris in bold, risky decisions that fly in the face of conflicting or negative evidence. We will see hubris in denying even the possibility that the enterprise could be at risk, imperiled by external threats or internal erosion. (Collins, p. 30)

Because of the arrogance and sycophancy of CEOs who lost sight of the objective situation of the business environment and self-interested and unmotivated organizational members and employees, GM and Toyota could not objectively discern the changes in the global business environments and make changes to their organizational structure. In particular, the motivation and morale of employees could not be improved and the best profit opportunity in the companies could not be created, since the wrong prospective opportunity was pursued and the situation was made more disadvantageous as a result of problematic organizational structures. It leads to hubristic and unscientific management behavior to believe the absolute controllability of uncertainty notwithstanding its impossibility. On the contrary, to think over the ceaseless existence of uncertainty and its relative controllability makes corporate management take a modest and prudent behavior.

4.6 Opportunity, Profit Opportunity, and Profit

The management cycle, from opportunity through profit opportunity to profit (or to lost profit opportunity and losses, as the case may be), mirrors the path from uncertainty through probability to reality. Accounting profit is not real profit, but a calculated profit that symbolizes reality. Profit materializes in markets only when planned products and services that are produced on the expectation of profit opportunity coincide with consumer demands and needs. Profit opportunity and budget profit are forecast under uncertainty before production actually occurs in markets. Even an orderly organizational structure administrated by excellent stratified management cannot avoid uncertainty and let consumer behaviors have its own way. At the same time, even most excellent top management cannot transform profit opportunity into profits by themselves. In comparison with profit, profit opportunity is closely related to understanding the true condition of an organization and the ability and willingness of its peoples within the production and management structures, as well as grasping the changing conditions of markets and competition (information on price, supply and demand, consumer needs, and other changing factors), and combining this organizational and market knowledge under a particular probability. However, all leadership and members of an organization should continue to be aware of uncertainty, since the required steps and activities to successfully pursue a profit opportunity remain uncertain before its completion. Therefore, profit opportunities require forecasting the connection of organizational structure (production and management structure) with the changing business environment as objectively as possible, whereas profit results from effectively and efficiently acting on profit opportunities to the best of the organization's ability within its structure. Presently, this management cycle is always estimated and carried out in businesses. Apart from whether uncertainty is controllable or not, we should, at present, examine the relationship among the three stages (opportunity, profit opportunity, and profit) in order to clarify enterprise strategic and risk management.

Top managers who are responsible for linking opportunities with the business organizational structure and for the decision-making on profit opportunities should directly look at the real changes in organizational structures and business environments and analyze the possibility of successfully making this combination. This process is concerned not only with the abilities of individuals, such as judgment, knowledge, and analysis ability and charisma, but also with organizational governance, including the selection of management, organizational decision-making, and motivation of all members. In this case, feed-forward control plays the most important role in securing profit opportunity, since top leaders must look forward and adopt preventive and proactive controls for understanding profit opportunity (Nishimura 2003, 2005; see a, b, and c in Fig. 4.2).[4]

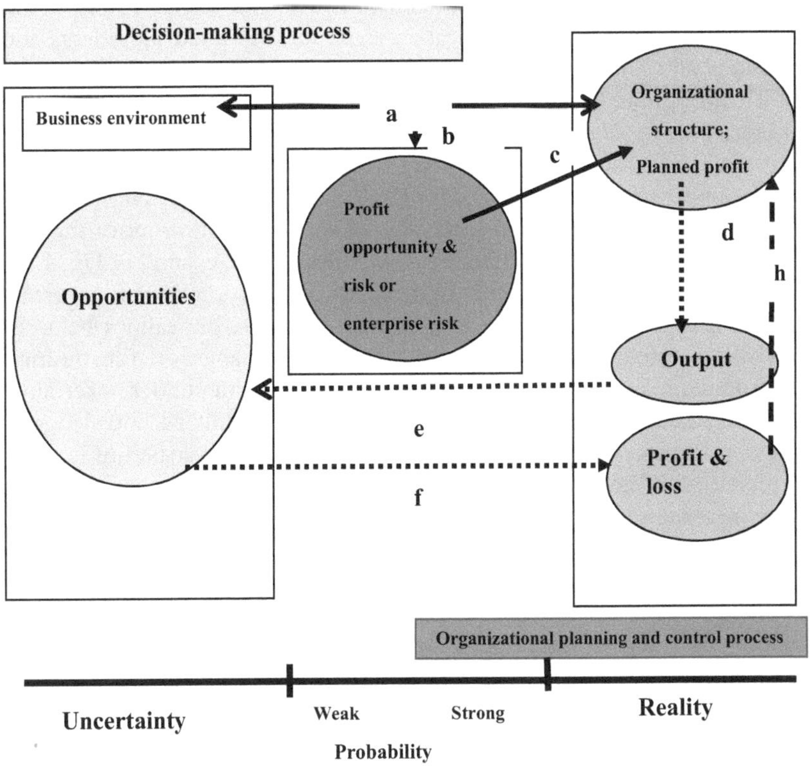

Fig. 4.2 Opportunity, profit opportunity, and profit (Note: The process from *a* through *b* to *c* represents feed-forward control and the processes from *d* through *e* and *f* to *h* represent feedback control. The control loop from *a* to *h* shows a business control cycle: the combined loop of feed-forward and feedback controls)

Regular management and production organizations that are directed by top managers should also carry out their assigned missions under relative certainty after a profit opportunity is identified. Their shared tasks are performed, controlled, and evaluated according to the plan as developed. At the same time, after performance evaluations, feedback control gives a full perspective on the actualization of expected plan for future profit planning. This feedback control is possible when organizations are relatively certain and stable. However, as long as uncertainty affects the whole management cycle until the point when products are actually sold, managerial and production structures (i.e., organizational structure) are also not completely free from uncertainty. Therefore, the loops of feed-forward and feedback controls are repeated under uncertainty. Physical and mental conditions in an organization that keep top leaders from making good judgments and decisions and a stagnant organizational culture always give rise to uncertainty throughout the whole business. Therefore, the ability of people in an organization to sense and understand risk, as well as well-structured management and production structures, is critical for the transformation of profit opportunity into profit and for good risk management. Thus, business culture gains momentum to make the whole organization move forward and function smoothly (Nishimura 2003, 2005; see d, e, and f in Fig. 4.2).

To summarize, profit opportunity exists between the initial, uncertain opportunity and the actual organizational structure, but cannot be accurately forecasted without objectively observing changes in the business environment, and having awareness of the opportunities under uncertainty and the actual organizational structure. Successfully linking knowledge of the opportunities with awareness of the organizational structure leads to exploitation of good profit opportunities. However, wrong decisions and poor awareness leads to terrible risks, or worse, to business crises.

4.7 Conclusion

As examined above, management and accounting scholars have researched and developed significant and ingenious tools and techniques that have contributed to improving the effectiveness and efficiency of management. However, in a strongly uncertain global economy, reexamining the fundamental framework of business management and accounting in reference to uncertainty seems to be of utmost importance. If the basic logic of management theory is weak, the whole structure is like a house of cards, even though each element and component of the system is elaborate and perfect. We should more scientifically study the basic logic of management accounting through following the path of the scientific forerunners of management. Although management and accounting scholars have opened many ways to transform uncertainty into certain conditions and invented systemized and specific management tools, in the present unstable economic society we must realize that business management cannot always eliminate the threats of uncertainty and must always prepare mentally and physically with preventive and proactive measures. At present, the modest behavior of top management and the goodwill and morale of organization members become increasingly important. Even if enterprise governance and internal control are thorough and complete, only human beings, as real persons, *can sense changes that are just about to happen* and work within and manage the system since management tools are used *subjectively and actively*. Arrogance and lack of attention weakens this feeling and makes everyone lose sight of changes in the organization and environment and causes the many excellent management tools to be used erroneously in a nonobjective manner.

This chapter surveyed the theoretical framework of the management cycle from uncertainty through probability of profit opportunity and enterprise risk to realization of profit by referencing representative literature and describing the relationship between opportunity, profit opportunity, and profit, all vital areas to which management accounting must pay attention. Viewed in this light, the management accounting of the day can be regarded as a science and the technologies that make use of the concepts on the path from opportunity through profit opportunity to profit can be seen as enhancing the relative stability and probability of management through feed-forward and feedback controls in an uncertain environment. This science and these technologies also lead to sustainable business growth in an enterprise. All these things make it clear that profit opportunity has a particular probability with which opportunity may transform into accounting profit under particular business environment and organizational structure during a fiscal period. Thus, we can forecast it as well as enterprise risk with some degree of certainty.

Notes

1. The argument on the relationship between uncertainty and its management is applied to socialist planning economies as well as capitalist market systems. Although socialist leaders had strongly believed in the controllability of uncertainty between production and consumption through a centrally

planned economy, in the end, nobody could control it. The lack of control occurs since as leaders become more dictatorial, the less objectively they can forecast production capacity and consumers' demand, as well as the true morale of members of society. This process is quite similar to lost profit opportunities in a private company in capitalist market economy.

2. Simon described as follows: "There is now good reason to believe that the processes of non-programmed decision making will soon undergo as fundamental a revolution as the one which is currently transforming programmed decision making in business organization" (Simon, p. 21). We, at the same time, should give ear to Simon's following words: "He (The operational research enthusiast) expects the managers to be so dazzled by the beauty of the mathematical results that he will not remember that his practical operating problem has not been handled" (Simon, p. 18).
3. Anthony said that "the uncertainties of the future may be so great that no one trusts the validity of assumptions incorporated in the model" (Anthony, p. 60).
4. See Nishimura (2003) on the concepts of feedback and feed-forward controls and Demski's model.

Bibliography

American Accounting Association. (1966). *A Statement of Basic Accounting Theory*. Evanston: AAA.

Anthony, R. N. (1965). *Planning and Control Systems: A Framework for Analysis*. Boston: Division of Research, Graduate School of Business Administration, Harvard University.

Berle, A. A., & Means, G. C. (1932). *Modern Corporation and Private Property*. New York: Macmillan.

Burnham, J. (1941). *The Managerial Revolution: What Is happening in the World*. New York: John Day.

Chandler, A. D., Jr. (1977). *The Visible Hand: The Managerial Revolution in American Business*. Cambridge, MA: Belknap Press of Harvard University Press.

Collins, J. (2009). *How the Mighty Fall and Why Some Companies Never Give in*. New York: HarperCollins Publishers Inc.

Demski, J. S. (1967, October). An Accounting System Structures on a Linear Programming Model. *Accounting Review, 42*(4), 701–712.

Demski, J. S. (1969, October). Decision-Performance Control. *Accounting Review, 44*(4), 669–713.

Ingrassia, P. (2011). *Crash Course: The American Automobile Industry's Road to Bankruptcy and Bailout—And Beyond*. New York: Random House trade Paperbacks.

Knight, F. H. (1921). *Risk, Uncertainty and Profit*. Chicago: University of Chicago Press. Reprint version: Cosimo Classic, New York, 2005.

Kumarasinghe, S., & Willett, R. (2010). What Can Management Accounting Practitioners and Academics to Improve Risk Measurement and Foreworn Impending Financial Crises? *Asia-Pacific Management Accounting Journal, 5*(2), 1–10.

Langlois, R. N. (2003). The Vanishing Hand: The Changing Dynamics of Industrial Capitalism. *Industrial and Corporate Change, 12*(2), 351–385.

Marx, K. (1867). *Capital: A Critical Analysis of Capitalist Production, Volume 1*. Moscow: Foreign Language Publishing House.

Marx, K. (1965). *Das Kapital: Kritik de politischen Ökonomie*, Erster Band, Dietz Verlag Berlin (*Capital: A Critical Analysis of Capitalist Production*, Volume 1, Moscow: Foreign Languages Publishing House).

Nishimura, A. (2003). *Management Accounting in Asia: feed forward and Asian perspectives*. Hampshire: Palgrave Macmillan.

Nishimura, A. (2005). Strategic Management and Contemporary Management Accounting. In A. Nishimura & R. Willett (Eds.), *Management Accounting in Asia* (pp. 1–8). Singapore: Thomson Learning. (A division of Thomson Asia Pte Ltd.).

Nishimura, A. (2006a). Enterprise Governance and Management Accounting from the Viewpoint of Feed Forward Control. *Asian-Pacific Management Accounting Journal, 1*(1), 1–17. Public Knowledge Project (Open Journal System). http://arionline.uitm.edu.my/ojs/index.php/APMAJ/issue/view/20.

Nishimura, A. (2006b). Analysis of Industrial Structure and Profitable Structure in China; Recent Development and Problems Chinese State-owned Enterprises: Structures of Industry and Deficit. *Business Administration and Management Accounting in Asia* (pp. 257–279 and 311–334), Tokyo: Chuou Keizai Publisher.

Nishimura, A. (2006c). *Business Management and Management Accounting in Asia (Japanese)*. Tokyo: Chuokeizai Publisher.

Simon, H. A. (1969). *The New Science of Management Decision*. New York/Evanston: Herper & Row, Publishers.

Smith, A. (1776). *An Inquiry into the Nature and Causes of the Wealth of Nations*, 423. New York: The Modern Library (reprinted in 1937).

Sommer, S. C., & Loch, C. H. (2004, October). Selectionism and Learning in Projects with Complexity and Unforeseeable Uncertainty. *Management Science, 50*(10), 1334–1347.

Sommer, S. C., Loch, C. H., & Dong, J. (2009, January–February). Managing Complexity and Unforeseeable Uncertainty in Startup Companies: An Empirical Study. *Organization Science, 20*(1), 118–133.

The Wall Street Journal (2010, March 5). Japanese Version. http://jp.wsj.com/layout/set/print/Business-companies/Autos/node_26986.

CHAPTER 5

Profit Opportunity, Strategic Innovation, and Management Accounting

5.1 Introduction

This chapter aims to reexamine the meanings of accounting profit as management information and its use in feed-forward management, which is a critical subject in contemporary management accounting. Therefore, the chapter investigates the source and process of profit creation retroactive to profit opportunity, rather than the measurement and usage of accounting profit, in order to adequately address contemporary problems of management accounting.

Management accounting is a cognitive and control activity that uses accounting concepts and calculation methods (Nishimura 2003). Fundamentally, it uses feedback information such as accounting profit, assets, liabilities, revenues, expenses, costs, and capital in order to plan for and control the long-term future of businesses. Although such accounting information is truly objective and reflects past economic phenomena through accounting methods, it is not directly relevant to decision-making and performance evaluation, given that the present economic and political situations completely differ from those in the past, and the business environment is characterized by strong uncertainty, complexity, and unknown/uncontrollable situations. Feedback accounting information must also join hands with feed-forward information on future changes in the business environment to be useful for proactive management in which an enterprise tries to cope with a changeable and uncertain future business environment. In the current environment, in which management

A. Nishimura, *Management, Uncertainty, and Accounting*,
https://doi.org/10.1007/978-981-10-8989-3_5

accounting must integrate feedback information with feed-forward information, management accountants and researchers are confronted with several new issues that businesses must address.

These problems cannot simply be resolved by adding supplementary physical or economic information to accounting information. The value and quality of such information is not disputed, but the source and process of creating profit information have remained controversial in contemporary management accounting, since management accounting cannot fulfill its function independently from the concept of profit. Management accounting cannot be separated from accounting profit, and cannot depend upon only its own data and its value. Therefore, this chapter seeks to examine the sources and processes of profit creation and develop a scheme of management accounting in which feed-forward information is combined with financial accounting or feedback information. Thus, the chapter makes an attempt to address key issues in the future of management accounting.

In Chap. 4, the author clarified the relationships between uncertainty and profit, entrepreneurship activities involving profit creation, and accountants' efforts in management and financial accounting to control uncertainty in the business environment. The importance of understanding the profit management cycle, from opportunity through profit opportunity to accounting profit, was also pointed out in the previous chapters. Consequently, in this chapter the author will explore in detail *how* it is that *entrepreneurs* can recognize and exploit opportunity in an uncertain environment where there are unknown and uncontrollable factors, known but uncontrollable factors, or controllable but unknown factors, and *how* to transform such an opportunity under uncertainty into a profit opportunity with some degree of probability. Thus, the chapter first classifies opportunity and profit opportunity into clear categories; second, it investigates practical innovations to exploit profit opportunity; and, lastly, it presents a vision of contemporary management accounting that makes use of profit opportunity–based variance analysis.

5.2 Opportunity and Profit Opportunity

Opportunity is slippery and vague because it exists in uncertainty and is unlimited in space-time. In reality, opportunity lies in chaos (Hopkins 2010). Thus, enterprises do their best to discover and exploit opportunity in chaos. However, opportunity, in the general and ambiguous sense, is meaningless for businesses, and it must take a definite form with some degree of probability (in case of either subjective or objective probability) because an enterprise has definite expectations of profit creation or enhanced business value. Opportunity does not take a deliberate form until such an enterprise's expectations are closely combined with some objective conditions and its organizational structure (resources, technology, and human power). Such a combination can be conducted in a completely unknown and uncontrollable situation, in an unknown but a controllable situation, or in a known but uncontrollable situation. The difference between opportunity and profit opportunity is quite similar to the difference between 'exploration and exploitation' that March (1991) discusses: "compared to returns from exploitation, returns from exploration are systematically less certain, more remote in time, and organizationally more distant from the locus of action and adaption" (p. 73).

Opportunity must emerge in a special form in space and time for an individual enterprise, even though its actualization cannot be confirmed (Grégoire et al. 2010). Under this situation, the enterprises assess not only the business environment (e.g., competitive markets) but also their own technology, resources, organizational competence, and development potential (hereinafter, collectively referred to as *organizational structure*) to discover, affirm, and exploit the opportunity. Such space-time limitations on opportunity are so difficult that the activity of addressing these factors is regarded as a special attribute of the *entrepreneur* (Shane 2000; Nishimura 2011), since it depends on prior experience, knowledge, and special intelligence in terms of the ability to foresee the opportunity and provide leadership in exploiting it. Shane (2000) thinks of opportunity from the two perspectives of discovery and exploitation, and attaches importance to the former. Because of discovery, an enterprise can connect new technology with the creation of new processes, new products, new markets, and new strategies. It is the *entrepreneur* who has sufficient useful knowledge and experience to discover and exploit opportunities. However, even if such is the case in theory, how can opportunities be searched for, discovered, and exploited? In regards to this question, the theories of Simons and Haynie provide valuable insight.

Simons's Concept of 'Opportunity Space'

Simons (1995) may be the first scholar to systematically analyze the relationship between opportunity and strategic management from an integrated viewpoint of strategy and the subsequent initiative of an organization.

According to him, *opportunity space* is "the unique set of opportunities that [an] organization can potentially identify or create at a point in time given its competences and resources" (p. 16). Opportunity does not have any meaning for organizations until it is transformed into special business value. Simons also refers to *organizational attention* as "the allocation of information processing capacity within the organization to a defined issues or agenda", which leads to the optimum distribution of attention in the organization. As a result of this allocation, an organization can maximize, not return on investment, but 'return on management' (ROM). In other words, ROM represents the advantageous opportunity that is produced by combining organizational attention with the most critical opportunities.

As he describes, "effective managers use control systems effectively to balance the inherent tensions between (1) unlimited opportunity and limited attention, (2) intended and emergent strategy, and (3) self-interest and the desire to contribute" (p. 28). Then, he gives a detailed account of "the four levers of the control", which he examines on the basis of opportunity and in reference to organizational attention and value creation (ROM). Therefore, his analysis of control can be seen as wide ranging and up to date, and provides clarification to the relationship between opportunity and control in business management. The features of "opportunity space" have a close relationship with the resulting types of innovation (Kornish and Ulrich 2011).

Haynie's Concept of Evaluation

Haynie et al. (2009) inquire more deeply into the discovery and exploitation of opportunity from the viewpoint of intelligence and highlight the importance of "evaluation" in recognizing "valuable economic opportunity" (Haynie et al. 2009). In their chapter, Haynie et al. summarize the relation between opportunity and resources as follows:

> We are not suggesting that opportunities *are* resources, but instead we suggest that for entrepreneurs engaged in opportunity evaluations, it is likely that the content of opportunity evaluation decision schemas is focused on both the resources at hand and the resources that must be marshaled (not currently under the firm's control) in order to exploit the opportunity under evaluation. Such resources can be intangible – such as new knowledge or organizational routines- or tangible outcomes that may generate the promising new goods and services that can be sold at greater than cost of production. (p. 341)

In order to convert opportunity into valuable economic opportunity, entrepreneurs must first recognize it in a tangible and visible form and specifically note how the opportunity relates to current and future resources.

According to their analysis, business management should deal with opportunity from the viewpoint of a cause-and-effect relationship, in which the cause is the situation of an opportunity and the effect is "the future-oriented outcome envisioned by the decision maker" (p. 340). Thus, evaluation is a useful means to match a valuable economic opportunity with current and future resources.

Condensation

From the two theories discussed above, the author can see the importance of "opportunity space", where opportunity is combined with resources and competences, "organizational attention" and the four levers of control in maximizing the creation of ROM. Further, it is the evaluation of valuable economic opportunity that makes the combination of opportunity and current and future resources possible. Valuable economic opportunities are future-oriented, resources related, and value (or ROM) creation. To achieve value for organization, opportunities cannot exist as general and abstract concepts, but instead must be synthesized for business outcomes with some degree of probability. It is appropriate to name such opportunities as "profit opportunities".

Opportunity space and valuable economic opportunity transform unclear and vague opportunities into comprehensive, fully formed opportunities in business management. Moreover, attention and evaluation take opportunities closer to being profit opportunity. In actuality, entrepreneurs may tacitly imagine profit opportunity at this stage, and most researchers have also studied methods to transfer opportunity into profit opportunity from various angles, even though they may not have consciously sought to do so (Gruber et al. 2008; Shane 2000). Profit opportunity is limited in time-space and should be considered opportunity with a certain probability (Morris 2005), which requires synthesis and systematic evaluation in relation to the business environment and *organizational structure* (technology, human and organizational strengths, resources, competencies, etc.). At the same time, it is clear that profit opportunity is closely related to strategic innovation based on current and future resources. In particular, innovation for exploitation converts opportunity from a general and vague form to a concrete and profitable one, although it should be noted that innovation is closely related to both the discovery and exploitation of opportunities.

As examined above, opportunity has been examined from the viewpoints of discovery and exploitation, and the importance of its identification to creating profit opportunity has also been discussed (see also, Reuer and Tong 2010; Gruber et al. 2008; Shane 2000). It may be better for enterprises to identify the optimal opportunity from a set of diverse opportunities, rather than to pursue several opportunities early on, since pursing a single opportunity more easily leads to exploitation (Grégoire et al. 2010). However, an enterprise must dedicate much time and resources for the investigation of opportunities to discover the single optimal opportunity, even though their prior experience and knowledge certainly play an important role in the discovery process. Moreover, profit opportunity is synthetic in terms of profitability and the results from synthesizing diverse opportunities depend on organizational structure, since opportunities such as potential revenue, technology development, and cost reduction are not connected directly with profit opportunity (Nagaike 2010). The concept of profit opportunity becomes clear in contrast to risk in terms of probability by virtue of 'opportunity space' concept and in its relationship with organizational structure. It, with risk concept, enables entrepreneurs to evaluate and manage future innovations by combining them with management accounting.

Opportunity is a fundamental key to grope about in the dark for a new innovation and is transformed into profit opportunity, or a definite opportunity in specific space-time, when opportunity is concretely combined with information system and organizational structure under the specified environment from the angle of profitability. On the basis of this profit opportunity, senior managers as entrepreneur decide on a planned profit for business directions, or annual target in each organizational unit, which presents a feasible and periodical business value. Moreover, when the innovation process actually starts, the planned profit becomes control indicators to actualize the process and standards for evaluating performance. Figure 5.1 reveals the relationship between innovation, profit opportunity, and planned accounting profit on the basis of what we have described. This relation also represents an ascending process to high probability from uncertainty.

With regard to practical development of feed-forward innovation[1] or strategic innovation, the next section will more deeply pursue this process

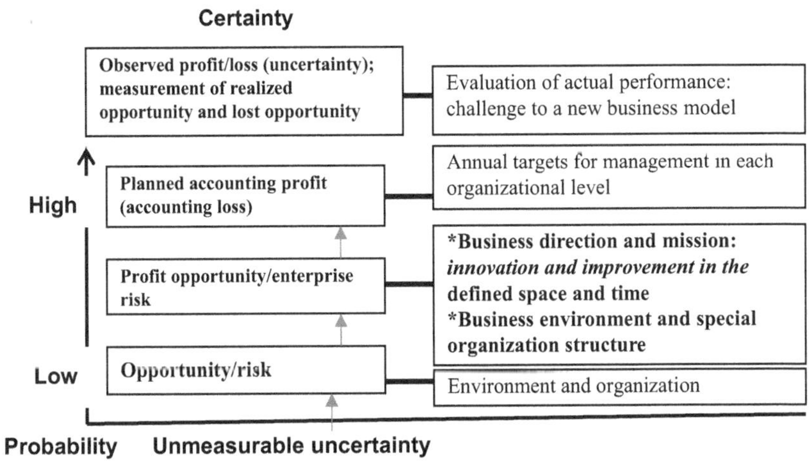

Fig. 5.1 Relationship between innovation and profit opportunity. (Note: uncertainty in a broad sense consists of unmeasurable uncertainty and risk (foreseeable uncertainty with some likelihood))

and the contents of innovations that increase the probability of success in the uncertainty of the real business world, in other words, the practical transformation process of opportunity into profit opportunity.

5.3 Strategic Innovation and Profit Opportunity

Profit opportunity–based management and accounting is a new phenomenon in the contemporary business environment with strong uncertainty (complexity and diversity). Traditional management and accounting could surely forecast future business opportunity assuming the continuation of the present situation. Generally, in relatively stable markets, enterprises mainly adopted mass production or cost control techniques to implement effective and efficient management. Such traditional innovation as the conveyor system and standard cost management was based on feedback information and control methods. However, new concepts and management innovation began to emerge in the 1970s. These were completely different from the traditional methods following the oil crisis that pushed many countries into a full-fledged recession and the spread of financial liberalization throughout the world economy.

In particular, under strong competition in the international market, Japanese manufacturers who had previously received strong government protection in trade and finance have to establish their competitive advantage by implementing new innovations. They broke free from the trade-off thought of cost and quality assumed in traditional management processes to create an integrated approach that achieved high quality, low cost, and timely delivery, which allowed for the discovery and exploitation of profit opportunity, and the successful combination of opportunity with current and future resources. This shift began the use of strategic innovation with the aim of discovering and exploiting profit opportunity by preventively and proactively using forward-looking information and developing production and management systems such as closely united supply chain and subcontracting systems, differently from the traditional methods of innovation. The international business society has developed new types of strategic innovation with the Japanese methods of production and management (e.g., cost design) as a turning point: agile supply chain management (external innovation) and global innovation (open external innovation) (Nishimura 1996, 2003, 2005, 2007).

Japanese Production and Management Systems: Lean Production

Toyota Motor Company, representative of the Japanese type of management, opened a new path of strategic innovation that has been pursued since the 1960s: innovation to create and exploit new markets without excess capacity or supply. This production and management system is characterized by the creation of demand in markets through the original development of new technology, and by closely united supply chain (subcontracting system), total quality control, and visible management in the internal organizations of the company. This system is also distinguished from the traditional systems of innovation by the use of preventive and proactive feed-forward information (target cost) and control systems (continual cost improvement). The traditional system started to reveal its brittleness under the severe uncertainty and complexity of global markets in the 1970s. Toyota adopted strict methods such as just-in-time (JIT) and made-to-order production to eliminate the risks of excess capacity and inventory, which contrasts with the mass production and optimal buffer stock systems in the traditional methods of innovation (Nishimura 2003).

Many Japanese companies have adopted this system as a model and globally expanded into new markets. Foreign companies have also introduced these systems to strengthen their competitive advantages. The Toyota system has come to be known as 'lean production'. Considered from the perspective of uncertainty, this system aims to exploit profit opportunity and control uncertainty by developing unique technology and management systems and promoting self-reliance on an internal supply chain (subcontractors or *Keiretsu*) within the company. Many firms who introduced lean production could enjoy their competitive advantage for a while because of the closed and feed-forward attributes of its management and production system.

However, the benefits vanish and the system becomes a hindrance when the aspirations of executives to expand globally to new markets go ahead of new innovations. As a result of such decision-making, excess investment and inventory in the supply chain can result before the creation of the new markets themselves. Overinvestment and oversupply break down the fundamental structure of this innovation, particularly when orders become stagnant and market demand shifts, since lean production always relies on made-to-order systems and tight methods and is only effective when there is growing demand in global markets. The enterprises that adopt lean production often puzzle over the high costs that result from overinvestment and excess inventory in the supply chain. If their subjective and immoderate expectations of demand in new markets and goal of being the worldwide sales leader are disjointed from reality, the benefits of closed self-reliance of innovation and the supply chain cannot be achieved (Nishimura 2011).

Recently, many Japanese manufacturers have again been hindered by uncertainty in the marketplace. The self-reliant innovation does not fulfill its function when the market suddenly changes and demand decreases, particularly when executives cling to subjective and immoderate goals that disregard the changing situation in the global markets and their limited innovative ability. Lean production can have a strong advantage in global markets, as long as an enterprise can continue to develop their own technology and production and management systems that reflect how markets respond to their products. However, in global markets a wide variety of demands can be found, with some markets fond of standardized articles with low quality and low price, whereas other markets lean toward environmentally friendly or charitable goods even at higher prices. Moreover, the diversity and complexity of global markets change every day. In such a global market and strong uncertainty, self-reliant innovation has its limit to discover and exploit profit opportunity globally. Under such conditions, self-reliance must shift to external innovation.

External Innovation: Agile Supply Chain Systems

In contrast with self-reliant innovation and the internal-company supply chains (internal innovation), agile supply chain systems tend to absorb changing demand in global markets through the use of flexible networks of supply chains and site-based communication. Such a system can be seen as external reliance of supply. An agile supply chain consists of many independent suppliers who share common information and goals and participate in a common networked system. The manufacturers of finished goods can flexibly respond to rapid changes in demands by introducing such flexible supply chains and modular production systems to quickly and flexibly produce goods tailored to meet the needs of customers. Thus, the flexible response of open supply chains in changing markets and site-based communication play an important role in agile supply management. Actual customer requirements are captured by 'direct feed-forward methods' and 'virtual supply chains' that are composed of 'geographic capacity allocation' and globally concentrated capacity based on 'collaborative demand planning' with customers, rather than feedback methods such as production orders based on market forecast information (Collin and Lorenzin 2006).

According to Rimienè (2011), supply chain networks must become more global and intricate in the contemporary business environment, as the level of market uncertainty increases. Specifically, uncertainty is driven by the increasing occurrence in the market of intense competition, short life cycles of goods, ever-changing demand, and unreliable suppliers. Consequently, changes in markets are too complicated to easily plan for and control risks and uncertainty. Thus, "enterprises no longer control all resources, necessary for full satisfaction of market demand. The companies noticed that agility is the essential condition for their survival and competition" (Rimienè 2011). Rimienè insists that agile manufacturing is required to effectively respond to unexpected rapid changes and uncertainty in the market through a combination of flexible innovation with lean production systems.

In an agile supply chain management, the close relationship between the assembler and constituent members of the supply chain is very important to flexibly respond to the short-term change in demand in markets. The assembler should equip itself with singular designs, technological capabilities, sales strategies, and a large network of suppliers, whereas the suppliers should always produce 'standard parts and components' or 'standard semi-finished products awaiting final assembly or localization' for the assembler. Suppliers must also always share common goals and information in the network. For this purpose, the assembler should give "the necessary technological, financial, logistical support required to achieve stringent time and quality targets" in order to flexibly cope with sudden changes in demand, "although production is always kept at a level slightly below expected sales to keep the stock moving" (p. 41).

Agile supply chain management adopts closed but broad supply chain networks and modular production to flexibly respond to changing markets and to control for uncertainty, which allows opportunity to be transformed into profit opportunity. As Christopher and Towill (2001) point out, "it has also become apparent that markets today are increasingly volatile and hence less predictable and so the need for a more agile response has grown" (p. 244). Therefore, speed and flexible response to volatile markets, modular production, and shared global information and goals play an important part in agile supply chain management. Naylor et al. (1999) define "agile" as follows: in contrast to "lean" production, agile production aims to develop a value stream by eliminating all waste, including time, and to ensure a *level* schedule; "agility means using market knowledge and a virtual corporation to exploit profitable opportunities in a *volatile* market place" (p. 108). Christopher focuses on the flexibility of agile supply chains more than their speed. Therefore, this production system is favorable for low-volume production of diverse products, because it relies upon "multiple levels of inventory between the parts of production and final market place, and its high variability and low volume against low variability and high volume in lean production". Certainly, "agility is a business-wide capability that embraces organizational structures, information systems, logistics processes, and, in particular, mindsets" (Christopher 2000, p. 37; see also Sharif and Zhang 1999).

Agile management made the increasingly global discovery and exploitation of profit opportunity possible by using external supply chains (external innovation) and site-based networks rather than the Japanese type of production and management. The 'opportunity space' of global, agile management systems is wider than that of the relatively more closed Japanese systems. Thus, agile supply chain management seems to overcome the problems of lean production and to build upon its strong points. However, implementing total inventory management and ensuring the mutual benefit of both assembler and suppliers remain key issues to be resolved in the case of external innovation. Even though there are advantages for the assembler, suppliers in an agile production system may suddenly face excess inventory when their parts and components are not useful to meet changing demand in the market.

Finding the balance between the optimization of the whole system and the benefits to individual members is the crux of the problem in agile supply management. Thus, innovation shifts from external to global innovation in order to actualize profit opportunity more globally in terms of individual and social optimization. However, the boundary between external and global innovations is so ambiguous that some companies that introduce agile supply management are also considered as examples of companies implementing global innovation. For example, Nokia, a leading mobile phone supplier in Finland, and Dell, an American multinational computer technology company, have been viewed as representing agile supply management and global innovation. At the same time, lean production and agile supply chain management are not mutually exclusive and can be complementary (Christopher and Towill 2001; Naylor et al. 1999). However, it is more critical in this chapter to define the conceptual difference of the three innovation types than to classify companies as practicing one of the three types.

Global Innovation

Social upheaval and financial crises are consistently present, and yet their impacts have become more severe and their reach more global. Consequently, the fundamental contradiction between production and consumption, discussed in Chap. 4 (see also Nishimura 2011), touches upon the fact that uncertainty in the market is worldwide and is intensified by the global synergism of financial manipulation and universal information network. Uncertainty becomes stronger and more severe in individual enterprise. Although the increase and diversification of consumption are accelerated by the globalization of consumer financing and information networks, manufacturers are also unsettled by the short life cycle of goods, sudden changes in demand preferences, and changing purchasing power. Under these conditions, lean production and agile supply management are insufficient for the global discovery and exploitation of profit opportunity. Some enterprises have started to adopt global strategic innovation that relies upon open innovation and an open business model (Chesbrough 2003, 2007).

Global companies have globally and socially introduced innovation and business models that other companies and individuals developed and are developing and also leave their own innovation and models open to global society. As a result, the companies can develop global innovation to discover and exploit global profit opportunity and transform them into marketable products by using unlimited supply chains and global information networks. The openness and socialization of this innovation differ from the limited and closed features in lean production and agile supply chain management.

Global innovation, which is also called “open innovation”, “structural innovation”, or “strategic innovation” (Chesbrough 2003, 2007; Govindarajan and Trimble 2004), is characterized as the usage of “crowd wisdom”, “social embedded innovation”, or “global network” (Simanis and Hart 2009). The Nintendo Wii platform resulted from people and third-party companies that were interested in “acquiring certain skills” for developing software “by participating in the innovation process” or by the “desire to advance a technology” (Boudreau and Lakhani 2009). In recent times, the exchange of innovation among rival companies has become a daily occurrence internationally, as these companies seek to increase profit opportunity compared with their common rivals. For example, NTT Docomo, Fujitsu, and other Japanese electronics companies cooperate with Korean Samsung, a strong rival to them, to establish a new company that develops, designs, and promotes the sale of core semiconductors for next-generation smartphones. However, within this consortium, the manufacturing of products is outsourced (Nikkei 2011a).

Dell has become one of the most successful personnel computer manufacturers, “not through P&D investment, but by making PCs easier to use, bringing products to market more quickly and innovating on process like supply-chain management, manufacturing and direct selling” (Sawhney et al. 2006, p. 29). The main point of global innovation is to find and exploit profit opportunity worldwide and give priority to the latent profit opportunity that exists in an unknown and uncontrollable environment. Therefore, many enterprises have recently shifted from lean production through agile management to a global innovation model or have developed their own hybrid systems. Global innovation also relates to embedded innovation of organizations, such as charitable or environmental activities, in which global knowledge, resources, and competence are used in relationship with wide stakeholders outside of companies from the perspective of long-term growth (Simians and Hart 2009).

This fundamental difference from lean production and agile management is to set up ‘open space for global innovation’ inside and outside a company, particularly through the Internet, in order to socially exchange various ideas, technologies, and designs. Such global innovation is also a 'space of global profit opportunity' that is fundamentally consumer oriented, and has attributes such as speed, variation, diversity, and flexibility. Enterprises organize supply chains, manufacturing processes, resource and technology arrangements, and logistics on the basis of what was discussed and decided through debate in the open space. An example of the use of the online space is IBM arranging a 72-hour "innovation Jam" on its corporate Internet where its employees, clients, and partners could debate about "new business opportunities" (Birkinshaw et al. 2011, p. 4). At the same time, the company donated "500 of its software patents to the open source community" (Chesbrough 2007, p. 72). Another example is Grameen Bank in Bangladesh, which successfully introduced the "village banking model" to combine villagers' unique knowledge, insights, and perspectives with profit opportunities through micro credit (Simanis and Hart 2009, pp. 9–10). The standardization and simplification of parts and components are also common features of external and global innovations, in spite of different conceptions of the opportunity space. Nissan Motor Co. in Japan adopted a policy to "develop a line of cars and sport utility vehicles with markedly different styles, performance and market positioning" based on a common set of components (Sawhney et al. 2006, pp. 30–31). The apparel retailer Zara in Spain made "counterintuitive choices in sourcing, design, manufacturing and logistics" and created "a fast and flexible supply chain". Zara did not adopt the full outsourcing of production, but rather retains half in-house in order to "locate its manufacturing facilities closer to its markets to cut product lead time". The company favors "small lot" production and "a plethora of designs" to economies of scale, allowing it to "refresh its design almost weekly" (Sawhney et al. 2006, p. 32).

Finally, open external innovation tends to strengthen sustainable business growth by distributing the outcomes of innovation to the stakeholders involved in the discovery and exploitation of new profit opportunities. Komatsu Co. in Japan, a manufacturer of machine tools, developed 'a machine tracking system' that can remotely control information on the operating situation and hours of Komatsu-made construction machinery, and monitor the amount of fuel remaining through the Internet by using Global Positioning System (GPS) satellites and mobile communication. The company can use the information from 100,000 machines input into this system to forecast future demand and production and to plan future inventories. Further, Komatsu gives their customers this information to promote new profit opportunities by providing opportunities for fuel savings and cost reductions to them. The company also holds a "Technical Skill

Competition" every year, in which 200 individuals participated, including more than 46 foreigners representing nine countries (Nikkei 2011b).

As the space of global innovation expands and the opportunity space enters into unknown and uncontrollable areas, the feed-forward capabilities in facilities and organization and the corresponding costs must also be large. Therefore, the evaluation of profit opportunity plays an important role in global innovation.

5.4 Strategic Innovations and Cost Design

The Three Innovations and the Creation of Profit Opportunity

As stated above, enterprises have continually exerted themselves to discover and exploit greater profit opportunity in order to cope with the strong uncertainty and complexity in the world economy. With regard to this issue, this book chapter has clarified the development process for innovations involving opportunity, including internal innovation, external innovation, and global innovation. However, this is also a process in which global companies compete to discover and exploit profit opportunities and, for this purpose, have established feed-forward, or strategic mechanisms of innovations including global information and networks, as well as new production, supply chain, and management systems (Table 5.1).

Uncertainty and probability in the real world can be schematized in a matrix of known, unknown, controllable, and uncontrollable factors. Perfect uncertainty fundamentally exists where one cannot know and control at all, whereas some degree of probability is possible through the use of knowledge and information or the development of control methods and technologies. The shift from internal to external innovation is to search for the latent opportunity potential that is hidden by uncertainty. In lean production and management, a car company could gain market share by developing a new production and control system, including cost design (target costing), where low costs are integrated with high quality, because no other firms would be privy to this information and would be left with the existing trade-off between cost and quality. Agile supply chain systems aim to promote flexible and speed responses to unknown future market changes by the reorganization and cooperation of a known supply chain.

In contrast with these innovations, the global innovation makes a challenge to discovering and exploiting latent profit opportunity under uncertainty generally considered as unknown and uncontrollable uncertainty by globally and socially adopting revolutionary knowledge and control methods.

Table 5.1 Feed-forward system of the three types of innovation

Type	*Production and management system*	*Communication, information, and network*	*Features*	*Opportunity pivot*
Internal innovation (Toyota system: Lean production)	Just-in-time (Zero inventory); made-to-order; total quality control; continuous improvement; closed subcontractor system; **cost design**	Visible management (Kanban); shared goals and norms of all members in organization	Market creation through integration of low cost and high quality (function) and value engineering	Internal development of innovated technology, management and organizational structure
External innovation	Agile supply chain; integration of modular production and flexible supply chain to respond to changing market conditions	Site-based shared information, goals and network among suppliers; concentrated design and strategy by the manufacturer of finished products	Mobility and flexibility of market-oriented supply chain and site-based information system	Market-oriented supply chain and the production of standardized parts and components
Global innovation	Social and open innovation including embedded innovation, through open modular system, relating with external global stakeholders (shared development and usage of technologies and resources)	Globally and socially shared information and outcomes shared by participants	Global creation of profit opportunity; socialization of potential profit opportunity and globally defined allocation of resources to the opportunities	Global development ability; simultaneous dispersion and concentration of profit opportunity

In practice, the three innovations become intertwined with one another, and no one can decide the best of the three with certainty because of the difficulty in measuring the true cost of strategic innovation and the amount of profit opportunity. However, every enterprise should reexamine and reform their existing framework of management accounting and researchers should also thoroughly probe the relationship between accounting profit and uncertainty.

Transfiguration of Cost Design in Japan

Now that we inquired into the three strategic innovations in connection with the creation and exploitation of profit opportunity, the next step is to examine how they have impacted on management accounting and its changes. Unfortunately, a new model of management accounting based on profit opportunity and risk management was not yet established. However, it will go to the core of the above problem to investigate how cost design (*Genka Kikaku;* target costing) in which target profit and target cost take a leading role in cost management has transfigured in Japan according to the development of the innovations, because this costing was established as "a feed-forward mechanism" (Cooper and Slagmulder 2004) and "a proactive cost reduction tool" (Shank and Fisher 1999) in company with the internal strategic innovation. Some transfigurations of cost design in global innovation will be clarified through analyzing present cost design practices, although the costing have not assumed a new form appropriate to the global innovation in spite of efforts such as "J cost theory"(Tanaka 2008, 2009) and life cycle cash flow accounting based on time (Kawada 2009). Our recent research suggests some different aspects from what it used to be in Japan, which have resulted from the internal to the global innovation.

A questionnaire was administered to 850 Japanese listed companies in Tokyo Stock Exchange in November 2011 in order to investigate 'target costing in the era of global management'. Although 12 replies were returned and were not enough to define the whole characteristics of Japanese companies, we can throw some light on the content and meaning of present cost design by analyzing them as case studies with reference to more detailed data of Annual Securities Reports. The list of their employee number, sales, and industrial sector is shown in Table 5.3 in Appendix at the end of this chapter.

Eleven companies answered 'effective' in Japanese factories in response to the question that asked whether cost design was even now effective or not. Of the 11 companies, 9 said it was also effective in Asia and it was also effective in 7 companies in Europe. Companies that did not answer had no factories there. Although cost design seemed to be effective in Japan, ten companies, including one company, which had adopted activity-based standard costing, planned to change it into cost design in future, answered 'newly improve its existing method' in the future. D and I companies, whose cost design was 'fully effective' in Japan and Asia, affirmed that it was useful for not only competitive advantage, profit planning, and cost planning but also the establishment of employees' cooperative relationship. They also intended to consider its improvement in connection to different cultures, environments, and customs in foreign countries. I company connected it with product life cycle costing (LCC) at the stage of materials and components purchase and product manufacturing process and at the same time was concerned about 'consumers' needs': reduction of maintenance and repair costs. E company whose cost design was fully effective in Japan and comparatively effective in Asia gave an affirmative answer that it was useful for cost reduction and competitive advantage in Japan and for the establishment of employees' cooperative relationship and competitive advantage in Asia, too. The company planned to further improve it from the viewpoint of LCC.

G company whose local factories in Asia implemented their own local management and which adopted cost design only in Japan for profit planning and cost planning used LCC at the stage of product manufacturing process to make decisions about competitive price, reduce cost, and evaluate the total profit of a product life cycle. Among C, E, G, K, and H, which connected cost design with LCC, E and D also implemented it for competitive advantage. C company made use of LCC not only for competitive price decision and cost reduction but also for environmental consideration and the shortening of product life cycle.

As stated above, the focus of cost design shifts from cost reduction and the shortening of lead time through Kaizen (continuous improvement) which is a distinctive feature in the original mode (Cooper and Slagmulder 1999, 2004; Shank and Fisher 1999) to a stronger aspect of strategy in terms of competitive pricing and the profit planning of a new product. The combination of cost design with LCC, whose application extends from internal costs (development/design cost and production cost) to external costs (user's and social costs and disposal/recycle costs), also intends to quickly respond to changing market needs and complexity by shortening product life cycle (Nakajima 2004, 2011), and to adopt competitively differential pricing policy. Regarding competitively differential pricing, Seiko Epson Corp., which produces ink-jet printers with short life cycle, sells a printer at a low price in price-competitive areas and makes up for its low profitability by selling ink-cartridges as consumption articles at a comparatively high price during its useful life, while it sells a printer with big ink-tank thrice as high as the price of the above area in developing countries. The analysis and evaluation of product life cycle profit may play an important role in competitively differential pricing (Nikkei 2011c; Seiko Epson Company 2012). We must also pay attention to the connection of cost design with LCC at the level of materials and components purchase and product manufacturing process. The recognition of total profit of product life cycle not only captures "information on social benefits and external opportunity costs" (Lim 2011) but also works well to reduce these costs for marketing.

As shown in Table 5.2, the ratio of material cost and expenses arising from outside manufacture amounts to about 60–95% of total manufacturing cost. For the reduction of total product cost, global companies should develop global supply chain management and supply chain costing in cost design. These costs must also be taken into consideration beforehand, keeping step with strategic profit planning. In Fuji Xerox Company, which has its production base in China, the estimation and portfolio of suppliers' costs are an important part of cost design at the case of developing a new product and also fulfills its function as a benchmark in cost management in overseas factories after going into mass production (Orita 2012a, b).

We can see from the above that cost design tends to focus on competitive pricing and strategic profit planning more strongly in connection with LCC and supply chain costing. With respect to our matter, this focus is

Table 5.2 Ratio of each cost element in total manufacturing cost (%), 2011

Company	*A*	*B*	*D*	*E*	*H*	*K*	*J*
Material cost	96.1	37	56.7	72.4	75.5	65.9	59.1
Labor cost	3.5	19.2	19.4	14.1	11.1	22.2	18.8
Other manufacturing costs	0.4	43.8	23.9	13.5	13.4	11.9	22.1
Expenses arising from outside manufacturers	(32.5)	(16.8)	(1.5)				

Note: As for concrete contents of each company, see Table 5.3 in Appendix

Source: *Statements of Manufacturing Costs in Annual Securities Reports of Seven Companies (2011 or 2012),* Ministry of Finance, Japan

closely related to the finding and exploitation of profit opportunity. With reference to these cost design practices, the author can tentatively propose a theoretical model of profit opportunity–based variance analysis from the viewpoint of strategic innovation management. Fundamentally, the closer the planned profit comes to profit opportunity, the more it is of an advantage to strategic innovation. Profit opportunity–based variance analysis also plays an important role in feedback management in order to reduce opportunity costs in the next period. Before turning to a closer examination of profit opportunity–based variance analysis, the two following remarks should be made concerning the relationship with cost design.

First, if cost design is closely connected to the profit opportunity–based variance analysis, it will become more strategic and play an important part as strategic cost design in the process of strategic innovation. Secondly, a product does not have only its inimitable target cost, but has manifold target costs according to different functions and price structures in different areas. The best among these target costs will be decided on the basis of differential profit opportunities in each area from the viewpoint of global innovation. At the same time, based on this target cost, cost management is also implemented in multifarious forms.

5.5 Profit Opportunity and Profit Opportunity–Based Variance Analysis

Meanings of Profit Opportunity–Based Variance Analysis

Regarding profit management, accountants have long recognized opportunity cost as a benchmark measurement (Samuels 1965; Demski 1967 1968, 1969). According to Demski's model (ex post system), forecast profit variance is measured by a comparison of ex ante (forecast profit) and ex post profits (the optimal profit in the current situation), and as a result, the planning ability of a manager can be evaluated. These concepts can be expressed in the following equations:

Ex ante profit − ex post profit = forecast profit variance
Ex post profit − actual profit = opportunity cost variance

Managers have incentives to precisely forecast profits and risks in future periods through such variance analysis. Next, organizations' attempt to use opportunity cost variance information by comparing the ex post profit with the observed profits and to generate business value through efficient improvements and a high degree of capacity utilization in the next period. As a result of such analyses, they can also foresee the nature of risks and subsequently adopt methods to mitigate them. Currently, such a model as this is usually considered to be mainly of theoretical interest, although many managers probably already informally control opportunity in this manner, even though the analyses may not be conducted in a systematic way. The ex post system described above relies on feedback control. The forecast variances of opportunity cost are recognized after the event. Furthermore, ex post systems advocate a simple feedback model that contrasts with the double-loop feedback of BSC (Kaplan and Norton 1996). In order to proactively develop profit and risk management as part of a systematic approach to strategic management accounting, it is necessary to adopt an integrated cycle of feed-forward and feedback controls, because profit opportunity and risk must be preventively and proactively controlled before the event.

The present object is not to pursue this ex post optimum, but to discover and exploit profit opportunity and control enterprise risk and opportunity cost beforehand. This integrated cycle in strategic management accounting is necessary for this purpose. However, some elements in the integrated cycle of feed-forward and feedback controls are suggested by the approach of the ex post system and Japanese management through cost design (Genka Kikaku), which embodies feed-forward control and the importance of the planning process during the cost design stage. Such considerations are very important for proactive and preventive project management.

Profit Opportunity–Based Variance Analysis in the Integrated Cycle of Feed-Forward and Feedback Management

The application of feed-forward information to management accounting has been discussed elsewhere (Nishimura 2003, 2011). This chapter therefore focuses on integrated information on target profit and costs and profit opportunity–based variance analysis in a development process of innovation, as embodied in a strategic viewpoint (see Fig. 5.2).

The cost design which Japanese enterprises created in the 1970s made it possible to develop feed-forward control in accounting. As shown in

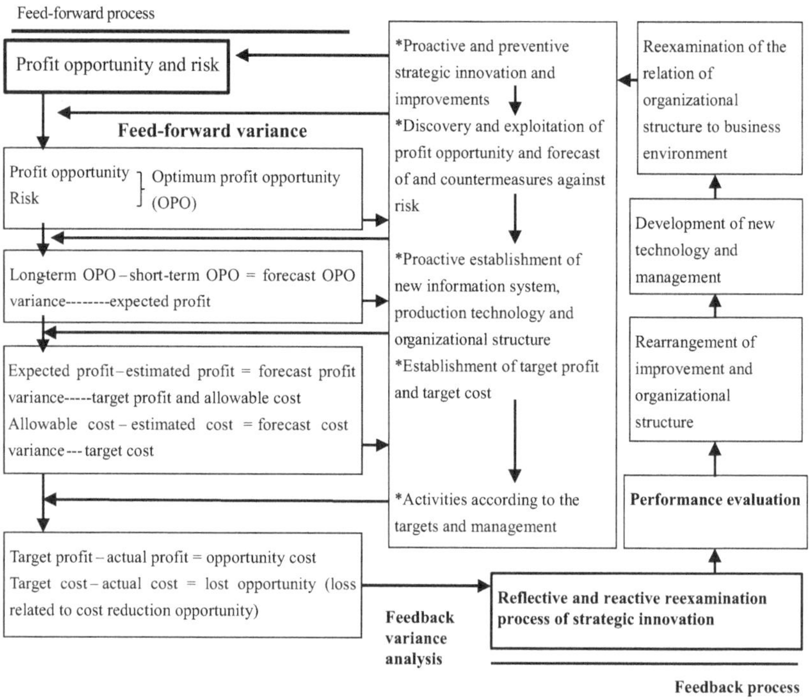

Fig. 5.2 Unified management of profit opportunity and risk with a feed-forward and feedback control loop. (Notes: (1) Long-term OPO is forecasted through examining profit opportunity and risk (optimum profit opportunity) under long-term strategy; (2) Short-term OPO is forecasted through optimum profit opportunity under short-term strategy; (3) Expected profit is forecasted on the basis of long-term OPO and sustainable growth expectation in the light of the past result; (4) Estimated profit is forecasted under the condition of present competitive strategy; (5) Allowable profit is calculated in relation to expected profit; (6) Estimated cost is calculated in the relation to estimated profit; (7) Target profit is planned through considering estimated profit and forecast profit variance in the light of past result; (8) Target cost is planned in relation to the target profit)

Fig. 5.2, which extends this framework, this feed-forward approach to control at the cost management stage is not designed to reactively reflect on profit opportunities and risks after they occur, but to accumulate long- and short-run information on innovation related to the business environment and organizational structure and to synthesize this information when possible. Information gathered in such a way is connected to multidimensional, planned values (target and budgeted profits, allowed costs and target costs based profit opportunity and expected risks) that reflect long-term strategic and short-term competitive plans, and business can proactively adopt the most suitable methods to realize practical target values. Senior managers can thus compare an annual target profit based on long-run strategy with estimated profit based on actual competition, and, through preparatory variance analysis, decide budgeted profit and adopt preventive and proactive improvement methods to better ensure that a satisfactory profit is realized. At the profit forecasting stage, they may also compare the target risk avoidance with the estimated risk avoidance at the same time as the comparison between target profit and estimated profit. In this way, preparatory variance analysis and preventive and proactive methods can be used to mitigate risk and enhance profit opportunity. Additionally, attention should be paid to the fact that all the variances in this model are measured in relation to profit opportunity and enterprise risk, and that the model also evaluates and controls methods to improve profit opportunity proactively and preventively. This relationship can be schematized as follows:

Annual target profit is calculated by dividing profit opportunity by the number of years after adding the above variance which may be resolved by supplemental strategic innovation. Estimated profit is deduced from yearly forecasting comprehensive factors related to present business environmental (competitive) and organizational conditions in reference to the annual target profit. Managers decide a definite budgeted profit after implementing proactive innovative and improvable management (changes in materials, production processes, or processing methods) beforehand to actualize the estimated profit. At the same time, it can calculate allowed costs and estimated costs according to profit variance analysis. The allowed cost is based on long-term business policy (investment and dividend policy). On the other hand, the estimated cost is decided by competitive strategy in markets or "reverse engineering method" (Mcmillan 1984, p. 258). Target cost is decided after comparing allowable cost with estimated cost and considering forecasted cost variance and its improvement methods.

Budgeted profit – actual profit = posterior opportunity cost
Target cost – actual cost = cost variance (lost opportunity variance)

Enterprises use feed-forward information on business performance and financial accounting results to rearrange existing resources and organizational structures and to guide future innovation management. Specifically, the variance between target profit and budgeted profit shows anticipated failure or success to control uncertainty, or indicates prior-opportunity cost related to the discovery and exploitation of profit opportunity and the wrong forecast of risk. On the other hand, variance between budget profit and actual profit represents posterior opportunity cost related to problems of practical organizational structure or organizational and individual performance. Senior managers use this variance to reexamine and rearrange existing organizational structure and develop more strategic and competitive technology and products in the next period. The cost variance as lost opportunity is an indicator to reexamine and improve the existing organizational structure and operating system in the context of the existing innovation in the next period. Profit variance analysis is also connected to cost variance analysis in the integrated cycle of feed-forward and feedback management.

If cost design in Japan is incorporated with this profit opportunity–based variance analysis, it will become more strategic and competitive, and be able to have multiphasic forms which can effectively correspond to global consumers' needs in different prices and functions, since it links directly with the space of profit opportunity and enterprise risk.

5.6 Conclusion

Businesses operate in unknown and uncontrollable uncertainty every day. As pointed out in the previous chapters, we cannot be confident of the absolute controllability of uncertainty, because we are surrounded by inexhaustible unknown and uncontrollable phenomena. Therefore, business managers should not be arrogant and unscientific to nature and society. The strategic innovations advocated in this chapter are only one attempt to control uncertainties. Management accounting has also to take part in the challenge. As a result, one can be confident of relative truth and controllability.

Regarding profit opportunity and uncertainty, in this chapter it was clarified that in the near future, all chief executives, managers, and other organizational members should be conscious of the implementation and evaluation of strategic innovations and the actual continuous improvements resulting from the analyses of prior and posterior variances involving profit opportunity. Contemporary management and accounting must also have a stronger integration of feed-forward (preventive and proactive) and feedback (reflective and reactive) looking. For example, when cost design is correctly positioned beneath profit opportunity–based variance analysis from this integrated proactive and reactive perspective, it becomes more strategic and competitive and can enable the senior manager to evaluate and exploit profit opportunities and for managers to plan for and control business activities based on strategic innovations.

Although the feed-forward (future-looking) aspect has been discussed in the fields of business management and management accounting (Ishikawa and Smith 1972 Belkoui 1983; Morgan 1992), it has not yet taken a definite form in accounting systems generally. The traditional management accounting systems have recently begun incorporating feed-forward and feedback ideas through cost design and cost improvement techniques established by Japanese enterprises and through the ABC and BSC approaches developed by innovators in strategic management accounting (Atkinson et al. 2001; Kaplan and Norton 1996). The possibility of applying feed-forward and feedback information more widely extends not only to cost management but also to profit opportunity and enterprise risk management, as strategic innovation is looked upon as more important.

This chapter gives only a framework for coping with the current issues of uncertainty and opportunity in management accounting. Others, such as Falta et al. (2006) and Kumarasinghe and Willett (2010), have used mathematical, statistical, and empirical approaches to analyze these new contemporary issues in business enterprises. Oshita (2012) also grapples with the difficult task of clarifying contemporary gaps in management accounting. These efforts to illuminate the fundamental problems in contemporary management accounting or to establish proactive and preventive management accounting will unite and open up new ways to establish new strategic management accounting. They will contribute to lessening the gap between practice and theory in contemporary management accounting as for which Scapens (1991) posed a problem for the scientific development of management accounting.

In the strongly uncertain and complicated society at present, the allure of organizational power and the intelligence of scientific-minded leaders make feed-forward and strategic innovations feasible and fruitful, and ensure the transformation of opportunity into profit opportunity and profit opportunity into profit, though the fuller study of these critical factors in organizational structure lies outside the scope of this chapter. As described in the previous chapters (see also Ingrassia 2011; Collins 2009), even a little arrogance in top leaders in large car companies has damaged their business performance over the long term and much money and time have been required for their recovery. Management accounting must also be more forward looking and more deeply and scientifically enter into the unknown and uncontrollable world, although it is very dangerous to unreasonably assume to control what nobody completely knows or can control.

Unfortunately, risk management cannot be discussed here for lack of space in spite of a serious question in relation to profit opportunity. This issue, linking the above activation of organization in corporate governance, will be examined in other chapters in order to clarify the role of management accounting in a very uncertain society.

Appendix

Table 5.3 Employee number (EN), sales, and industrial sector of the investigated companies (2011) (money amount in 100 million yen)

	EN	*Sales*	*Sector*		*EN*	*Sales*	*Sector*
A	198	798	Electric machinery and tools	**G**	1050	1647	Food processing
B	3581	4210	Precision machinery	**H**	1542	1800	Food processing
C	800	448	Transport equipment	**I**	6700	4541	Food processing
D	17,465	2078	Electric and communication machinery	**J**	1468	461	Medicines
E	5200	4309	Lighting fixtures for cars	**K**	1480	500	Food processing
F	32,598	7000	Chemistry	**L**	1026	875	Food processing

Source: *Ministry of Finance, Japan, Annual Securities Reports* of the investigated companies 2012

Note

1. This book uses the term 'feed-forward innovation' more roughly than as used in cybernetic science. In this context, the word means proactive and preventive information and management /production system in which global information, knowledge, resources, competence, and technologies are used for self-reliance (internal innovation), agile supply chain management (external innovation), and global innovation. Enterprises have invested large amounts of money and time for establishing this feed-forward innovation. Thus, it would be better to say '*strategic innovation*' in this chapter, because it is strategic and we are not familiar with 'feed-forward innovation'. For example, a leading mobile phone manufacturer, Nokia, adopted integrated project management, which consists of collaborative demand planning with customers, site-based ordering by progress, professional cost management, and performance metrics with an integrated platform. The supply chain is flexibly decentralized according to changing markets on the basis of concentrated demand planning and site-based ordering, whereas parts and components are standardized and modularized for finished products in response to changes in demand in markets. Its goal is "to provide customers with more speed, efficient and cost effective deliveries by better orchestrating the end-to-end supply chain" (Collin and Lorenzin 2006). In the case of Zara, each of the more than 300 small contractors specializes in one particular part of the production process or one particular garment type. They work exclusively for Zara's parent company, Inditex SA. In return, they receive the necessary technological, financial, and logistical support required to meet the stringent time and quality targets (Christopher 2000).

Bibliography

Atkinson, A. A., Banker, R. D., Kaplan, R. S., & Yong, S. M. (2001). *Management Accounting*. Upper Saddle River: Prentice Hall.

Belkoui, A. (1983). *Cost Accounting: A Multidimensional Emphasis*. Chicago: The Dryden Press.

Birkinshaw, J., Bouquet, C., & Barsoux, J-L. (2011, Winter). The 5 Myths of Innovation. *MIT Sloan Management Review*, 1–8. Sloan-select Collection.

Boudreau, K. J.. & Lakhani, K. R. (2009, Summer). How to Manage outside Innovation, *MIT Sloan Management Review*, 50–57. Sloan-Select Collection, Winter 2011.

Chesbrough, H. W. (2003, Spring). The Era of Open Innovation. *MIT Sloan Management Review*, 35–41. Sloan-select Collection.

Chesbrough, H. W. (2007, Winter). Why Companies Should Have Open Business Models, *MIT Sloan Management Review*, 68–74. Sloan-select Collection.

Christopher, M. (2000). The Agile Supply Chain: Competing in Volatile Markets. *Industrial Marketing Management, 29*, 37–44.

Christopher, M., & Towill, D. (2001). An Integrated Model for the Design of Agile Supply Chains. *International Journal of Physical Distribution & Logistics Management, 31*(4), 235–246.

Collin, J., & Lorenzin, D. (2006). Plan for Supply Chain Agility at Nokia: Lessons from the Mobile Infrastructure Industry. *International Journal of Physical Distribution & Logistics Management, 36*(6), 418–430.

Collins, J. (2009). *How the Mighty Fall and Why Some Companies Never Give in*. New York: HarperCollins Publishers Inc.

Cooper, R., & Slagmulder, R. (1999). Develop Profitable New Products with Target Costing. *MIT Sloan Management Review, 40*(Summer), 23–33.

Cooper, R., & Slagmulder, R. (2004). Achieving Full-Cycle Cost Management. *MIT Sloan Management Review, 46*(Fall), 45–52.

Demski, J. S. (1967, October). An Accounting System Structures on a Linear Programming Model. *Accounting Review, 42*(4), 701–712.

Demski, J. S. (1968, October). Some Observations on Demski's Ex Post Accounting System: A Reply. *The Accounting Review, 43*(4), 672–674.

Demski, J. S. (1969, October). Decision-Performance Control. *Accounting Review, 44*(4), 669–713.

Falta, M., Gallagher, L., & Willett, R. (2006). Modeling 'Hard-To-Measure' Costs in Environment Management Accounting. *Asia-Pacific Management Accounting Journal, 1*(1), 127–125.

Govindarajan, V., & Trimble, C. (2004, Winter). Strategic Innovation and the Science of Learning, *MIT Sloan Management Review*, 19–27. Sloan-select Collection.

Grégoire, D. A., Barr, P. S., & Shepherd, D. A. (2010, March–April). Cognitive Processes of Opportunity Recognition: The Role of Structural Alignment. *Organization Science, 21*(2), 413–431.

Gruber, M. M., Ian, C., & Thompson, J. D. (2008, September). Look before You Leap: Market Opportunity Identification in Emerging Technology Firms. *Management Science, 54*(9), 1652–1665.

Haynie, M. J., Shepherd, D. A., & McMullen, J. S. (2009, May). An Opportunity for Me? The Role of Resources in Opportunity Evaluation Decision. *Journal of Management Studies, 46*(3), 337–360.

Hopkins, M. S. (2010, Spring). The Four Ways IT Is Revolutionizing Innovation (Interview), *MIT Sloan Management Review*, 75–80. Sloan-select Collection.

Ingrassia, P. (2011). *Crash Course: The American Automobile Industry's Road to Bankruptcy and Bailout—And Beyond*. New York: Random House Trade Publishing Group.

Ishikawa, A., & Smith, C. H. (1972). A Feed Forward Control System for Organizational Planning and Control. *ABACUS, 8*(2), 163–180.

Kaplan, R. S., & Norton, D. P. (1996). *The Balanced Scorecard: Translating Strategy into Action*. Boston: Harvard Business School Press.
Kawada, M. (2009). From *Profit* to *Profit Potential*: Redesign the Performance Indicator to Support Toyota Production System, *Contemporary Issues of Management and Accounting in the World Financial Crisis*. Proceedings of the 5th Asia-Pacific Management Forum in Japan, the Asia-Pacific Management Accounting Association.
Kornish, L. J., & Ulrich, K. T. (2011, January). Opportunity Spaces in Innovation: Empirical Analysis of Large Samples of Ideas. *Management Science, 57*(1), 107–128.
Kumarasinghe, S., & Willett, R. (2010). What Can Management Accounting Practitioners and Academics to Improve Risk Measurement and Foreworn Impending Financial Crises? *Asia-Pacific Management Accounting Journal, 5*(2), 1–10.
Lim, M. (2011). Full Cost Accounting in Solid Waste Management: The Gap in the Literature on Newly Industrialized Countries. *Journal of Applied Management Accounting Research, 9*(1), 21–36.
March, J. G. (1991, February). Exploration and Exploitation in Organizational Learning. *Organizational Science, 2*(1), 71–87.
Mcmillan, C. J. (1984). Cost Information and Competitive Strategy: Lessons from Japan. In L. C. Rosen (Ed.), *Topics in Managerial Accounting* (3rd ed.). New York: McGraw-Hill Ryerson.
Morgan, M. (1992). Feed Forward Control for Competitive Advantage: The Japanese Approach. *Journal of General Management, 17*(Summer), 41–52.
Morris, D. (2005). A New Tool for Strategy Analysis: The Opportunity Model. *Journal of Business Strategy, 25*(3), 50–56.
Nagaike, K. (2010, October). Rising Global Horizontal Integration Business Network Systems in Electronics Industry and Reorganization Strategies of Japanese Electronics Companies. *Journal of Strategic Management Studies, 2*(1), 29–37.
Nakajima, H. (2004). Treatment of Life Cycle Costs in Target Costing; A Review of Past Research and Examination of Unsettled Subjects. *Study of Business Management, 21*, 119–139.
Nakajima, H. (2011). *Life Cycle Costing: Development in UK*. Sosei Publisher.
Naylor, B. J., Naim, M. M., & Berry, D. (1999). Legality: Integrating the Lean and Agile Manufacturing Paradigms in the Total Supply Chain. *International Journal of Production Economics, 62*, 107–118.
Nikkei (Nihon Economic Newspaper) (2011a, September 13). Japanese and Korean Cooperation for Development of Smartphone Semiconductors. *Nikkei (Nihon Economic Newspaper)*.
Nikkei (2011b, September 13). Komats Searches for its Course (1). *Nikkei*.
Nikkei (2011c, December 12). Why is Ink-jet Expensive? *Nikkei*.

Nishimura, A. (1996). New Development of Japanese Management Accounting: From Cost Design to Strategic Cost Design. *Journal of Political Economy (Kyushu University)*, *62*(1–6), 241–251.

Nishimura, A. (2003). *Management Accounting in Asia: feed forward and Asian perspectives*. Hampshire: Palgrave Macmillan.

Nishimura, A. (2005). Strategic Management and Contemporary Management Accounting. In A. Nishimura & R. Willett (Eds.), *Management Accounting in Asia* (pp. 1–8). Singapore: Thomson Learning (a Division of Thomson Asia Pte Ltd).

Nishimura, A. (2007). Conceptual Analysis of Value-based Management and Accounting: with Reference to Japanese Practices. *Asian-Pacific Management Accounting Journal*, *2*(1), 71–87. Public Knowledge Project (Open Journal System). http://arionline.uitm.edu.my/ojs/index.php/APMAJ/issue/view/54.

Nishimura, A. (2011). Uncertainty and Management Accounting: Opportunity, Profit Opportunity and Profit. *Asia-Pacific Management Accounting Journal*, *6*(1), 81–101. Public Knowledge Project (Open Journal System). http://arionline.uitm.edu.my/ojs/index.php/APMAJ/issue/view/13.

Orita, Y. (2012a). The Whole Company's Improvement Process of Cost Management, Reexamination of Management Accounting for Manufacturing, *Report in the Third Forum* (December 8, Tokyo), Japanese Association of Management Accounting.

Orita, Y. (2012b). *The Whole Company's Improvement Process of Cost Management: Reexamination of Management Accounting for Manufacturing (Case Study of Fuji Xerox Company)*. Report Presented in the Third Forum (December, Tokyo), The Japanese Association of Management Accounting.

Oshita, J. (2012, December). Paradox of Control and Management Accounting. *Annual Report of Economics Science, Kyushu Association of Economic Science*, *50*, 19–31.

Reuer, J. J., & Tong, T. W. (2010, January–February). Discovering Valuable Growth, Opportunities: An Analysis of Equity Alliances with IPO Firms. *Organization Science*, *21*(1), 201–215.

Rimienè, K. (2011). Supply Chain Agility Concept Evolution (1990–2010). *Economics and Management*, *16*, 892–899.

Samuels, J. M. (1965). Opportunity Costing. *Journal of Accounting Research*, *3*(2), 182–191.

Sawhney, M., Wolcott, R. C., & Arroniz, I. (2006). The 12 Different Ways for Companies to Innovate, *MIT Sloan Management Review*, Winter (ibid., 28–34).

Scapens, R. W. (1991). *Management Accounting: A Review of Contemporary Developments* (2nd ed.). London: Macmillan Education Ltd.

Seiko-Epson Corporation. (2012), *Annual Securities Report*. www.epson.jp/IR/library/yuho/yuho-bbn.htm.

Shane, S. (2000, July–August). Prior Knowledge and the Discovery of Entrepreneurial Opportunities. *Organization Science, 11*(4), 448–469.

Shank, J. K., & Fisher, J. (1999). Case Study Target Costing as a Strategic Tool. *MIT Sloan Management Review, 41*(Fall), 73–82.

Sharif, H., & Zhang, Z. (1999). A Methodology for Achieving Agility in Manufactring Organizations: An Introduction. *International Journal of Production Economics, 62*, 7–22.

Simanis, E., & Hart, S. (2009, Summer). Innovation from the Inside Out. *MIT Sloan Management Review*, 9–18. Sloan-select Collection.

Simons, R. (1995). *Levers of Control: How Managers Use Innovative Control Systems to Drive Strategic Renewal*. Boston: Harvard Business School Press.

Tanaka, M. (2008). Report on Practical Improvement of Accounting for Manufacturing: Practices of J Cost Theory, *MMRC Discussion Paper*, No. 208, Manufacturing Management Research Center, Tokyo University.

Tanaka, M. (2009). *Accounting of Toyota Type of Improvement (Kaizen)*. Tokyo: Chukei Publisher.

CHAPTER 6

Strategic Management Accounting and Feed-Forward Management: With Reference to the Unified Management of Profit Opportunity and Risk

6.1 Introduction

Strategy planning plays an increasingly important role in business management, with managers seeking to gain competitive advantage over rivals in strongly uncertain environments. Although management accounting has contributed to strategic management through providing decision-makers with financial data, traditional management accounting methods based on financial information (budgetary control and standard costing) have been judged from the 1980s to the 1990s by some accounting researchers to be inadequate for today's strategic needs under fierce market competition and a rapid pace of technological change. For the contemporary strategic management, management accounting must certainly provide the management with more useful information closely related to economic activities and organizational mission, or future-oriented data. Many who advocate strategic cost management or management accounting have searched for ways to satisfactorily incorporate nonfinancial information into internal reporting processes and to keep an appropriate balance between financial and nonfinancial perspectives. However, could this focus on nonfinancial information essentially change the substance of management accounting and strengthen its strategic character? This chapter inquires into the implication of information and control in contemporary

A. Nishimura, *Management, Uncertainty, and Accounting*,
https://doi.org/10.1007/978-981-10-8989-3_6

management accounting, and reexamines the strategic space-time expansion of information and control from the viewpoint of current strategic management practices. For this purpose, the relationships of profit opportunity and enterprise risk with strategic management are clarified and the unified management of profit opportunity and risk is addressed in connection to comprehensive risk management as their integrated concept to understand the contemporary characteristics of management accounting. Last, in this chapter the framework of strategic management accounting will be further explored with reference to a management loop involving feed-forward and feedback.

6.2 Strategic Cost Management and Accounting Information

Strategic Management and Nonfinancial Information

Many scholars of strategic management accounting have described strategies and tactics for achieving competitive advantage in markets. This focus seems to be based on Porter (1985), who considers the value chain as a core category and discusses strategic competitive advantage from the perspectives of cost leadership, the differentiation of business, and its uniqueness. Performing activities generates costs, but cost advantage arises from one business performing particular activities more efficiently than its competitors (Porter 1998). For Porter, differentiation arises from both the choice of activities and their performance. In this sense, activities are the basic units of competitive advantage, and an overall advantage or disadvantage results from a company's total activities, not from just a few activities. In connection to these activities, Porter centers his attention on their nonfinancial aspects rather than the role of financial reports in the development of strategic management. Moreover, Shank and Govindarajan (1993), Kaplan and Norton (1996), and Kaplan and Cooper (1998) have related strategic cost management to Porter's concept of competitive advantage. In particular, Shank and Govindarajan developed Porter's idea of competitive advantage from the perspectives of the value chain, cost drivers, and strategic location analyses. They assert that cost data is used to develop superior strategies en route to gaining substantial competitive advantage, and that financial measures only reflect the results of past decisions, not the actionable, future-oriented steps needed to survive in a competitive environment. Shank and Govindarajan (1993) thereupon state the following:

> [...] we see the rise of non-financial measures as an attempt to reassert the primacy of being operations driven. Non-financial measures try to capture progress on the actionable steps that lead to company success, because first, the non-financial measures were more directly traceable to the strategy (key success factors) of firms. [...] Management felt that progress on these measures directly affected the success of firm strategy. (pp. 138–9)

They try to shift from traditional financial information to the nonfinancial information reflected in the accounting data and to relate it more closely to strategic management. They do not separate the former from the latter, since financial information is a critical component for clarifying the practical relationships between strategy and objective information gained through accounting system. For example, as represented in ABC, cost cannot be disregarded and plays a more important role in strategic profitability management in combination with activity information and cost drivers.

Many advocates who have focused their attention on nonfinancial information and strategic cost management have surely contributed to the reform and improvement of traditional management accounting by providing a realistic recognition of strategy and the practical research methods such as case studies and empirical research. However, the problem is how much their theories can contribute to the development of strategic management accounting. Let us move next to look at the value of information and organizational structure in relation to strategic management.

Strategic Aspect of Nonfinancial Information

In recent years, new types of nonfinancial information in management accounting have emerged. Scholars have studied cost design (function), quality costing, ABC (activity), product life cycle costing (environment), value-chain costing, and benchmarking from a strategic viewpoint (Drury 2001). These nonfinancial approaches differ from the traditional thought since cost considerations shift from a close focus on the financial effects of production and cost relationships with suppliers and customers to an increased emphasis on understanding physical and economic activities as a basic attribute of cost (e.g., cost drivers, product life cycle, value analysis, value engineering, organizational mobility, consumer satisfaction, supply chain, and education and training systems). In particular, ABC and BSC show the strategic expansion toward enterprise value (profitability) and organizational mission (target). Nevertheless, although the new school of thought views traditional management accounting as playing a declining role in strategic management, it remains to be seen to what extent this belief is true and what function traditional information will continue to serve in strategic management accounting, not only useless aspect.

Kobayashi (1993), who has studied the development of strategic cost management in Japan from its beginnings, points out that surprisingly few empirical studies have been reported that show to what extent costing and management accounting systems assist managers in making strategic decisions. It appears that little further progress has been achieved since Kobayashi's study. Drury points out that "in particular, strategic management accounting has been identified as a forward way. However, there is still no comprehensive framework as to what constitutes strategic management accounting" (p. 485). This point is very important when examining the present state of management accounting practices and when questioning what the shift from financial information to the nonfinancial means for strategic management (Nishimura 2005, 2008).

It is not yet clear if "strategic management accounting" in any true sense of the term is actually being practiced by businesses. For example, a survey by Guilding et al. (2000) of business in the United States, United Kingdom, and New Zealand found that although strategic uses of accounting (e.g., monitoring locations, evaluating the performance of competitors based on published financial statements, and conducting cost evaluation of competitors) are evident, other strategic uses of costing (e.g., quality costing, value-chain costing, product life cycle costing, and attribute costing) are less commonly shown. Thus, they concluded their analysis by stating:

> Shank and Govindarajan (1993) have suggested that strategic accounting will supplant managerial accounting as a framework for decision-making. With the exception of strategic pricing and some aspects of competitor accounting, the evidence uncovered in this study falls well short of providing vindication for Shank and Govindarajan's prophesy prophency. (p. 129)

We must recognize the whole framework of contemporary management accounting and its relationships to strategic management to clarify the central conception of strategic management accounting: its significance and characteristics.

A Controversial Point

Neither traditional accounting nor financial information can *directly* reflect the true situation of business organizational activities, since they both have the special attributes of calculating stock and flow situations of business value or profit by using particular accounting methods and concepts. In this sense, we can understand that advocates of strategic management accounting prefer nonfinancial information to financial information for strategic planning and control, because nonfinancial information *directly* reflects the actual and objective situation of business organization. However, as Drury (2001) and Guilding et al. (2000) suggest, the key question is why strategic cost accounting or a hybrid accounting of physical and financial information cannot assume a greater role in strategic management accounting. The point of this discussion is not to judge whether financial or nonfinancial information is more useful or to think of ways to integrate both types of information, but to assess the value of each type of information for management needs. Therefore, points of controversy remain as to whether traditional management accounting can be transformed into strategic management accounting by adding supplementary nonfinancial information to accounting systems and how nonfinancial information can change the fundamental framework of traditional management accounting into a future-oriented and forward-looking one.

As long as strategy must be forward-looking and future-oriented, information for strategic management must also do the same. Even if the focus shifts from financial information to nonfinancial information, the fact remains that the information is feedback; the fact that not only financial information but also nonfinancial information here is feedback, not feed-forward-looking, is crucial for us to consider. If we take the feed-forward standpoint and reexamine information from the perspectives of profit opportunity and enterprise risk (Nishimura 2011, 2012), we can open a new way in strategic management, when we consider them in combination with accounting profit concept. Of course, these new methods would be most beneficial if we can recognize and use physical and organizational activities as well as accounting information from a feed-forward viewpoint. At present, because uncertainty and complexity are strongly present in business environments, strategic management also cannot continue to rely only on present and past information, but must look ahead and think more toward the future.

6.3 Roles of Information and Organizational Efforts

Another important aspect in strategic management is the effect of organizational structure and its constituent members on strategic management, although having the relevant information for strategic management can surely stimulate organizational efforts to implement a business vision. Even if an organization has useful information for strategic management, it cannot be put to optimal use if the organization and its constituents are too inactive and timid to cope with the strong uncertainty and fluctuation of the contemporary business environment. For this reason, researchers have focused their attention on the relationship between strategy management, information, and organizational efforts. Thus, the literature has discussed the penetration of strategic goals into organizations, which can result from a combination of top-down decision-making and bottom-up learning, organizational vitality, and the integration of financial measurers and the nonfinancial.

Balanced Scorecard Approach and Organizational Mobility for Strategy

Kaplan's works are representative of those who advocate strategic management accounting. His researches, including ABC and BSC approach, are noteworthy in the accounting literature in that they relate traditional management accounting to strategic management. Kaplan and Norton (1996) systematically analyze the activities that generate costs and emphasize the balancing of external and internal measures from the viewpoint of business strategy. They recommend the 'change of strategy into action' where strategy is formed by the whole organization and made to permeate its entirety. They argue that, in the BSC, financial and nonfinancial measures must be part of the information system for employees at all levels of the organization. Not only must the frontline employees understand the financial consequences of their decisions and actions but senior executives must also understand the drivers of long-term financial success, or nonfinancial information:

> The objectives and the measures for the Balance Scorecard are more than just a somewhat ad hoc collection of financial and non-financial performance measurers. [...] The Balanced Scorecard should translate a business unit's mission and strategy into tangible objectives and measures. (Kaplan and Norton 1996, pp. 9–10)

Kaplan and Norton (1996) deem a vision or strategy to be a core component of company management. A business strategic system containing financial and nonfinancial information that accounts for customers, business internal processes, learning and growth, and financial goals is necessary to change business strategy into action in every section of the organization. As a result, accounting information is situated in the relative, not absolute, place of management accounting in relation to nonfinancial information. Such novel methods as ABC and BSC have certainly contributed to making management accounting relevant to practical organizational needs.

BSC is a balance between the external and internal measures which derive from an organization's strategy and vision. This balance of measures can be impossible without incorporating financial and nonfinancial information into the practices of constituent members throughout an organization. As a result, BSC provides a practical foundation for developing strategy based on business environmental measures (customer and shareholder information) and internal business activities (learning and growth, and internal business processes). Simultaneously, the approach provides not only balance in the present but also the ability to balance future-oriented information involving sustainable growth that adjusts with change, or opportunities and threats. In order to actualize the balance of external and internal information, a single-loop feedback process, or the linear process of establishing a vision and strategy which is implemented by traditional top-down command-and-control model, must shift to a double-loop learning process in which the strategy is revised to confront changes. BSC is a future-oriented system that uses a double-loop learning (feedback) process to reactively grapple with the continual changes of environmental and internal factors (Kaplan and Norton 1996, pp. 16–17).

Controversial Points

In the strong uncertainty and increasing complexity of the current global economy, we should once more reexamine the framework of BSC from the feed-forward, not feedback, viewpoint. First, regarding the new appreciation of nonfinancial information, BSC instills this information, as well as financial information, into each member's mind of an organization to urge attention to company financial targets based on frontline activities, customer's need, and strategy. Thus, all activities throughout the organization related to scorecard measures can be ultimately linked with financial performance. This is in striking contrast to the traditional model in which the financial information of senior managers is completely separate from the physical and nonfinancial information of the lower- and mid-level employees at local sites. A new concept of cost in the case of ABC is created as a result of integrating financial information with nonfinancial information. This concept not only represents economic resources spent on manufactured goods but also reflects and measures physical information and activities related to each product, which can facilitate the profitability management of products: distinguishing value-creative activity from the nonvalue added. BSC spreads the use of nonfinancial information as well as financial target to the whole organization, while ABC creates a new model of costing by incorporating nonfinancial information into traditional costing. The issue that we must consider next is that neither of the two approaches is based on feed-forward thought.

Second, Kaplan and Norton (1996) advocate a double-loop feedback and learning process, in which the four actions of "clarifying and translating the vision and strategy, communicating and linking, planning and target setting, and strategic feedback and learning" are circulated (p. 11), in order to achieve a balance between strategies and other management factors or measures. They emphasize that a comparison of desired performance goals with current levels identifies the existence of any performance gap, and hold that strategic initiatives can be designed to close the gap. Thus, according to them, "the Balanced Scorecard not only measures change; it fosters change" (p. 16). This change results from the learning and communication that occurs in the double-loop feedback process. In such cases, organizational consensus plays an important role in this double-loop feedback process. This feedback process is a necessary component for any strategy to spread into all the levels of a business organization and enhance their mutual understanding, if the strategy is to engender a consistent, high degree of motivation and morale among personnel and thus increase the probability that the organization becomes or remains efficient, profitable, and adaptable in a rapidly changing environment.

There remains an important concern: for management in the highly changeable environment and global innovation age, has the extension of traditional management accounting to nonfinancial information and double-loop feedback or learning processes become an effective tool? According to them, low-level feedback management first begins with cost controls, budgetary controls, and market forecasting, and is a reflective and reactive process that is repeated through learning. However, more important is high-level feedback management that closely relates to strategic goals or vision. Feedback systems are interconnected with one another from low to high levels. Such a loop makes organizational energy vital through the sharing of financial and nonfinancial information. In contrast to the single-loop feedback, which may be adequate in stable economic environments, the double-loop feedback process speculates on the information that managers need to receive about increasingly complicated strategies in continually changing environments. Kaplan and Cooper (1998) suggest that cost management and performance evaluation can function adequately in a feed-forward system if they are integrated with an organizational reporting system and are prominently built into the structure of the management process. However, the application of feed-forward information to accounting concept is still in controversy.

Third, Kaplan and Norton (1996) also argue that business enterprises should balance expected returns management against risk management, although they are not specific on exactly how to achieve the required balance. Because this point is also related to the feed-forward aspect of strategic management accounting systems, it is important to examine the structure of feed-forward and feedback control loop and the integrated management of profit opportunity and risk. Thus, the question now arises: What relationship does profit opportunity or enterprise risk management have with strategic management? Are ABC and BSC useful enough for controlling the serious uncertainty? At the same time, we should meditate on what IFAC (2004) points out as follows:

> We also concluded that the balanced scorecard, which is a respected performance management tool, could not be used to fill the strategic oversight gap. Although it is invaluable in helping business to translate agreed strategy into action and/or to bring non-financial key performance indicators into better focus, it is less successful in addressing the ambiguous, uncertain, complex decisions required to formulate the strategy at times of transformational change. (p. 6)

We have discussed the meaning of information and the strategic energy or efforts of organizations in regard to implementing strategic management accounting and have pointed out some key points of dispute in contemporary management accounting. This chapter will look more carefully into the synthetic loop of feed-forward and feedback controls from the angle of profit opportunity and risk management in Sect. 6.5.

There is one further point that we must not ignore. Regarding the relationships between organization and profit opportunity or enterprise risk management, we should more deeply look at the meanings of organization. The relationship between the organization and individuals is very complicated. Any organization is itself a form of authority and has the power of silence. Some persons can use the organization to restrict other members' benefits and further their own interests, while others strive to make the most of organizational opportunities to enhance both organizational and individual benefits at the same time. Therefore, only as long as "opportunity space" (Simons 1995) is made to be a human space with organizational and individual opportunities, it can promote promising and sustainable growth. Arrogance and sycophancy are not traits confined only to individuals but can also be negative characteristics of the organization, which weaken overall organizational energy and vitality: 'risk space'. Any organization in which arrogance and sycophancy are prevalent will break down eventually, whether sooner or later (Nishimura 2011; Collins 2009; Ingrassia 2011). In this sense, the common consciousness of profit opportunity and enterprise risk among all members of an organization and their vital and human relations within the organization where they can measure themselves with 'opportunity space' are important factors in strategic management. Considered from this viewpoint, until recently management accounting has been challenged by some gaps between information value and organizational needs (strategic control under uncertainty).

6.4 Opportunity Space or Risk Thought and Strategic Management

Opportunity or Risk Management and New Gaps

It is plain from the above discussion that both the BSC and ABC approaches are essentially based on feedback thought. In contrast, Simons (1995) advocates "four levers of control" from the viewpoint of "opportunity space" in order to spur the strategic energy of organizations. Because strategy is future-oriented and forward-looking, opportunity space is where organizational power and attention must connect with the future direction of the organization in order to create business value. Simons refers to the combination of organizational power, attention, and direction as ROM. His "four levers of control" is based on feed-forward and proactive and preventive standpoint. This standpoint not only focuses on the future-oriented aspect of strategy but also considers the "space" in which organizational opportunity is joined with individual opportunity. Within the opportunity space, the "four levers of control" can fulfill their strategic function throughout the whole organization.

According to him, an organization and its members use their attention to define the boundary of unlimited opportunity space: its subset or specific domain. Their attention to ideas related to the space triggers problems for whose solution innovation is created and developed. Opportunity seeking is also limited by defined business risk as a boundary system. These balanced activities between core value (opportunity space) and boundary system (risks to be avoided) lead to maximizing ROM.

In contrast to such focus on opportunity space, Smith and Merritt (2002) focus on risk management as a fundamental concept of project management and use it to effectively control uncertainty. They grasp risk in the dual sense of "a potential for loss" and "an opportunity for gain" and emphasize the loss aspect to "eliminate the surprises that go with such losses" (p. 182). Positively, the comparison of net expected loss among projects is also useful for better decision-making. Therefore, they also consider risk an essential characteristic of product innovation (p. 4).

Simons as well as Smith and Merritt emphasize the proactive concept of opportunity or risk, not planned profit and loss based on experience, to plan and carry out a strategy under uncertainty, differently from Johnson and Kaplan (1987). This situation forces management accounting into recognizing a gap between its traditional feedback system and the new loop of feed-forward and feedback control that weaves opportunity or risk into accounting planning and evaluation system.

As discussed above, at the start, risk management did not take a synthetic and comprehensive form in which risk management was carried in harmony with profit opportunity management by using probability thought, because risk was also understood and managed disconnectedly with opportunity. This piecemeal and specialized approach to risk was caused under a situation where, for strategic decision-making, enterprises were first compelled to cope with uncertainty by means of risk management. As the gap increases between traditional management accounting and the strategic opportunity or risk management, management accounting also inclines toward feed-forward perspective and began to be reconstructed in the framework of enterprise risk management.

However, in the 2008–2009 financial crisis, such piecemeal risk management has been criticized on the grounds that it depended too upon quantitative and unpractical measurement to operate well for the control of global uncertainty and the corporate governance that tried to cure managers of unjust and unlawful activities in larger companies (Richardson 2010; Mikes 2011). Company-centered viewpoint begins to shift to the holistic and social one, where risk is simultaneously managed with profit opportunity to proactively and synthetically control uncertainty through comprehensive risk management and enhance corporate governance through the transparency and controllability of enterprise risk management. As a result, the more comprehensive and trustworthy risk management has been advocated, in which the risk management is incorporated in corporate governance and internal control and keeps step with profit opportunity management to simultaneously control uncertainty (risk) and strategically create enterprise value (COSO 2004; Power 2007). The comprehensive risk management connected to profit opportunity management has taken an important part in corporate governance, strategic innovation, and organizational management. At the same time, the strategic innovation has also made managers and researchers recognize the concept of opportunity or risk and shift the risk management movement to the comprehensive risk management including profit opportunity.

As for profit opportunity and enterprise risk, three innovations are worth special mention in the recent development of global economy: internal innovation such as Toyota production system, external innovation such as agile supply chain, and global innovation. As shown in Table 6.1, each innovation essentially aims to find and exploit large profit opportunity. However, it cannot also be avoidable from risk because of close connection with this profit opportunity. The development process of the three innovation types also represent the extension of risk management from the piecemeal standpoint disjoined with profit opportunity to the holistic and comprehensive one.

It follows from what has been said that there are three gaps between information and organizational needs (managerial direction), as indicated in Fig. 6.1. The first gap is "relevance lost", which Johnson and Kaplan (1987) proposed in terms of informational irrelevance to organizational needs and which ABC and BSC were developed to address through many case studies. The second gap is the disconnection between feedback information and the proactive and preventive opportunity or risk recognition to mitigate fierce uncertainty as effectively as possible or to maximum

Table 6.1 Profit opportunity and enterprise risk in the three innovations

Innovation	*Exploitation of profit opportunity*	*Enterprise risk control*
Internal innovation (e.g., Toyota production system)	Development of unique production and management systems such as JIT, Kanban, zero inventory, total quality management, and cost design	Coincidence between market and production capacity through make-order method, zero inventory, and pull method (JIT) **Problem**: sluggish response to the change of market
External innovation (e.g., agile supply chain)	Construction of market-oriented and flexibly speedily respondent supply chain and module production	Dispersion of risk among suppliers through standardization and normalization of suppliers products and sharing target and information among suppliers **Problem**: balancing of benefit and cost between a demander and suppliers
Global innovation and social innovation	Opened innovation to society, free participation of citizens and unspecified firms in the innovation of a specified company, and connection profitability with charitable or social undertakings	Sharing a company's risk among invisible individuals and firms **Problem**: balancing of opportunity and risk between a company and participated persons

profit opportunity. The third gap is between existing management accounting and the corporate governance (social responsibility) that unites with the comprehensive risk management. All enterprises should be requested to establish accounting measurement and evaluation models which not only clarify profit opportunity and enterprise risk and enhance the strategic energy and vitality of organizations but also make senior managers strongly conscious about social responsibility of environment, safety, and stability in an era of global innovation and the unstable financial world (see Nishimura 2011, 2012).

In relation to corporate governance and internal control, contemporary management accounting takes an integrated form of holistic risk management and social responsibility, which is called enterprise risk management, or the comprehensive risk management. This chapter inquires more closely into management accounting in the unified management of profit opportunity and risk rather than the comprehensive risk management, because the above unified management is more general in every firms and

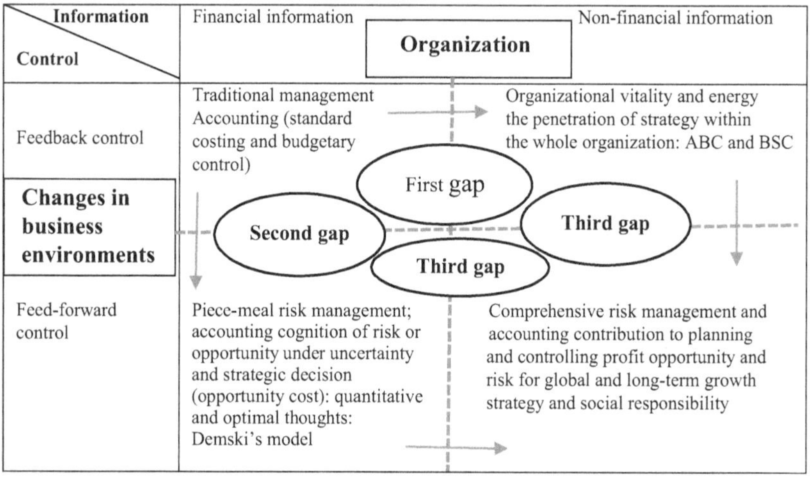

Fig. 6.1 Gaps between management accounting, and environment and organizational structure

a fundamental structure which lies at the root of the comprehensive management. This inquiry may also be useful for clarifying a holistic meaning of the comprehensive risk management. Next, we shall focus our attention on feed-forward management accounting in the unified management.

Comprehensive Risk Management and Feed-Forward Management Accounting

When considering business strategy, managers must compete with rivals in the development and creation of new product models and technology. Enterprises that fail to compete are forced out of markets. However, while the profit opportunity from innovation may be enormous, the enterprise risks and potential losses are large as well. In the current economy, the globalization of businesses that seek increased profit opportunity enhances risks, particularly country risk (e.g., overseas riots, labor disputes, and sudden changes in regulations), since business expands to subcontracting systems, supply chain, and factories in foreign countries. Therefore, existing information systems are also inadequate to deal with the need for the reliable forecasts of profit opportunities and risks that are produced through global research and development activity and growing business. Managers will be required to adopt new philosophies and use more dynamic management styles than at present, and must pay attention not only to profit opportunities that are produced by good strategies but also to the risks that accompany them. As Borge (2001) puts it:

> [...] the world is getting more competitive, interconnected, and complex. Events seem more unpredictable and are moving with greater speed and force. Many of the old safety nets enjoyed by organizations and individuals are badly frayed or gone altogether. The level and nature of risks in the world are constantly changing. Those without access to good risk management are in greater danger than before. (p. 225)

Risk is a particular probability of a phenomenon occurring that is contrary to one's wishes, or, in other words, the expected loss in business. This expected loss or the level of risk is calculated by multiplying the probability of the risk event and the probability of impact (risk likelihood) by the total amount of the loss at the occurrence of the risk (Smith and Merritt 2002). Therefore, risk management must gather feed-forward information and execute proactive and preventive management to minimize the expected loss. Risk management not only makes use of superior computer hardware and social information network but also organizational structure that sensitively perceives the up- and downstream risks of an organization. At present, it is more important to transform risks into profit opportunity than simply to evade them. As a result, risk management combines with profit opportunity management. Profit opportunity management directly and positively binds strategic innovation together with risk management. Thus, the contemporary strategic management, in which profit opportunity management is combined as one body with the risk one, has a more positive meaning than minimizing opportunity cost and risk probability, or its object is to transform risk into profit opportunity and optimize profit opportunity for business value creation (see Figs. 3.3 and 3.4 in Chap. 3). Therefore, management accounting needs to develop methods to measure and control opportunity cost and expected risk.

Risk management is closely related to profit opportunity management (Nishimura 2011) in either case of the unified or the comprehensive management and these profit opportunity and enterprise risk management systems exist both in front of and behind strategic management in the process of business value creation (IFAC 2004). At present, enterprises should pay more attention to feed-forward information and control in formatting their strategy rather than looking to the past. In particular, 'opportunity space' should ultimately result in the creation of 'profit opportunity space' in business enterprises that not only provides organizational and individual benefits but also has a high confidence of probability in terms of risks. Consequently, managers can compare profit opportunities with enterprise risks and estimate optimum profit opportunity. Thus, enterprises should also strive to discover and exploit this optimum profit opportunity (by comparing profit opportunities with risks) and devote their attention and evaluation to the 'optimum profit opportunity space'.

To date, however, most management accounting theories have focused on either accounting profit (return) or loss for strategic decision-making. Contemporary management accounting should deeply pursue future-oriented or feed-forward information and integrate information on both profit opportunities and risks, although indeed it is difficult to envision an integrated system for measuring enterprise risk and profit opportunity as a probability simultaneously, since the level of risk and profit opportunity is normally too wide and vague to be grasped easily by basic feedback control. As Culp (2001) stated, in the past, managers could run stable and profitable businesses when confronted by risks, since they could allocate the requisite resources, and exert sufficient control, either to avoid or to minimize the risks. Now, as risks are entangled with strategies under the striking change and growing complexity of business environment, they cannot be controlled without the holistic and comprehensive management systems: for example, Strategic Scorecard that is aligned with risk management (IFAC 2004). Only managers who better understand the tangled relationship between risks and profit opportunities may expect to gain a competitive advantage. Thus, an integrated system of controlling profit opportunities and risks assumes more importance under the present unstable and uncertain conditions and is an essential part of what should be termed 'strategic management accounting'.

As shown in Fig. 3.3 in Chap. 3, risk management and profit opportunity management exist in both sides of the contemporary strategic management for business value creation. In order to turn the risks associated with credit, interest rates, currency, commodities, stocks, operations, and asset liquidity into profit opportunities, managers must quantitatively measure and rank their risks under uncertainty. As for the importance of both business and financial risks, Borge (2001) states as follows:

> At a strategic level, we know that a firm is a complex of business and financial risks. The results from this aggregate portfolio determine the success or failure of the company. The top management of the firm, especially the CEO, can view and manage this portfolio as a whole, trading off one risk against another, reducing risks that are peripheral to the company's long-term strategy, or adding risks (and opportunities) that are central to that strategy. Strategic risk management can help a business achieve its primary business goals without endangering its financial stability. (p. 230)

Regarding profit management, accountants have long recognized opportunity cost as a benchmark measurement (Samuels 1965; Demski 1967, 1968, 1969). According to Demski's model (*ex post* system), forecast profit variance is measured by a comparison of *ex ante* (forecast profit) and *ex post* profits (the optimal profit in the current situation), and as a result, the planning ability of senior managers can be evaluated. These concepts can be expressed in the following equations:

$$\textit{Ex ante}\ \text{profit} - \textit{ex post}\ \text{profit} = \text{forecast variance}$$

$$\textit{Ex post}\ \text{profit} - \text{actual profit} = \text{opportunity cost}$$

Managers have incentives to precisely forecast profits in future periods through variance analysis between *ex ante* and *ex post* profit. Next, organizations attempt to use opportunity cost variance information by comparing *ex post* profit with the observed profits and to generate business value through efficient activities and a high degree of capacity utilization in the next period. As a result of such analyses, they can also foresee the nature of risks and subsequently adopt innovation and improvement methods to mitigate them. Currently, such a model as this is usually considered to be mainly of theoretical interest, although many managers probably already informally control opportunity in this manner, even though the analyses may not be conducted in a systematic way.

The *ex post* system described above relies on feedback control, as does the BSC approach. The variances of opportunity cost are recognized after the event. Furthermore, the *ex post* system advocates a single-loop feedback that contrasts with the double-loop feedback of BSC. In order to develop the proactive management of profit opportunity and enterprise risk as part of a systematic approach to strategic management accounting, it is necessary to adopt a 'synthetic loop of feed-forward and feedback control'. Risk must be proactively and preventively controlled before the event. In the words of Borge (2001), "The purpose of risk management is to improve the future, not to explain the past" (p. 6). The present object of management is not to pursue optimum after the fact, but to control enterprise risk and profit opportunity beforehand. The synthetic loop of feed-forward and feedback controls in strategic management accounting systems are necessary for this purpose. Such elements in an accounting system are suggested by the approach of '*proactively manufacturing cost and quality*' in Japanese *Genka Kikaku* (cost design) (see Nishimura 1996, 2001, 2003; Tanaka 1995), which embodies feed-forward control and are very important for proactive and preventive project management. The unified management of profit opportunity and enterprise risk with a feed-forward and feedback control loop, and the role of accounting in this management is shown in Fig. 5.3 in Chap. 5.

6.5 Feed-Forward Management Accounting in the Unified Management of Profit Opportunity and Risk

The application of feed-forward information to management accounting was discussed in previous chapters (see also Nishimura 2003, 2011). This chapter therefore focuses on the meaning of target profit and costs in the unified management of profit opportunity and risk with a feed-forward and feedback control loop.

The cost design which Japanese enterprises created in the 1970s made it possible to develop feed-forward control thought in accounting. As shown in Fig. 5.3 in Chap. 5, which extends this framework, this feed-forward approach is not designed to reactively reflect on profit and loss after they occur, but to accumulate long- and short-run information on the business environment and to synthesize this information when possible. Information gathered in such a way is connected to multidimensional, planned values (target and budgeted profits, target and estimated costs, or profit opportunity and enterprise risk) that reflect long-term strategic and short-range competitive plans, and business can proactively adopt the most suitable methods to realize practical target values. Senior managers can thus compare an expected profit on the basis of long-run strategy with estimated profit based on actual competition, through proactive variance analysis, and adopt proactive and preventive methods to better ensure that a satisfactory profit is realized. At the optimum profit forecasting stage, complementarily, to effectively control risk in detail, they could also compare the expected risk avoidance with the estimated risk avoidance at the same time as the comparison between estimated profit and estimated profit. In this way, proactively variance analysis and evaluation methods can be used to mitigate risk and enhance profit opportunity. Additionally, attention should be paid to the fact that all the variances in this model are measured in relation to profit opportunity and enterprise risk and that the model also evaluates and controls activities and resources to proactively improve optimum profit opportunity.

The system of feed-forward and feedback control loop brings the unified management of profit opportunity and risk together. Profit opportunities and risks are assessed and recognized in relation to information on the business environment and organizational structure. Effective and efficient methods are implemented in regards to comparisons of multidimensional planned values, and all activities are controlled and evaluated by using practical targets.

After the target profits are determined in relation to profit opportunity and enterprise risk under the feed-forward perspective, this profit approach then considers cost design and cost improvement issues. All firm personnel are then directed to achieving target costs in each division and department. Standard costing also fulfills its function in connection with the target profit and risk avoidance. As feed-forward management is implemented, the whole system becomes multilooped. As a result, a cooperative, voluntary type of organizational culture is encouraged in human resources management by using the feed-forward approach. The formation of strategy and the recognition of profit opportunity and enterprise risk at every level of the organization help to reduce the possibility of management overconfidence and reliance on habit, although a vibrant atmosphere within the organization based on mutual reliance and shared benefit must be established for this to occur. Present management accounting practices are only distantly connected to these strategic developments. The realization of a strategic management accounting system will become more of a reality when target profits and risk avoidance are connected with the unified management of profit opportunity and enterprise risk with a feed-forward and feedback control loop described above. Variance analysis must be proactively and preventively implemented at the level of profit opportunity and enterprise risk management, not just cost management but also in relation to assessment and evaluation of the innovation process (see Nishimura 2011).

6.6 Conclusion

Although the idea of feed-forward control has long been discussed in the fields of business management and management accounting, it has not yet taken a definite form in accounting systems generally. The traditional management accounting systems have recently begun incorporating this idea into profit opportunity or enterprise risk idea through the cost design and cost improvement techniques established by Japanese enterprises and partly through the ABC and BSC approaches developed by innovators in strategic management accounting. The possibility of applying feed-forward information extends not only to cost management but also to profit opportunity and enterprise risk management (profit design).

This chapter has reexamined the value of information and organizational efforts, based on the existing literature on strategic management, and addressed feed-forward management in regards to cost design in Japanese auto companies. Cost design is also addressed in terms of "the second or third gap", which reveals its limitations in globalized markets and in an increasing uncertain and diverse environment (see Nishimura 2011, 2012; see also Chap. 3). Enterprises have developed agile supply chain and global innovation instead of Japanese type of management to globally discover and exploit profit opportunities. On the basis of these experiences and practices, management accounting must take a more firmly future-oriented and forward-looking form. Researchers should clarify the limitations of planning for and controlling global business by using feedback information and control methods, and should establish a new feed-forward strategic management accounting system together with profit opportunity and enterprise risk perspective to relevantly respond to contemporary business needs.

This chapter gives only a framework for coping with the current issues in management accounting. Others, such as Falta et al. (2006) and Kumarasinghe and Willett (2010), have used mathematical, statistical, and empirical approaches to analyze these new contemporary issues in business enterprises. These efforts to establish proactive and preventive management accounting will unite together and open up new ways to establish new strategic management accounting. When Monden (1994) introduced the Toyota production and management systems, the former vice-president of Toyota Motor Corporation, Taichi Ono, expected the system would lead to advances in strategic management accounting. It is not yet clear whether this expectation has been met. Although Japanese-style management accounting has been considered by many at times to be more strategic than its Western counterparts, the nature of the relation between management accounting and strategy remains unresolved. It is interesting to consider whether it may be possible to better develop strategic management accounting by clarifying the fundamental framework of feed-forward cost control that Japanese enterprises have created. The evolution of current practices requires us to resolve more troublesome problems and establish a new research outcome and a scientific perspective. It is most important to integrate existing and growing ideas into a scientific framework, or a fundamental concept. In this sense, the study of Japanese-style management accounting, international comparative studies of management accounting practices and theories, and the study of the relationship between these cognate disciplines from the viewpoint of feed-forward thought and an integrated viewpoint of feedback and feed-forward controls may play an important role in clarifying the strategic nature of management accounting.

Discussion for Further Research

This chapter discussed the feature and structure of today's management accounting in relation to strategic management from the viewpoint of feed-forward management. On the basis of the aforesaid discussion, two points seems to be helpful in attention to sketch out the contemporary management accounting. One is a new idea of extending management accounting information from financial data to nonfinancial one, which tried to regain the relevance of management accounting lost to strategic directions or targets. In management accounting, this idea takes such a definite form as ABS or BSC that is based on the concept of enterprise value or activity. This concept of nonfinancial information is used in wide area from cost to the whole organization.

Another point is related to 'a relevant idea' that extends management accounting information and control from feedback standpoint to the feed-forward. In this case, managers plan for and control profit opportunity or enterprise risk proactively for enterprise value creation. Cost design or the comprehensive risk management is the application of this idea to the contemporary strategic management. However, it is an unsettled question to clarify what part management accounting plays in the comprehensive risk management.

Environmentally conscious cost design (Nishimura 2014), as well as the holistic and comprehensive risk management in internal control, is developed from the socioeconomic point of view, according to which corporate profitability strategy and sustainable business growth are combined with corporate responsibility and consciousness of social issues (e.g., environmental protection, safety, and social welfare). As regards the comprehensive risk management accounting, much still remains how to strengthen the transparency and accountability of risk management from the socioeconomic viewpoint as well as how to effectively control uncertainty by means of risk management and its related accounting.

Bibliography

Borge, D. (2001). *The Book of Risk*. New York: Wiley.

Collins, J. (2009). *How the Mighty Fall and Why Some Companies Never Give in*. New York: HarperCollins Publishers Inc.

COSO. (2004, September). *Enterprise Risk Management-Integrated Framework: Executive Summary Framework*, The Committee of Sponsoring Organizations of the Treadway, NJ (US).

Culp, C. (2001). *The Risk Management Process: Business Strategy and Tactics*. New York: Wiley.

Demski, J. S. (1967, October). An Accounting System Structures on a Linear Programming Model. *Accounting Review, 42*(4), 701–712.

Demski, J. S. (1968, October). Some Observations on Demski's Ex Post Accounting System: A Reply. *The Accounting Review, 43*(4), 672–674.

Demski, J. S. (1969, October). Decision-Performance Control. *Accounting Review, 44*(4), 669–713.

Drury, C. (2001). *Management Accounting for Business Decisions*. Bedford: Thomson London.

Falta, M., Gallagher, L., & Willett, R. (2006). Modeling 'Hard-To-Measure' Costs in Environment Management Accounting. *Asia-Pacific Management Accounting Journal, 1*(1), 127–125.

Guilding, C., Cravens, K. S., & Tayles, M. (2000). An International Comparison of Strategic Management Accounting Practices. *Management Accounting Research, 11*(1), 128.

Ingrassia, P. (2011). *Crash Course: The American Automobile Industry's Road to Bankruptcy and Bailout— And Beyond*. New York: Random House.

Johnson, H. T. & Kaplan, R. S. (1987). *Relevance Lost; the Rise and Fall of Management*. Boston: Harvard Business School Press.

Kaplan, R. S., & Cooper, R. (1998). *Cost and Effects: Using Integrated Cost Systems to Drive Profitability and Performance*. Boston: Harvard Business School Press.

Kaplan, R. S., & Norton, D. P. (1996). *The Balanced Scorecard: Translating Strategy into Action*. Boston: Harvard Business School Press.

Kobayashi, T. (1993). *Current Costing Theory-Approach to Strategic Cost Management (in Japanese)*. Tokyo: Chuo Keizai Publisher.

Kumarasinghe, S., & Willett, R. (2010). What Can Management Accounting Practitioners and Academics to Improve Risk Measurement and Foreworn Impending Financial Crises? *Asia-Pacific Management Accounting Journal*, *5*(2), 1–10.

Mikes, A. (2011). From Counting Risk to Making Risk Count: Boundary-work in Risk Management. *Accounting, Organization and Society*, *36*(4–5), 226–245.

Monden, Y. (1994). *Toyota Production System: An Integrated Approach to Just-In-Time* (2nd ed.), Chapman and Hall, Foreword, London.

Nishimura, A. (1996). New Development of Japanese Management Accounting: From Cost Design to Strategic Cost Design. *Journal of Political Economy*, *62*(*1–6*), 241–251.

Nishimura, A. (2001). Feed Forward Cost Accounting and Strategic Management, *International Journal of Accounting Literature*, *1*(2, 3 and 4), 117–136.

Nishimura, A. (2003). *Management Accounting in Asia: feed forward and Asian perspectives*. Hampshire: Palgrave Macmillan.

Nishimura, A. (2005). Strategic Management and Contemporary Management Accounting. In A. Nishimura & R. Willett (Eds.), *Management Accounting in Asia* (pp. 1–8). Singapore: Thomson Learning. (A division of Thomson Asia Pte Ltd.).

Nishimura, A. (2008). Effect of Management System on Management Accounting: The Case of Chinese Cellular Phone Terminal Unit Manufacturers. *Asian-Pacific Management Accounting Journal*, *3*(1), 87–105. Public Knowledge Project (Open Journal System). http://arionline.uitm.edu.my/ojs/index.php/APMAJ/issue/view/18.

Nishimura, A. (2011). Uncertainty and Management Accounting: Opportunity, Profit Opportunity and Profit. *Asia-Pacific Management Accounting Journal*, *6*(1), 81–101. Public Knowledge Project (Open Journal System). http://arionline.uitm.edu.my/ojs/index.php/APMAJ/issue/view/13.

Nishimura, A. (2012). Profit Opportunity, Feed Forward Innovation, and Management Accounting. *Asian-Pacific Management Accounting Journal*, *7*(2), 65–98. Public Knowledge Project (Open Journal System). http://arionline.uitm.edu.my/ojs/index.php/APMAJ/issue/view/12.

Nishimura, A. (2014). Transforming Cost Design Into Environmentally Conscious Cost Design in Japan: Likelihood and Problems for Further Development. *Journal of Management Control*, *25*(*1*), 55–75. https://doi.org/10.1007/s00187-014-0190-x.

Porter, M. E. (1985). *Competitive Advantage, Creating and Sustaining Superior Performance*. New York: Free Press, a Division of Simon and Schuster, Inc.

Porter, M. E. (1998). *On Competition, Harvard Business Review Book Series.* Boston: Harvard Business School.
Power, M. (2007). *Organized Uncertainty: Designing a World of Risk Management.* New York: Oxford University, Press.
Richardson, J. G. (2010). The Certainty of Uncertainty: Risk Management Revisited. *Foresight, 12*(4), 49–64.
Samuels, J. M. (1965). Opportunity Costing. *Journal of Accounting Research, 3*(2), 182–191.
Shank, J. K., & Govindarajan, V. (1993). *Strategic Cost Management: The New Tool for Competitive Advantage.* New York: Free Press, A Division Simon and Schuster, Inc.
Simons, R. (1995). *Levers of Control: How Managers Use Innovative Control Systems to Drive Strategic Renewal.* Boston: Harvard Business School Press.
Smith, P. G., & Merritt, G. M. (2002). *Proactive Risk Management: Controlling Uncertainty in Product Management.* New York: Productivity Press.
Tanaka, M. (1995). *Theory and Practices of Cost Design.* Tokyo: Chuo-keizaisha Publisher, Co.

CHAPTER 7

Transforming Cost Design into Environmentally Conscious Cost Design in Japan: Likelihood and Problems for Further Development

7.1 Introduction

Global warming and changing ecological systems have led to increased environmental consciousness among enterprises and consumers. In particular, enterprises that participate in material exploitation, processing, distribution, and disposal may not be viewed favorably by stockholders, employees, and consumers unless those enterprises provide environmentally friendly products. Because of this, environmental management has become an important part of enterprise strategic management. Recently, there have been many studies on environmentally conscious manufacturing (ECM), the recovery and reuse of materials and products, and waste and pollution control (Gungor and Gupta 1999; Henri and Joumeault 2010; Ilgin and Gupta 2010; Pondeville et al. 2012). However, a great deal of research on environmental costing and environmental cost management remains to be done.

Enterprises should make efforts to reduce their environmental impact even as they try to balance these efforts with profitability efforts. These enterprises should therefore establish a model that integrates environmental costs into their cost management strategy while maintaining profitability. Toward this end, some study of environmental costing and environmental cost management has been conducted (Kreuze and Newell 1994; Parker 2000; Steen 2005; Ito 2006; Hunkeler et al. 2008; Horváth

A. Nishimura, *Management, Uncertainty, and Accounting*,
https://doi.org/10.1007/978-981-10-8989-3_7

and Berlin 2012; Gabriel et al. 2014). In regard to this subject of study, Horváth and Berlin (2012) in particular offer insight on integrating the costs of environmental requirements with target costing and take a proactive view of 'green target costing'.[1] They also divide green target costing activities into six steps, such as the evaluation of target selling price including green price premium and green *kaizen* (continuous improvement) costing, mirroring the six principles of target costing: price-led costing, focus on customers, focus on design, cross-functional involvement, life cycle orientation, and value-chain involvement. As a result, a comprehensive product design approach is built, in which environmental costs and impacts are identified and improved by incorporating them into the steps, and customers' requirements can be met along with environmental requirements and cost constraints together with product design. Their views motivate this study of environmentally conscious cost design.

In Japan, researchers have only just begun to examine the integration of environmental consciousness with cost management, although some large companies are said to have developed environmentally conscious management to gain a competitive advantage or better utilize limited natural resources (Sarkis 1995; Ito 2007) and the Japanese Ministry of Economy, Trade and Industry (METI) (2002) threw a comprehensive light on the subject of environmentally conscious cost design (ECCD) and its status as a new stage of cost design in their investigation, the results of which were published as *A Workbook for Environmental Management Accounting* by METI (see also Ito 2006). Kajihara et al. (2009) also conducted a factual survey on design for environment (DFE) and cost design in the general machine, electrical machine, transportation equipment, and precision machine industries in Japan. They found that 79.2% of firms had implemented DFE, 73.1% had implemented cost design, and 59.7% had implemented both (see Park 2007, 2009). Although these studies suggest the possibility of evolving conventional cost design into a comprehensive environmental cost design, a relation between DFE and ECCD, as well as a concrete procedure for carrying out this cost design, remains a subject of debate, as these studies have clarified neither the relation between DFE and life cycle costing and eco-procurement (EP) nor the difference between DFE and ECCD.

The purpose of this chapter is to clarify the relation between environmental management and cost design and describe the current state of ECCD. Some remaining problems whose solution will advance ECCD are also described. Our analysis depends primarily on the social and environment reports of companies listed on the Tokyo Stock Exchange in the electric machine and transportation equipment industries. This is because these companies have long histories of implementing cost design (82.5% in the electric machine industry (2002 data), 76.5% in the transportation equipment industry (2002 data), and 81.5% in the manufacturing industry (2009 data)) and are more likely to evolve cost design into ECCD (Yoshida et al. 2012; JAMS 2005, 2009).

We must first define the concept of cost design to understand how it can become ECCD. We therefore begin by comparing cost design with standard costing practices and explain the fundamental characteristics of cost design. In Sect. 7.3, we will discuss product life cycle, environmental management, and the extension of cost design to global supply chains and the complete life cycle. In Sect. 7.4, we analyze the relation between cost design and environmental consciousness, investigate the actual state of ECCD, and list some of the problems that should be addressed for the further development and generalization of ECCD. To conclude, we examine a fundamental framework for ECCD to allow both high value (high function at low cost) and minimal environmental impact from a socioeconomic angle. This chapter aims to clarify the present state of Japanese green cost design and its structure and meanings. In clarifying, the implication of comprehensive cost management, upon which Horváth and Berlin (2012) touched in relation to the absorption of environmental awareness into target costing, should be kept in mind, and inquiry into further development and problems of environmentally friendly cost design in Japan will adopt the social well-being viewpoint in this study.

7.2 Cost Design and Its Space-Time Expansion

Comparison of Cost Design with the Standard Cost System

Cost design was energetically discussed in the Japanese academic literature of the 1990s. Because it has been discussed from multiple angles, including costing, cost management (cost planning and control), cost engineering, and profit management, there is not yet a universal definition of the term (IMA 1994; Sato 2009). However, here we should define cost design before launching a discussion of ECCD since the recognition of ECCD is influenced by the understanding of cost design.

Monden and Hamada (1991) first used the management practices of Toyota Motor Corporation to define cost design as proactive cost reduction at the design stage[2] of a new product, contrasting this with reactive cost reduction at the manufacturing stage (see also Monden 1999): that is, cost reduction by using the standard cost system. In connection with this issue, Tanaka (1992) used the following equation to compute target costs and clarify the difference between cost design and standard costing, or budget control (see also Tanaka 1993; Sakurai 1989, 1991).

> This equation is $g = (S_p - C_t)\,Q_y - (S_p - C_e)Q_y = (C_e - C_t)Q_y$, where g is cost variance, S_p is the target selling price, Q_y is the target sales volume, C_t is the target cost, and C_e is the estimated cost.

In this equation, it is most important to minimize cost variance by means of proactive *kaizen* (improvement) and innovation, which help to achieve target costs. These are especially important when the target cost is lower than the estimated cost. In such cases, the category of product *value*, which motivates the above equation, is understood as the ratio of function to cost and becomes an effective index to improve product function with minimum cost. This proactive control view, which is based on exhaustive value engineering, is fundamentally different from the reactive view of standard costing, in which actual cost is evaluated on the basis of standard cost as the true cost. Thus, the proactive view analyzes variance and enacts the remedial measures for that before production to realize target cost, while the reactive view controls activities in the next period by ex post fitting to the standard cost of the previous period. In seeking to explain the concept of value in cost design, Tani (1994, 1995) also noted the engineering aspects of proactive cost management, including simultaneous engineering, concurrent engineering, and cooperation with suppliers (see Tani et al. 1994; Yoshikawa 1994). Tanaka (1985) stressed design-stage value engineering, using a cost table[3] for feed-forward cost estimation. Cost design that is founded on these engineering methods and includes cost management can be regarded as total profit management in the whole organization of a company (see Kato 1993a, b; Kato et al. 1995; Tanaka 1985, 1995, 2002; JAMS 2009).

Table 7.1 shows the fundamental features of cost design as discussed in the literature above and compares those features with those of the standard cost system.[4]

On the basis of the contents of Table 7.1, this chapter defines cost design as cost management to proactively manufacture new value (high function at low cost) into a product at the design stage to gain a competitive

Table 7.1 Cost design in comparison with the standard cost system

	Cost design	*Standard cost system*
Object	To proactively manufacture value (cost and function) into a product at the design stage	To actualize standard cost at production stage
Methods	Proactive cost management by using ex ante cost variance analysis with value engineering and improvement	Feedback cost control by means of ex post cost variance analysis with efficient physical and scientific management
Analysis	Target cost based on value or on target sales and target profit Estimated cost (competitive future cost) is evaluated on the basis of target cost (long-term planned cost) and measures to improve its variance from the target cost are proactively prepared during the cost design stage	Standard cost based on standard volume, standard unit price, and standard capacity Actual cost is evaluated on the basis of standard cost as determined by time study (time standard of each task), and activities to reduce the variance, defined through ex post cost variance analysis, are retroactively implemented at the production stage
Actions	Proactive alteration or improvement of existing cost elements, production processes, methods, and organization styles, based on the concept of value	Changing purchasing methods or efficient and effective usage of cost elements or increasing productivity, given existing cost elements and manufacturing processes

Source: Nishimura (2003); Tanaka (1995)

advantage. This idea is called *tsukurikomi* in Japanese and can be translated as 'built-in cost and quality' in English. This definition will later be seen to be closely related to ECCD, since enterprises must tackle various problems to proactively reduce environmental impact without sacrificing cost and quality. Thus, the following subsection examines how this cost design has been extended to global supply chains and the whole product life cycle from an environmental viewpoint.

Extension of Cost Design to Supply Chains and the Product Life Cycle

Cost design in Japan was originally supported by subcontractors who cooperated in industrial groups (the *keiretsu* system), in contrast to the openly contracted supply chains in the West (Bhimani 1995; Ellram 2000, 2006; Cooper and Slagmulder 1997, 1999). In Japan, suppliers (subcontractors) to whom their parent company gives financial, technological, and informational support may find it difficult to supply other companies with their products because suppliers are dependent not only on the parent company but also on the parent company's production plan. In contrast, Western-style suppliers are independent of purchasers and can select the most favorable purchaser through mutual agreement. However, this situation in Japan is recently becoming less prevalent, as we shall see in Sect. 7.4.

To make effective and efficient use of scarce materials and provide customers with highly functional and cheap products, finished product manufacturers in Japan must establish global cooperation with suppliers. The supplier contracting system in Japan was considered a pyramid, where a large assembly company took a vertex position over the broader base of the supply tiers. For example, supply chains in the automotive industry were composed of stratified supply groups (tiers) in which entire car manufacturing companies (14 firms) closely related to their suppliers and cooperated on information and technology; first tier (about 800 firms), second tier (about 4000 firms), and third tier (about 20,000 firms) suppliers provided functional parts, exterior and interior decors, detailed parts, metal parts, and plastic parts both up the supply chain and laterally within a tier (Nabeyama 2011). In this system, suppliers who enlarge their businesses also expand their own supply chain networks. Supply chains in the transportation equipment and electric machine industries have also extended their businesses overseas, keeping step with the overseas expansion of finished product manufacturers (METI 2008; Otsuka and Ichikawa 2011; Nishimura 2008). This expansion of cost design into the global supply chain results from corporate strategy to increase manufacturing *flexibility* as a means of coping with the uncertainty that competitive environmental change causes (Rimienė 2011; Grigore 2007).

As recently rising fuel price, mass consumption economy, and strict environmental regulations cause increases in user and disposal costs of a product in comparison with manufacturing costs, enterprises and consumers begin to think about the total lifetime cost of a product from production to disposal or recycling (Kobayashi 1996; Nakajima 2004). Although engineers may have planned and designed target costs at the design stage on the assumption that the manufacturing and selling stage is the final stage of cost design, they must now proactively build in the costs and functions across the whole product life cycle, from material procurement to production, use, and disposal. Generally, the connection between life cycle costing and cost design results from business activity to offer consumers satisfaction at a cost and quality that gives a sustainable competitive advantage (Seuring 2004, 2010; Goldbach 2010). The process of expanding cost design into the global supply chain and the whole product life cycle is represented in Fig. 7.1.

Cost design was originally used to refer to a process of proactively manufacturing value in a production process, whereby the costs and functions of materials and parts from domestic suppliers and their processing costs were controlled at the design stage of a new product. In this process, as shown by *dotted arrows A and B*, the costs of domestic suppliers and other costs in manufacturing stage are estimated at the cost design stage, when their production conditions are relatively certain. When it extends to the whole product life cycle (*bold arrow C*), the company should also proactively manufacture at the design stage to control the costs and functions of a product

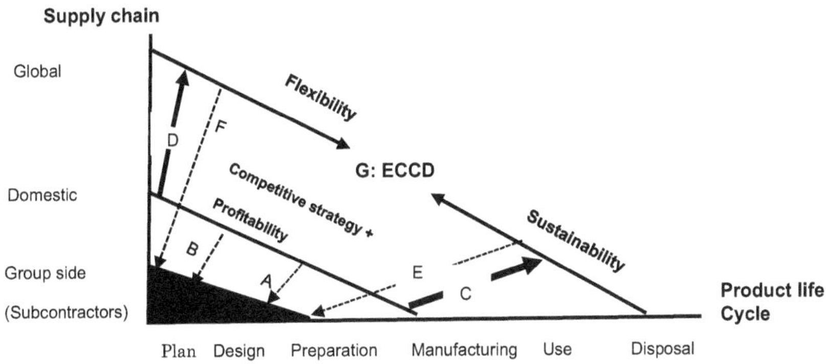

Fig. 7.1 Expanding cost design into environmentally conscious cost design (Note: The black triangle shows the actual state at the stage where the cost design is carried out (supply from the group of the company or subcontractors and production preparation), *dotted arrow A* represents estimated product life cycle until the manufacturing stage in the initial cost design, and *dotted arrow B* represents the estimated domestic supply chain in the initial cost design. Both are structured from the viewpoint of profitability and competitive strategy. *Dotted arrow E* shows the estimation sphere of the whole product life cycle in the expanded cost design, which is a result of expansion of cost design into the whole product life cycle (*bold arrow C*), while *dotted arrow F* shows the estimated global supply chain in the expanded cost design, which is a result of expansion of cost design into the global supply chain (*bold arrow D*). G indicates the function of ECCD into which C's sustainability and D's flexibility are integrated from the viewpoint of environmental consciousness.)

in the complete life cycle (*dotted arrow E*) with an eye toward sustainability. When a supply chain becomes global (*bold arrow D*), a company should proactively manufacture to control the costs and functions of materials and parts in the global supply chain (*dotted arrow F*) by using manufacturing flexibility to cope with uncertainty. In the area of ECCD (G), a company must take steps to reduce the environmental impact, from the material procurement stage up to the use and disposal of products by customers.

This necessitates managing quality, costs, and delivery from the viewpoints of environmental protection, particularly as it relates to resources recycling, global warming prevention, and compliance (NEC 2012). Figure 7.1 shows the global supply chain on the vertical axis and product lifetime along the horizontal axis. The cost design stages are spread along the horizontal and vertical directions, which are indicated by *bold arrows C and D*, signifying an expansion of cost design to cover the product lifetime and the global supply chain. Proactive manufacturing that creates new value (or proactively building-in value) enables wider and longer processes to control costs, functions, and environmental impact at the design stage, and this result is shown as the actualization of environmental consciousness in cost management based on flexibility and sustainability.

More importantly, it is the global development of environmental consciousness that has caused cost design to simultaneously expand to global supply chains and the complete life cycle of a product. As environmental regulations become more stringent and both stockholders and consumers become more sensitive to environmental issues, enterprises should also make efforts to use environmentally friendly, functional, and cheap materials and parts so as to reduce the environmental impact across the product life cycle and produce more environmentally conscious products (ECPs). Finished product manufacturers therefore tend to rely on suppliers who can offer cheaper and more environmentally friendly materials and parts. Manufacturers may also implement strict environmental assessments in the production and disposal processes of products. Enterprises are concerned with ECCD and try to proactively implement the desired reduction of environmental impact, including cost, quality, and delivery targets, at the design stage of a new product. Socially responsible design, such as the safety of products, is considered in the same way as ECCD.

Enhanced environmental consciousness stimulates the need to combine cost design with global supply chain and product life cycle management organically, so that high quality and environmental impact reduction becomes integrated with cost reduction. In the following sections, we consider how cost design can evolve into ECCD.

7.3 Cost Design and Environmentally Conscious Manufacturing of Japanese Companies in Electric Machine and Transportation Equipment Industries

The Present State of Environmentally Conscious Management

To begin, we will examine ECM, which includes ECPs, DFE, life cycle assessment (LCA), and EP. Data related to ECM were collected from corporate social and environmental reports disclosed mainly in 2013 (or in 2012 when undisclosed in that year) on the Internet by 137 companies in the electric machine industry and 58 companies in the transportation equipment industry. These industries were chosen for discussion because the available data allow us to recognize the present advanced practices of cost design (particularly, ECCD) in Japan and to forecast its future direction because they are representative industries that have underpinned the Japanese economy for a long time and have both long experience of cost design practice and experience leading the way in ECCD. The companies investigated represent 85.8% and 95.2%, respectively, of each of the companies from each industry that is listed on the Tokyo Stock Exchange. Generally, ECP[5] refers to a product manufactured by a firm that has adopted mainly any or all of DFE, LCA, and EP to fulfill standards of environmental impact reduction across the product life cycle. DFE is a design process that considers environmental impact reduction across the entire product lifetime, from material procurement to production, distribution, use, recycling, and disposal of a product.

As stated above, EP (sometimes called green procurement) plays an important role in ECP and is now a decisive standard of judgment by which upstream suppliers and finished product-makers select suppliers with whom to subcontract. Manufacturers and upstream suppliers give preference to those suppliers who positively address environmental issues on the basis of environmental assessment, presuming that the assessed standards will be included in the appraisal of quality, delivery, cost, and technological development and reliably achieved (Sumida Group 2012). LCA refers to activities to quantify environmental impact over the complete product lifetime, from materials procurement to product disposal (Mitsubishi Electric Corporation 2002, 2010). Table 7.2 shows how the investigated companies carry out ECM. The relation between ECP and other environmental manufacturing methods is indicated in Table 7.3. Here, we see that ECP (60.5%) is linked closely with EP (61.5%) and LCA

Table 7.2 Present state of environmentally conscious manufacturing

Industry (number of investigated companies)	*ECP*	*DFE*	*LCA*	*EP*
Electric machine				
Number of companies (out of 137)	76	46	59	86
Ratio	55.5%	33.6%	43.1%	62.8%
Transportation equipment				
Number of companies (out of 58)	42	29	28	34
Ratio	72.5%	50%	48.3%	58.6%
Total				
Number of companies (out of 195)	118	75	87	120
Ratio	60.5%	38.5%	44.6%	61.5%

Abbreviations: *ECP*, environmentally conscious product; *DFE*, design for environment; *LCA*, life cycle assessment; *EP*, eco-procurement. Source: corporate social and environmental reports in the two industries

Table 7.3 Relations between ECP and other environmental manufacturing methods

Industry	***ECP+DFE +LCA+EP***	***ECP+DFE +LCA***	***ECP+DFE +EP***	***ECP+LCA +EP***	***ECP+EP***
Electric machine	40	3	1	13	18
Transportation equipment	26	1	2	1	5
Total (**110**)	**66**	**4**	**3**	**14**	**23**

Note: In addition to the companies indicated in the table, there are 8 companies that report carrying out only ECP without identifying any other methods. As a result, we can see that 118 companies implement ECP conjointly with any or all of DFE, LCA, and EP, or only EP (= 110 + 8). We may note, in passing, the situation of other environmental manufacturing methods: one company in DFE+LCA+EP, 2 in LCA+EP, 1 in DFE, and 11 in EP. Sixty-two companies identify nothing about environmental manufacturing

(44.6%). This situation suggests that overall ECP is never implemented in a systematic form based on DFE. Where ECP strongly connects with DFE, LCA, and EP, the probability of ECCD implementation is assumed to be high since DFE is easily connected to cost design at the design stage.

In Table 7.3, we see that 66 companies from among 195 (about 33.8%) implement ECP in a form strongly connected with DFE, LCA, and EP, while the rest (44) of 110 companies that report any relation of ECP to other environmental manufacturing methods do so in a partial form, where it is supported mainly by an environmentally conscious supply chain network. It is also important to consider that ECP is strongly supported by

EP. It may be inferred from Table 7.3 that 26 (44.8%) of the 58 investigated companies in the transportation equipment and 40 (29.2%) of the 137 in the electric machine industry may carry out ECP in a comprehensive form based on DFE, LCA, and EP, which may also be related to ECCD (setting aside what type of cost design the companies adopt), since another survey (Park 2009) showed that 82.6% of companies in the transport equipment industry carry out DFE and 87% implement cost design. This is in contrast to 85.7% and 67.6%, respectively, in the electric machine industry. In this research as well as that of Kajihara et al. (2009), when recycling, design, and environmental assessments are regarded as DFE, the research shows a higher rate of implementation for DFE than that shown in our results, in which DFE is separated from LCA and EP. The rate of ECCD implementation would thus be lower in our study than in the findings by Kajihara et al. if DFE represents ECCD; this is because DFE in our study has a narrower definition than in their studies: 38.5% as a whole, and 33.6% in the electric machine industry and 50% in the transportation equipment industry. Additionally, as discussed in Sect. 7.2, we must consider the function of ECCD, or integration of flexibility and sustainability based on profitability and competitive strategy, in process in which cost design expands into global supply chain and the whole product life cycle. Therefore, ECCD may certainly take a comprehensive shape through the connection of DFE with LCA and EP. We cannot assume a rate of ECCD implementation higher than about 35%. This may also be supported by the research of JAMS in 2009, when only 20–24% of the investigated companies included costs for environmental preservation in target costs (JAMS 2009).

Even if we assume an implementation rate of ECCD at about 35% on the presumption that ECCD is carried out when ECP is closely connected to DFE, LCA, and EP, it is debatable what form of ECCD each company adopts and what procedures enterprises follow when integrating low cost, high quality, and environmental impact reduction with ECCD.

Structures and Problems of Environmentally Conscious Cost Design

Ito (2007) and METI (2002) present two types of ECCD: a unified type, which proactively targets costs based on the value concept and targets environmental impact reduction simultaneously at the design stage, and a two-layer type, in which the target level in DFE is decided on the basis of business policy before product development, separating items of expenditures related to DFE from target cost allocation (Ito 2007). Sony, a major electrical manufacturer that adopts the unified type, "has added environmental quality considerations to Sony's procurement system, while quality, cost, delivery and service are obviously essential" (Sony Corporation 2001, p. 22). Already in 1991, the corporation, acting on the belief that product quality is inseparable from environmental quality, launched "a full-scale product assessment program that included environmental factors in its overall definition of product quality" (Sony Corporation 2001, p. 28). At Toyota, which has created and developed its own cost design system, the chief engineer responsible for development of a particular vehicle also sets environmental impact reduction targets for that vehicle in accordance with a comprehensive environmental impact assessment system that functions for the systematically assessing a vehicle's impact on the environment over the entire life cycle from the design stage through to the production, use, and disposal stages (Toyota Motor Corporation 2011, 2013).

Figure 7.2 shows "Sony's comprehensive approach to environmentally conscious operations begins with product assessment during product planning and design" (Sony Corporation 2001, p. 28). For the first assessment of environmental impact (labeled (a) in Fig. 7.2), five significant items of environmental impact in the hypothetical scenario of a Camcorder TSE/3000 (a video camera) are picked according to an environmental management system related to ISO 14001, which concerns electrical consumption, electricity used during standby, the number of parts used, the solder, and packing materials. Each environmental impact reduction target (labeled (b) in Fig. 7.2) is then compared with similar models available at the time of conception and design. Changes such as a reduction in electrical consumption from 10 to 8 W and a switch to lead-free solder are examples of the types of changes made to reduce environmental impact (Ito 2007). In addition, the priority given to these items is decided and the cost of production is reexamined as compared with the initial target cost (functional and cost targets). Concretely, target costs are closely connected with each stage—concept design, trial design/plan, trail production, assessment, and mass production—in product design: in each stage, activities to mitigate environmental impacts are also planned, controlled, and assessed in association with cost and function. As a result, cost design is transformed into ECCD, while product design into environmentally conscious product design (ECPD) (see Fig. 7.4).

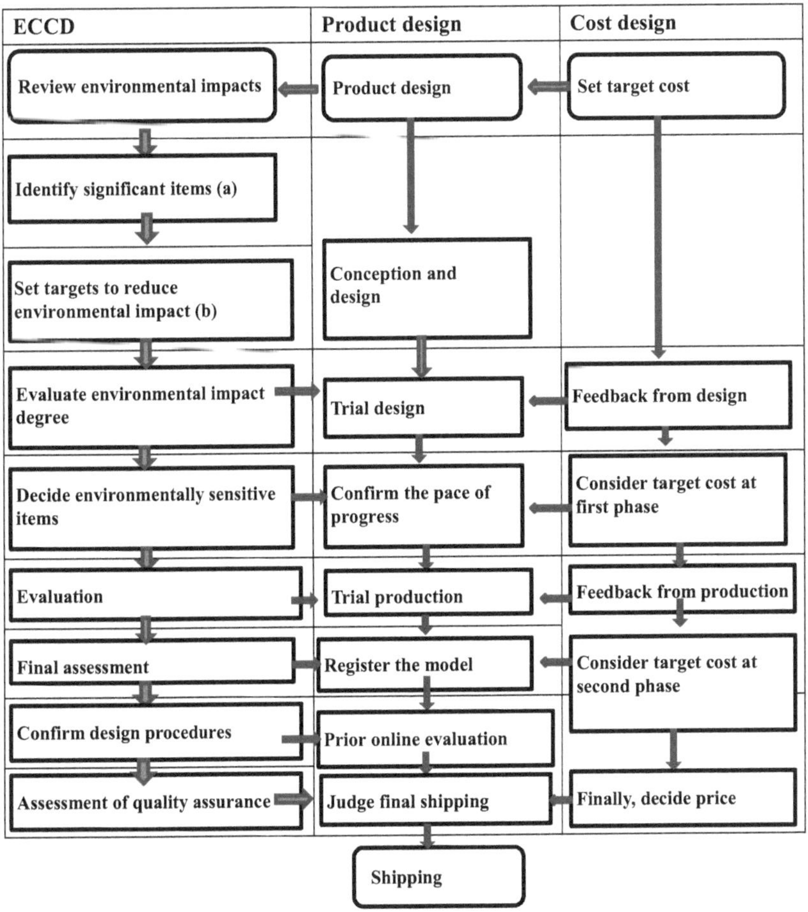

Fig. 7.2 Unified type of ECCD in Sony Corporation. (Source: Ito 2007; METI 2002, p. 64)

Sony computes the monetary conversion of the environmental impact reduction performance "by applying Sony's original monetary conversion coefficients as well as by comparing the environmentally conscious design cost with the environmental impact reduction performance in terms of such factors as energy conservation, and weight, polystyrene foam, and leaded solder reduction" (Sony Corporation 2001, p. 31). Denso Corporation, an

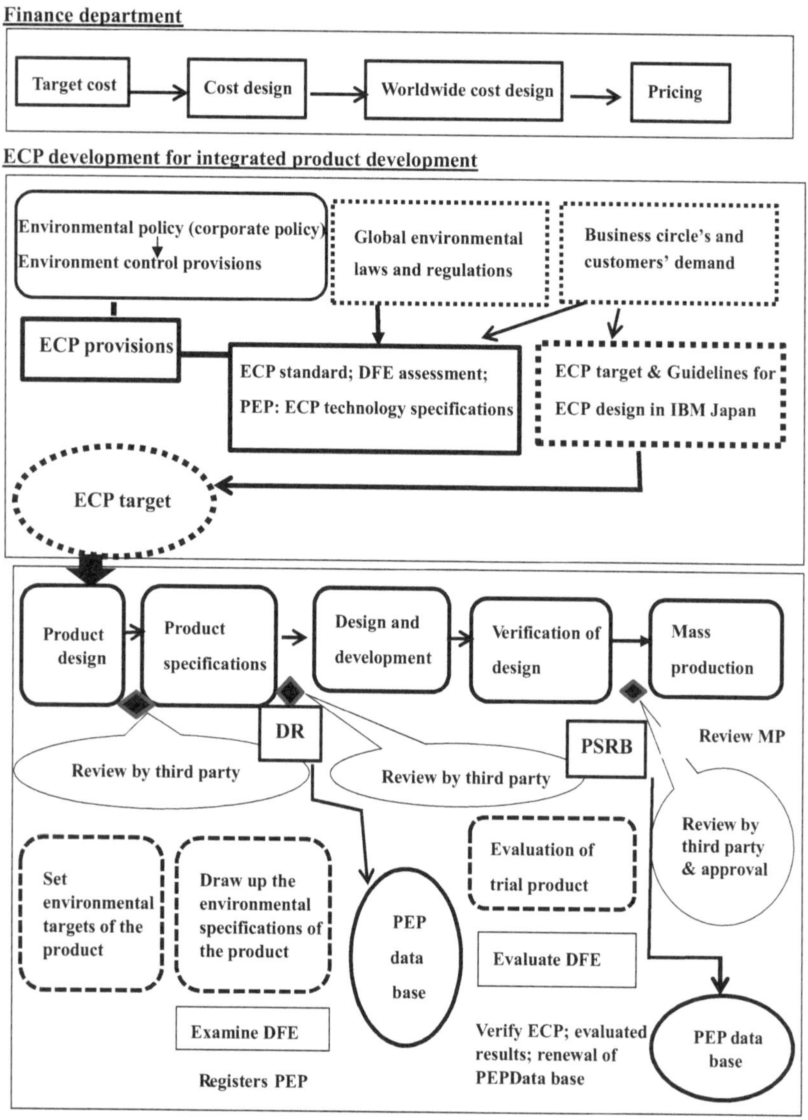

Fig. 7.3 The two-layer type of ECCD in IBM Japan. (*Abbreviations*: *PEP*, product environmental profile; *ECP*, environmentally conscious product; *DFE*, design for environment; *DR*, design review; *PSRB*, Product Safety Review Board. Source: Ito 2007; IBM Japan 2001)

automotive parts manufacturer, also uses environmental efficiency index to compare new and existing products to balance between environmental impact reduction and product *value*. Regarding the index, product value (a positive factor) and environmental impact (a negative efficiency index to compare new and existing products to provide an environmental impact reduction factor) of the new product are normalized to the values for existing products to create an index number (Denso Corporation 2010, 2014).

As stated above, Sony implements ECCD by combining environmentally conscious design, product design, and cost design (Figs. 7.2 and 7.4; see also Nishimura 2014). In contrast, IBM Japan implements our definition of DFE, formally separating it from cost design system, although the target of environmental impact reduction and LCA links closely with cost design in terms of ECCD (Fig. 7.3). IBM Japan, which carried out environmental impact assessment programs in 1978, extended this to ECP programs and started implementing simple and easy-to-handle DFE in 1991 (IBM Japan 1999, 2000; Yamamoto and Kokubu 2001). In ECCD, the corporation's finance department implements "accurate and impartial costing, and uses the whole value related to the procurement of materials and parts in the whole company, not departmental costing, to establish a scheme for cost design" (Ito 2007, p. 54). However, DFE and cost design are connected by the Integrated Product Development Plan (see Fig. 7.4). DFE is implemented under the Integrated Product Development Plan, in which new products are developed under a global standard and the applicable scope includes all life cycle processes of a newly developed product. During implementation, it is important to set up and actualize targets of quality, cost, and delivery, while realizing environmental targets. In developing a new ECPD, the need to 'proactively manufacture' the product at the early stage of development plays a critical role in determining the environmentally conscious level of a finished product. At the same time, IBM Japan began to emphasize EP (IBM Japan 2001).

As shown in Fig. 7.4, the unified type of ECCD in Sony Groups may be more synthetic and fine-grained in terms of cost design based on 'value' (environment, function and cost) than the two-layer type in IBM Japan. At present, Sony makes environmentally conscious design more elaborate through positioning it in the framework of plan-do-check-act cycle (Sony Corporation 2017, pp. 283, 322). First, at design/plan stage of ECP, key factors to consider—observation of relevant laws in individual countries, reduction of energy consumption, resource conservation, management of

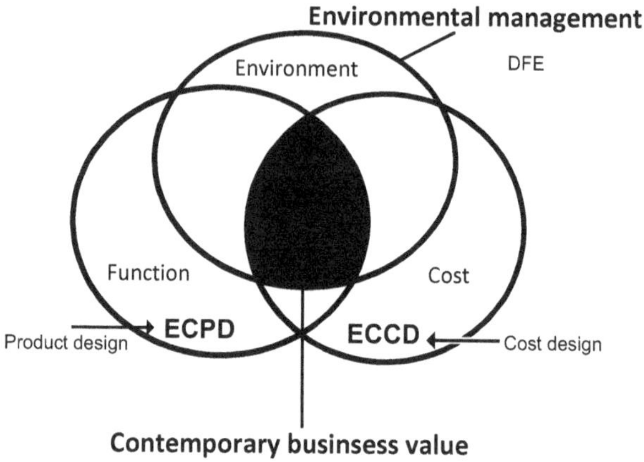

(1) Unified Type of Design for Environment in Sony Corporation
DFE: Design for environment: environmentally conscious design

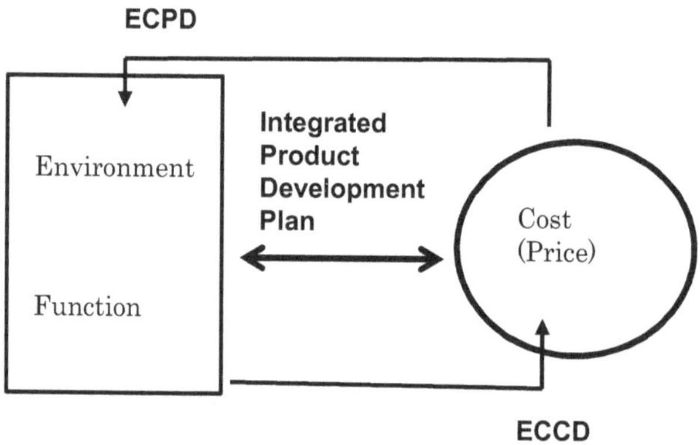

(2) The two-layer type of design for environment in IBM Japan

Fig. 7.4 Comparison between the unified type and the two-layer type of ECCD. (*Abbreviations*: *ECCD*, environmentally conscious cost design; *ECPD*, environmentally conscious product design)

chemical substances, assessment of products' environmental impact over their entire life cycle, and disclosure of pertinent information—are incorporated into initial design plan. These targets and measures are efficiently and effectively implemented and controlled through evaluation and improvements: implementation of environmental management based on the annual business plan (Do) and audit and review of annual business plan and environmental mid-term targets as well as performance assessments and decisions regarding awards (Check). Then information on these performances is fed to designing and target-setting for subsequent models: review by top management (Act). In this process, Sony's corporate headquarters (department in charge of environmental functions) annually assesses the environmental impacts of the entire Sony Group and, "after identifying risks and opportunities" feedback its information to "mid-range environmental targets and annual plans" and continues to promote improvements (Sony Corporation 2017, p. 283). Further, it must be noted that Sony not only endeavors to minimize the risk of chemical substances for human health and the environmental protection but also considers 'grappling with environmental issues' to create and expand business opportunities through providing environment-friendly products with consumers who deepen environmental consciousness and healthy orientation (Sony Corporation 2017, pp. 260–262). Environmentally conscious management system PDCA cycle and the close unification of product design and cost design quantitatively and qualitatively elaborate ECCD system through the extension and substantiality of business value concept (an integrated concept of environment, function, and cost). We must especially draw attention to the fact that ECCD in Sony is integrated with risk and opportunity management and continual improvements, since this leads us to consider society-oriented business management and

Table 7.4 Rate of material costs and suppliers' processing costs in manufacturing costs

Cost elements	*Material costs*		*Suppliers' processing costs*	
Industry	Transportation equipment (%)	Electric machine (%)	Transportation equipment (%)	Electric machine (%)
Median	69.5	57.6	4.6	9.4
Standard deviation	15.1	20.8	9.6	17.5
Minimum	22.9	0.8	0.03	0.03
Maximum	88.1	96.1	37.9	82.3
Sample points	55	133	55	133

Data were collected from corporate social and environmental reports in the manner described in Section "The Present State of Environmentally Conscious Management" contemporary business value as the key concept of this management. This consideration surely goes to the very core of discussion in this book. Before returning to the next section, we take a general view of ECCD practices in Japanese manufacturing companies.

As indicated in Tables 7.2 and 7.3, about 35% of the companies investigated in the 2 industries (75 in Table 7.2 and 66 in Table 7.3 out of 195) are assumed to carry out either of the two types of ECCD discussed above, assuming that ECP based on DFE and connected with some of other three factors represents ECCD. We also note that the success or failure of ECCD is highly dependent on finished product manufacturers' environmental management and their cooperation with suppliers, since ECCD has a critical need to proactively build in low cost, high quality, and minimum environmental impact of materials and parts at the design stage and to proactively assess the above factors over the complete product life cycle. This is because expenditures to suppliers are a large portion of production costs, as shown in Table 7.4 of Sect. 7.4. Although we can understand the general state of ECCD from the figures shown, we do not have a great deal of information on concrete practical models (in particular, a fundamental category combining the three factors) and their detailed procedures. We should extend our observation to include the relation between ECCD and EP to investigate the likelihood of adoption and problems for its further development. In practice, EP plays an important role in realizing DFE effectively.

7.4 Eco-Procurement and the Future Development of Environmentally Conscious Cost Design

Problems and Challenges

It is worthwhile to quantify the expense of materials and supplier's processing costs[6] within the manufacturing costs of finished product manufacturers in the electric machine and transport equipment industries as a means of clarifying the importance of supply chains for ECCD. Table 7.4 shows how companies in both industries depend strongly upon suppliers, despite a difference between concentrated dependency in the transportation equipment industry and the more dispersed type in the electric machine industry. One of the more critical aspects in ECCD for finished product manufacturers and upstream suppliers is the selection of subordinate suppliers (or subcontractors) in parallel with innovation of their own manufacturing processes and methods. IBM Japan points out the importance of green supply chains for ECP as follows. Cost competitiveness is an important factor for the corporation and it is critical to minimize production costs by becoming a more environmentally conscious enterprise. The reduction of environmental countermeasure costs in material cost through the elimination of waste and the minimization of energy costs through the reduction of the energy used for production are necessary for this purpose. Speedy correspondence with parts and materials manufacturers along the supply chain, including the development of information technology, is essential to proactively manufacture environmental quality in the development of a new product under ever-changing materials and parts (IBM Japan 2001).

Toyota also requires materials and high-quality parts at low cost with quick delivery and assurances of environmental safety from suppliers according to their *Green Purchasing Guidelines*: "Toyota expects its business partners to ensure 'long-term and stable procurement of the best products at the lowest price in the most speedy and timely manner,' based on thorough compliance with all applicable laws, regulations, and social norms and consideration for the environment. From the standpoint of customers who purchase our products, we ask you to 'build quality' into all processes for Toyota products, from development to production and shipment/logistics" (Toyota Motor Corporation 2011, p. 2). A green supply chain and its management play an important role in the development of ECP or ECCD in Japan as well as in the West (Kajüter 2002; Cooper and Slagmulder 1997).

Questions and Possible Solution Under Complicated Supply Chain System

The Great East Japan Earthquake of March 2011 marked a change in the relationship between finished product manufacturers and suppliers. Although before the earthquake all Japanese auto manufacturers were thought to control all supply chains from tier 1 to tier 3, these chains were cut into pieces and manufacturers were compelled to suspend business for several months as they were unable to control the new supply chain (Nabeyama 2011). The supply chain has since changed from a closed, simple structure, such as the pyramid type previously described, to a multilayered and complicated structure, such as a diamond or a mesh structure, where the enhanced diversification and concentration of production, as well as the loose relationships among suppliers, has made the whole supply chain both invisible and uncontrollable (Otsuka and Ichikawa 2011). As advancing technology increases the specialization and division of work, suppliers have not only shifted from the supply of parts inside the same group (e.g., Toyota) to diversified supply to other groups (e.g., Nissan or Honda), but they have also accelerated the extensive division of work wherein a supplier in the first or second tier not only directly provides an entire car manufacturing company with parts but also sells parts to other suppliers. The intensive tendency of supply chains is also increased through mergers and reorganization undertaken to improve productivity and raise value added after the Great East Japan Earthquake. This tendency of big suppliers in the first and second tiers gives rise to more intricate relationships among suppliers, who use multifarious methods and networks to establish an efficient and effective supply chain system (Otsuka and Ichikawa 2011).

As a result, the weakness of the close and visible supply chain, in which a supplier served a finished product manufacturer in a crucial capacity and other suppliers in the related group, was exposed after the earthquake. The invisibility and uncontrollability that arose caused increased complexity and weakened relations among suppliers. In addition, the search for rich resources and cheap labor prompted many suppliers to move to East Asia (METI 2008), touching off a price war that has only increased the complexity and invisibility of the supply chain structure. Those enterprises that carried out cost design on the basis of close and visible relation to suppliers are now faced with the problem of how to make visible and control the wide and long-term relations to suppliers and other interested parties, such as carriers and collecting/recycling dealers, in a way that ensures manufacturing flexibility and sustainability.

ECCD is a system to surmount not only the problem of lowering costs while increasing quality but also the antagonistic relation between these two factors and the problem of reducing environmental impact (Beppu 2005). ECCD is a process to proactively build in the three factors over a wide supply chain and the whole life cycle of a product. The reason we cannot find many definite models of ECCD is due to the difficulty of estimating the costs related to wide and complicated supply chains and the entire life cycle of a product at the design stage.

The diversified and complicated nature of supply chains can make the cost estimating process obscure and uncontrollable, even as large finished product manufacturers strengthen the unity of their groups in order to control the whole supply chain through group-internal cooperation. Because of this, enterprises find it difficult to estimate and proactively manufacture for cost, quality, and the environmental impact of supplier materials and parts at the design stage. Moreover, enterprises must work to not only estimate the costs over the product lifetime but also cope with the changing life of the product in competitive markets (Orita 2012). Finished product manufacturers should establish a strongly green and socially responsible partnership with suppliers (Lavastre et al. 2012; Thun and Hoenig 2011; Cheng et al. 2012) to develop improved competitiveness, profitability, and long-term sustainability (Lockamy and Smith 2000).

However, in Japan where there is little room left in the cost design for cost reduction, this often leads to a deterioration of quality, which can in turn lead to product recalls, since enterprises may compel suppliers to produce parts at lower cost to achieve the target cost of a product (Kato 2010). At times, severe curtailment of costs (by setting strict cost targets in factories or through requiring lower costs of suppliers) and stricter environmental requirements lead to a reduction in the level of functioning of the vehicles. Recall-related costs are a pure waste of social resources that the suppliers, managers, and workers of an assembly firm could otherwise use in an effort to manufacture cheap, functional, and environmentally friendly products. Thus, in effect, these costs are also environmentally unfriendly activities. Under the prevailing cost design systems in Japan, it is most critical to find ways to proactively manufacture costs, quality, and environmental impact reduction into products and tackle recall-level problems from the viewpoint of profitability, competitive strategy, and social responsibility. Although auto manufacturers and big electronics companies seek to increase the uniformity of their supply chain through information sharing and technological and financial support, there still remain some problems of visibility and control in cost design. Even today, recalls by auto manufacturers of defective vehicles is a serious problem. The recall of 1.9 million Prius automobiles was the result of improper programming for the hybrid control system, which Toyota produced from March 2009 to February 2013 and sold globally (The Nikkei 2014). From among Honda hybrid cars, 81,353 of two different types produced from July 2013 to February 2014 were also recalled (Nikkan Kogyo Shinbun 2014). According to an analysis of automobile recall notifications published by the Road Transport Bureau of METI, 59.5% (122) of all notified recalls (205) in 2011 resulted from 'design problems', and 109 recalls (53.2% of the whole and 89.3% of the 122) were caused by lax evaluation standards (Road Transport Bureau 2013). The average results over five years, from 2007 to 2011, show almost the same tendency as that in 2011. The recall of defective vehicles by Japanese auto manufacturers that are the result of design problems exemplifies the difficulty of balancing cost design with environmental impact reduction in ECCD.

At the individual company level, the most important aspect of ECCD implementation is to find and establish a *fundamental category*, analogous to *value* in the initial cost design, which will make it possible to simultaneously quantify and evaluate the cost, functions, and environmental impact of a product. However, some skepticism about the development of this fundamental category seems reasonable, since we depend here on the efforts of companies, changes in social environmental consciousness, and the strong support of governments and industrial circles, which will all play a role in resolving the environmental problems that have resulted from global socioeconomic development. For example, to effectively implement ECCD, individual companies must use cost tables at the functional level that are prepared with the aid of product environmental information and databases on regulated chemical substances, prohibited materials use, and energy-conserving technologies in each industrial sector. These tables are also indispensable for the ultimate goal of sustainability, which is to "achieve a better balance of environmental protection and social equity" in the economy (Swarr and Hunkeler 2008, p. 85). Information on these items from each industrial sector, even if the cooperation of firms, industrial groups, and national governments is necessary in terms of finance and activities, may help nurture the development of ECCD in the same way that Japanese motor companies could hasten to produce environmentally friendly vehicles on the model of the International Material Data System[7] and the Global Automotive Declarable Substance List.[8] In the electric machine industry, the recycling cost table[9] of the office machine and optical instrument manufacturer, Ricoh (Kokubu and Nakashima 2003), which makes use of life cycle costing in ECCD, could be more effectively supported not only by industrial group (e.g., by PC3R, an association to promote the *reduction, reuse, and recycling* of personal computers and their related machinery and tools) but also by governments as a source of information (PC3R Promotion Association 2014).

7.5 Conclusion

In ECCD, Japanese companies must solve the problem of proactively and reliably manufacturing cheaper and more functional products with minimal environmental impact at the design stage under increasing uncertainty and complexity caused by broadening supply chains and the diverse, intricate relationships among suppliers and other dealers (producers, users, retailers, and collecting/recycling dealers) in the life cycle process. ECCD, when used on the basis of the initial cost design with the intention of profitability and competitive strategy, performs its social and environmental duties by integrating flexibility and sustainability into it as a result of the initial cost design's expanding to global supply chain and the whole product life cycle. Therefore, ECCD becomes more complicated than the initial cost design. The core of all the questions is whether Japanese enterprises continually follow management thinking to solve the inherently antagonistic relation between low cost and high quality and minimal environmental impact in ECCD by proactively manufacturing for all of these factors at the design stage or whether they modify its thinking and use a trade-off between cost and environmental impacts to seek a well-balanced combination. Thanks to the success of cost design, the idea of cheap, high-quality goods has taken root in the minds of Japanese consumers. Consumers have become accustomed to enterprises taking efforts toward environmental protection without passing on these costs, even as producers wrestle with the problem of producing a low-cost product that has minimal environmental impact. Japanese enterprises should continue to look inward and outward for cost and quality improvements.

The most important point is to deepen national environmental awareness and for each person to bear the social and environmental costs in his or her own way. In this situation, enterprises can use ECCD to proactively manufacture with *reasonable target costs*, at high quality, and with low environmental impact. For example, they may use a metric such as social well-being based value, in which functional improvement and environmental impact reduction curves will intersect at an optimum cost. However, this problem is not only on the company side. Industrial organizations and governments must also contribute to the realization of the goals of ECCD. Although difficult, both enterprises and consumers in Japan must now embark on a new path in which they must contribute to environmental protection in their own ways since environmental problems take a long time and global effort to solve. The efforts of the government and industrial organizations have led to several advances in environmental manufacturing and management in Japan. These include tax breaks for eco-friendly cars and energy-saving household electric appliances, environmental regulations, and public environmental protection activities.

As Japanese enterprises begin to implement ECCD, there will be room after several years for further investigation of its practical state. However, the framework and fundamental concepts of ECCD have already been implemented in some companies and will be further refined in the future. At the same time, future study in management accounting will considerably shift viewpoints from thinking in divisions or units of company (the unitary systematic approach) to a systems-thinking approach (Rebitzer 2010), including environmental and, perhaps, social aspects (Lichtenvort et al. 2008). This chapter examined the possibility for cost design to transform into ECCD and pointed out the difficulty of this transition and problems for its further development. The fundamental thinking discussed in this chapter may be in line with social well-being based studies in management accounting, which accounting researchers must undertake when they investigate socioeconomic issues such as the safety of products and environmental consciousness focused on profitability and competitive strategy.

Notes

1. Although cost design in Japan is expressed as target costing in other countries, this book uses 'cost design' to focus on its main characteristic—proactive cost management, or 'proactively manufacturing cost and quality into a product' (*tsukurikomi* in Japanese)—from the standpoint of profitability rather than of costing. The distinction between cost design and target costing and its effects needs further discussion. Ito (2006) also points out that cost design is by no means a kind of costing, but is instead cost management to proactively manufacture 'the conditions of cost occurrence'.
2. 'Design stage' in this chapter is used in a broad sense that includes conception, planning, development and design, trial manufacture, and preparation for production.
3. The cost table (cost estimator's reference manual) sets functions, the characteristic values of specifications, processing characteristics, and volumes of similar articles against the normal actual costs of the similar articles. This is used as a handy and speedy tool for cost estimation (Tanaka 2002).
4. "[T]he actual costs are compared against standard costs for performance evaluation and the deviations are investigated for remedial actions. Cost

control is also concerned with feedback that might change any or all of future plans, production method, or both" (Siegel and Skim 2000, p. 106).

5. Toshiba group describes ECP in its environmental report as follows: "We will accelerate the creation of ECPs with high levels of environmental performance in all product areas through 'Greening of Products' initiatives aimed at minimizing the environmental impact of products throughout their entire life cycles and 'Greening by Technology' initiatives aimed at providing a stable power supply and mitigating climate change worldwide using low-carbon energy supply technology" (Toshiba 2013, p. 23).
6. Here, the amount paid to subcontractors and processing expenses arising from outside manufacturing is simply defined as suppliers' processing costs.
7. IMDS is a system that collects information on about 30,000 types of parts and chemical substances contained in supply chains (Hewlett Packard 2014).
8. GADSL has the purpose of facilitating communication and exchange of information regarding the use of certain substances in automotive products throughout the supply chain (GADSL 2011).
9. A recycling cost table is used to evaluate environmental costs on the basis of the relation between cost analysis induced by life cycle costing and physical analysis based on the evaluation of product environmental impacts (Kokubu and Nakashima 2003).

Bibliography

Beppu, Y. (2005). Environmental Management and Business Strategy: The Case Studies of Japanese Companies in Oceania (3). *The Teikyo University Economic Review, 38*(2), 25–73.

Bhimani, A. (1995, June). Target Excellence: Target Cost Management at Toyota in the UK. *Management Accounting, 73*(6), 42–45.

Cheng, T. C. E., Yip, F. K., & Yeung, A. C. L. (2012). Supply Risk Management Via *Guanxi* in the Chinese Business Context: The buyer's Perspective. *International Journal of Production Economics, 139*, 3–13.

Cooper, R., & Slagmulder, R. (1997). *Target Costing and Value Engineering*. Portland: Institute of Management Accounts, Productivity Press.

Cooper, R., & Slagmulder, R. (1999). Develop Profitable New Products with Target Costing. *MIT Sloan Management Review, 40*(Summer), 23–33.

Denso Corporation. (2010). *Supplier CSR Guidance*, April, 6.

Denso Corporation. (2014). *Product-Environmental Management*.http://www.denso.co.jp/ja/csr/environment_report/management/product/index.html/. Accessed 9 Apr 2014.

Ellram, L. M. (2000). Purchasing and Supply Management's Participation in the Target Costing Process. *The Journal of Supply Chain Management, 36*(Spring), 39–51.

Ellram, L. M. (2006). The Implementation of Target Costing in the United States: Theory Versus Practice. *The Journal of Supply Chain Management, 42*(Winter), 13–26.

Gabriel, M., Tschandl, M., & Posh, A. (2014). Sustainability-Oriented Lifecycle Costing. *International Journal of Engineering, 12*(1), 33–40.

GADSL. (2011). *Global Automotive Declarable Substance List: Guidance Document, 2011–2012.* http://plastics.americanchemistry.com/Stand-Alone-Content/Global-Automotive-Declarabble-Substance=Document/. Accessed 14 Mar 2014.

Goldbach, M. (2010). Organizational Settings in Supply Chain Costing. In S. Seuring & M. Goldbach (Eds.), *Cost Management in Supply Chains* (pp. 89–108). Heidelberg: Physica-Verlag.

Grigore, S. D. (2007). Supply Chain Flexibility. *Romanian Economic and Business Review, 2*(1), 66–70.

Gungor, A., & Gupta, S. M. (1999). Issues in Environmentally Conscious Manufacturing and Product Recovery: A Survey. *Computers & Industrial Engineering, 36*, 811–853.

Henri, J.-F., & Joumeault, M. (2010). Eco-control: The Influence of Management Control Systems on Environmental and Economic Performance. *Accounting, Organizations, and Society, 35*(1), 63–80.

Hewlett Packard. (2014). *International Material Data System to Automotive Industry.* http://h50146.www5.hp.com/solutions/industry/manufacture/sol/imds/. Accessed 14 Mar 2014.

Horváth, P., & Berlin, S. (2012). Green Target Costing; Getting Ready for the Green Challenge! *Cost Management, 26*(3), 25–36.

Hunkeler, D., Lichtenvort, K., & Rebitzer, G. (Eds.). (2008). *Environmental Life Cycle Costing.* Florida: CRC Press, Taylor & Francis Group, and the Society of Environmental Texicology and Chemistry.

IBM Japan. (1999). *Environment & Well-being Progress Report 1999.* Environment & Safety/Sanitation/Health, 10–11.

IBM Japan. (2000). *Environment & Well-being Progress Report 2000*, 16–17.

IBM Japan. (2001). *Environment & Well-being Progress Report 2001*, 24–25; As for the Relation Between Product Development and ECP Based on Integrated Product Development Plan, and Green Supply Chain, See the Released Documents on Green Supply Chain: IBM Environmental Conscious Product Design (Green PLM). http://www-06.ibm.com/services/bcs/jp/solutions/sc/menu/green_plm.html. Accessed 17 Feb 2014.

Ilgin, M. A., & Gupta, S. M. (2010). Environmentally Conscious Manufacturing and Product Recovery (ECMPRO): A Review of the State of the Art. *Journal of Environmental Management, 91*, 563–591.

IMA. (1994). Implementing Target Costing. *Statements on Management Accounting*, Institute of Management Accountants (Canada).

Ito, Y. (2006). Subjects of Environmentally Conscious Cost Design. *Accounting, 170*(4), 485–499.

Ito, Y. (2007, May). *Investigation and Research on Environmentally Conscious Cost Design*, Report to Japan Society for Promotion of Science, pp. 37–40.

JAMS. (2005). *The Situation and Subjects of Cost Design in Japanese Leading Companies*, Research Report to Japan Society for Promotion of Science, 2004–2005: Japanese Association of Management Researchers (JAMS).

JAMS. (2009). *The Situation and Subjects of Cost Design in Japanese Leading Companies*, 2008–9's Survey by JAMS.

Kajihara, T., Park, K. Y., & Kato, Y. (2009). Environmentally Conscious Design and Cost Design: Preparatory Investigation on Survey Research. *Kokumin-Keizai Zasshi (Journal of National Economy), 199*(6), 11–28. Kobe University.

Kajüter, P. (2002). Proactive Cost Management in Supply Chains. In S. Seuring & M. Goldbach (Eds.) (ibid., 31–51).

Kato, Y. (1993a). Target Costing Support Systems: Lessons from Leading Japanese Companies. *Management Accounting Research, 4*, 37–47.

Kato, Y (1993b). *Cost Design: Strategic Cost Management*, Nikkei Newspaper Office.

Kato, N. (2010). Discussion on Impoverished Problems of Suppliers in Cost Design. *Oita University Economic Review, 62*(1), 23–49.

Kato, Y., Böer, G., & Chow, C. W. (1995). Target costing: An Integrative Management Process. *Journal of Cost Management, 9*(Spring), 39–51.

Kobayashi, T. (1996). Life Cycle Cost and Cost Design. *Kokumin-Keizai Zasshi (Journal of National Economy), 173*(3), 1–13. Kobe University.

Kokubu, K., & Nakashima, M. (2003). Environmental Accounting in Ricoh Company. *Kokumin-Keizai Zasshi (Journal of National Economy), 188*(3), 41–56. Kobe University.

Kreuze, J. G., & Newell, G. E. (1994, February). ABC and Life-Cycle Costing for Environmental Expenditures. *Management Accounting, 75*(8), 38–42.

Lavastre, O., Gunasekaran, A., & Spalanzani, A. (2012). Supply Chain Risk Management in French Companies. *Decision Support Systems and Electronic Commerce, 52*, 828–838.

Lichtenvort, K., Rebitzer, G., Huppes, G., Ciroth, A., Seuring, S., Schmidt, W-P., Günther, E., Hoppe, H., Swarr, T., & Hunkeler, D. (2008). History of Life Cycle Costing, Its Categorization, and Its Basic Framework, In D. Hunkeler, K. Lichtenvort & G. Rebitzer (ibid.)

Lockamy, A., & Smith, W. (2000). Target Costing for Supply Chain Management: Criteria And Selection. *Industrial Management+Data Systems, 100*(5), 210–218.

METI. (2002, June). *Environmental Management Accounting (EMA) Workbook.* Tokyo: Japanese Ministry of Economy, Trade and Industry.

METI. (2008, June). *White Paper on Manufacturing Industry (Monotsukuri) in 2007.* Joint Project with Ministry of Health, Labor, and Welfare, and Ministry of Education, Culture, Sports, Science and Technology, pp. 18–45.

Mitsubishi Electric Corporation. (2002). *Environmental Sustainability Report.*

Mitsubishi Electric Corporation. (2010). *Corporate Social Responsibility Environmental Report.*

Monden, Y. (1999). Cost Design Schedule of Automobile Industry. In Y. Monden, K. Hamada, & K. Lee, (Ed.), *Japanese Cost Management* (pp. 115–127), in Japanese, Dobunkan Publisher.

Monden, Y., & Hamada, K. (1991). Target Costing and Kaizen Costing in Japanese Automobile Companies. *Journal of Management Accounting Research, 3*(Fall), 16–34.

Nabeyama, T. (2011, September). Examination of Supply Chain Reconstruction after the Great East Japan Earthquake, *Joyo ARC*, AREA Research Center, pp. 6–11.

Nakajima, H. (2004). Treatment of Life Cycle Costs in Target Costing; A Review of Past Research and Examination of Unsettled Subjects. *Study of Business Management, 21*, 119–139.

NEC. (2012). *Environmental Activity. Report, 2012*: http://www.nec.com/en/global/eco/product/eco_pro/index.html/. Accessed 19 Feb 2014.

Nikkan Kogyo Shinbun. (2014, February 11). *Recall of the Two Types of Cars in Honda: Fit Hybrid Cars*, Daily Industry Newspaper, Ltd. http://www.nikkan.co.jp/. Accessed 22 Feb 2014.

Nishimura, A. (2003). *Management Accounting in Asia: feed forward and Asian perspectives.* Hampshire: Palgrave Macmillan.

Nishimura, A. (2008). Effect of Management System on Management Accounting: The Case of Chinese Cellular Phone Terminal Unit Manufacturers. *Asian-Pacific Management Accounting Journal, 3*(1), 87–105. Public Knowledge Project (Open Journal System). http://arionline.uitm.edu.my/ojs/index.php/APMAJ/issue/view/18.

Nishimura, A. (2014). Transforming Cost Design Into Environmentally Conscious Cost Design in Japan: Likelihood and Problems for Further Development. *Journal of Management Control, 25*(*1*), 55–75. https://doi.org/10.1007/s00187-014-0190-x.

Orita, Y. (2012, December). *The Whole Company's Improvement Process of Cost Management: Reexamination of Management Accounting for Manufacturing (Case Study of Fuji Xerox Company).* Report Presented in the Third Forum. Tokyo: The Japanese Association of Management Accounting.

Otsuka, T., & Ichikawa, Y. (2011). How Is Japanese Supply Chain Judged? *Mizuho Research Institute Review, 3*, 1–9.
Park, K. P. (2007, March). Subjects on Environmental Conscious Development. *Economic Review, 79*(4), 87–108. Kagawa University.
Park, K. P. (2009). Fact Finding of Environmental Conscious Product Issues. *Research Report, 49*, 73–93.
Parker, L. D. (2000). Green Strategy Costing: Early Days. *Australian Accounting Review, 10*(1), 46–55.
PC3R Promotion Association. (2014). Guideline of PC3R Promotion Association. http://www.pc3r.jp/association/index.html/. Accessed 14 Mar 2014.
Pondeville, S., Swan, V., & Rongé, Y. D. (2012). Environmental Management Control Systems: The Role of Contextual and Strategic Factors. *Management Accounting Research, 24*(4), 317–332.
Rebitzer, G. (2010). Integrating Life Cycle Costing and Life Cycle Assessment for Manufacturing Costs and Environmental Impacts in Supply Chains. In S. Seuring, & M. Goldbach (Eds.) (ibid., 127–146).
Rimienè, K. (2011). Supply Chain Agility Concept Evolution (1990–2010). *Economics and Management, 16*, 892–899.
Road Transport Bureau. (2013). *The Analyzed Results of Contents Notified as Recall of Cars*, Road Transport Bureau, Japanese Ministry of Land, Infrastructure, Transportation and Tourism, April 19.
Sakurai, M. (1989, Summer). Target Costing and How to Use It. *Journal of Cost Management*, 39–50.
Sakurai, M. (1991). *Change in Business Environment and Management Accounting*. Tokyo: Dobunkan Publisher.
Sarkis, J. (1995). Manufacturing Strategy and Environmental Consciousness. *Technovation, 15*(2), 79–97.
Sato, Y. (2009). The Soul of Cost Design (1): *Nikkei Monotsukuri (Manufacturing)*, September, 113–116.
Seuring, S. (2004). Industrial Ecology, Life Cycles, Supply Chains: Differences and Interrelations. *Business Strategy and the Environment, 13*, 306–319.
Seuring, S. (2010). Supply Chain Target Costing: An Apparel Industry Case Study. In S. Seuring & M. Goldbach, (Eds.) (ibid., 111–125).
Siegel, J. G., & Skim, J. K. (2000). *Dictionary of Accounting Terms* (3rd ed.). Hauppauge: Barron's Educational Series, Inc.
Sony Corporation. (2001). *Environmental Report 2001: Entertaining the World, Caring for the Future*. http://www.sony.co.jp//SonyInfo/csr_report//2001/qfhh7c00000d76pv_att/copy_of_2001_all.pdf. Accessed 15 Aug 2013. (2014). Annual Securities Report, June, EDINE.
Sony Corporation. (2017). *Sony CSR Report*. Retrieved from Sony.co.jp/SonyInfo/csr-report/issues.

Steen, B. (2005). Environmental Costs and Benefits in Life Cycle Costing. *Management of Environment Quality, 16*(2), 107–118.
Sumida Group. (2012). *Guideline for Green Procurement*, July, Sumida Corporation.
Swarr, T., & Hunkeler, D. (2008). Life Cycle Costing in Life Cycle Management. In D. Hunkeler, K. Lichtenvort & G. Rebitzer (Eds.) (Ibid., pp. 77–90).
Tanaka, M. (1985, July/August). New Approach to the Function Evaluation System in Value Engineering, *International Journal of Production Research, 23*(4), 625–638.
Tanaka, T. (Ed.). (1991). *Contemporary Management Accounting System.* Japan: Chuou-keizaisha.
Tanaka, T. (1992). *Field-Study: Contemporary Management Accounting System.* Tokyo: Chuo-keizaisha Publisher, Co.
Tanaka, T. (1993). Target Costing at Toyota, *Journal of Cost Management*, (Spring) 4–11.
Tanaka, M. (1995). *Theory and Practices of Cost Design.* Tokyo: Chuo-keizaisha Publisher, Co.
Tanaka, M. (2002). *Profit Strategy and Value Engineering: How to Implement Practical Cost Design.* Tokyo: Sangyo Noritu University Publisher.
Tani, T. (1994). Interactive Control in Cost Design: Significance. *The Kokumin-Keizai Zasshi (Journal of National Economy), 169*(4), 19–38. Kobe University.
Tani, T. (1995). Interactive Control in Target Cost Management. *Management Accounting Research, 6*, 399–414.
Tani, T., Okano, H., Shimizu, N., Iwabuch, Y., Fukuda, J., & Cooray, S. (1994). Target Costing Management in Japanese Companies: Current State of the Art. *Management Accounting Research, 5*, 67–81.
The Nikkei. (2014, February 12). Recall of 1.9 Million Hybrid Cars in Toyota in Japan and Abroad, *Nihon Keizai Shinbun* (Japan Economy Newspaper) Inc. http://www.nikkei.com/article/DGXNASDG1203y_SaA210CR8000/. Accessed 22 Feb 2014.
Thun, J., & Hoenig, D. (2011). An Empirical Analysis of Supply Chain Risk Management in the German Automotive Industry. *International Journal of Production Economics, 131*, 242–249.
Toshiba Group. (2013). *2013 Environmental Report.* http://www.toshiba.com/csr/docs/env_report13_all.pdf. Accessed 10 Jun 2014.
Toyota Motor Corporation. (2011). *Toyota Green Purchasing Guidelines*, December.
Toyota Motor Corporation. (2013). *Report for the Planet: Toyota's Environmental Initiatives*, 22–23.
Yamamoto, K., & Kokubu, K. (2001). *Environmental Management in IBM.* Tokyo: Toyo Keizai.

Yoshida, E., Fukushima, K., & Senoo, T. (2012). *Studies of Japanese Management Accounting*, Chuo Keizaisha.

Yoshikawa, T. (1994). Some Aspects of the Japanese Approach to Management Accounting. *Management Accounting Research*, 5, 279–287.

CHAPTER 8

Comprehensive Opportunity and Lost Opportunity Control Model and Enterprise Risk Management

8.1 Introduction

As the development of global competition leads to a changeable and complicated economic environment where technological innovation accelerates and consumer needs rapidly change, enterprises must always consider uncertainty when planning business strategies. Measurement and control of uncertainty is a critical problem for contemporary business management. Value creation in enterprises, in particular, is strongly influenced by financial uncertainty. Uncertainty stems not only from environmental complexity and diversity but also from the information and control level of management. In a global, finance-oriented economy, accounting as an information system also plays an important part in controlling uncertainty, in conjunction with the judgment and experience of senior managers.

In examples such as the Enron bankruptcy in December 2001 and the collapse of the WorldCom group in July 2002, charismatic senior managers who had previously been considered independent of financial oligarchies and shareholder influence (Berle and Means 1932) had stained their hands with financial manipulation and related financial instruments (derivatives), sacrificing long-term value for short-term profits (Richardson 2009, 2010). This resulted in a dramatic rise in uncertainty in the international economy. At the same time, it was found that window dressing accounts that had concealed their dangerous business results were created in conspiracy with

A. Nishimura, *Management, Uncertainty, and Accounting*,
https://doi.org/10.1007/978-981-10-8989-3_8

certified public accountants, adding further fuel to the fire (Stuart and Stuart 2004). Moreover, as the production structure and lifestyle in some capitalistic economies became more finance-oriented, some senior managers in global businesses became arrogant (Collins 2009) and lost sight of true profit opportunities, instead treading a path toward failure by keeping step with Lehman Brothers in 2008 (Ingrassia 2011). These events shook the financial and monetary base not only in the United States but also in some European economies (Richardson 2009). The bankruptcy of automobile companies such as GM and Chrysler in 2009, the long-running depression in Europe, and Japan's 'two lost decades' show the serious nature of current uncertainty in the global finance- and information-oriented society.

Enterprises should wrestle with such uncertainty for stable and durable business growth and, as a matter of social responsibility, give an account of its management to stakeholders including investors; such management not only influences corporate destiny (potentially including bankruptcy) but can also decrease social uncertainty or economic stagnation. At present, companies tend to balance short-term competitive strategy with a long-term growth strategy to create business value for sustainable business growth. To effectively and synthetically control opportunity and risk that connect closely to business value creation strategies under uncertainty, enterprises should establish effective and efficient management systems to find and exploit opportunities (hereinafter 'profit opportunities' when clarifying the relation with accounting profit and risk; see also Chaps. 5 and 6) and correspondently mitigate risk that is deeply related to control of uncertainty. They should furthermore strengthen mutual understanding with stakeholders and society about enterprise governance through transparent and trustworthy disclosure of risk management processes to maintain sustainable growth and dispel social uncertainty (see IFA 2004).

This raises the question of how management accounting wrestles with risk and what control models accountants should build for risk management and its social application. Unfortunately, accounting control systems have not so far included enterprise risk and profit opportunity information in their control models, comprehensively controlled enterprise risks related to uncertainty, or given stakeholders a clear account of management processes for discharging accountability and controllability. Therefore, this chapter builds a feed-forward accounting control system based on opportunity and lost opportunity and examines contemporary management accounting from the comprehensive perspective of enterprise risk management to clarify needed structural changes and future directions.

8.2 Basic Framework of the Accounting Control System

Before discussing the role of accounting control systems in enterprise risk management, we should clarify the relation between accounting income and profit opportunities and risks. As COSO (2004) points out, 'uncertainty presents both risk and opportunity, with the potential to erode or enhance value' (p. 3). Therefore, risk and opportunity must be holistically[1] managed with *business strategy* as an axis of business value management. Note that here 'opportunity' refers to profit opportunity in a qualified sense, since enterprises aim at finding and exploiting opportunities that lead to *accounting profit,* not opportunities in general, and simultaneously have an internal and external relation to risk. Thus, profit opportunity is recognized as opportunity with a certain objective and subjective probability that is transformed into accounting profit in the near future (Nishimura 2011), in the same way as risk, or the possibility of a disappointing result (accounting loss) under the condition. Risk in a quantitative sense is considered as expected loss, which can be calculated by multiplying the likelihood of the event by the total loss experienced when the event occurs (Smith and Merritt 2002).

Risk management is also considered *enterprise risk* management, rather than management of risk in general. The result is that like 'profit opportunity', it is dealt with as part of enterprise governance for ensuring sustainable value creation; risk management follows profit opportunity management as a comprehensive form of enterprise risk management. In traditional management accounting, enterprises have focused mainly on accounting income and used this information to plan for and control business activities. However, in order to meet profit targets under uncertain conditions, management should be proactive in the *process* by which profit is created, not just in its result. Management accounting not only yields feedback on variance information to planning process in the following accounting year, but must also proactively find and explore profit opportunity and control enterprise risk for optimum value actualization. Therefore, management accounting should also measure profit opportunities and enterprise risks to fulfill its function in proactive strategic decision-making and evaluate the results of proactive countermeasures against risks and opportunity exploitation in the *process* of transforming profit opportunity/enterprise risk into accounting income.

As indicated in Fig. 8.1, business processes that ultimately result in profit or loss are composed of many strategic and managerial activities that involve profit opportunity and enterprise risk (see COSO 2004; Schneier and Miccolis 1998). Accounting profit results not only from positive value creation management, which aims to maximize profit opportunities and minimize lost opportunity, but also from risk management, which seeks to avoid or minimize events that may preclude profit opportunities or value creation. Although loss is traditionally recognized in an accounting book when an enterprise does not succeed in actualizing its plans, lost profit opportunity or opportunity cost that dilutes business value in the working process of these plans is not accounted for. Under strong uncertainty, it is important that accounting control systems take a new approach to the comprehensive recognition of opportunity and lost opportunity to create business value as planned. Enterprise risk management and accounting control systems use different approaches to realizing the common goal of maximizing business value (Holmquist 2012). As Rasid et al. (2014, p. 132) point

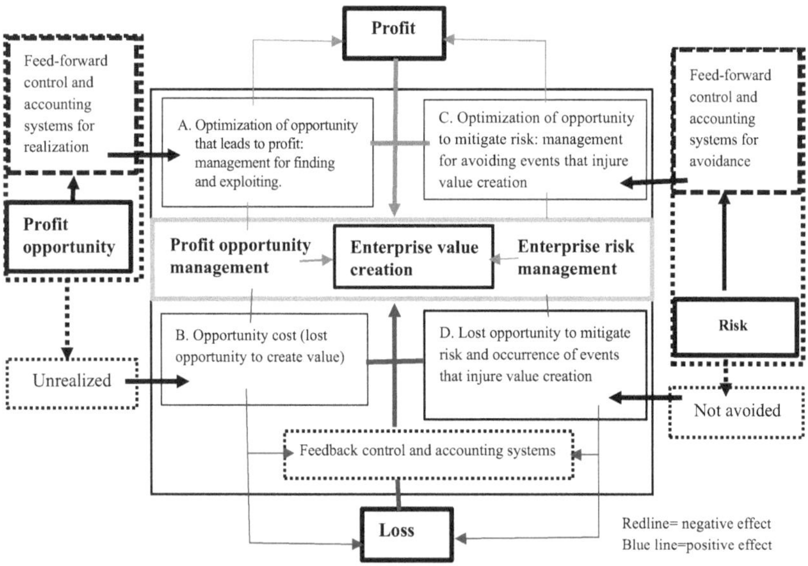

Fig. 8.1 Transformation process of profit opportunity and enterprise risk into accounting profit and loss

out, "In fact, risk management and management accounting are integral to strategic planning and performance assessment" (see also Grote 2014). If managers incorrectly control for risks, profit opportunity can instead transform into lost opportunity (see Fig. 8.1). Therefore, successful strategy implementation requires that risk management is carried out in parallel with profit opportunity management. Enterprises should proactively measure and control risks for profit management in feed-forward accounting control systems. Therefore, strategic-level enterprise risk management acquires a more important role than low-level management, which is focused on downside risks and risk avoidance, because it "incorporates a focus that goes beyond addressing downside risks to a strong focus on upside risks—an offensive strategy of identifying and seizing opportunities" (Arnold et al. 2011, p. 174). Risk management moves together with profit opportunity management along the main axis of business strategy. As risk management is closely connected with whole activities from strategic planning to management and operational controls, an accounting control system as a feed-forward form of management accounting must also comprise comprehensive and enterprise-wide risk information in its daily measurement and evaluation (see Shank and Miguel 2009; Seal 2006; Schneier and Miccolis 1998). Because accounting is conceptually structured around the concept of profit, and profit opportunity and enterprise risk too embody future information related to this concept, feed-forward accounting control systems must also be constructed on this fundamental concept and its future-oriented information. Thus, when comprehensively implementing enterprise risk management, enterprises should plan for and control management activities from the aspect of opportunity and lost opportunity, not of past profit and loss, and should build a new comprehensive opportunity and lost opportunity control (COLC) model. Figure 8.1 indicates that enterprises must pay attention to measurement and evaluation of opportunity and lost opportunity for business value creation.

As illustrated in Fig. 8.1, contemporary management accounting presents a synthetic system in which feed-forward control process from proactive management (profit opportunity and enterprise risk management) to reactive accounting (recognition and control of profit and loss) is integrated with feedback control process from the latter to the former.

8.3 Development of Accounting Control Systems

Uncertainty has influenced the mode of management accounting as well as business management (Knight 1921), and recently its influence was clarified in enterprise risk management. Uncertainty represents objectively and subjectively unstable conditions for beginning an action without complete information, or "an unknown probability of occurrence of an event" (Jaafari 2001, p. 101). In contrast, risk represents the probability of a disappointing result under this condition. Thus, enterprises can take some countermeasures against risk (e.g., buying insurance), unlike threat and unrest under uncertainty, and so have tried to develop risk management and risk-related accounting control systems to mitigate uncertainty (Nishimura 2011). Accounting control systems founded on globally finance-oriented and competitive economies have had to control uncertainty more sensibly and commit more deeply to risk management than before. In the following subsections, we further explore the state of accounting control systems that enterprises and researchers have devised to address changes and diversity in uncertainty. We describe it in the development process from the traditional accounting control system to Demski's ex post model and cost design. We then focus on COLC model and *profit design* as an expanded form of cost design to define the functions of contemporary management accounting in enterprise risk management.

Traditional Accounting Control System

In relation to diversity and complexity, the traditional accounting control system does not include "all inputs to the decision model" (Demski 1967, p. 701), instead consistently using a first-formed plan as a target and an evaluation basis for actual value, despite a changeable environment. This system cannot give any control direction to management beforehand in relation to change of environmental factors, and deviation between planned and observed values cannot display all changes of environmental factors or give variance information for interim performance evaluations, since this is due to a static model like the following: Enterprises can analyze profit or cost variance as price variance and volume (or hour) variance only after the fact and provide them as information feedback for the next-period budget profit and standard cost; furthermore, when planning for business direction, they do not take the optimum and future-changing conditions into consideration, despite trust in the absolute truth of the planned value. Because they have no "optimum adjustment to changed conditions", the traditional accounting control system cannot "gauge significance by determining the opportunities foregone as a result of deviation and failure to respond to it" (Demski 1977, p. 233). No proactive and preventive control information is provided. In this sense, such system is not conscious of irremediable changes and complexity.

Forecast (standard) observed deviation
Budget profit – Actual profit = Profit variance
100 – 80 = 20 (U)
Standard cost – Actual cost = Cost variance

Note: The above numerical values are hypothetical

Abbreviation: *U*, unfavorable variance

Accounting control systems are intrinsically founded on bookkeeping, with duties consisting of recording accounting transactions in various journals, posting them in ledgers, and preparing a trial balance. Therefore, while the traditional system can inform planning processes for the next accounting year of variances between plans and actual results, it cannot do so within the current year because of its "planning–control dichotomy" (Demski 1977, p. 233). In this book, feedback and feed-forward strictly refer to the control function of variance analysis in the current accounting year. In this sense, the traditional accounting control system fulfills a cognitive function in this variance analysis for the next-period control, but cannot make opportunity cost clear for want of optimum thought.

Demski's Model: Ex Post System

Considering feedback thought in the action of variance analysis to optimum profit planning, Demski developed a unique accounting control system based on the viewpoint of opportunity and opportunity cost—the ex post system. This system inputs all information to the model and calculates optimum profit after the fact using a liner programming method to recognize various changes in environmental factors and to clarify profit forecast variance (opportunity) and opportunity cost. This model allows recognizing opportunity cost variance through comparing optimum (ex post) profit with actual profit in the current period (Nishimura 2003). Forecast profit (opportunity) variance is measured by comparing ex ante profit at the forecast stage with ex post profit at the actual evaluation stage. These two variances make it possible to measure managers' forecast ability to the optimum profit and the maladjustment of corporate resources to optimum usage. It also allows for model revision in the following period (Demski 1967, 1977). This model also has a feedback function for opportunity cost variance, as shown in the following formulation:

Feedback accounting control process			
Forecast	**Target**	**The observed**	**Deviation**
Ex ante profit	– **Ex post profit**		= Forecast profit variance
100	— 120 (2nd)	(1st)	= –20 (F)
	Ex post profit	– Actual profit	= Opportunity cost
variance			
	120	- 80	= 40 (U)
(100 – 120) + (120 – 80) = –20 + 40 = 20 (U)			

Abbreviations: *F*, favorable; *U*, unfavorable

This ex post accounting system assumes (1) application of some well-defined formation in the planning process, (2) management ability to distinguish between avoidable and unavoidable variances or deviations, (3) the usefulness of feedback control information, and (4) limitations on searching for possible opportunities (Demski 1967, p. 702). In this case, ex ante and ex post profits are structured as optimum profit by using linear programming that includes various data or variable inputs (contribution margin, production volume of products, limited resources, per-unit production requirements, etc.) in the profit-maximization model, and ex post profit is calculated under the same conditions as observed profit determined at the end of the accounting period. This accounting control system can thus measure environmental change and complexity to indicate "the efficiency of the planning process" and "the need for additional forecasting efforts" through deviation between ex ante and ex post profits, and indicates "the opportunity cost of non-optimal capacity utilization" with opportunity cost variance (Demski 1967, pp. 704 and 711; see also Demski 1969). This variance analysis facilitates learning and remedial action in wide-ranging aspects of the planning and control process because of the linear programming structured in the system. This accounting control system carries out feedback control functions for variance cognition in the current accounting year and for control in the next. This cognitive function is qualitatively more advanced in specifying opportunity cost and opportunity than the traditional accounting control system.

Cost Design and the Feed-Forward Control Model

Unfortunately, in the ex post system, although the variances give significant indicators to management, they cannot be connected with the revision of forecast process in the current accounting year on account of feedback system, so learning and revision in the intra-period is controversial (see Cushing 1968; Demski 1968). Thus, an accounting control system that can fulfill its function for proactive measurement and evaluation of planning and controlling process should include feed-forward control and information in plural ex ante profits. That is, feed-forward control system must be adopted in the model, not only with regards to information. Incidentally, the term 'feed-forward' can be defined as the following meaning: before executing a plan, a manager has information on factors or conditions that will disturb its realization, and adopts some proactive control methods to alter and improve them, in contrast to 'feedback' in which the manager reflects on actual results and carries out reactive action to get close to the expected target. We can see this in cost designs that Japanese automobile companies developed and practiced in the 1970s, referred to as target costing in English, where cost design tends to include all competitive strategic information based on value (relative relation between function and cost) in the model and determines target cost as an evaluation standard through cost variance analysis. This target cost is extracted through comparing two planned costs (allowable cost and estimated cost or piling-up cost) and considering prior cost improvement that the prior cost variance urges management to do.

As shown in the following formulation, cost design as well as COLC model described is feed-forward, since it integrates prior cost variance with a competitive strategic plan (estimated cost) beforehand to search for target cost through proactive improvement and to evaluate performance from opportunity and opportunity cost.

Feed-forward accounting control process					
Forecast (1)	***Forecast (2)***	***Deviation***	**Target**	**Observed**	**Deviation**
Target profit – Estimated profit					
Allowable cost – Estimated cost = prior variance					
Estimated cost > Allowable cost – Improvement					
(Estimated cost – Prior improvement = Target cost)			**Target cost**	– Actual cost = Posterior variance	

Note: Forecast (1) = Primary long-term plan; Forecast (2) = Secondary competitive plan

Target profit is defined as the planned profit that must be achieved in the total life cycle of a designed product and leads to allowable cost in one period or per one product, while estimated profit is calculated by making the most of practical data on future profitability from the viewpoint of short-term competitive strategy and, on the basis of this calculated profit, estimated cost is also decided by piling up improved functions and costs on an existing product cost similar to the designed product from the same viewpoint as the profit (see Tanaka, T. 1992). Allowable cost must also be realized in the life cycle of the product to attain the target profit. Therefore, prior cost variance is a proactive indicator with which cost should be improved beforehand. Target cost, which is calculated after considering estimated cost and prior cost improvement, works as the strategically optimum evaluation standard to actual cost as well as posterior cost improvement targets. As a result, posterior cost variance also means opportunity cost or profit opportunity forgone, in which organizational ability and resources cannot achieve the optimal cost for competitive strategy, although it feeds back to the planning process in the next accounting year.

This feed-forward accounting control system aims to forecast profit opportunity (or opportunity to mitigate risk) from sustainable growth and competitive strategy and fix target cost through prior and intra-period improvement, and to evaluate performance in terms of the attachment degree of the target (optimal strategic target). Performance is evaluated by the attainable capacity standard for competitive strategy. As a result, this system, which includes all information on function, quality and cost in the two optimal cost models in the long-term growth strategy and the short-term competitive strategy, intends to cope with changes and complexity in business environments for the actualization of profit opportunity maximization and enterprise risk minimization of a product; the integration of high quality and low cost by means of just-in-time systems, zero inventory, and total quality control. Although cost design thinks much of such a risk control method as zero inventory, it as well as the ex post system does not refer to opportunity to mitigate *risk* and lost opportunity (C and D in Fig. 8.1) in accounting control system, apart from recognizing opportunity and opportunity cost related to profit opportunity (A and B in Fig. 8.1).

When comparing this variance analysis with that of ex post system, we find one fundamental difference. Although the ex post system makes opportunity cost variance clear, variances explain profit variance in the traditional accounting system in details from the viewpoint of opportunity and opportunity cost. The evaluation of actual profit after the fact is regarded as more important than the prior decision of optimum target.

$$\begin{aligned}&\text{So in the traditional system profit variance}\\&= \text{budget profit} - \text{actual profit, while in ex post systems, profit variance}\\&= \text{forecast profit variance} + \text{opportunity cost variance}\\&= (\text{ex ante profit} - \text{ex post profit}) + (\text{ex post profit} - \text{actual profit})\end{aligned}$$

In contrast, cost variance analysis in cost design does not divide traditional cost variance into parts, but rather gives variance analysis a new meaning for deciding target cost, because it newly draws out two peculiar variances or indicators for prior and posterior cost improvement, and gives management an optimal target as an interperiod standard for control by using the former improvement (variance) and as an evaluation standard to actual cost through the posterior cost variance for competitive strategy. Of course, posterior variance feedback to the planning process is for the next accounting year. Logically, cost design can also adopt linear programming for deciding optimal cost and practically use some well-defined formulations for applications such as industrial engineering, value engineering, quality management, or design review to lead to a strategically fittest cost (Tanaka, M. 1985, 1995). This new idea is founded on a feed-forward control system. However, this system focuses mainly on target *cost* for cost management based on opportunity and opportunity cost thought, even while connecting with profit planning. As stated at the beginning, as actual business environments have recently influenced by increased changes and complexity (uncertainty), risk management has become increasingly important for the whole of business activity. All enterprises should wrestle with this uncertainty and look for more future-oriented and comprehensive target information (comprehensive opportunities, opportunity cost, and lost opportunity from A to D indicated in Fig. 8.1) beyond target cost (opportunity and opportunity cost in A and B in Fig. 8.1) in order to effectively carry out enterprise risk management and governance. Management accounting tends to emphasize risk information over cost (Kim and Collier 2013).

8.4 COLC Model and Profit Design as an Amplified Form of Cost Design

Structure and Characteristics

Enterprises should effectively manage profit opportunity and enterprise risk for dispelling uncertainty and maintaining long-term business growth, while conforming to corporate governance regulations. For this purpose, they should incorporate comprehensive feed-forward control and information into models and carry out profit opportunity and risk management beyond profit and cost management. The feed-forward accounting control system that is founded on COLC model intends to recognize and control profit opportunity and risk from a long-term viewpoint for sustainable growth strategies and short-term viewpoints for immediate competitive strategy. It assumes the form of *profit design*: an amplification of cost design. It uses variances in these profit opportunities and risks to search for optimal target profit for the control of business activities and the evaluation of actual profit.

Concretely, variances between expected (long-term) and estimated (short-term) profit opportunities or risks lead to forecast profit opportunity or enterprise risk variance. On the basis of these variances, enterprises try to proactively implement some improvement activities (*Kaizen* in Japanese)[2] and decide expected profit as an optimum profit for long-term sustainable growth and short-term competitive strategy by considering the revision and improvement of expected or estimated profit opportunity and risk. For example, when exchange rate, interest rate, or price changes alter enterprise risk, improved profit opportunities are added to the original estimated profit opportunity or the expected one, while some risks mitigated by the improvement are deducted from the original estimated risk. As a result, expected profit is calculated by considering these improvement results on expected or estimated value for profit opportunity and enterprise risk. At the same time, estimated profit is forecasted by compiling various factors (data) under present competitive conditions. Moreover, they can recognize forecast profit variance by subtracting estimated profit from expected profit when the latter is larger than the former. After proactively carrying out improvement activities with reference to forecast profit variance, they can acquire the target profit through adding this improved amount to the estimated profit. This target profit becomes a standard to control interim activities and evaluate actual performance.

Lost opportunity that is given by its comparison with actual profit becomes an index for this posterior performance evaluation. As a result, this control process leads to the best actualization of business values on the basis of the unified management of profit opportunity and risk.

Although planned profits may be calculated by using quantitative formulations such as linear programming and normal distribution, professional managers' judgment must be adopted in calculating these planned values (see Borison and Hamm 2010; Mikes 2011; Jaafari 2001). This feed-forward accounting control system is distinguished from the feedback system in comprehensively measuring and controlling multilateral profit opportunities and risks beforehand, in which the forecast ability of management about uncertainty is evaluated beforehand, and actual performance is measured and evaluated from the viewpoint of profit opportunity, enterprise risk, and lost opportunity (including opportunity cost). At the same time, COLC model and profit design can be connected to a cost design model to establish a long-term and more future-oriented cost design. Therefore, lost opportunity or posterior variance can also be recognized in detail in terms of both profit and cost. Target profit leads to allowable cost and target cost is calculated based on this allowable cost, estimated cost, and prior cost variance (= prior cost improvement). Here, estimated cost is not led directly from estimated profit but is deduced from the piling-up cost and estimated profit. The fundamental structure of profit design based on the COLC model can be presented in a simple diagram like the following for comparison with the other control models:

Feed-forward (proactive) accounting control process	
Forecast process and variance analysis	**Target**
Expected profit opportunity- Estimated profit opportunity= forecast profit opportunity variance	
Expected risk – Estimated risk (expected loss) = forecast risk variance	
Expected profit opportunity>Estimated profit opportunity }	
Expected risk<Estimated risk } ------ **Improvement** ←	
(Estimated profit opportunity + improvement = EOPI)	
(Estimated risk – improvement = ERI)	**Expected profit**
Examination of EOPI and ERI →	
Expected profit – Estimated profit = **Forecast profit variance**	
Estimated profit>Expected profit------------------------**Improvement**	**Target profit**
Estimated profit + Improvement =Target profit →	
Target profit – Actual profit = Opportunity cost variance	

Note: Expected profit opportunity and risk show planned values from a long-term and sustainable growth viewpoint, while estimated profit opportunity and risk indicate planned values from a short-term and competitive viewpoint; the above assumes that risk increased during the current year

Abbreviations: *EOPI*, estimated profit opportunity after profit opportunity improvement; *ERI*, estimated risk after improvement to mitigate risk

This COLC model may seem to be only a theoretical idea, but some Japanese companies focus on opportunity when implementing risk management. Some companies indicate opportunity loss and business opportunities in relation to business risk in their annual securities reports: "There are possibilities of *sales-opportunity loss* and inventory adjustment that give rise to a confusion of production plans, with the result that an inaccurate forecast of consumer demand and insufficient business management cause excess or short inventories" (Hitachi Manufacturing Company, Annual Securities Report 2015, p. 12); "The company establishes a system that can smoothly respond to consumer and local needs by appropriately seizing *business opportunities* when overseas business strategic points develop and promote business strategies" (Sony Corporation, Annual Securities Report, June 2014, p. 28); and "There is a possibility that we will not gain *new business opportunities* to the extent expected" (Kyosera, Annual Securities Report, March 2014, p. 24). The systematization and theorization of these practices play a critical role in fostering comprehensive and effective enterprise risk management.

COLC Model and Its Historical Implication

As management is strongly aware of uncertainty in business environments, it is proper that greater importance has been attached to feed-forward control information than to the feedback. Thus, risk management is thoroughly colored by feed-forward control information. In the traditional accounting system where past financial data was used for planning and control, uncertainty was ex post facto recognized as the difference between planned and actual values by means of variance analysis. Information on uncertainty was not inserted into control model, because managers convinced themselves that the situation in the future would follow the same trajectory as the present. The planned value was therefore considered a "true cost" (Emerson 1909; see Scholes 2000). However, sometimes expectations do not coincide with actual results. For example, managers might not be certain of fluctuations in material prices until price variance was recognized in cost variance analysis after the fact. They use this feedback information to control the changed price in the next period. This, judging from a function over two accounting years, was the feedback control system for uncertainty in the era when managers seemed able to control uncertainty by using such a reactive and reflective management accounting system (Nishimura 2011).

In the mid-1960s, many managers began to recognize that planned value was relative, rather than absolute, because business conditions were continuously changing. They therefore incorporated unprogrammed scenarios into the planning process, adopted alternatives to respond to changing business conditions, and established optimum models for decision-making. They perceived that value in planning was relative and conditional and used a known-alternatives model to make optimum decisions. However, uncertainty was not completely controlled. In those days, many quantitative and mathematical models indirectly reinforced accounting control systems for this optimum decision-making (Nishimura 2003). Although accounting control systems were intended to recognize the multifarious changes common to business environments and cope with uncertainty closely related to these changes, there was no system for proactively and preventively controlling uncertainty. Although Demski (1967, 1969) introduced the ex post system, in which ex ante profit (the optimum profit before a price change) was compared with ex post profit (the optimum profit after a price change), forecast profit variance was recognized after the measurement of actual profit, and managers' forecasting ability in the planning process was evaluated and controlled from the angle of opportunity and opportunity cost by using such an optimum formulation as linear programming and ex post facto variance analysis. This was fundamentally a feedback control system, because this variance could not be measured until actual profit was calculated. However, this consideration of opportunity cost suggested a significant step toward the development of feed-forward control models (Nishimura 2003). Demski pioneered measuring and evaluating environmental changes and management ability to respond to them from the viewpoints of opportunity and opportunity cost.

Alongside such academic research, under the influence of global market competition some automobile companies in Japan created 'cost design', which adopts a complete feed-forward process (prior and posterior cost variances that lead to improvement movements) to actualize high-profit opportunities (products at low cost and high quality) with minimum advance risk (zero inventory) (Nishimura 2003).

As stated above, the present global finance-oriented economy intensifies the uncertainty of the business environment and makes it difficult to ascertain the future direction of business. Mismanagement of uncertainty not only is damaging to the enterprise but also results in social unease and confusion. Regulatory authorities have therefore required enterprises to strengthen their governance and risk management to protect stakeholders from uncertainty and to secure social stability. As a result, management accounting, which is closely related to risk management, is also changing its structure and functions, as shown in the COLC model and profit design.

Figure 8.2 shows how the COLC model combines with profit opportunity/risk management and fulfills its function in creating enterprise value and adequately conducting enterprise governance. The transformation of accounting information into a comprehensive feed-forward form (i.e., profit design) is given more weight in constructing the COLC model, because business strategy and risk management tends toward strong dependence on proactive information of profit opportunity and enterprise risk. The most important function of contemporary management accounting is to recognize and control uncertainty beforehand through the unified management of profit opportunity and risk, protecting business from risks and driving it in an advantageous direction through feed-forward control methods such as optimal programs, proactive variance analysis, and profit/cost design. The structure of management accounting is also being reorganized, not only from the viewpoint of efficiency and effectiveness but also from the long-range and global integrated viewpoint of profitability, sustainable growth, and social responsibility. Enterprises must now improve the transparency and trustworthiness of their financial statements and integrate risk management information into them. Additionally, they should use information on variances between profit opportunity/ risk and actual accounting income to control business value with proactive efficiency and effectiveness. In this sense, the contemporary accounting control system should adopt a completely feed-forward-oriented system. As a result, an accounting control system strengthens its socioeconomic flavor in enterprise risk management as well as environmentally conscious cost design (Nishimura 2014) through the integration of profitability with social responsibility. As a result of a pivotal junction between risk management and enterprise governance, accounting control systems have become

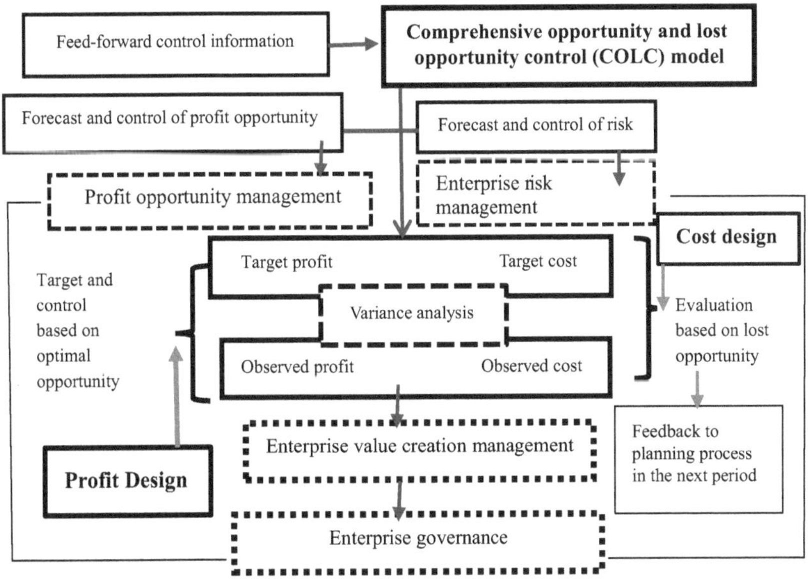

Fig. 8.2 COLC model, profit design, and enterprise governance

more sensitive to the control of uncertainty than before and have taken on new structures and features.

8.5 COLC Model and Risk Management Report

Risk Management Report Under the COLC Model

Risk strategy and efforts of the whole organization to realize it are fundamental factors in enterprise risk management, as failure and carelessness can endanger the value of an enterprise and reduce social confidence in the long term. In more serious cases, this can cause social disaster and economic crisis. In this sense, the evaluation of risk management performance as well as profitability has an important part in organizational efforts to business value creation. Therefore, an enterprise should give stakeholders a full account of not only indications of risk events that influence its goal but also their management process. This enhances the transparency and social confidence of financial statements.

Although we have described the unified management of profit opportunity and risk to clarify the role of the COLC model in comprehensive enterprise risk management, a risk management report must further be prepared for the development of socially trustworthy communication in enterprise governance, with reference to this control model. For this purpose, under the framework of the COLC model, a unified management statement of profit opportunity and risk is prepared in Tables 8.1 and 8.2 and then a risk management report can be contrived in Table 8.3.

We can know from Tables 8.1 and 8.2 that this company could attach 495 profit opportunity with 15 unsettled risk through proactive improvements (150) under the primary conditions of 500 primarily forecasted (expected) profit opportunity and 100 expected risk and evaluate company performance in positive business value creation (480) and risk mitigation effort (105) and the new exploitation of profit opportunity (45). Moreover, it is necessary to give a full account of the practical meaning of the risk management in the contemporary business environment. As shown in Table 8.3, the report can give an explanation of the company's risk management process to stakeholders, through which shareholders and other stakeholders can understand the true situation of business risk and company efforts to proactively and preventively minimize the risk.

With regard to the situation and problems of international financial instrument risk disclosure, Papa and Peters (2011) describe clearly from findings by literature review, direct survey feedback from users of financial statements or respondents to survey questionnaire, and the analysis of International Financial Reporting Standards (IFRS) reporting companies that, notwithstanding voluminous disclosure, there are some problems such as inadequacy of relevant and complete information, difficulty of access, and insufficient understandability and comparability in financial statements. They point out a need "for financial statement preparers to shift away from 'tick-box mere-compliance' with disclosure requirements" and "adopt a meaningful mindset aiming to convey risk exposures and risk management policy effectiveness, as well as to foster a dialogue with investors" (p. 23). Management accountants as well as the statement preparers should be farsighted enough to think of their indication to provide users and society with substantially useful risk information. In this sense, a risk management report needs to be the executive "summary that distills key information on entity-wide risk exposures and effectiveness of risk management practices" across different risk types (Papa and Peters 2011, p. 18).

Table 8.1 Unified management statement of profit opportunity and enterprise risk (units: million yen)

	Forecast value		*Variance*	*Countermeasures to the variance*	*Data for target profit*
	Long term	*Short term*			
1. Profit opportunity Expected profit opportunity	500				
Estimated profit opportunity		450		(+45)	495
Forecast opportunity variance			50	(−45)	(5)
Proactive improvement				45	
Total	500	450	50	45	495
2. Enterprise risk Expected risk	100			(−90)	10
Estimated risk		120			
Forecast risk variance			20	(−15)	5
Proactive improvement				105	
Total	100	120	20	105	15

Hypothesis: In this table, it is assumed that a company invests in a project which yields a profit of 500 per year over ten years and whose likelihood of risk is 20%. Therefore, expected risk per year is 100 per year under 500 primarily forecasted (expected profit) opportunities. There occurred a change in risk probability (20% increase) owing to a supplier problem at planning in this period from the short-term viewpoint and, at the same time, in price change that pulls down yearly profit by 10% (to 450). As for proactive management of profit opportunity and enterprise risk, the company adopted new proactive countermeasures or improvements (e.g., changes in materials and parts, organizational structure, and manufacturing method) against 100 expected risks and 20 forecast risk variances, while it decided to strive for stronger improvement to get back 50 lost profit opportunities or forecast profit opportunity variance beforehand. As a result, 105 risks were mitigated, but there remained 15 unsettled risks as lost profit opportunity. As for profit opportunity, the company could not actualize 50 proactive improvement targets and lost 5 profit opportunities (i.e., occurrence of 5 opportunity costs). Information on these lost profit opportunity and opportunity cost will serve as a reference for making a decision on expected or estimated risk and profit opportunity in the next period

Risk Management Report and Corporate Accountability

To clarify the contribution of a feed-forward accounting control system to risk transparency and corporate social responsibility, we inquire into the actual state of risk disclosure by analyzing the financial statements of listed

Table 8.2 General statement of profit opportunity and risk management

Practically forecasted values in present period	*Forecast value*	*Proactive improvement*	*Data for target profit*	*Unsettled planned value*
Estimated profit opportunity	450	45	495	5
Estimated risk	120	105	−15	15
Optimum profit opportunity	330	150	480	20

Table 8.3 Strategic risk management report (units: million yen)

Items	**Forecast**	**Variance & improvement**		
1 Forecast risk from long-term perspective (sustainable value growth)	**100**			
2 forecast risk from short-term perspective (competitive strategy)	**120**			
3 Forecast risk variance		**20**	**(15)**	
4 Primary improvement target		**100**	**(90)**	
Expected improvement of risk in this year		**120**		
5 Total proactive improvement				
(1) Improvement of the primary planned risk			**90**	
(2) Improvement of the variance			**15**	
Total			**105**	
6 Unsettled risk in this year		**(120 – 105=)**		**15**
7 Countermeasure against the above risk (Contract insurance: expense in this income account)				**15**

Japanese companies and, for increased improvement of its situation, propose a risk management report including profit opportunity management to which the COLC model leads (see Tables 8.1, 8.2, and 8.3).

Table 8.4 indicates the actual state of risk disclosure in listed Japanese companies, where the average number of risk items per company disclosed by the top 100 Japanese companies by sales amount in fiscal year 2013 is shown. Risk items are divided into four categories according to Tokyo Marine Risk Consulting, Co. Ltd. (TRC) (2004): strategic, financial, hazard, and operational risks. We can see from Table 8.4 that generally risks

Table 8.4 The disclosed risk items of top 100 Japanese companies by sales amount: Disclosed risk items per company in fiscal year 2013

Industry (companies, average sales)	*Strategic risk*	*Financial risk*	*Hazard risk*	*Operational risk*	*Total risk*
Mining (6; 1778.3)	5.67	1.83	1.17	1.17	9.83
Manufacturing (55; 3835)	9.6	2.13	1.64	3.22	16.56
Electric power and gas (7; 2893.6)	6.00	0.29	3.14	3.29	13.71
Information (5; 5546.2)	9.8	0.80	1.60	3.60	15.80
Transportation (7; 1864.3)	8.86	1.29	2.00	1.71	13.86
Commercial (16; 5484.7)	9.06	3.13	1.81	2.38	16.38
Others (4; 1625.3)	11.75	2.5	0.75	1.5	16.5
Total (100; 3769.3)	9.07	2.1	1.73	2.81	15.71

Note: *Strategic risk*: risks related to business strategy, market marketing, personnel system, politics, economy, society, media, and capital and liabilities; ***financial risk***: risks related to assets management, settlement of accounts (including changes in interest and exchange rates), and liquidity; ***hazard risk***: risks related to natural disaster, accidents and trouble, and information systems; ***operational risk***: risks related to products and services (including recall and intelligence leakage), legal affairs/ethics, environmental protection, labor management, the management team (including turbulent management and scandals)

Source: TRC (2004); EDINET (2005; 2013)

are strongly recognized in connection with strategic planning, managerial and operational control, or the whole management activity, although, in the common situation, commercial companies tend to focus more on financial risk than do other industries, while companies in the electric power, gas, heat supply, and waterworks industries have been very concerned with hazard risks since the Fukushima nuclear power accident and tsunami in March 2011. This is also confirmed by a comparative analysis of risk items between the 2005 and 2013 fiscal years.

Table 8.5 presents the difference in risk items in 2005 from those found in fiscal year 2013. We can see that in general corporate risk consciousness has risen since the global financial crisis of 2008. In particular, companies in the mining and information industries have become more sensitive to financial risk, while companies in the electric, gas supply, and commercial industries are more sensitive to hazard risk. These changes are influenced by natural and social disasters such as the Great East Japan Earthquake and Tsunami and the Fukushima nuclear disaster of March 2011, but the current tendency of the enhanced risk disclosure seems to be caused by an amendment of the Company Act in 2006 and the enforcement of the

Table 8.5 Comparison of disclosed risks of top 98 Japanese companies by sales amount between the 2005 and 2013 fiscal years

Industry (companies, average sales)	*Strategic risk*	*Financial risk*	*Hazard risk*	*Operational risk*	*Total risk*
Mining (6; 1778.3)	1.50	0.83	0.17	0.33	2.83
Manufacturing (54; 3677)	1.78	0.41	0.46	0.56	3.20
Electric power and gas (7; 2893.6)	0.71	0	0.71	1.29	2.71
Information (5; 5546.2)	1.80	0.80	0.40	1.60	4.60
Transportation (7; 1864.3)	2.57	0	0.29	0.29	3.14
Commercial (15; 5754.1)	1.87	0.07	0.87	0.87	3.67
Others (4; 1625.3)	0.25	−0.25	0	−0.75	−1.25
Total (100; 3769.3)	1.67	0.32	0.49	0.62	3.1

2009 Financial Instruments and Exchange Act. These laws aim to increase the transparency of financial statements and company compliance through more effective internal control, risk management, and external auditing. The Company Act requires 'large companies'[3] to maintain and improve the internal rules that govern their preventive procedures and systems of countermeasures that guard against risk, while the Financial Instruments and Exchange Act puts listed companies under an obligation to prepare internal control reports and external auditing. It also requires them to clearly state the risks of their financial instruments and the risk management systems related to these instruments as notes to the financial statements.

As discussed above, all listed or 'large' companies must warn shareholders and other stakeholders of risk events. These stakeholders must be aware of corporate risks and, at the same time, accept investment losses in the near future if strategic and operational activities don't work out or an accident occurs. Moreover, according to Japanese Auditing Standards, external auditors should also conduct an audit of *internal control and risk management* with 'professional skepticism' from the viewpoint of '*rationally low auditing risk*'. Internal control, or the internalized audit (or self-regulation) of business operations that was independent of external accounting audits, can be externalized through disputes over corporate governance and risk management. This means that all business activities in these listed companies are inspected by external professional auditors, because of the combination of risk management and business strategy. This externalization is one way to promote good governance, since stakeholders, in particular stockholders, generally have greater confidence in external professional auditors than in their own judgment. Is there another way to internalize the "self-regulation" of corporate management and strengthen stakeholders' commitment toward a "participatory democracy" (Drori 2006, p. 110)? Is there a positively voluntary way for a company to charge itself with social accountability and controllability?

Although, as indicated in Tables 8.4 and 8.5, risk events are increasingly disclosed in financial statements, little is disclosed about how each company plans to manage these risk events. Therefore, stakeholders and society in general cannot know what misfortune will happen in the very near future, or what relation there is between risk and accounting profit, even though this may also be a general trend in other countries (Gates et al. 2012). When risk-taking and management processes for dealing with it are not elucidated in financial statements, stockholders and society may feel uneasy maintaining their relation with the company unless they can depend on the opinions of external auditors. At times, investors may wash their hands of the business, and potential investors may wish to stay out of the oncoming disaster, since signs of risk only serve to arouse caution in stakeholders. This seems to be an inducement to the increased social uncertainty.

Most of the surveyed companies did not disclose their risk management process or its result in their financial statements at all. In spite of the upsurge of enterprise risk consciousness, "For a financial institution, a conventional balance sheet does not provide adequate information to insiders or to outsiders such as investors or creditors as to the risk" (Scholes 2000, p. 18). Even now there may be no dramatic change in this situation for financial or other organizations. If a more general and simpler report based on the "unified management statement of profit opportunity and risk"[4] (see Tables 8.1, 8.2, and 8.3), or if quantitative information on risk management is included with the internal control report in notes to the financial statements, corporate transparency and social confidence will increase in a small way. As joint-stock companies and disclosure are a product of democracy in modern capitalism, high-quality transparency (intelligible and concrete explanations) and accountability (responsibility for quantitative and qualitative substantiation) of the risk management process can not only accelerate "better communication with management" (Gates et al. 2012) but also become part of the general corporate culture, even to the extent that all listed and "large" companies can keep step with society toward the goal of sustainable growth through "participatory democracy" (Drori 2006, p. 110), social commitment (see Power 2007), and criticism. If society becomes sensitive to enterprise risk and these listed companies communicate their corporate and risk management strategies to the society, the conversion of enterprise risk into social risk (or uncertainty) can be moderated (see Heath et al. 2009). Business risks may also be reduced or mitigated, as companies can absorb effective ideas from society and improve their management. Society can also examine methods to mitigate the social risks that arise from corporate risks. The choice between greater internalization of 'internal risk control' (self-regulation of risk) and its externalization for effective enterprise risk management depends on each nation's political, economic, and social structure. However, even in the former case, management accounting should be reformed to follow not only a more holistic and future-oriented but also socialized and dialogical form.

8.6 Conclusion

Since the financial crisis as symbolized by the globally linked, finance-oriented economy, and senior managers' abuse of accounting systems, management accounting has become more conscious of uncertainty and its control and has shaped feed-forward accounting control systems to serve enterprise risk management and governance. This has called on accountants and researchers to generalize the relationship between management accounting and risk management (see Bhimani 2009, p. 2). In this chapter, a feed-forward accounting control system incorporated profit opportunity and enterprise risk information into a proactive and feed-forward control model and made it possible to perform holistic risk management. This chapter is intended as a tentative investigation of COLC model and its managerial and social functions. At the same time, the significance of profit design is examined in relation to this model. Contemporary accounting control systems should be useful not only for effective enterprise risk management but also for carrying out social and democratic functions through the accountability and disclosure of risk management. However, to achieve this subject, enterprises must be strongly conscious of social responsibility and strengthen quality transparency and the voluntary disclosure of risk management, while stakeholders who are concerned with corporate risk management and governance should look to construct a social space in which they can participate and discuss these issues from a variety of viewpoints.

This chapter seeks to serve future accounting science by clarifying the feed-forward structure of the COLC model as it shifts from reactive feedback information to proactive feed-forward information and from piecemeal and partially optimum functions to holistic and social functions, corresponding with the holistic perspective of risk management (see Drori 2006; Power 2007; Mikes 2011; Grote 2014; Rasid et al. 2014). It also examines the contribution of contemporary management accounting to the control of uncertainty as well as governance in enterprise risk management.

Notes

1. A holistic approach is one that assesses, explores, monitors, and controls risks from all sources of an organization in more integrated and comprehensive manner than do piecemeal approaches (Leung and Isaacs 2008; Clarke and Varma 1999; see also Stockstrom and Herstatt 2008; Abrams et al. 2007).
2. Improvement is used as an inclusive means that shows ameliorative and alternative response to profit opportunity and risk variances. Concretely, it clears up their factors and causes, and takes measures to raise the probability of profit opportunities and to lower the risk likelihood. The situation of strategic innovations is modified or altered for profit opportunities, while avoidance (such as buying insurance), compensation (agreement), or dissolution (cooperation) is considered for risk. At the same time, organizational structure and opportunity/risk consciousness among constituents in the organization must be improved, and risks must be kept from triggering risks in other areas (Dickinson 2000; COSO 2004; Clarke and Varma 1999; Leung and Isaacs 2008; Arena et al. 2010). Although *Kaizen* (improvement) in Japanese means activities which inspect and reexamine all product factors and production process for proactively manufacturing high quality/function and low cost into a product, here it takes in a broader sense, including the reexamination of strategy and innovation process.
3. Here, 'large companies' means companies whose capital stock is more than 500 million yen and whose liabilities are more than 20 billion yen. For details about the Company Act, the Financial Instruments and Exchange Act, and auditing standards in Japan, see 'regulations' in Data and Materials from Websites. As for Japanese National Laws, see the following; Minister of Justice: Japanese Law Translation: http://www.japaneselawtranslation.go.jp/?re=01; Financial Instruments and Exchange Act (Tentative translation): http://www.japaneselawtranslation/go.jp/law/detail_print; Companies Act (Part V, Part VI, Part VII, and Part VIII): http://www.japaneselawtranslation/go.jp/law/detail_print; Business Accounting Council, 2009, Opinion on the Revision of Auditing Standard, April 9, Financial Service Agency, The Japanese Institute Public Accountants: http://www.fsa.go.jp/en/news/2009/20090525-1/01 pdf

4. The 'unified management statement of profit opportunity and risk' and the risk management report are only examples to heighten the quality transparency of comprehensive risk management. A more exhaustive and easy-to-understand report of risk management is contrived by using the basic framework of the statement, even when it includes more complicated conditions.

Bibliography

Abrams, C., von Känel, J., Mäller, S., Pfitzmann, B., & Ruschka-Taylor, S. (2007). Optimized Enterprise Risk Management. *IBM System Journal, 46*(2), 219–234.

Arena, M., Arnaboldi, M., & Azzone, G. (2010). The Organizational Dynamics of Enterprise Risk Management. *Accounting, Organizations and Society, 35*(7), 659–675.

Arnold, V., Benford, T., Canada, J., & Sutton, S. G. (2011). The Role of Strategic Enterprise Risk Management and Organizational Flexibility in Easing New Regulatory Compliance. *International Journal of Accounting Information Systems, 12*, 171–188.

Berle, A. A., & Means, G. C. (1932). *Modern Corporation and Private Property.* New York: Macmillan.

Bhimani, A. (2009). Risk Management, Corporate Governance and Management Accounting: Emergence Interdependences. *Management Accounting Research, 20*(1), 2–5. https://doi.org/10.1016/j.mar.2008/11.002.

Borison, A., & Hamm, G. (2010). How to Manage Risk (After Risk Management Has Failed). *MIT Sloan Management Review, 52*(Fall), 51–57.

Clarke, C. J., & Varma, S. (1999). Strategic Risk Management: The New Competitive Edge. *Long Range Planning, 32*(4), 414–424.

Collins, J. (2009). *How the Mighty Fall and Why Some Companies Never Give in.* New York: HarperCollins Publishers Inc.

COSO. (2004, September). *Enterprise Risk Management-Integrated Framework: Executive Summary Framework*, The Committee of Sponsoring Organizations of the Treadway, NJ (US).

Cushing, B. E. (1968, October). Some Observations on Demski's Ex Post Accounting System. *The Accounting Review, 43*(4), 668–671.

Demski, J. S. (1967, October). An Accounting System Structures on a Linear Programming Model. *Accounting Review, 42*(4), 701–712.

Demski, J. S. (1968, October). Some Observations on Demski's Ex Post Accounting System: A Reply. *The Accounting Review, 43*(4), 672–674.

Demski, J. S. (1969, October). Decision-Performance Control. *Accounting Review, 44*(4), 669–713.

Demski, J. S. (1977). Analyzing the Effectiveness of the Traditional Standard Cost Variance Model. In G. J. Benston (Ed.), *Contemporary Cost Accounting and Control* (2nd ed., pp. 222–236). Encino: Dickenson Publishing.

Dickinson, G. (2000). Risk Role Grows to Enterprise Scale: Enterprise Risk Management Provides Control Over Disparate Risks in the Business Environment. Gerry Dickinson Explains How: [Surveys ed.], *Financial Times*, London (UK), 13 November; 8.

Drori, G. S. (2006). Governed by Governance: The New Prism for Organizational Change. In G. S. Drori, J. W. Meyer, & H. Hwang (Eds.), *Globalization and Organization: World Society and Organizational Change* (pp. 91–118). New York: Oxford University Press.

EDINET (Electronic Disclosure for investors 'NET-work.: http://disclosure.edinet.fs.go.jp and 'kabupro.jp': http://www.kabupro.jp: *Concerning Annual Securities Reports* (fiscal year 2005 and fiscal year 2013) of the Japanese 100 companies.

Emerson, H. (1909). *Efficiency as a Basis for Operation and Wages*. New York: The Engineering Magazine, 131.

Gates, S., Nicolas, J. L., & Walker, P. L. (2012). Enterprise Risk Management: A Process for Enhanced Management and Improved Performance. *Management Accounting Quarterly, 13*(3), 28–38.

Grote, G. (2014). Promoting Safety by Increasing Uncertainty-Implications for Risk Management. *Safety Science*. https://doi.org/10.10176/j.ssci.1014.02.010.

Heath, R. L., Lee, J., & Ni, L. (2009). Crisis and Risk Approaches to Emergency Management Planning and Communication: The Role of Similarity and Sensitivity. *Journal of Public Relations Research, 21*(2), 123–141.

Hitachi Manufacturing Company Ltd. (2015). *Annual Securities Report*: http://www.kabupro.jp/edp/20150625/S10055M4.htm; see also EDINET, 2014.

Holmquist, E. (2012). Risk Management and Business Strategy. *The RMA Journal, 94*(10), 40–45.

IFA. (2004). *Enterprise Governance: Getting the Balance Right*, booklet prepared by the Professional Accountants in Business Committee (PAIB). New York/UK: International Federation of Accountants (IFA)/CIMA.

Ingrassia, P. (2011). *Crash Course: The American Automobile Industry's Road to Bankruptcy and Bailout—And Beyond*. New York: Random House trade Paperbacks.

Jaafari, A. (2001). Management of Risks, Uncertainties and Opportunities on Projects: Time for a Fundamental Shift. *International Journal of Project Management, 19*, 89–101.

Kim, S., & Collier, R. (2013). Risk and Risk Management in Management Accounting and Control. *Management Accounting Research, 24*(2), 82–87. https://doi.org/10.1016/j.mar.2013.04.003.

Knight, F. H. (1921). *Risk, Uncertainty and Profit*. Chicago: University of Chicago Press. Reprint version: Cosimo Classic, New York, 2005.

Kyosera. (2014, March). Annual Securities Report. *EDINET*.

Leung, F., & Isaacs, F. (2008). Risk Management in Public Sector Research: Approach and Lessons Learned at a National Research Organization. *R&D Management, 38*(5), 510–519.

Mikes, A. (2011). From Counting Risk to Making Risk Count: Boundary-work in Risk Management. *Accounting, Organization and Society, 36*(4–5), 226–245.

Nishimura, A. (2003). *Management Accounting in Asia: feed forward and Asian perspectives.* Hampshire: Palgrave Macmillan.

Nishimura, A. (2011). Uncertainty and Management Accounting: Opportunity, Profit Opportunity and Profit. *Asia-Pacific Management Accounting Journal, 6*(1), 81–101. Public Knowledge Project (Open Journal System). http://arionline.uitm.edu.my/ojs/index.php/APMAJ/issue/view/13.

Nishimura, A. (2014). Transforming Cost Design Into Environmentally Conscious Cost Design in Japan: Likelihood and Problems for Further Development. *Journal of Management Control, 25*(*1*), 55–75. https://doi.org/10.1007/s00187-014-0190-x.

Papa, V. T., & Peters, S. J. (2011). *User Perspectives on Financial Instrument Risk Disclosure under International Financial Reporing Standards (IFRS).* http://www.cfainstitute.org/ethics/Documents/financial_instruments_risk_disclosure_report_volume_1.pdf.

Power, M. (2007). *Organized Uncertainty: Designing a World of Risk Management.* New York: Oxford University, Press.

Rasid, S. Z., Isa, C. R., & Ismail, W. K. W. (2014). Management Accounting Systems, Enterprise Risk Management and Organizational Performance in Financial Institutions. *Asian Review of Accounting, 22*(*2*), 128–144. https://doi.org/10.1108/ARA-03-2013-0022.

Richardson, J. G. (2009). Uncertainty, the Critical Basis of Risk Management. *Foresight, 11*(6), 42–56.

Richardson, J. G. (2010). The Certainty of Uncertainty: Risk Management Revisited. *Foresight, 12*(4), 49–64.

Schneier, R., & Miccolis, J. (1998). Enterprise Risk Management. *Strategy & Leadership, 26*(2), 10–16.

Scholes, M. S. (2000). Crisis and Risk Management (the Near Crash of 1998). *The American Economic Review, 90*(2), 17–21.

Seal, W. (2006). Management Accounting and Corporate Governance: An Institutional Interpretation of the Agency Theory. *Management Accounting Research, 17*(4), 389–408.

Shank, J. K., & Miguel, J. G. (2009, January/February). Merging Financial and Managerial Accounting, Strategic Cost Management and Enterprise Risk Assessment Under SOX, *The Journal of Corporate Accounting & Finance, 20,* 83–99.

Smith, P. G., & Merritt, G. M. (2002). *Proactive Risk Management: Controlling Uncertainty in Product Management.* New York: Productivity Press.

Sony Corporation. (2014, June). *Annual Securities Report*, EDINET.

Stockstrom, C., & Herstatt, C. (2008). Planning and Uncertainty in New Product Development. *R&D Management, 38*(5), 480–490.

Stuart, I., & Stuart, B. (2004). *Ethics in the Post-Enron Age*. Cincinnati: Thomson South-Western College Pub.

Tanaka, M. (1985, July/August). New Approach to the Function Evaluation System in Value Engineering, *International Journal of Production Research, 23*(4), 625–638.

Tanaka, T. (1992). *Field-Study: Contemporary Management Accounting System*. Tokyo: Chuo-keizaisha Publisher, Co.

Tanaka, M. (1995). *Theory and Practices of Cost Design*. Tokyo: Chuo-keizaisha Publisher, Co.

TRC. (2004). *The Definitive and Digestible Book on Risk Management: The Newest Version*. Tokyo: Tokio Marine Risk Consulting, Co. Ltd.

CHAPTER 9

Foreign Exchange Risk and Profit Improvement in the Comprehensive Opportunity and Lost Opportunity Control Model

9.1 Introduction

The function and content of management accounting has been changing since the world financial crisis of 2008. For example, in Japan, cost design (also known as target costing in English) has contributed to innovation in manufacturing activities and improvement in business results through organically integrating low cost with high quality (effective function) since the 1960s. In recent years, this tool is now taking a new form that is more suitable for coping with financial risks and can adapt to changes in the business environment (Nishimura 2014; Imai 2010, 2014; Tanaka 2015). Manufacturing enterprises that adopt cost design now face a critical problem: how to protect their manufacturing activities from financial risks, primarily market risks such as foreign exchange risk, interest rate risk, and commodity price risk. At present, management accounting cannot exist independently of risk management, derivatives strategy, and hedge accounting, as these must be controlled and disclosed. Management accounting, beyond its original functions of efficiency and effectiveness, should also be a tool for planning for and controlling financial risks that may harm manufacturing activities. The profit opportunities of derivatives can act as a countermeasure against these risks. Before and after the recent world financial crisis, many enterprises had the bitter experience of sacrificing sustainable and long-term manufacturing performance to the speculation

A. Nishimura, *Management, Uncertainty, and Accounting*,
https://doi.org/10.1007/978-981-10-8989-3_9

of short-term derivatives. In this sense, all manufacturing enterprises are now confronted by a critical problem: how to manage the relations between manufacturing activities and external financial risk (particularly foreign exchange risk) by using effective management and accounting systems. This problem is also related to derivatives strategy and enterprise risk management.

Although management accounting, with the original goal of efficient and effective management, did not include risk as a main subject in the past, management accounting has now always been influenced by uncertainty. Enterprises have managed uncertainty in management accounting by means of variance analysis (the ex post recognition of prior uncontrollable factors) and improved decision-making and performance evaluation methods (relativized planned value and the acceptance of nonprogrammed activity) since the beginning of the twentieth century. At present, uncertainty is deeply intertwined with financial risk, including foreign exchange risk, which is the primary and inextricable issue on the agenda of contemporary management accounting. In contrast, in the past, risk was generally recognized as controllable through the amelioration of traditional planning and control systems (Nishimura 2011). Management accounting is shifting from the partial modification of decision-making and performance evaluation to the proactive and perspective systematization and synthetization of decision-making and performance evaluation with enterprise risk management and hedge accounting.

Against this background, manufacturing enterprises should pay greater attention to market risks, and particularly to the risk of foreign exchange volatility, which strongly influences manufacturing activities. This attention should be paid not only to protect their activities from these negative effects but also to build up a stable manufacturing foundation that overcomes external financial risks by means of profit improvements in terms of revenue, purchasing, and cost improvements. Therefore, those employing management accounting in globally competitive manufacturing enterprises must also recognize the relations between market risks, derivatives as countermeasures against those risks, and manufacturing activities, using this recognition to insert them into a newly transformed planning and control system to improve the use of information, measurement, and communication (Nishimura 2015a).

In this chapter, we aim to clarify the problems and roles of contemporary management accounting in connection with foreign exchange risks, derivatives and profit improvements, and their relations. Therefore, to make clear the actual situation of foreign exchange risks and derivatives, we first analyze the financial statements and data of major listed manufacturing enterprises in Japan. We also examine the prior literature on the general interrelation between risk management and management accounting and, with reference to this issue, introduce the COLC model, which was addressed in Chap. 8 (Nishimura 2015a). Second, on the basis of this COLC model, we examine hedge accounting and foreign exchange risk management from the viewpoint of profit opportunity and lost opportunity, using this to further clarify the more practical and specialized form of the useful model in today's risk environments. Lastly, through this investigation, we elucidate the main purpose and the changing features of contemporary management accounting.

9.2 Prior Research and Literature

Literature on the Interrelation Between Risk Management and Management Accounting

Management accounting researchers have not fully elucidated "the general relationship between management accounting and risk management" (Bhimani 2009, p. 2) and have clarified the relation between management accounting and some specific risks (such as foreign exchange risk) even less. Developing this understanding is important to allow basic recognition of the effects of external risks on manufacturing activities. As Kim and Collier (2013) point out, because of our weak recognition of the operational risks and external risks facing organizations during the world financial crisis, "with a few exceptions, we have relatively little understanding about the (complex) interrelation between risk, risk management, and management accounting and control practices" (p. 84). Few studies have been carried out on this topic, and it is important that, as a first step, we understand the interrelations.

Shank and Miguel (2009) propose that management accounting provides managers with a comprehensive and enterprise-wide information system that can warn of impending disasters. Management accounting makes it possible to prepare broad information, including both financial and nonfinancial information, on past and future performance. Rasid et al. (2014) also mention that "besides information that is broad in scope, management accounting information that is timely, integrated and aggregated is essential for risk management" (p. 140). At the same time, as Kim and Collier (2013) point out, management accounting is more strongly inclined to consider risk information than cost.

Woods (2008) contends that strategy is organizationally combined with risk information by integrating four perspectives (financial, customer, internal business process, and learning and growth) in a balanced scorecard with risk management. Through these perspectives, senior managers can plan for and control strategic direction on the basis of risk awareness, while those at the operational level not only carry out the enterprise strategy and objectives but also control operational risks, maintaining strategic and risk awareness in doing so. Seal (2006), on the basis of institutional theory of agency, notes the routine aspect in management accounting and discusses its important role in restricting senior managers' arbitrary heroic decisions, strategically controlling their subordinates, and providing nonexecutive directors with pertinent strategic and risk information. Here, risk, as well as strategy, is also managed across the whole organization through this routine system and the creativity of senior managers.

As discussed above, the main attempts made by some researchers have been to demonstrate the interrelation between risk management and management accounting from informational, functional, and organizational viewpoints: broad nonfinancial and timely information, the routine function, and the balanced scorecard. However, it is unclear how information on both risk and opportunity, as oppositional aspects of strategy, should be synthesized with accounting profit and loss in management accounting systems as well as how management accounting fulfills its function in the decision-making and performance evaluation processes. Further, it is not clear how this synthesis strengthens the proactive and prospective features of management accounting.

Proposal of the COLC Model

In the light of the controversial issues above, in the preceding chapter we constructed a model in which profit opportunity and enterprise risk information is proactively integrated into accounting profit and loss as part of the decision-making and performance evaluation processes. In the model, strategic activities related to profit opportunities and risks are controlled toward a profit target through multiple planned (long-term and short-term) values, preparatory variance analyses, and indicators of improvements (organizational and structural improvements, including cost improvement) for exploiting profit opportunity and minimizing enterprise risk. This model is called the COLC model. In the model, a proactive and preventive planning process links to profit and cost design systems on the basis of the concepts of profit opportunity and enterprise risk, while each aspect of performance is controlled with the unified feed-forward and feedback management for lost opportunity or opportunity cost. The COLC model is simply revealed in the following equations (Nishimura 2015b):

$$\begin{aligned}&\textit{Expected}\left(\textit{from the viewpoint of long-term or sustainable value growth}\right)\\&\textit{profit opportunity} - \textit{estimated}\begin{pmatrix}\textit{from the viewpoint of short-term}\\\textit{or current competitive strategy}\end{pmatrix}\\&\textit{profit opportunity} = \textit{forecast profit opportunity variance}\end{aligned}$$

$$\begin{aligned}&\textit{Expected risk}\begin{pmatrix}\textit{ExR;from the viewpoint of long-term}\\\textit{or sustainable value growth}\end{pmatrix}-\\&\textit{estimated risk}\begin{pmatrix}\textit{EsR;from the viewpoint of short-term}\\\textit{or current competitive strategy expected loss}\end{pmatrix}\\&= \textit{forecast risk variance}\end{aligned}$$

Profit improvements are proactively examined by using quantitative and qualitative variance analyses, and effective measures exploiting profit opportunity and mitigating impending enterprise risks are incorporated. For example, measures and factors that may be taken into account include external and internal improvements; the external improvement is related to the reorganization of overseas business points or supply chains and the reexamination of import and export policies, while the internal one to new product design, technological innovation, the reorganization of manufacturing and management, new cost design, and cost improvement. We should further note in relation to the main subject of this paper that the speculative exploitation of profit opportunity through derivatives and other financial instruments is also considered part of external profit opportunity improvements, even if it aims at risk-hedging. The expected or target profit decided after this improvement examination can be schematized via the following equations:

$$\begin{aligned}&\begin{pmatrix}\textit{Estimated profit opportunity}\left(\textit{EsPO}\right)+\\\textit{improved profit opportunity}\end{pmatrix}-\\&\left(\textit{EsR} - \textit{risk reduction by improvement}\right) = \textit{expected}\left(\textit{or target}\right)\\&\textit{profit} : \textit{in the case of expected profit opportunity}\\&\left(\textit{ExPO}\right) > \textit{EsPO or ExR} < \textit{estimated risk}\end{aligned}$$

Enterprises can decide the expected or target profit with reference to these profit opportunities and enterprise risks. In specific cases, the expected profit from the long-term strategy gives the target profit as a practical goal after comparing it with the presently estimated profit from the current competitive strategy and adding some improvements to the estimated profit when the former is higher than the latter. This target profit provides managers with indicators of opportunity cost for performance evaluation by comparison with actual profit. Before making this comparison, managers can further obtain basic data based on target profit to help in deciding the allowable cost or target cost in cost design.

For manufacturing activities under today's financial risks, it is practical to apply the COLC model to the most influential market risk, namely foreign exchange risk, to clarify the relations between market risks, derivatives, and manufacturing activities. We can then develop the model into a more proactive form, which would allow organizing proactive and preventive measures against potentially disastrous risks and their negative effects on manufacturing activities.

9.3 Effects of Foreign Exchange Rate Risks on Manufacturing Performance in Japanese Manufacturing Companies

Recently, the risk of foreign exchange fluctuation has had a strong influence on corporate performance in Japan. The exchange rate between the Japanese yen and the US dollar has fluctuated from a high of 76.19 yen per dollar in January 2012 to a low of 134.56 yen per dollar in January 2002, well below the annual mean value of 105.55 yen from January 1999 to January 2015. It is clear that the business performance of Japanese manufacturing companies was strongly influenced by this fluctuation. In the 17 years from 1999 to 2015, the yearly rate of the yen was higher than average in 10 years and lower in 7 years.[1] Judging from the exchange rate of the yen against the dollar, a 10-yen depreciation appears to increase operational profit by 658.2 billion yen for the all listed companies in the transportation machinery industry and 886.7 billion yen in the general machine and electric machinery industry. In contrast, operational profits are estimated to decrease by 36.3 billion yen in the hardware and other manufacturing industry and 72.8 billion yen in the wholesale and retail sale industry, which depend strongly on import trade. In the opposite case, the appreciation of the yen might similarly have a negative impact on the business earnings of strongly export-oriented manufacturing companies. According to an investigation by Ueno and Aoyama in the NLI Research Institute (2011), the negative effect of the appreciation of the yen was generally strong in manufacturing industries in January 2011, among which the general machine and precision machine industries were most strongly influenced, followed by the iron, transportation machinery, and electric machine industries (see also Mizuho ISD 2014).

Because the transportation machinery, electric machinery, and industrial equipment industries are representative of overall Japanese manufacturing activities, we aim to clarify the relations between foreign exchange risks and manufacturing activities by examining financial statements and related information from those industries.[2] Further, we examine the foreign exchange earnings and the countermeasures taken against related risks by representative companies in these industries. For this, we chose representatives from the top 100 Japanese companies (by sales volume as of March 2015) and some representative companies in the industrial equipment industry that have a much smaller sales volume but have a high level of overseas sales. The results are presented in Tables 9.1 and 9.2.

Comparing foreign exchange earnings of the chosen companies in fiscal year 2014 with those earnings in 2008, we can see that in 2008 (strong yen), 70.6% of these companies were subject to the negative influence of foreign exchange fluctuation and 44.1% (15) had worse foreign exchange earnings than in the previous year. In contrast, in fiscal year 2014 (weak yen) about 72% companies were positively affected and had earnings better than in the previous year. In particular, many companies (83%) in the transportation machinery industry were favorably affected by the yen's depreciation in fiscal year 2014, showing improved exchange earnings. However, on the whole, many companies were more unfavorably affected by the yen's appreciation in fiscal year 2008, with some companies unable to escape the adverse circumstances resulting from overlapping problems of exchange rate fluctuation and strong price competition from other Asian countries.

At present, generally export-oriented manufacturing companies have increased their revenues following depreciation of the yen and are now strengthening their countermeasures against foreign exchange risks in order to cope with future situations, taking a lesson from the trying experiences of the financial crisis of 2008. As shown in Table 9.2, most major manufacturing companies conduct hedge accounting and hold nonhedged

Table 9.1 Foreign exchange earnings of key manufacturing industrial companies in fiscal years 2008 and 2014

Industry (number of researched companies)		*Companies that reported foreign exchange profit*	*Companies that reported foreign exchange loss*	*Companies with higher exchange profit or lower loss than in previous year*	*Companies with lower exchange profit or greater loss than in previous year*
Transportation machinery (12)	2008	5	7	7	5
	2014	10	2	10	2
Electrical machinery and apparatus (11)	2008	1	10	6	5
	2014	8	2	6	4
Industrial equipment (11)	2008	4	7	6	5
	2014	5	5	7	4
Total (34)	2008	10	24	19	15
	2014	23	9	23	10

Note: One company is excluded in the electrical machinery and apparatus category in fiscal year 2014 because it did not include information on foreign exchange profit or loss in its financial statements. One company is also excluded in the industrial equipment in fiscal year 2014 because it reports zero foreign exchange earnings in its financial statements for fiscal year 2014

derivatives. This trend mirrors that of other Japanese industrial companies whose ratio of export dependency is high and is strongly influenced by the risk of foreign exchange fluctuation (Ito et al. 2013).

Most of these companies would accept following idea from Panasonic: "risk management activities are closely connected with the planning and implementation of business strategy to surely accomplish business purpose that leads to the advancement of enterprise value" (Panasonic Corporation 2014, 2015). Similarly, Hino Motors points out in its financial statements that the company may potentially have reduced profit, compared with what could have naturally be achieved, as a result of derivatives trading that was partially undertaken to mitigate the risk of foreign exchange fluctuation but which may instead have exerted a negative influence on business results and the firm's financial condition when purchasing raw materials and selling finished products at home and abroad (Hino Motors 2015).

Yamaha Motor (2015) also describes the potential for hedge trading to cause the loss of profit opportunity due to fluctuation in the foreign exchange rate opposite to what the company assumes. Even though it adopted countermeasures against the risk of foreign exchange fluctuation, Hitachi (2015) rightly notes the potential for ineffective hedge accounting

Table 9.2 Derivatives in major manufacturing companies in Japan in fiscal years 2008 and 2014

Industries	*Hedged derivatives*						*Nonhedged derivatives*						
Risk	*Currency*		*Interest rate*			*Price*	*Currency*			*Interest rate*			*Price*
Methods	*EC*	*CS*	*IS*	*ICS*	*SO*	*CF*	*EC*	*CS*	*CO*	*IS*	*IO*	*Others*	
Transportation machinery (12)	8	2	8	1		1	12	3	3	5	2		
Electrical machinery and apparatus (11)	8	2	7		1		8	3		4	1	ICS 1 SF 1	CF 1
Industrial equipment (11)	10	2	10	1		2	9	3		3		SF 1 CCS1	CF1
Total (34)	26	6	25	2	1	3	29	9	3	12	3	4	2

Abbreviations: *EC*, exchange contract; *CS*, currency swap; *IS*, interest rate swap; *ICS*, interest rate and currency swap; *SO*, stock option; *CF*, commodity futures; *CO*, currency option; *IO*, interest rate option; *SF*, stock futures; *CCS*, cap crossing currency swap

and countermeasures adopted to mitigate the risks of foreign exchange fluctuation, specifically because these measures only put off the negative effects of the risks or give only temporary relief from them. As described above, despite the adoption of hedge accounting, most of the companies cited in Tables 9.1 and 9.2 have tried to create a stronger business foundation that is not influenced by external environmental risks. Steps in this direction include the reorganization of bases and supply chains for production and overseas trade, the reexamination of import and export policies, the promotion of new product designs and technological innovation, the reorganization of internal business structures, and the reinforcement of cost design and cost improvement.

For example, to protect against the risk of future foreign exchange fluctuation, Toyota Motor Corporation (2015) has taken steps to strengthen its business foundation through such internal improvements as cost design, cost improvement, and fixed expense reduction under the presently favorable condition of the yen depreciation (see also Toyota Industries 2015). Imai (2010, 2014) designates this fundamental idea as "Toyota-style performance management accounting" and uses the concept of "proactive slack" to shed light on its structure and specific characteristics.

As described at the beginning, in this chapter we intend to apply the COLC model to foreign exchange risk management and clarify the new cognitive and control functions of management accounting in risk management. This goal drives us to the question of what accounting form the concepts of hedge accounting, derivatives, and internalized improvements should take in the COLC model and of how foreign exchange risks can be planned for and controlled together with internal profit improvements.

9.4 COLC Model and Hedge Accounting

Derivatives and Risk Management

Derivatives are considered as a useful tool to transform or avoid risk, although their speculative nature and risk are becoming clear as the globalization of their trading, the diversity of financial instruments, and the deregulation of finance/insurance sectors advance. For example, Phillips (1995) considers the complexity of derivative activities as a driver of revolution in risk management practices and states that derivative markets give opportunities to transform market risks (p. 240; see also Gibson 2007).

However, as the key roles of derivatives in Asian financial crisis and the world financial crisis of 2008 and their serious negative influences on global economy became clear, there were many warnings against the dangerous nature of derivatives. For example, Buffett (2002) warns us that "derivatives are financial weapons of mass destruction, carrying dangers that, while now latent, are potentially lethal" (p. 15). He also compares the derivatives business to a "time bomb" and a "hell" that is "easy to enter and almost impossible to exit" (p. 13). According to Sipko (2011), this financial crisis was more serious in its scope and depth than the Great Depression in the 1930s. Moreover, the growth of the global derivatives market was much faster than that of global real gross domestic product (GDP) (p. 40). Therefore, their transparency and hedge effectiveness have become a strong point of focus (Kawaller 2002; see also Johnson et al. 1994) in order to control derivatives speculation and strengthen the counterbalance function of derivatives against risk. The synchronic social control and stronger transparency of derivative activities, along with comprehensive risk management, are required for the protection of the real economy and manufacturing foundation. This results not only in the establishment of "new requirements that better reflect the risks and returns from derivatives and other trading activities" (Phillips, p. 245; see also Cowell 2006) but also the systematic requirement of comprehensive and effective balancing between derivatives and risks.

These requirements are pushing forward more comprehensive development of risk management and the systemization of an effective economic relation between derivatives and risks, including disclosure, corporate governance, and internal controls. We find these in their most representative form in international accounting standards.

Hedging and the COLC Model

The main purpose of hedge accounting is to insure against market risks by means of derivatives or speculative profit or, alternatively, to use a speculative measure to protect manufacturing activities from external risks (see Frestad and Beisland 2015). However, as shown in Table 9.2, typically companies clearly describe in their financial statements that their derivatives trading is by no means speculative because they conform to accounting standards that allow them to use derivatives as part of risk management strategy. Thus, derivatives are not presently considered as speculative in business circles when they are connected with risk management, even though they cannot intrinsically be separated from speculation. Under IFRS 9, which will take effect in 2018, derivatives are entered into from the viewpoint of enterprise risk management in which enterprise positive practices, not a formal obedience, the restriction of speculation, and sustainable enterprise value creation are included. At the same time, IFRS 9 shifts the fundamental nature of the standard from rules to *principles* and imposes an effective check on period-income expression distorted by derivatives through the close alignment of derivatives with enterprise risk management and the distinction between fair value hedges and cash flow hedges. Each enterprise, in return for being allowed to use subjective judgment in carrying out hedge accounting and risk management, should prepare definite documents related to hedge measures, hedge objectives, the nature of the hedged risks, how the hedge effectiveness is judged, and the hedge ratio when starting hedge accounting. Additionally, they should retrospectively disclose the objectives, methods, and effectiveness of risk management in financial statements. Consequently, the judgment of hedge effectiveness shifts from a bright-line test of hedge ratio (0.8–1.25) to demonstration of a clear economic relation between hedging measures and hedged items. Risk management must be more intensively implemented from a prospective standpoint rather than a retrospective one (IASB 2014; McCarrol and Khatri 2014; Lombardi 2010).

As mentioned above, hedge accounting in the near future will be based not only on the reinforcement of prospective and proactive risk management but also on its close alignment with strategic business planning. Specifically, enterprises should proactively examine profit opportunities and risks that are brought about by enterprise strategy and plan for and control the profit opportunities of derivatives that correspond to enterprise risks (Mercy 2006). We can represent this relation as follows:

$$\begin{aligned}&\textit{Hedge effectiveness ratio} = \textit{the fluctuation range of hedging measure value}\\&/\textit{the fluctuation range of hedged item value} \simeq 1\end{aligned}$$

That is, the effective economic relation in hedge accounting implies that the effectiveness ratio approaches 1 toward infinity, and so it more clearly captures a satisfactory economic relation. According to the COLC model, the hedge effectiveness ratio is shown as follows:

Hedge effectiveness ratio = profit opportunities of derivatives / risks of hedged assets and liabilities $\simeq 1$

Therefore, hedge accounting can also be incorporated into the relation between profit opportunity and enterprise risk in the COLC model and thereby become part of the decision-making and performance evaluation process for strategic and risk management. In practice, it may be rare for the return (or profit opportunity) of a hedging measure to be completely balanced against the risk of the hedged item because the objective movement of market risks cannot be guaranteed to coincide with managers' forecast, and speculative inclination cannot be entirely eliminated from entrepreneurs in the present financial environment (see Fujita 2003; Frestad and Beisland 2015; Russell-Jones 2014). Accordingly, to protect manufacturing activities from derivatives speculation and risks, the profit opportunity and enterprise risk of derivatives and their effective relation must be managed and disclosed prospectively and retrospectively (Cowell 2006; Smistad and Pustylnick 2012; Kawaller 2004; Kawaller and Koch 2013; see also Metzger 2009).

More Proactive Countermeasures Against the Risk of Foreign Exchange Fluctuations

Many companies cannot conceive of thoroughly coping with market risks by using only hedge accounting, but instead view it as only a temporarily method of delaying market risks. Accordingly, they emphasize building up a stable business foundation that is protected against the risk of fluctuation in foreign exchange rates and interest rates. Toyota carries out an advanced form of this method that focuses on proactively strengthening business adaptability to changing risks in the external business environment by using preventive cost design and cost improvement. Imai (2014) systemizes this idea and method as the concept of "proactive slack" (p. 45). Proactive slack protects against future external business environmental risks, provides sustainable business growth, and contributes to the preservation of the preconditions (revenue drivers) related to the external business environment in profit planning and control processes. Further, it strengthens adaptability to changing external business environmental risks by devising cost reduction schemes connected to the preconditions (Imai 2014).

Next, we investigate proactive slack, which in Imai's scheme is designated as the "Toyota-style performance management accounting" (2014, p. 44; see also Imai 2010), by using presumed figures with some amendments to the numerical values and framework to understand it from the angle of the COLC model. In addition, this approach will clarify the model's role in planning for and controlling profit opportunities, risks, and profit improvement activities. Table 9.3 shows a diagram in which Imai's proactive slack table is reorganized according to the COLC model.

In Table 9.3, a company expects profit opportunities of 15,000 million yen (all currencies here are assumed to be yen) from the viewpoint of long-term and sustainable business growth. The profit opportunity consists of 10,000 million in base profits calculated on past reliable business results, 4000 million in internal profit improvements (2000 million from the sales side and 2000 million from the manufacturing side), as well as anticipated foreign exchange profits of 1000 million from the favorable influence of a slumping yen. However, to draw up a more practical plan of profit opportunities and risks, the company should estimate short-term and practical (competitive) profit opportunities and risks to cope with impending enterprise risks through the examination of actual and future economic data on the business environment and organizational ability. As a result of this examination, the company finds that there is the possibility of sudden appreciation in the yen, which would adversely affect the expected improvements in sales volume and selling price. (Although the negative change in these improvements may arise from such internal causes as incorrect planning and control on the revenue side, study of that issue lies outside the scope of this chapter.) The effect of this shift causes the company not only to incur the new risk of foreign exchange fluctuation (1000) but also a decrease of 1500 million in profit opportunity, consisting of the disappearance of the 1000 million in anticipated foreign exchange profits and a reduction of 500 million from the negative effect of the new risk on improvements in the sales side. However, the company should actualize the incipient expected profit opportunities to maintain sustainable business growth.

In Table 9.3, Imai's concept of proactive slack, in which internal profit improvements outweigh external environmental risks, is also incorporated into the general framework of profit opportunity and risk planning, The company should undertake new endeavors to realize internal profit improvements in areas such as product design, cost design, and cost improvements to protect the manufacturing foundation from risks, which

Table 9.3 Foreign exchange risk and internalized improvement in the COLC model (1) (Millions of yen)

Planning	*1. ExPO and ExR*		*2. EsPO and EsR*		*3. Target internal improvements against EsR and (ExPO-EsPO)*	*4. Expected or target profit (= EsPO + 3)*
Improvements and risks	*ExPO*	*ExR*	*EsPO*	*EsR*		
1. Forecast profit based on past performance	(10000)		(10000)			10000
2. Profit improvements and negative effects of risk on them						
(1) Sales side	2000		1500			1500
(Sales volume)	(1000)		(800)			(800)
(Selling price)	(1000)		(700)		2500	(700)
(2) Manufacturing side	2000		2000		(1250)	4500
(Product design)	(1000)		(1000)			(2250)
(Cost design)	(600)		(600)		(750)	(1350)
(Cost improvement)	(400)		(400)		(500)	(900)
3. External improvements and risks						
(1) Market environment	1000		0	1000		
(foreign exchange rate)	(1000)			(1000)		
Total	15000		13500	1000	2500	16000

Note: Positive fluctuation of foreign exchange rate (yen depreciation) shows foreign exchange profit in the profit opportunity column, while the negative fluctuation (yen appreciation) shows foreign exchange loss in the risk column; *Abbreviation*: ExPO, Expected Profit Opportunity; ExR, Expected Risk; EsPO, Estimated Profit Opportunity, EsR, Estimated Risk

in this scenario will yield profits of 2500 million. For example, the company develops new products of high quality (function) and low cost through new cost design and cost engineering and further works to curtail manufacturing costs and fixed expenses through reexamining the production structure, business organization, and supply chain system. It is because a decrease of the ExPO (1500) and the new risk of foreign exchange fluctuation (1000) would inflict a serious damage on the expected business growth. After this, the company sets a strategically expected profit or target profit of 16,000 million through the further internal improvements so that it can lessen foreign exchange risks and their negative influence on manufacturing performance while strengthening its manufacturing foundation against future business environmental risks.

In our model, profit opportunity can be defined as the probability that internal profit improvements and external favorable changes in the business environments will yield corporate profit, while risk is the probability that external unfavorable changes of business environment and their negative effects on internal enterprise improvements will result in accounting loss, although risk is generally understood more widely.

Given this context, the terms in the COLC model are concisely explained as follows, using the example from Table 9.3 (in millions of yen):

$$ExPO - EsPO = \textit{forecast profit opportunity variance}$$

$$15{,}000 - 13{,}500 = +1500$$

$$ExR - EsR = \textit{forecast risk variance}$$

$$0 - (1000) = -1000$$

$$\textit{Improvement target} = \textit{forecast profit opportunity variance} - \textit{forecast risk variance}$$

$$2500 = 1500 - (-1000) = 2500$$

These two variances show the forecast error of profit opportunities and risks related to some changes in the business environment. The forecast profit opportunity variance is related to favorable or unfavorable changes in the business environment and forecast error concerning them, while the forecast risk variance deals with the new occurrence of risk, the transformation of ExPO to enterprise risk, their negative effects on expected profit opportunities and profit improvements, and errors in these forecasts. For the year shown, the EsPO results in 1500 million less than the incipient expected amount as a result of forecast error concerning foreign exchange fluctuation (1000) and a decrease of the expected improvement on the sales side (500) negatively influenced by the new risk of foreign exchange fluctuation (1000), which is shown on the risk side of the estimation column and by means of additional internal improvements, the company should cope with as well as the decreased expected profit opportunity. It is clear from these formulations that expected profit opportunities are influenced by foreign exchange fluctuation and its effects on internal profit improvements.

Therefore, the company should pursue more comprehensive improvements (product design, cost design, and cost improvement) totaling 2500 million more than the estimated profit opportunities in order to establish a strong business foundation for the future against external environmental risks and their negative effects while preserving sustainable business growth. For example, if actual profit were 13,500 million and the expected profit equaled the target profit, even though the company could eliminate foreign exchange risk and the associated negative effects, the substantial business foundation at the incipient expectation stage would be damaged seriously. Therefore, it must concretely examine lost profit opportunity by using variance analysis and make a program to eliminate external risks and encourage profit improvements more strongly in the next year.

$$\textit{Target profit} - \textit{actual profit} = \textit{opportunity costs variance}$$

$$15{,}000 - 13{,}500 = 1500$$

If actual profit were 16,000 million, or the same as the target profit, in contrast with the estimation stage, the company could not only establish the same sustainable manufacturing foundation assumed in the incipient expectation stage but, after making good risks of foreign exchange fluctuation, could also further invest 1000 million from additional internal improvement (the same amount as the expected profit of favorable foreign exchange fluctuation in the incipient expectation stage) to establish a stronger manufacturing foundation. Even if actual profit were 15,000 million, the company could maintain the substantial business foundation. In the case of 16,000 million, 1000 million could be dealt with as 'proactive slack' to cope with future risks or exploit more advantageous improvements in the next period. The COLC model recognizes the interrelation between the fluctuation risk of foreign exchange rate and profit improvements from the angle of profit opportunity and opportunity cost and provides managers with effective information for risk management and internal improvement. Moreover, its target profit further plays a significant role in estimating target cost for cost design.

9.5 Synthetic Development of the COLC Model in Foreign Exchange Risks and Derivatives

Next, we consider the case where the company suffers a 1000 million foreign exchange risk from yen appreciation as well as risks of 400 million from the negative influence on planned improvements of the sales side (200 million from sales volume and 200 million from selling price). The company then conducts hedge accounting (a 1400-derivative transaction against these risks). We can also present this alternate situation using the COLC model, the results of which are shown in Table 9.4.

Before turning to Table 9.4, we must note that the table includes different content from Table 9.3. "Improvement activities on the purchasing side" has been added to the internal profit enterprise improvements in the first column. This addition is made because most of the manufacturing companies identified in Table 9.1 establish stable and firm supply chains at home and abroad, where they have strong strategic cooperation with suppliers. As a purchaser, the company synchronizes the development and design of new products with suppliers as producers of parts and components through joint cooperation in value engineering. Therefore, these manufacturing companies can internalize suppliers' improvements into their improvement program through the joint development of product design, cost design, and cost improvement (Tanaka 2015; Nishimura 2014).

In Table 9.4, we can see from the second column that the 1400-million profit opportunity from derivatives is forecasted as hedge accounting against a 1000-million expected loss from expected foreign exchange dealings plus a 400-million expected loss from the resulting negative effects on sales-side improvements (200 million from its negative effect on sales volume improvement and 200 million from its negative effect on selling price improvement). The original amount of improvements on the sales side (2000 million) is still effective because even though 400 million of the 2000 expected amount may be unfavorably influenced by foreign exchange rate risks, these risks are counterbalanced by the profit opportunities of derivatives hedging. In the next column, the practical short-term (competitive) estimation of profit opportunities and risks shows the probability that the 1400-million profit opportunities from derivatives hedging will change to an unfavorable situation or risk, while, at the same time, the risks of previously hedged items related to foreign exchange risk and their negative influence on the sales side are untied from the derivatives. At the same

Table 9.4 Foreign exchange risk and internalized improvement in the COLC model (2) (millions of yen)

Planning / *Improvements and risks*	*1. ExPO and ExR*		*2. EsPO and EsR*		*3. Target internal improvements against EsR and (Expo-EsPO)*	*4. Expected profit or target profit (= EsPO + 3)*
	ExPO	*ExR*	*EsPO*	*EsR*		
1. Forecast profit based on past performance	(10000)		(10000)			10000
2. Internal improvements and negative effects of risks on them						
(1) Sales side	2000	400	1600			1600
(Sales volume)	(1000)	(200)	(800)			(800)
(Selling price)	(1000)	(200)	(800)			(800)
(2) Manufacturing side	2000		2000		1800	3800
(Product design)	(1000)		(1000)		(900)	(1900)
(Cost design)	(500)		(500)		(450)	(950)
(Cost improvement)	(500)		(500)		(450)	(950)
(3) Purchasing side	1000		1000		1000	2000
(Purchasing volume)	(600)		(600)		(500)	(1100)
(Purchasing price)	(400)		(400)		(500)	(900)
3. External improvements and risks						
(1) Market environment						
(Foreign exchange rate)		1000		1000		
(Interest rate)						
(Price change)						
(2) Derivatives	1400		0	1400		
Total	16400	1400	14600	2400	2800	17400

time, the probability of the dealings' failure increases more definitely than before and its negative effect is manifesting itself in sales side. The EsPO amounts to 1800 million less than the expected as a result of the failure of derivative trading and the negative effect of foreign exchange rate risk on the sales side and at the same time, the EsR results in 1000 million more than the expected in consequence of the transformation of favorable derivative trading to the unfavorable or risk. Therefore, the company should cope with these risks and their negative effects as well as the decrease of profit opportunity by further strengthening of internal profit improvements on the manufacturing and purchasing sides to establish the long-term stability of its manufacturing foundation. As for the improvement in the sales side, it must be replaced by other improvements unaffected largely by foreign exchange risk. Therefore, the new improvement target in product design, cost design, and cost improvements becomes 2800 million, consisting of the original risks (1000 million), the original negative influences of these risks on the expected profit improvements (400 million), and the new risks of derivatives trading failure (1400 million). As a result, this relation between the expected and estimated amounts leads to an expected or target profit of 17,400 million. If this expected profit materializes, the company will be able to establish a solid real-manufacturing foundation against external business environmental risks by using internal profit improvements, even though serious damage is caused by losses from derivatives trading.

However, we should not overlook that this target profit is not directly to actual accounting profit, since it must account for accounting losses as a definite form which the above risks of foreign exchange dealing failure and its negative influence will take in the not-far distant future.

The COLC model plays an important part in planning for and controlling business activities in these processes by taking into account information on profit opportunities, risks, and lost opportunity (opportunity cost). Moreover, expected profit is compared with estimated profit calculated using practical accounting information and data from middle- and lower-level managers. After considering their variances and proactively undertaking revised countermeasures against risks, this process leads to the target profit and lays the foundation for allowable cost in cost design. Consequently, this internalization of external environmental risks into profit opportunities is carried out through the COLC model and internal profit improvements based on product design, cost design, and cost improvement. The following equations summarize the process above and highlight the figures (in millions of yen) from our example company in Table 9.4.

ExPO – EsPO = forecast profit opportunity variance
16,400 – 14,600 = 1800 (error of judgment about derivatives trading effectiveness and the erosive amount of improvements in sales side that are negatively influenced by foreign exchange risks and should be replaced by other internal improvements: decrease in profit opportunity or lost profit opportunity)

ExR – EsR = forecast risk variance
1400 – 2400 = –1000 (risk amount that must be counterbalanced by new improvement in relation to the derivatives trading failure: increase in enterprise risk.)

Thus, the forecast profit opportunity variance and the forecast risk variance show the new necessity for establishing stronger internal improvements to cover lost profit opportunity and the foreign exchange risk restored by the failure of derivatives trading, and to replace the foreign exchange risk-fragile improvements by risk-unaffected improvements. Accordingly, the company must introduce new additional improvements against the lost profit opportunity and the newly reappeared risks as follows:

Improvement target = forecast profit opportunity variance and forecast risk variance

$$2800 = 1800 + 1000$$

This improvement target of 2800 results from the failed derivatives trading and the definite restoration of original foreign exchange risk and its negative effects on sales-side improvements, or the reappearance of the negative effects of foreign exchange risks on sales-side improvements that were counterbalanced or hidden at the incipient expected stage by derivatives, and the amount of 2800 must be now covered by new internal improvements or new exploitation of profit opportunity to maintain the originally expected sustainable value growth. As 400 (the negative influence of the foreign exchange risk on sales side) among 2800 is made good by other improvements in unaffected manufacturing side (400), the relation between the ExPO before risk-hedging and the expected profit after improvement planning against risks is illustrated as follows: 15,000 = 17,400 – 2400 – (400–400). It must be noted that although the total amount in the ExPO is secured by the expected profit (or the target profit) from which the risk amount may be deducted, the content and structure of improvements at the former stage is completely different from that at the latter stage: some of the incipient improvements on sales side are replaced by the internal improvements on manufacturing and purchasing sides.

The variance analysis of profit opportunity and risk clarifies the decrease in profit opportunities by the ineffectiveness of derivatives (1400), the reappearance of the negative effect of foreign exchange risk on profit improvements (assets or liabilities) of 400 million, against which the company originally hedged with derivatives, and the restored foreign exchange risk as a result of being separated from the derivatives trading (1000). This risk variance information, together with forecast profit opportunity variance, warns managers against risks that exceed this decrease in the expected profit opportunity. Therefore, the company should plan to increase internal profit improvements by 2800 million beyond the incipient EsPO to establish a stronger manufacturing foundation that can withstand external environmental risks and their negative effects. This information on the lost profit opportunities and the increased risks informs managers of the necessary internal level of improvements needed to maintain a durable manufacturing foundation. If the company achieves this target profit of 17,400 million based on this 2800 million in profit opportunities and risks, it can establish a stable and durable manufacturing foundation by internal profit improvements, irrespective of the ineffectiveness of derivatives and the appearance of foreign exchange risk. However, the company should always preserve 'slack' with which external business environmental risks can be internalized into profit improvements. In this sense, it should also always establish the manufacturing and management structures needed to implement external and internal improvements. Additionally, the planning process for profit opportunity and enterprise risk leads to target profit and target cost as follows:

$$EsPOs + internal\ profit\ improvements = expected\ profit\ (or\ target\ profit)$$

$$14,600 + 2800 = 17,400$$

The expected and estimated profit opportunities and risks, along with the improvement target through variance analysis, give the calculation foundation for target profit. To make sure, we indicate the relation between the COLC model and cost design (target costing) as follows:

$$\textit{Expected profit} - \textit{estimated profit} = \textit{forecast profit variance} \rightarrow \textit{proactive profit improvements}$$

$$\textit{Estimated profit} + \textit{proactive improvement amounts} = \textit{target profit}$$

$$\textit{Target profit} - \textit{actual profit} = \textit{profit variance}\left(\textit{opportunity cost variance}\right)$$

$$\text{Target profit} \rightarrow \text{allowable cost}$$

$$\textit{Allowable cost} - \textit{estimated cost} = \textit{forecast cost variance} \rightarrow \textit{proactive cost improvements}$$

$$\textit{Estimated cost} - \textit{proactive cost improvement amount} = \textit{target cost}$$

$$\textit{Target cost} - \textit{actual cost} = \textit{cost variance}\left(\textit{lost profit opportunity}\right)$$

Incorporating the COLC model into management accounting gives profit and cost targets for proactive and reactive business improvements on the basis of information about profit opportunities and risks, controls business activities according to these targets, and evaluates their performances in terms of opportunity and lost opportunity (opportunity cost). These planned values are always collated with actual data and information from middle- and lower-level management and from workers.

As mentioned above, practical improvements are estimated after multiple planned (long-term/ideal and short-term/practical) values of profit opportunities and risks are examined and compared from the viewpoint of opportunity and lost opportunity. This then gives decision-makers more practical information on estimated profit opportunities and risks by connecting these profit improvements to the original estimated values. This process allows companies to identify a target profit and target cost and to make better use of cost design and cost improvements, backed with profit opportunities and lost opportunities (opportunity costs). In a strong finance-oriented economy, this model incorporates market risks into systems of management accounting and urges managers to develop strong improvement activities to protect their manufacturing foundation from external risks. The approach put forth in this chapter may give impetus to not only the protection of firms' manufacturing foundations from market risks but also improvements and innovation in manufacturing technology and organization. At the same time, a company can compile a strategy and risk report in a simpler form for stakeholders on the basis of the COLC model and its table (see also Chap. 8; Nishimura 2015a).

9.6 Conclusion

The COLC model uses the comparison and analysis of profit opportunity and enterprise risk to identify improvement measures, proactively arrange for and implement such measures, and connect the optimum value of profit opportunity with the traditional methods of profit and cost management. The inclusion of the COLC model in management accounting can broaden managers' global and long-term outlook on decision-making and performance evaluation. This also contributes to the protection and strengthening of manufacturing activities under the strong uncertainty and financial risks of the contemporary global economy.

Concerning market risk management in management accounting, much remains to be argued and discussed because enterprises cannot perfectly manage external risks by using hedge accounting and the COLC model. Not only do risks in the external business environment ceaselessly increase both in quantity and in scope, but these changes also rise above the ability of humans to forecast completely. Derivatives, by their complicated and nontransparent nature, can act as a ticking 'time bomb' in the economy, with the resulting damage worse than in the Great Depression of the 1930s. Because at present management accounting cannot manage market risks alone by looking at internal business effectiveness and efficiency, management accountants should broaden their horizons toward global and long-term changes in social and economic structures. At the same time, just as hedge accounting and derivatives should be carried out as part of a comprehensive strategy of risk management, corporate governance and internal controls, and in close conformity with international and domestic accounting standards, so should management accounting adhere more closely to financial accounting and be more socially and economically oriented. Management accounting should strive to be sufficiently conscious of not only efficiency, effectiveness, and profitability but also disclosure, transparency, and social responsibility. It should shift from a retrospective, explanatory, and procedural standpoint to a prospective, proactive, socially aware, and creative one (Nishimura 2015a). Management accounting science, like other social science, goes on a journey from contradiction to harmony. In a system where the COLC model joins hands with such global and long-term perspectives and methods, it may contribute toward such new direction in management accounting, even though it is only a step for harmony and balance among the many contradictable and uncertain conditions present.

Notes

1. The data that are quoted here come from Yahoo! Finance: Japanese yen to American dollar [USDTP]Foreign Exchange. Each exchange rate is the closing price (mean value) on January 1 of each year from 1999 to 2015. Average rates also depend on these prices. http://info.finance.yahoo.co.jp/history/?code=USDJPY%3DX&sy=199
2. Annual securities reports of companies in Tables 9.1 and 9.2 are obtained from the data of EDINET (Electronic Disclosure for investors' NET work): http://disclosure.edinet.fs.go.jp and KABUPROP: http://www.kabupro.jp

Bibliography

Bhimani, A. (2009). Risk Management, Corporate Governance and Management Accounting: Emergence Interdependences. *Management Accounting Research, 20*(1), 2–5. https://doi.org/10.1016/j.mar.2008/11.002.

Buffet, W. (2002). *Warren Buffett's Letters to Berkshire Shareholders.* Omaha: Berkshire Hathaway, Inc. http://www.berkshirehathaway.com/letters/2002.html.

Cowell, F. (2006, November). Risk Management for Derivatives. *Derivatives Use, Trading & Regulation, 12*(3), 228–243.

Frestad, D., & Beisland, L. A. (2015). Hedge Effectiveness Testing as a Screening Mechanism for Hedge Accounting: Does it Work? *Journal of Accounting, Auditing & Finance, 30*(*1*), 35–56.

Fujita, K. (2003). Effectiveness and Limitation of Hedging Accounting. *Ritsumeikan Keieigaku, 42*(*2*), 1–18.

Gibson, M. S. (2007). Credit Derivatives and Risk Management, *Economic Review, Fourth Quarter*, pp. 25–40.

Hino Motors Ltd. (2015). *Annual Securities Report.* http://www.kabupro.jp/mark/2015622/S10050CE.h.

Hitachi Ltd. (2015). *Annual Securities Report.* http://www.kabupro.jp/edp/20150625/S10055M4.htm (2014). *EDINET.*

IASB (International Accounting Standard Board). (2014, July). *IFRS 9 Financial Instruments.* http://www.iasplus.com/en-gb/standards/ifrs-en-gb/ifrs9.

Imai, N. (2010). Proposal of Dual Mode Management Accounting Model: With a View to Dissolve "Accounting Lag". *Meijo Journal, 10*(4), 61–87.

Imai, N. (2014). Concept of Proactive Slack: A Study on Essence on Toyota's Performance Accounting. *Journal of Japan Management Diagnosis Association, 14*, 41–46.

Ito, T., Koibuch, S., Sato, K., & Shimizu, J. (2013, April). Exchange Rate Exposure and Exchange Rate Risk Management: The Case of Japanese Exporting Firms, *The Research Institute of Economy, Trade, and Industry, Discussion Paper Series, 13-E-025*.http://www.rieti.go.jp/en/.

Johnson, L. T., Bullen, H. G., & Kern, V. W. (1994, January). Hedge Accounting: Is Deferral the Only Option? *Journal Accountancy, 177*(1), 53–58.

Kawaller, I. G. (2002, September/October). Hedge Effectiveness Testing: Using Regression Analysis, *AFP Exchange, 22*(5), 62–68.

Kawaller, I. G. (2004, May/June). Ways to Test Hedge Effectiveness: Reconsidering Regression Analysis, *AFP Exchange, 24*(3), 62–63.

Kawaller, I. G., & Koch, P. D. (2013). Hedge Effectiveness Testing Revisited. *Journal of Derivatives, 21*(1, Fall), 83–94.

Kim, S., & Collier, R. (2013). Risk and Risk Management in Management Accounting and Control. *Management Accounting Research, 24*(2), 82–87. https://doi.org/10.1016/j.mar.2013.04.003.

Lombardi, L. J. (2010). Monitoring Changes in Capital and Hedge Effectiveness Under Fair Value Accounting Principles. *North American Actuarial Journal, 14*(*1*), 1–15.

McCarrol, J., & Khatri, G. R. (2014, April). Aligning Hedge Accounting with Risk Management. *Accounting Ireland, 46*(*2*), 36–38.

Mercy, S. (2006). Failures Continue Evaluating Hedge Effectiveness, SEC Official Says. *Accounting Policy & Practice Report, 2*(*25*), 1–2.

Metzger, L. (2009). Measuring Hedging Effectiveness for Derivatives. *The Journal of Government Financial Management, 58*(4, Winter), 48–53.

Mizuho ISD. (2014). How Do We Consider Weak Yen' s Influences? *Mizuho Short Industry Focus, Oct. 120*, Industrial Survey Division (ISD) of Mizuho Corporate Bank, 1–5. http://www.mizuhobank.co.jp/corporate/bizinfo/industry/pdf/msif_120.pdf.

Nishimura, A. (2011). Uncertainty and Management Accounting: Opportunity, Profit Opportunity and Profit. *Asia-Pacific Management Accounting Journal, 6*(1), 81–101. Public Knowledge Project (Open Journal System). http://arionline.uitm.edu.my/ojs/index.php/APMAJ/issue/view/13.

Nishimura, A. (2014). Transforming Cost Design Into Environmentally Conscious Cost Design in Japan: Likelihood and Problems for Further Development. *Journal of Management Control, 25*(*1*), 55–75. https://doi.org/10.1007/s00187-014-0190-x.

Nishimura, A. (2015a). Comprehensive Opportunity and Lost Opportunity Control Model and Enterprise Risk Management. *International Journal of Business and Management, 10*(*8*), 73–87. https://doi.org/10.5539/ijbm.v10n8p73.

Nishimura, A. (2015b). Strategic Management Accounting and Feed-forward Management: With Reference to the Unified Management of Profit Opportunity and Risk, *Global Management, 3 & 4 (combined)*, 1–19

Panasonic Corporation. (2014). *Sustainability Report, 2014*, 20–25. http://www.panasonic.com.jp/corporate/sustainability/downloads/back_number/pdf/2014/sr2014j.pdf.

Panasonic Corporation. (2015). *Annual Securities Report*. http://www.kabupro.jp/mark/2015626/S100562ZF.htm.

Phillips, S. M. (1995). Derivatives and Risk Management: Challenges and Opportunities. *Northwestern Journal of International Law & Business, 15*(2), 239–247.

Rasid, S. Z., Isa, C. R., & Ismail, W. K. W. (2014). Management Accounting Systems, Enterprise Risk Management and Organizational Performance in Financial Institutions. *Asian Review of Accounting, 22*(2), 128–144. https://doi.org/10.1108/ARA-03-2013-0022.

Russell-Jones, M. (2014, March). Financial Risk Management: Derivatives. *Governance Directions, 66*(2), 81–84.

Seal, W. (2006). Management Accounting and Corporate Governance: An Institutional Interpretation of the Agency Theory. *Management Accounting Research, 17(4)*, 389–408.

Shank, J. K., & Miguel, J. G. (2009, January/February). Merging Financial and Managerial Accounting, Strategic Cost Management and Enterprise Risk Assessment Under SOX, *The Journal of Corporate Accounting & Finance, 20*, 83–99.

Sipko, J. (2011). Derivatives and the Real Economy. *Creative and Knowledge Society/Industrial Specific Journal, 1*(*1*), 33–43. https://doi.org/10.2478/10212-011-0003-7.

Smistad, R., & Pustylnick, J. (2012). Hedging, Hedge Accounting and Speculation: Evidence from Canadian Oil and gas Companies. *Global Journal of Business Research, 6*(*3*), 49–62.

Tanaka, M. (Ed.). (2015). *Cost Design and the Development Strategy of Purchasing*. Tokyo: Chuokeizai Publisher.

Toyota Motor Corporation. (2015). *Annual Securities Report*. http://www.kabupro.jp/mark/20150624/S1005156.htm.

Ueno, T., & Aoyama, S. (2011). Influences of Strong Yen on Enterprise Management: Findings of Questionnaire Research by Nissay Co. in January, *NLI Research Institute Report*, April, 16–21.

Woods, M. (2008). Linking Risk Management to Strategic Controls: A Case Study of Tesco plc. *International Journal of Risk Assessment & Management, 7*(*8*), 1074–1088.

Yamaha Motor Co. Ltd. (2015). *Annual Securities Report*. http://www.kabupro.jp/mark/2015327/S1004DPT.htm.

CHAPTER 10

Synthesis of Environment, Risk, Function, and Cost in Profit Design

10.1 Introduction

This book has theoretically and positively inquired into how management and management accounting have developed during the current period of increasing uncertainty, and has discussed what their harmonious forms (in the sense discussed in this book) are in terms of functions for coping effectively with uncertainty. This chapter offers conclusions on these subjects by examining the possible development of management and management accounting in a future in which uncertainty further increases. In particular, it surveys the relationship of environment and risk with cost design as the symbolic figure of this development. This concluding examination will make reference to certain cases of Japanese manufacturing companies.

Today, besides the instability of international political affairs and the serious issues related to global warming, the globalization of the finance-oriented economy and the intensification of global competition make business management considerably unstable. Accordingly, risk and environment are truly critical issues that all enterprises must confront by building effective management and management accounting systems. This is necessary because even when a firm develops a product of high function and low cost, no enterprise can realize its profitability in markets without settling these issues first. Thus far, this book has studied the three aspects of cost design, green management, and enterprise risk management separately, but now we seek to elucidate a synthesis of their relationship, since

A. Nishimura, *Management, Uncertainty, and Accounting*,
https://doi.org/10.1007/978-981-10-8989-3_10

in actuality enterprises try to control them in concert according to their business strategy. This examination may lead us to a better understanding of the future shape of management and management accounting.

10.2 Environmentally Conscious Management and Supply Chain

As analyzed in Chap. 7, many Japanese enterprises have recently shown a strong interest in environmental preservation, and some of them have connected environmental improvement with product design and cost design. For example, Panasonic conducts compliance management through product quality management, with establishing a product environmental management scheme, including the evaluation and certification of chemical substances, energy efficiency, the '3Rs' (reduce, reuse, and recycle), and recycling regulatory compliance. This combined process ensures that the product complies with the required environmental standards through the following steps: (1) an outline of achievement targets is created at the decision-making stage of product design; (2) definite conceptual design and compliance targets are conformed with each other at the design stage; (3) an intermediate evaluation is conducted when the design stage is completed; and (4) a final evaluation is done at the decision stage prior to mass production (Panasonic Corporation 2017, p. 18). At the same time, such large companies also proactively and voluntarily grapple with environmental accounting and publish information on the carbon dioxide (CO_2) emissions of their factories across the supply chain. NEC, for example, shows the purpose of its accounting and disclosure in the following four activities: (1) evaluating the economic results of environmental activities and heightening cost consciousness; (2) identifying environmental activities that are effective and recognizing the importance of sustainable business growth; (3) sharing environmental information with interested parties; and (4) making operational improvements and reforms within the company (NEC 2017). The Ministry of Economy, Trade, and Industry (METI) and the Ministry of the Environment (MOE) of Japan enacted the 'Law Concerning the Promotion of Measures to Cope with Global Warming' in 1998 and appealed to everyone to "take this challenge [mitigating global warming] voluntarily and actively" (Ministry of the Environment 1998). In particular, this law asks enterprises, including their related parties, to formulate plans with measures to mitigate greenhouse gas emissions (or to enhance carbon sinks) in their business activities and to publicize these plans. It is noteworthy that some companies in Japan have proactively conformed to this law, voluntarily expanded management and disclosure for greenhouse gas emission, and developed new types of environmental management (e.g., environmentally conscious cost design and green accounting).

NEC provided information on CO_2 emission across the supply chain through multiple years, as shown in Table 10.1, to all people who were interested, such as shareholders, creditors, consumers, and the general public. Moreover, Table 10.2 compares NEC with Panasonic in terms of CO_2 emission in 2016.

These tables indicate the concentration of CO_2 emission in external production and consumption processes outside the companies (Scope 3), with these indirect CO_2 emission accounting for 95–97% of the total emissions in the companies and their related companies, including the supply chain. In 2016, the emissions from the use of products sold account for more than 70% of total emissions, which is followed by emissions from purchased goods and services (about 11% in NEC and 16% in Panasonic). As shown in Table 10.1, direct emission from production and consumption in internal

Table 10.1 CO_2 emission across the supply chain in NEC

Items	*2012*	*2014*	*2016*	*2017*
Scope 1: Direct emission from facilities owned and controlled within the company	8 (1)	8 (1)	6 (1)	5 (1)
Scope 2: Emission from production of energy for consumption in the above facilities	41 (5)	30 (4)	30 (3)	30 (4)
Scope 3: Other indirect emission, excluding Scopes 1 and 2 and including the supply chain[a]	**765 (94)**	**718 (95)**	**929 (96)**	**741 (95)**
Category 1: Purchased goods and services	106 (13)	83 (11)	104 (11)	104 (13)
Category 10: Processing of sold product	49 (6)	38 (5)	7 (1)	5 (1)
Category 11: Use of sold products	488 (60)	537 (71)	707 (73)	568 (73)
Other categories (excluding Categories 1, 10, and 11)	122 (15)	60 (8)	111 (11.5)	63 (8)
Total emission	814 (100)	756 (100)	965 (100)	776 (100)

Unit = 10,000 tons (%)

Source: NEC (2017). *Annual Environmental Report*: nec.com/en/global/eco/annual/index.html

[a]Scope 3 consists of 15 categories and shows the volume of greenhouse gas emission in the supply chain

Table 10.2 CO_2 Emission across supply chain in NEC and Panasonic[a]

Items	*NEC*	*Panasonic*
Scope 1: Direct emission from facilities owned and controlled within the company	6 (1)	44 (1)
Scope 2: Emission from production of energy for consumption in the above facilities	30 (3)	197 (2)
Scope 3: Other indirect emissions, excluding Scopes 1 and 2 and including the supply chain[a]	**929 (96)**	**7957.9 (97)**
Category 1: Purchased goods and services	104 (11)	1291 (16)
Category 10: Processing of sold product	7 (1)	–
Category 11: Use of sold products	707 (73)	6350 (77)
Other categories (excluding Categories 1, 10, and 11)	111 (12)	317 (4)
Total emission	965 (100)	8199 (100)

Unit = 10,000 tons (%)

Source: NEC, *Ibid*; Panasonic Corporation (2017). *Sustainable Data Book*, p. 22

[a]Panasonic reports all greenhouse gas emissions, so there may be other greenhouse gases that are included in their data after being converted into the CO_2-equivalent amount

factories within the company is decreasing, and the company must focus on the green procurement of materials and services and the production and marketing of products with low environmental burden arising from their use and disposal. By actively measuring and publishing data on CO_2 emission across its supply chain, NEC adds ecology and compliance to the conventional concepts of quality, cost, and delivery at the product development stage and copes with the reduction of environmental burden over a product life cycle from product design and production to disposal. In this case, ecology and compliance include global warming prevention (CO_2 reduction through energy-saving design), resource recycling (promotion of recycling through 3R conscious design), and environmental consciousness (control of hazardous materials through management of chemical substances included in products). To meet these objectives, the company purchases materials, parts, and services from suppliers that the company has granted a green certification in terms of high environmental consciousness and manufacturing processes, products, materials, and parts with low environmental burden (NEC 2017).

However, even though a company can maximize the relative amount of green material, parts, and products produced or purchased, the company is required to harmonize the reduction in environmental burden with its effect on production costs to ensure profitability. Therefore, social requirements for mitigating CO_2 emission necessitates that enterprises examine environmental activities across supply chains together with product life cycle costing and enterprise risk management. In other words, environmentally conscious products require not only environmentally conscious (green) procurement, green factories, and green marketing but also proactive design and planning of cost and profit at the design stage.

10.3 Green Factories and Green Products

This book has already inquired into the general situation of environmental management, in Chap. 7. However, now we examine green factories as a new phenomenon in recent years to clarify the relationship of environmental activities with cost design and profit design. Green factories are not only a keystone of product life cycle costing and of environmental activities for reducing CO_2 emission across supply chains but also a primary driver of capacity for green procurement and marketing. The aim of the 'Green Factory' is to mitigate emission of CO_2, methane, nitrogen dioxide, specified hydrofluorocarbons and perfluorocarbons, and sulfur hexafluoride—all of which are classified as 'greenhouse gases' under Japanese law (see Ministry of Environment 1998). Enterprises must convert their emissions into CO_2-equivalent amounts and publish this data. All factories in Panasonic have engaged in 'green factory activity' to reduce the environmental burden in the product manufacturing processes (Panasonic Corporation 2017, p. 27). Since 2003, Sharp has also evaluated and certified each factory in terms of hardware specifications by designating highly effective machinery and tools and appropriate approaches for using software and management to establish 'super green factories' that lead to the production of 'super green products' (Sharp Corporation 2011, pp. 39–40; 56–57).

In the case of Panasonic, its green factory model incorporates environmental activities proactively and voluntarily. Each factory makes a plan for reducing every environmental burden in production activities in regards to CO_2 emission, waste matter, generation of valuable substances, water consumption, and emission and movement of chemical substances. Each factory carries out the plan and seeks to improve its overall reduction in emission and its progress management through basic unit management, and attempts to reconcile environmental activities and business activities (Panasonic Corporation 2017, p. 27). At the same time, the company has begun to implement a green factory assessment system in which each factory evaluates itself in terms of reduction in total emissions, reinforcement of its stated objectives, efforts to reduce and mitigate risk, and human resource creation and management. Then, the factory compares its progress with that of another key factory and its self-assessment, which is meant to prompt consideration of new ideas and methods for improvement. Environmental and business improvements are carried out through 'visualization'. Fujitsu also has built a scheme that equally evaluates cost and environment burden in the production processes. These 'green process activities' aim to reduce resource input and energy consumption per manufacturing line unit and to expand activities to reduce environmental burden, the use of chemical substances such pharmaceuticals and gasoline, and the use of other energy sources in the manufacturing process (Konno et al. 2008, pp. 185–186).

Environmental activities in Panasonic's green factories have given rise to further improvement processes that have resulted in green products, which have expanded to strategic green products and super green products. In the Panasonic scheme, *green products* means products or services that pass the company's evaluation standards for advanced environmental capability in more than one of global warming mitigation, chemical substance management, effective use of resources and water, and biodiversity, while *super green products* accelerate progress toward increased environmental capability and the realization of sustainable society. In comparison, *strategic green products* contribute to accelerating the shift to a sustainable society by mitigating global environmental burden with top-class environmental capability in the business world to mitigating global environmental burden through its popularization and promotion and, in some areas, to mitigating global environmental burden or coping with the environmental burden (p. 24). The development of the green factory feeds back to production of different high-grade green products through concrete and detailed green management in each level and section of the factory. However, in practice, it is not easy to incorporate these detailed environmental activities under cost design at the product design stage.

Next, we focus our attention on the structure and problems of environmentally conscious cost design.

10.4 Structure and Problems of Environmentally Conscious Cost Design

In a cost design system, about 80% of the product life cycle cost must be estimated at the design stage. As a practical matter, since product managers and cost accountants cannot quite accurately estimate costs, some staff at Panasonic have proposed support systems for 'Front Loading of Target Cost Management' (cost design management), in which, to reduce processing costs, the estimated cost at the design stage is broken into pieces and reestimated for each product at the detailed planning stage and for each product factor at the production preparation stage by using 'comprehensive cost estimation methodology'. Each part must be redesigned through these processes, and parts are selected for effective cost improvement by using the 'redesign problem extraction method' (Yagi et al. 2009). This technique seeks to improve the precision of the estimation and detect practical and effective improvements when the estimated cost has not yet reached the target cost. Although such reforms to the cost design model may make the merging of environmental factors into cost design possible, there now exists no theory or method that can connect environmental activities with cost design except for the judgment and experience of professional managers, engineers, and cost accountants. This framework may be more theoretically and practically solidified by using value concept and value engineering.

It may well be that the accuracy and specificity of value concepts and value management will open paths together with recent efforts to deepen and refine environmental management and establish an accurate and practical cost design system such as 'Front Loading of Target Costing'. Figure 10.1 tentatively seeks to capture a possible framework in which value concept and value management help incorporate environmental management under a cost design system. This figure indicates that traditional management and costing fans out along three directions—environmental management, value management, and cost design—toward the production of green products and environmentally conscious cost design in the broad sense when viewed in terms of production flow. However, in environmentally conscious cost design (in the broad sense), enterprises typically start from sales management and green marketing and end at green procurement and purchasing management through the most important stage, green factory and target cost management. At present, environmentally conscious cost design may be examined at the stage of value creation (see Japan Environmental Management Association for Industry 2014) without linking environmentally conscious cost design at the procurement and selling stages. During purchasing management, when acting as buyers, enterprises generally first ask suppliers to provide innovative materials and high-quality parts at low cost at the appointed delivery day and then examine whether these supplies are environmentally consciousness and produce a low environmental burden. In other cases, this order

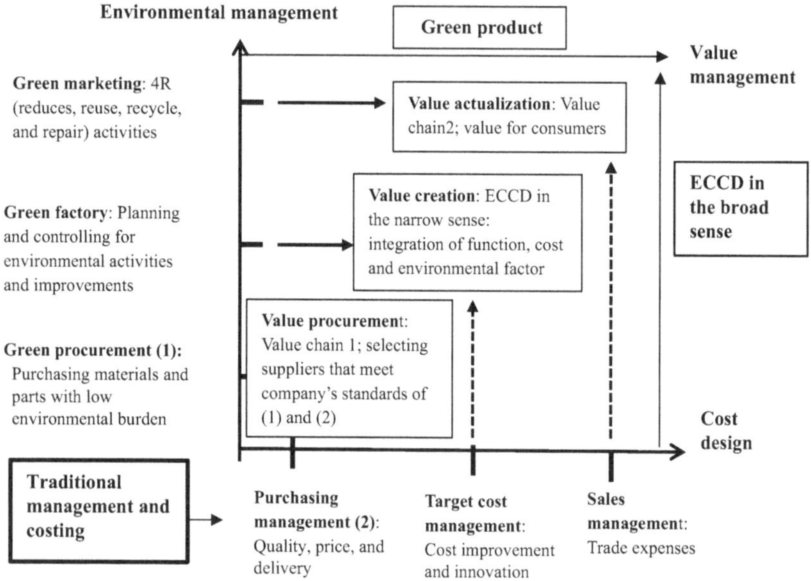

Fig. 10.1 Environmentally conscious cost design based on value. (Note: value is considered the sum total of the following ratios: the ratio of product function divided by use cost and the ratio of function of reducing environmental burden divided by countermeasure cost against it (see Industrial Environmental Management Institute 2014). (*Abbreviation*: *ECCD*, Environmentally conscious cost design)

may be inverse. In either case, at present, buyers and suppliers do not share a common environmentally conscious cost design system. Environmentally conscious cost design across the supply chain has not yet been built through mutual cooperation and support. Creating such a system is made all the more difficult at the selling stage because price is strongly influenced by changes in supply and demand. Thus, at present we must consider environmentally conscious cost design in a narrow sense. Environmentally conscious cost design cannot be implemented in a broad-based manner until an environmentally conscious cost design system is created across the whole supply chain and in related companies through the alignment and cooperation of parent companies, purchasers, and other parties. However, it is first necessary to establish environmental factors and functions that are integrated with a value concept as an axis with cost at each stage of purchasing, manufacturing, and selling before the three values can be designed and planned at the product design stage.

Further development of environmentally conscious cost design in a broad sense may be strongly influenced not only by enterprise and governmental efforts but also by strong consumer and citizen environmental consciousness. While we can now imagine environmentally conscious cost design only in its early form, management and management accounting should be further redesigned from the social and macro viewpoint.

10.5 Conceptualization of Profit Design in Relation to Environment, Risk, and Function

Reduction of environmental burden is also closely linked with the mitigation of environment burden risks, as well as with the increase in countermeasure cost against this burden. Production and consumption processes in the product life cycle are also the very processes that generate environmental burden and risks. At the same time, the product life cycle is always threatened by business environment risks such as market risk. Therefore, contemporary management and management accounting must pursue their duties to harmonize environment, risk, function, and cost to create sustainable value growth. Environmental management, enterprise risk management, and cost design must all play a specialized role in planning and controlling business activities efficiently and effectively. Simultaneously, they must be organically synthesized for sustainable business value growth from the viewpoint of harmonization and balancing beyond conflict. Moreover, cost design should also be positioned as the basis for environment- and risk-conscious cost design for affluent value creation from the proactive angles of profit opportunity and enterprise risk. At the same time, it is important to keep in mind that such synthesis and organization are also related to the organic and synthetic balancing against uncertainty that arises from the present social and natural environmental changes.

This book has analyzed key issues relating to corporate governance, uncertainty, cost management, cost design, environment, and enterprise risk management in the previous chapters. Now it is time to summarize them in a general framework for further development of management and management accounting. In particular, recent risk management and its relationship with profit design (and cost design) were analyzed in detail in

Chaps. 8 and 9. On the basis on this analysis and the contents, which theretofore have been examined in relation to uncertainty, Table 10.2 highlights the contemporary development of cost design and profit design as their roles have expanded.

As shown in Fig. 10.2, contemporary management and management accounting are made up of the two axes: market strategy (enterprise profitability) and sustainable growth strategy. Cost design in the former (indicated by the solid line) has exploited new markets through the development of new products whose cost and function (quality) are organically integrated in response to consumer demand, while profit design in the latter (indicated by the dotted line) results from the expansion of cost design over time and space to supply chain cost management and the product life cycle. In the latter, profit design, including cost design, must consider environmental and risk issues to ensure sustainable business value growth under contemporary serious uncertainty. Environment and cost are incorporated into environmentally conscious cost design, and risk and cost are also part of profit design based on the COLC model (enterprise risk management), with value as a center concept in the same way that cost and

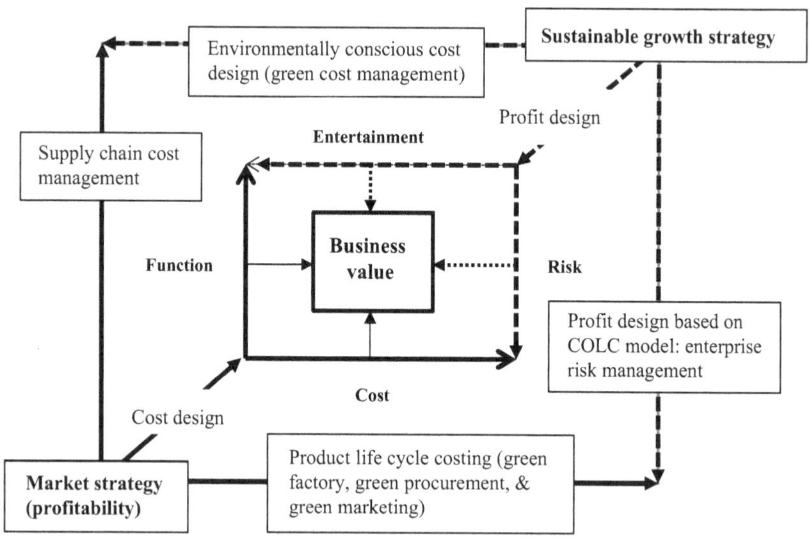

Fig. 10.2 Extension of cost design to profit design

function are united in cost design. There is a further possibility that the four concepts of function, environment, risk, and cost may be integrated under business value concept. At the same time, profit design based on the COLC model may also be integrated with environmentally conscious cost design in the form of environment- and risk-conscious profit design.

Profit design in this book is outlined as follows. At the first stage, target profit is calculated through the forecast and comparison of long-term and short-term profit opportunities and risks, with the proactive implementation of profit improvement using the framework of the COLC model. At the second stage, allowable cost is forecasted from a long-term perspective on the basis of this target profit, and estimated cost is calculated by using the piling-up method of practical data on business value ([reduced environmental burden/countermeasure cost + product function/use cost] and countermeasure cost against risks). Then target cost for controlling business activities is decided after proactively carrying out cost improvement when it is less than the allowable cost (long-term planned cost). At the same time, this process is deployed in a manner that allows the circulation of feed-forward and feedback control. This synthesis of profitability strategy and sustainable business growth strategy implies not only the contemporary evolution of harmonious function in management and management accounting but also the present deepening of uncertainty (fast change and growing complexity).

Bibliography

Japan Environmental Management Association for Industry. (2014). *IIB Environmental Management Accounting. Text in Environmental Management Practical Course.* http://meti.go.jp/policy/recycle/main/3r_policy/pdf/text_2.2.b.pdf.

Konno, J., Yashima, K., & Mizunaga, K. (2008). Environmental Improvement Activities in Semiconductor Factories. *FUJITSU, 52*(2), 185–189.

Ministry of the Environment. (1998). *Law Concerning the Promotion of the Measures to Cope with Global Warming.* https://env.jo.jp/en/laws/global/warming.html.

NEC (2017). *Annual Environmental Report.* Nippon Electronic Corporation. https://nec.com/en/global/eco/annual/index.html; Environment Accounting: https://nec.com/en/global/eco/announce/accounting/calculate.html.

Panasonic Corporation (2017). *Sustanability Data Book 2017.* https://www.panasonic.com/jp/corporate/sustanability/pdf/sdb2017/pdf.

Sharp Corporation (2011). *Environmental and Social Report.* https://www.sharp.world.com/eco/report/backnumber/pdf/esr2011e.pdf.

Yagi, K., Araki, H., & Akiyma, K. (2009, September). Support Systems for Front Loading of Target Cost Management. *Panasonic Works' Technical Report, 57* (3), 76-82.

CHAPTER 11

Recent Development and Features of Management System in China: The Case of Cellular Phone Handset Manufacturers

11.1 Introduction

The aim of this chapter is to clarify the general tendency and the background of recent developments in management system including management accounting in China with reference to the cellular phone handset manufacturing industry. Chinese production and management systems are examined in contrast with the Japanese situation, and, at the same time, a bipolar divergence occurring between the prosperous and the defeated enterprises in Chinese cellular phone handset production is analyzed. It is clarified that the driving force behind the emergence of a new management system in China is the global expansion of Chinese multinational enterprises. The process whereby state-owned enterprises reorganize the defeated enterprises by broadly raising social capital is worthy of attention since such activities will drive management system development forwards.

This chapter fundamentally makes clear the present general framework and the future of Chinese management system. It begins by examining the background as well as the recent tendencies of Chinese management system through an analysis of Chinese economic and business growth. The features of the Chinese management systems are then compared with those of the Japanese systems. Lastly, it is concluded that the current reorganization occurring in Chinese enterprises will produce a strong driving force for the emergence of a new third wave of development in international management system.

A. Nishimura, *Management, Uncertainty, and Accounting*,
https://doi.org/10.1007/978-981-10-8989-3_11

11.2 Background and Present Features of Chinese Management System

Chinese management system, when considered from the angle of its international relationships, has developed in three stages, from nationality (independence and autonomy, and commodity economy) during the period 1949–1990 through introduction and learning from the West (conformity to international standards), and shifting to market economy during 1990–2000 to nationality based on internationalization at present time (Table 11.1). After the adoption of reform and open policy in 1978, the Chinese government, enterprises, and academic circles, intent on joining the World Trade Organization (WTO) in 2001, started not only to introduce advanced methods and theories of management system from Western countries but also to modernize its management system differently from the strong ethnic characteristics isolated earlier from Western countries. Chinese contemporary management system is characterized as nationality based on internationalization or the integration of nationality and internationalization.

Recently, Chinese enterprises and management have shown strong interest in value-chain management, value-based management, balanced scorecard (BSC), activity-based costing (ABC), and corporate governance, and tend to favor more strongly American-type management methods over the Japanese methods which are characterized by cost design, cost improvement (Genka Kaizen), and total quality control.

Table 11.1 Relations between Chinese management system and the West

- **First Stage (1945–2000): Management system isolated from the West; the period of responsibility accounting**

1. 1945–1978: cost responsibility (cost control); productivity; enterprise budget as part of national planning; accounting as part of statistics
2. 1978–1985: profit responsibility; profit contracting system; joint-stock company
3. 1985–2000: cost responsibility based on market price: market principle; simulated market and rejection by cost evaluation; strong direction toward market economy

- **Second Stage (2000–present): Introduction of Western management system; entering the WTO**

ABC; BSC; value added; performance evaluation; Just-In-Time

- **Third Stage (present to future): Nationality based on internalization**

Generalization; trans-management science; conformity; empirical study; speed economy (enterprise governance, internal control, risk management)

At the same time, they also stress the generalization of various management methods, conformity with international standards, trans-economy, empirical study, and speed economy. These concepts thoroughly embody the contemporary general features of Chinese business management and accounting.

It is noteworthy that this latest trend of management system basically originated from the global development of Chinese enterprises and their strong desire for dominant control over the international market. Thus, their internationalization does not require simply adapting their management systems to international standards, but also actualizing the most suitable combination of international management methods from the global viewpoint. As a result, in efforts to identify and select the best from among international practices and theories, researches on management system in China have broadened in scope and become more practical, tending toward a general and common approach in order to develop a Chinese type of management system that is universally useful.

11.3 The Recent Chinese Economy and Enterprise Globalization

In order to make clear how such a general and global tendency for development came about, it is important to examine recent economic circumstances and the situations in which enterprises are operating in China. The growth rate of the Chinese economy has been very high and stable over the past ten years (Sakamoto 2007); the annual growth rate has consistently been higher than 7.5% of GDP and shows a tendency to ascend due to the increase in fixed capital formation and trade balance: in terms of the contribution rate to GDP, the fixed capital formation was 42.31% in 2006 against 34.35% in 1995, while the trade balance was 5.59% against 1.64, respectively (see Table 11.2).

At present, the export structure, which relies upon the heavy and machinery industries, is completely different from the previous export-led economy which mainly depended upon light industries such as textile goods and toys. As Table 11.3 shows, the increased fixed capital investment which is closely related to export is concentrated on the machinery and processing industries, consisted mainly of manufacturers of communication and information machinery, electronic apparatus, automobiles, and steel. Among them, the liquid crystal television and the cellular phone

Table 11.2 Contribution of each expenditure to GDP

Factors	*1995*	*2001*	*2006*
Final private consumption expenditure	46.67	46.22	38.73
Final governmental consumption expenditure	13.78	15.79	14.21
Total fixed capital formation	34.35	34.11	42.31
Increase of inventory	7.5	1.01	1.14
Net trade balance of money, property, and service	**1.64**	**2.41**	**5.59**

Source: Sakamoto (2007)

Table 11.3 Production growth of main electrical machines, motorcar, and steel

	2000	*01*	*02*	*03*	*04*	*05*	*06 (Production volume)*
Mobile telephone	1	1.5	2.3	3.5	**4.5**	**5.8**	**9.2** (480 million)
Micro-computer	1	1.3	2.2	**4.8**	**8.9**	**12.0**	**13.9** (93 million)
Integrated circuit	1	1.1	1.6	2.5	**4.0**	**4.6**	**5.7** (33,575 million)
Color television	1	1.0	1.3	1.7	1.9	2.1	2.1 (83.8 million)
Motorcar	1	1.1	1.6	2.2	2.5	2.8	3.5 (7.3 million)
Steel	1	1.2	1.5	1.8	2.4	2.9	3.6 (469 million ton)

Source: National Bureau of Statistic of China (2007)

industries are important contributors to the increased GDP. This table also shows the rapid increase in mobile phone, micro-computer, and integrated circuit productions after 2000.

At the same time, the export of office electronics supplies and computer machinery shows an increase, contributing strongly to increased total exports (Table 11.4).

Chinese big businesses in the electronic machinery industry have developed under such conditions and since Western multinationals launched into this sector. These Chinese and Western enterprises are presently driving the global increase in production and export of communication and information machinery and appliances. Figure 11.1 shows the rapid growth of the main Chinese cellular phone manufacturers, although they as yet have failed to dominate the domestic market; the share of Western firms was 59.4% against the 40.6% share of domestic firms in 2005 (Xu and Imai 2007).

The fortunes of these Chinese companies are characterized between 2000 and 2003 by rapid growth and development, both domestically and internationally. Such growth owes much to the governmental assistance,

Table 11.4 Exports of communication and information machinery products

(US$ billions)

Items	1995	1998	2001	2004	2006 (times of 95)
Total amount	148.8	183.8	266.1	593.3	**971 (6.5)**
Machinery	21.07	27.38	35.6	45.21	47.07 (2.23)
Office electronics supplies, computer machinery	3.23	6.44	8.86	14.68	**13.81 (4.28)**
Communication machinery	5.65	6.04	8.93	11.54	12.79 (2.26)

Source: Sakamoto (2007)

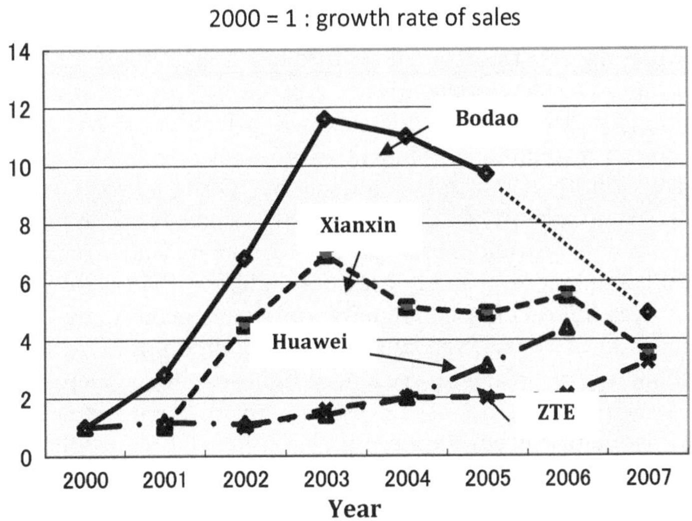

Fig. 11.1 Sales trend of the main Chinese cellular phone manufacturers. (Data for each cellular phone manufacturer are quoted from their financial reports and edited for the purpose of this article: http://www.chinabird.com/zh-cn/about/; http://money.finance.sina.com.cn/corp/go.ghp/vFD_FinancialGuideLine/stocid/600057/displaytype/4.pthml; http://www.cinafo.com.cn/gszx/gszx000100.html; http://www.cinifo.com.cn/gszx/gszx6000057.html; http://share.jrj.com.cn/cominfo/ggdetail_2008-06-07_600,057_648490_stock.htm: ZTE Corporation Annual Report, 2007 and its Summary; Xiaxin Electronic Joint-Stock Company Annual Report 2005, Annual Report Summary 2006 and Annual Report 2007: Huawei Technologies Co., Ltd. Annual Report 2004, 2006 and 2007)

the production systems employed, and the plentiful supply of foreign currency brought in through exports. Specifically with regard to production systems, in principle, every country at the present time has the capability to easily produce a finished product of low cost and high quality by combining modules (parts) thanks to the development of advanced and widely modular parts (appliances). Chinese enterprises have also made the best use of their status as a newcomer into the mature industry by introducing the best technologies and parts from overseas before developing their own technological and design capabilities adequately. Through this strategy, they can use cheap domestic labor to penetrate the international market. Communication equipment (particularly handset) manufacturers in China have depended upon overseas outsourcing and modularization of design, technology, and parts and expanded their sales from domestic markets (from rural districts to urban cities) through Asia and Africa to America and Europe. This development is just a process of national strategy from 'absorbing foreign power' to 'going abroad', which also shifts from closed stable economy to unstable competitive economy (see also Chap. 12).

In addition, the Chinese government has supported some enterprises of good standing by strictly limiting the establishment of communication enterprises and providing financial aid to nurture and strengthen the national communication and information industry while exercising social control over information communication simultaneously. In 1999, the promulgation of 'Some Proposals for the Promotion of Development in the Mobile Communication Machinery Industry' by the Department of State covered such issues as the prohibition of overinvestment in the cellular phone machinery industry, the licensing of production and marketing of cellular phone handsets, control over the extensive foreign capital investment, encouragement for domestic manufacturers to develop their businesses, and the investigation into and permission for the enhancement of production capacity (Xu and Imai 2007). These regulations were aimed at accelerating the development of the Chinese mobile communication machinery industry and control over antisocial information for reasons of national defense. Thus, Chinese cellular phone machinery manufacturers had more advantageous conditions for business expansion than their counterparts from overseas. Chinese enterprises also took a positive attitude to comply with national policies. For example, Huawei[1] has maintained a strong connection with the national defense force and conforms closely to the doctrines of the Communist Party and the state, despite its private company status. Private enterprises autonomously and positively utilize the Communist Party's or government's ideas and rules to awaken a spirit of nationality and build an enterprise community bound together by common fate. According to Cheng and Liu (2008), Ren Zhengfei, president of Huawei, which started business as 'a civil science and technology company' based on 'employee stock ownership' in 1987, says with reference to nationality in business: "Employees should do their best for Chinese prosperity, the development of Chinese nationality, and the fortune and happiness of themselves and their families." He also states the following: that the independence of technology is a fundamental problem; the independence of industry would simply be groundless without its own main prop of science and technology; there is no independence of a nation without national industry; and only the Chinese can resolve this issue themselves. On the basis of this notion, he set a target for his firm to achieve: "the development of national industry should depend on the development of its own science and technology and catch up with the most forefront technologies in the world in order to occupy the Chinese domestic market, find a new overseas market, and cope with competitors of the same industry overseas". With regard to the relationship between opportunity and technology, he holds that a person can realize an opportunity by himself, but there must be a tool for him to realize that opportunity. The tool is simply technology, where technology creates a new product and opens up a new market to create another opportunity afresh. This is an ascending spiral. According to Huawei, technology is only a means and the goal is market entry.

Globalization of Production and Markets in ZTE and Its New Third Wave in International Management System

As shown in Fig. 11.1, Bodao and Xianxin, whose mobile phone manufacture grew up depending on a French firm for handset parts and assembling production line and on Korean manufacturers and design houses for cellular phone handsets and exploiting a new market of low-end models in rural districts, began to lose their dominant position in 2003, when other firms started to establish their own design houses and exploit new markets of middle- and high-end models according to newly rising consumer demand. ZTE and Huawei, which had close relationship with telecommunication carriers, came to the fore toward the international market by entering into high-end and multifunctional model markets (Kimura 2010;

Marukawa 2009). Let us now examine the globalized development of mobile phone production and its sales in ZTE, which is famous for a successful 'government-owned and civil-operated' business model, to clarify fundamental characteristics of Chinese mobile phone industry and backgrounds that raise a new wave in international management system.

As Tables 11.5 and 11.6 indicate, the sales of handset and its contribution to the whole revenue began to increase from 2007 in contrast to the previous stagnant situation and they continued to grow up with higher speed. Handset products became one of the major sources of revenue for the company. In 2012, its contribution ratio to the total revenue became 30.68% (see Table 11.6). Handset manufacturing played an important role in developing business strategy as compared with other product segments. On the one hand, ZTE depended upon Korea in development of handsets, and the design and research of integrated circuits are the same as Bodao and Xianxin; on the other hand, it had already established a controlling subsidiary in the United States for research and development of soft-switch technologies in 2004 (ZTE Annual Report 2004, p. 135), and started to secure a strongpoint in Shenzhen for development and design

Table 11.5 Growth of each product segment's revenue and its ratio to total revenue in ZTE (2004–2007) (Unit: million RMB)

Product segments	*Growth rate of revenue by products*				*Ratio of each product revenue to the total revenue (%)*			
	2004	*2005*	*2006*	*2007*	*2004*	*2005*	*2006*	*2007*
Wireless communications systems	1 (9640.4)	0.93	0.95	1.54	42.5	41.1	39.9	42.7
Wireline switched and access system	1 (2851.1)	0.97	0.80	0.47	12.6	12.8	9.9	3.9
Optical and data communications systems	1 (2562.2)	1.31	1.51	2.48	11.3	15.5	16.8	18.3
Handsets	**1 (6015)**	**0.72**	**0.75**	**1.27**	**26.5**	**20.1**	**19.6**	**22**
Telecommunication software systems, services, and other products	1 (1629.5)	1.35	1.95	2.8	7.2	10.2	13.8	13.1
Total	1 (22698.2)	100	0.95	100	100	100	100	100

Source: *ZTE Corporation Annual Report*, 2004, 2005, 2006, 2007

Table 11.6 Growth and ratio of each product to total revenue (2008–2014) in ZTE (unit: billion RMB)

Product segments	*Growth rate of revenue by products (the base of 1: 2008)*				*Ratio of each product revenue to the total revenue (%)*			
	2008	*2010*	*2012*	*2014*	*2008*	*2010*	*2012*	*2014*
Carrier's networks	1 (29.96)	1.40	1.39	1.56	67.65	59.76	49.40	57.40
Terminal	**1 (9.69)**	**1.85**	**2.67**	**2.39**	**21.88**	**25.51**	**30.68**	28.37
Telecommunication software systems, services, and other products	1 (5.64)	1.84	2.98	2.06	12.73	14.72	19.92	14.22
Total	1 (44.29)	1.59	1.90	1.84	100	100	100	100

Note: Terminal is also used as 'Handsets terminals' in annual report 2014, including mobile phone handsets, data card products, and so on

Source: *ZTE Corporation Annual Report*, 2008, 2010, 2012, 2014

of mobile phone and its components and sales points in the United Kingdom, Brazil, Thailand, Russia, and so on. ZTE adopted a different strategy from such a traditional one as Bodao, which mainly focused on exploiting domestic immature markets, and fixed its eyes on the international market on the basis of close connection with communication industry from early on (Kimura 2010, 192–3; ZTE Annual Report 2004, pp. 135–143).

ZTE group has implemented 'differentiation and cost-leadership strategy' and enhanced 'financing capabilities and market-driven research and development capabilities' to pursue stable business development. In the production of handsets, the group depends on outsourcing of liquid crystal modules to a specialized subsidiary company (Shenzhen Lead communications Company, Limited) for their production and independent third companies for purchasing of various electronic components in place of the subsidiary company to fast produce handsets with effective cost and high quality on a large scale. Because assembling liquid crystal display with various electronic components by its own company was a low-value-added work, ZTE adopted outsourcing and modularization to transform its work into a cost-effective and flexible one. As a result, the group could "serve carriers' requirement for bulk purchases by providing quality low-end product as well as high-end intelligence/differentiation products and mobile broadband products" (ZTE annual report 2008, pp. 60–77, 98–99.) This outsourcing and the specialized production of liquid crystal modules to a subsidiary company and third manufacturers aimed at being not only cost-effective but also "steady, reliable, and quality supplies of liquid crystal modules for the group handset products" (p. 99).

Tables 11.7 and 11.8 show that increasing sales and low cost of sales resulted in advantageous profit margin from 2005 to 2010. As the cost of sales in handset products declines, their profit margin continues to grow up from 2005 to 2010 in contrast to the declining margin of the whole products in the company. This also results from the company's market strategy shifting from the domestic market through Asia and Africa to America, Europe, and Oceania on the basis of 'differentiation and cost-leadership strategy' or 'cost advantage and technological edge'. The company could globally expand the international market by using 'quality low-end products and high-end intelligence/differentiation products' properly (ZTE

Table 11.7 Revenue and cost of handset in ZTE (Unit: million RMB)

	(a) Operating revenue	*(b) cost of sales*	*b/a %*	*(c) % total*
2003	3623.7	2951.7	83.8	63
2004	6015	5150.8	85.6	63.3
2005	4333.1	3575	82.5	64.6
2006	4510.5	3375.2	74.8	65.9
2007	7645.1	5939.8	77.7	66.1
2008	9692.6	7393	76.3	66.6

Note: c shows the ratio of the cost of sales to sales (revenue) in the whole products in ZTE

Source: *ZTE Annual Report from 2003 to 2008*

Table 11.8 Revenue and cost of terminals in ZTE (Unit: million RMB)

	(a) Operating revenue	*(b) cost of sales*	*b/a %*	*(c) %*
2009	13,080.9	9770.9	74.7	69.1
2010	17,928.2	14,288.8	79.7	69.2
2012	25,838.8	21,498.7	83.2	76.1
2014	23,117.1	19,549.6	84.6	68.4

Note: c shows the ratio of the cost of sales to sales (revenue) in the whole products in ZTE; terminals include handsets, data card, fixed terminals, and so on

Source: *ZTE Annual Report, 2009, 2010, 2012, 2014*

Table 11.9 Growth and ratio of operational income to the total income by geographic segments in ZTE

	Growth of revenue (the base of 1:2004) Unit: billion RMB							*Ratio of revenue in each area to the total*						
	2004	*2005*	*2006*	*2008*	*2010*	*2012*	*2014*	*2004*	*2005*	*2006*	*2008*	*2010*	*2012*	*2014*
China	1(17.8)	0.77	0.72	0.98	1.81	2.22	2.28	78	54	56	39	46	47	50
Asia	1(2.63)	1.74	**2.19**	**3.97**	**4.82**	**6.10**	4.61	12	21	25	24	18	19	15
Africa	1(1.62)	1.75	1.58	**5.75**	**6.57**	4.83	3.81	7	13	11	21	15	9	8
Europe, America, and Oceania	**1(0.65)**	**0.46**	**2.97**	**10.98**	**22.86**	**32.22**	**35.02**	3	1	**8**	**16**	**21**	**25**	**28**
Total	1(22.7)	0.95	1.01	1.95	3.10	3.71	3.59	100	100	100	100	100	100	100

Annual Report 2008, 13, 60, 77, 99). Table 11.9 indicates the successful situation of this market strategy. The company counterbalanced the reduction of sales in the domestic market with increased sales in Europe, America, and Oceania. Although sales in Europe, America, and Oceania continue to increase, the sales and profit margin of handset products as well as the whole products begin to decline from 2014 with their rising cost of sales and to expose themselves to sever international competition.

The development process of ZTE business puts itself into step with the national strategic shift from 'absorbing foreign power' to going abroad' and at the same time expresses a new epoch when global firms such as ZTE and Huawei should compete with Western global enterprises for struggling for a larger share of the international market under an unstable and uncertain economy. Nowadays, ZTE establishes corporate governance, internal control, and risk management to dispel various uncertainties in the same way as Western enterprise. At the same time, all global firms in the world may be confronted by much severer competition and should grapple with much severer uncertainty and risks than they used to. In a sense, at present all global enterprises live in a new epoch of very unforeseeable uncertainty.

Chinese enterprises can also avail themselves of outstanding technologists as a result of strengthened education in science and technology and utilize in cooperation with local governments or social capitalists the huge funds to support their business operations. On the basis of the above analysis, the following section will discuss and compare the structure and features of Chinese with Japanese management system.

11.4 Structure of the Chinese Production and Management System in Reference to that of the Japanese

Structure and Features of Chinese Production and Management System

As such new production departments as cellular phone and liquid crystal television evolved in China, their manufacturers must also actively introduce some modern systems and thoughts from the West for modernization of management and accounting that supported these productions. Their management styles are now shifting to a new integration of nationality and internationalization, a process which shows potential for starting the third wave in international management system. This third wave can be compared with the first wave of Western management system distinguished by strategic decision-making, expansion of management accounting to nonfinancial information (ABC), organizational identity (BSC), and future-looking thought, and with the second wave of Japanese type management system characterized by the integration of low cost and high quality, cost design, and feed-forward control. The third wave absorbs the outcomes of the first and the second waves to formulate a new combination type of management system, which originated from the production strategy of Chinese enterprises aimed at integrating high quality, low cost, and quick delivery through the import of advanced technologies and modules from foreign countries on the basis of cheap domestic labor and plentiful economic resources. This aims to pursue maximum profit opportunity by using advanced methods which foreign companies have developed to exploit profit opportunity and minimize enterprise risk. A special feature of Chinese business management is that this pursuit is implemented under strong governmental leadership.

Contemporary management in China does not merely take the modular-type dealing with the import and combination into the manufacturing process of advanced and cheap parts, facilities, and technologies (Huang 2006). More important is the global integration of market and production strategies, which is in contrast to the business integration found in Japan where enterprises have integrated cost management with market strategy and created cost design from the feed-forward viewpoint. Chinese enterprises identify and select advanced design, apparatus, and technologies from across the world, combine them, and use or transform them into the cheapest and highest quality goods by using their own cheap labor and resources according to the international market condition, selling them first in the domestic market and continually extending their business to Western countries through the Asian and African markets. Their production and market strategy depend upon Mao Zedong's doctrine of rural revolution (revolution from rural to urban communities). Cheng Dongsheng and Liu Leilei (2008) explain Huawei's technology strategy as follows: "Its purpose is not to become the technology leader, but to weaken, give a blow to, and annihilate a rival in a market. Therefore, we adopt different methods and develop different levels and kinds of technologies against different rivals under different situations." This way of thinking is derived from Mao Zedong's martial strategy. According to this doctrine, Chinese enterprises try to reap everything they can from the international market. Their main strategy is price oriented, since quality is guaranteed by the advanced parts and technologies imported from foreign countries and abundant cheap domestic labor. As a result, the strategy is short term in nature and rather similar to America where the stockholders' standpoint is regarded as important. Their business growth is very strong and fast, although short-term price competition can drive some of them into dangerous situations or indeed just nothing short of bankruptcy. Indeed, the law of the jungle extends from the domestic to the international market, naturally creating a bipolar division between successful and defeated enterprises in the domestic market. This type of management system is known as the 'combined or modular management system', which not only optimally combines a system of advanced parts and technologies introduced from foreign countries but also harnesses internationally superior technologies and markets just like a 'combine harvester'.

The Comparison of the Chinese Management System with the Japanese

As already mentioned, strategic management system is simultaneously global and aggressive in Chinese enterprises. Japanese management system, on the other hand, is characterized by the proactive integration of market strategy and cost management and feed-forward control, in which cost design is carried out on the basis of virtual or estimated markets by establishing its own development and design of technologies and products. The long-term virtual cost is reciprocally collated with short-term competitive cost in the target cost at the level of product design prior to production. This is altogether long-term strategic cost management, characterized by self- development and design of the production system based on market strategy. We can sum up these features in Fig. 11.2 (Nishimura 2003).

By contrast, the contemporary production and management system of Chinese enterprises are characterized by feedback control and are a modular in which the best parts and technologies harnessed globally are combined with cheap domestic labor and resources in the most suitable design for differentiated demand. This integration of foreign advanced technologies and cheap labor has produced a fan-shaped market strategy in which marketing has gradually spread from the domestic to the Western markets through the Asian-African markets. Therefore, this short-term and aggressive strategy with feedback as its control, which is characterized by repeated

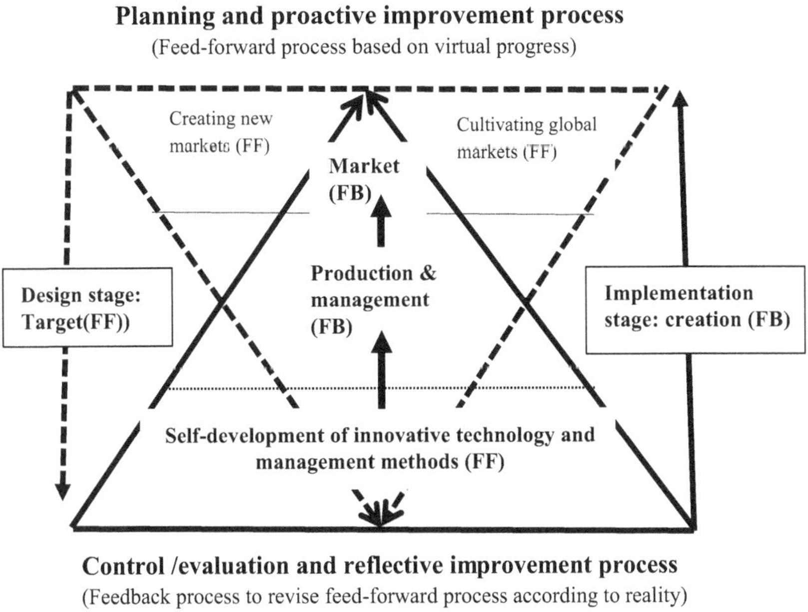

Fig. 11.2 Framework of Japanese management system

'trial and error' (practices and reflections) based on Tables 11.7 and 11.8, show that increasing sales and low cost of sales resulted in advantageous profit margin from 2005 to 2010.

Chinese cellular phone handset manufacturers have been strongly concerned with technology superiority, since they believed that it could lead to the monopolistic dominance over the international market. Because market strategy was not integrated with strategies of original technology development beforehand, in other words, it relied on the feedback strategic system, the immoderate dependency on overseas technology caused a bipolar diversity between the defeated and undefeated enterprises.

Although foreign enterprises also use cheap labor and resources in China and combine them with their own technologies to produce strategic competitive goods and promote their sales in the Chinese market, at present Chinese enterprises more effectively and more efficiently use foreign technologies from the global viewpoint of combining them with their labor and other resources in order to place their price-competitive goods

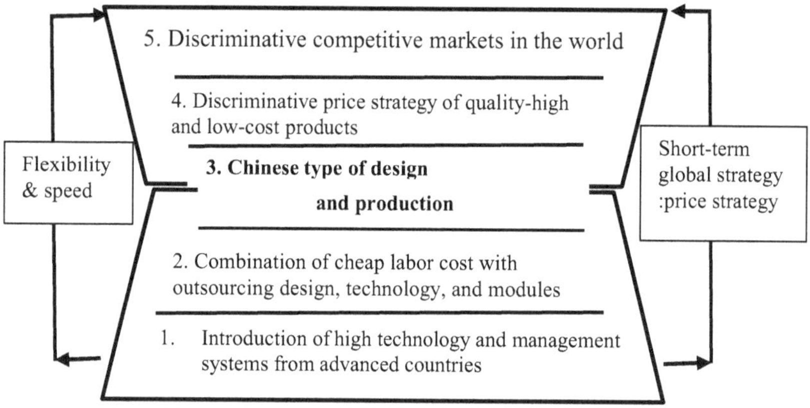

Fig. 11.3 Framework of Chinese management system

in the international market (Fig. 11.3). In particular, TCL group[2] placed priority on the internationalization of product manufacturing ahead of product marketing, and Ai Xinnan (2008) viewed such a strategy as the cause of this company's ultimate downfall. Bodao[3] also adopted the internationalization of technologies and parts under governmental support and extended its market into small rural towns in China (Kawamura 2008). Placing greater importance on production internationalization rather than marketing internationalization has become a general trend among cellular phone manufacturers (Li 2007).

While many Chinese enterprises can easily make inroads into new markets helped by short-term technology development, price competition, and the import and application of foreign design technology and parts, most of them promptly fall into a bad situation. The reason for this is the big investment risks entailed in developing a practically indistinguishable technology under competition conditions of severe cost reduction when the demand of the market is supplied by those enterprises which are in a more advantageous position in terms of price competition. Such a situation aptly illustrates the operation of 'the survival of the fittest' in the Chinese market and its related markets. In the production area of cellular phone machinery, Huawei[4] and ZTE[5] continue to be prosperous and to grow, while Bodao, Xiaxin,[6] and TCL struggle with adversity (Tables 11.10 and 11.11). Right now, huge multinational corporations such as Huawei and ZTE, which have tremendous capital

Table 11.10 Financial conditions from 2002 to 2007 in ZTE

Items	*2002*	*2003*	*2004*	*2005*	*2006*	*2007*
Sales (hundred million yuan)	1 (108)	1.58	1.96	2.00	2.13	3.22
Cost of sales	1 (69.2)	1.62	2.00	2.04	2.20	3.32
Operating profit	**1 (10.2)**	**1.43**	**1.70**	**1.75**	**1.16**	**0.98**
Gross profit	1 (38.7)	1.50	1.91	1.93	2.01	3.04
Gross profit rate of sales (%)	1 (35.8)	0.95	0.98	0.97	0.94	0.95
Cost rate of sales	1 (64.1)	1.03	1.02	1.02	1.03	1.03
Operating profit rate of sales	**1 (9.4)**	**0.91**	**0.86**	**0.88**	**0.54**	**0.3**
Net profit rate of sales	**1 (6.5)**	**0.93**	**0.92**	**0.92**	**0.51**	**0.64**
Gross profit rate of gross assets	**1 (7.6)**	**1.03**	**1.00**	**0.94**	**0.51**	**0.58**
Turnover of total assets	1 (0.9)	1.15	1.12	1.07	0.96	0.99

Net profit: disposable profit

Source: Annual Report in ZTE: see note (5)

Table 11.11 Financial conditions from 2002 to 2007 in Xiaxin

Items	*2002*	*2003*	*2004*	*2005*	*2006*	*2007*
Sales (hundred million yuan)	**1 (44.87)**	**1.52**	**1.13**	**1.07**	**1.21**	**0.77**
Cost of sales	1 (28.11)	1.60	1.42	1.51	1.55	1.11
Operating profit	1 (16.77)	0.33	0.62	0.34	0.64	0.19
Net profit	**1 (6.07)**	**1.01**	**0.02**	**−1.08**	**0.00**	**−0.01**
Operating profit rate of sales (%)	1 (37.36)	0.22	0.55	0.32	0.53	0.25
Cost rate of sales	1 (62.64)	1.05	1.26	1.41	1.28	1.45
Net profit rate of sales	**1 (13.53)**	**0.67**	**0.02**	**−1.01**	**0.00**	**−0.02**
Gross profit on gross asset	**1 (21.98)**	**0.64**	**0.01**	**−0.70**	**−0.11**	**−1.16**
Turnover of total assets	1 (1.63)	0.97	0.73	0.69	0.78	0.70

Net profit: disposable profit

Source: Annual Reports in XiaXin: see note (6)

power and tie up with governmental policies, are emerging from China to shape the third wave of management and management accounting globally (see Tables 11.5–11.9).

When we come to think of the characteristics of Chinese type of management system from not the historical but the spatial viewpoint, it is speedy and the cheapest based on world marketing strategy and modular management as opposed to profitability and efficiency based on strategic decision-making and organizational identity in the United States as well as integration of low cost and high quality based on marketability (market share) and technological development in Japan. Thus, the Chinese management system stresses speed economy, value chain, and conformity: selection and concentration, and nationality and internationality of management system. The modular or combined system of Chinese management system focuses particularly on a global and practical viewpoint, which is more in favor of the American management accounting methods (e.g., Activity-based Management [ABM], Balanced Scorecard [BSC], value chain, and Economic Value Added [EVA]) than the Japanese methods, and, simultaneously, it is interested in the concepts of speed economy, multilateral and cross economy, empirical study, corporate governance, and conformity. Presently, Chinese enterprises encounter intense international competition as a result of joining the WTO (the international market), although they have undoubtedly learnt much about the aforementioned advanced management methods used overseas. Thus, they recognize the advantages and disadvantages of these new methods and are busy creating a new type of management system based on internationalization.

The fundamental nature of feedback control which lays a foundation for Chinese management system may also hold fast to the traditional management accounting such as standard costing and budgetary control and be more strongly attracted to American management accounting, which has developed novel systems (e.g., ABC) based on feedback control, than to Japanese cost design based on feed-forward control.

11.5 The Bipolar Diversity of Chinese Enterprises and Reorganization

There exists bipolar diversity in the cellular phone industry between firms showing sustainable growth and firms that have experienced defeat as a natural consequence of short-term severe price competition. As shown in Tables 11.5–11.9, although all the companies were more or less influenced in the period from 2002 to 2007 by global economic conditions, there was obviously difference in their influence on individual company. It is clear that the four companies in the tables generally weakened the rate of earnings on total capital particularly from 2004 to 2007, but their weakening degree vary with each sales power and cost performance. Bodao, TLC, and Xiaxin companies very rapidly fell into decline and since 2004 have yet to recover. Conversely, Huawei as well as ZTE also continue to grow as world companies. These tables indicate the continually stable financial situation of ZTE against the rapid drop in sales and profits of Bodao and Xiaxin (Tables 11.12 and 11.13).

Table 11.12 Financial conditions from 2002 to 2007 in Bodao

Items	*2002*	*2003*	*2004*	*2005*	*2007*
Sales (hundred million yuan)	**1 (63.68)**	**1.70**	**1.61**	**1.42**	**0.72**
Cost of sales	1 (48.48)	1.85	1.79	1.73	0.93
Net profit	**1 (2.16)**	**1.13**	**0.96**	**−2.18**	**−2.75**
Operating profit rate of sales (%)	1 (16.87)	0.72	0.65	0.32	0.05
Cost rate of sales	**1 (76.13)**	**1.09**	**1.11**	**1.21**	**1.3**
Net profit rate of sales	**1 (3.39)**	**0.67**	**0.6**	**−1.54**	**−3.84**
Gross profit rate of gross asset	1 (20.61)	0.93	0.54	−1.7	−3.81
Turnover of total assets	1 (1.67)	1.64	1.20	1.07	0.99

Net profit: disposable profit

Source: Annual Reports in Bodao: see note (3)

Table 11.13 Financial conditions from 2002 to 2007 in TCL

	2002	*2003*	*2004*	*2005*	*2006*	*2007*
Net profit (hundred million yuan)	**1 (4.42)**	**1.35**	**0.58**	**−2.69**	**−4.56**	**1.55**
Net profit rate of equity capital	**1 (2.92)**	**1.23**	**0.27**	**−1.42**	**−3.01**	**1.09**

Source: Annual Reports in TCL: see note (2)

As Tables 11.14 and 11.15 show, a fundamental difference of cost rate to sales exists between the former and the latter groups. The rates of the former (Xiaxin, Bodao, and TCL) ranged from 80.1% to 92.4% in 2006 and 83.5% to 98.66% in 2007, respectively, while those of the latter (Huawei and ZTE) were 63.8% and 64.1% in 2006 and 66.1 in 2007. In addition, although the turnover of total assets in the former was relatively higher than that in the latter group, profits were reduced, because of the high cost ratio to sales, as profit margin per product is too low to cover fixed capacity cost even when sales increased. When fixed assets reduced, the business of the former worsened because of incompetent technology development and a high turnover of total assets, leading to the need to downsize. As a result of such circumstances, not only the former fared badly in terms of cash ratio, liquid ratio, and return on total assets than the latter but also their return on total assets fell into the red within a period of just two years.

Table 11.14 Business comparison of the main Chinese producers of cellular phone terminal devices for 2006

Items	*Xiaxin*	*Bodao*	*TCL*	*Huawei*	*ZTE*
Cash ratio %[a]	13.95		23.87	22.2	64.83
Liquid ratio %	92.95	120	97.38	132.5	145.6
Return on total assets %	−2.45	−11.21	−8.8	7.56	6.25
Cost ratio to sales %[b]	80.13	92.42	84.97	63.8	64.07
Turnover of total assets (times)	1.26	2.15	2.13	1.13	1.03

[a]Cash or its equivalent/liquid liability
[b]Sales cost/total sales revenue
Source: Annual Reports in Xiaxin, Bodao, TCL, Huawei, and ZTE (2006): see note (1–6)

Table 11.15 Business comparison of the main Chinese producers of cellular phone terminal devices for 2007

Items	*Xiaxin*	*Bodao*	*TCL*	*Huawei*	*ZTE*
Cash ratio % (1)	6.56		33.79		43.11
Liquid ratio %	66.41	114	122.08	140	180.53
Return on total assets %	−25.40	−24.97	3.88	6.39	5.83
Cost ratio to Sales % (2)	90.64	98.66	83.47	66.1	66.1
Turnover of total assets (times)	1.14	1.92	1.89	1.19	0.9

(1) = cash or its equivalent/liquid liability; (2) = sales cost/total sales revenue
Source*:* Annual Reports in Xiaxin, Bodao, TCL, Huawei, and ZTE (2007): see note (1–6)

11.6 Possibility of a New Potential in World Management System and Uncertainty

Third Wave of Business Management

If we evaluate the present management system in China from the perspective of its component parts rather than as a whole, we can variously point out weak points. However, no one can ignore Huawei's global strategy of combination (modular) system. From the global viewpoint, Huawei as well as ZTE, with its strong capabilities in development and design, which it combines with the most advanced technology and parts while utilizing cheap domestic labor and other resources, should be able to attain its full growth potential as one of the strongest multinational companies. At present, the possibility clearly exists for a global enterprise from China such as

Huawei or ZTE to establish a new wave of management system that will spread globally, even though such a huge multinational enterprise will eliminate many weak enterprises along the way and further the bipolar divergence of enterprises in China. Even Bodao, through its complete transformation to a state owned company with broadly raised social capital and strong ties between its board and the government, could become a huge multinational enterprise and also push forward the third wave if it establishes such a strong presence in terms of design and development as Huawei and adopts a global combination strategy.

As shown in Fig. 11.4, Bodao was originally an advanced collective company of cellular phone handsets manufacturing, which was established in September 1992 by Daqiao town government (5.1 million stocks, 51% of the whole capital) and four founders as personal shareholders as well as engineers (4.9 million stocks, 49%) at Fenghua city. In 2000, as the ownership of social public stocks whose right to vote is floating increased to 25% of the whole company and the founders' ratio of ownership and their right

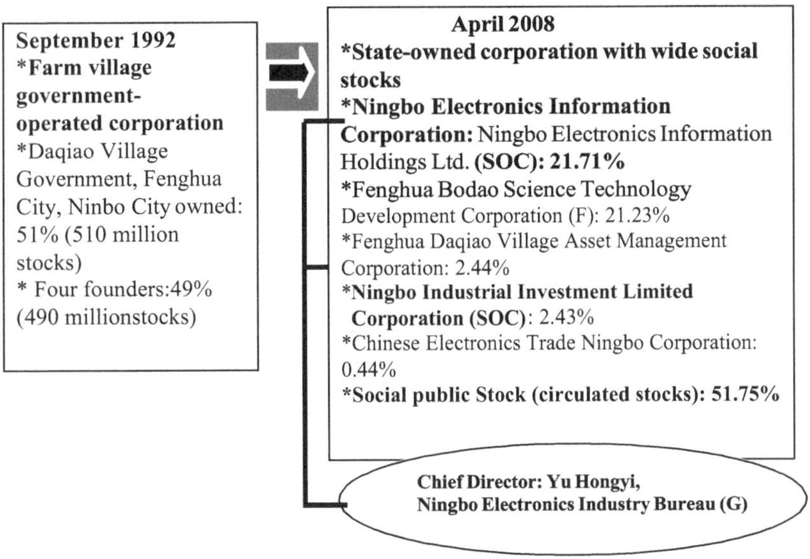

Fig. 11.4 Reorganization of Fenghua Bodao Company (*Abbreviations*: SOC, state-owned corporation; F, founders; G, government; *Source*: Bodao Annual Reports 2004 and 2008 (see note 2))

to vote became weaker, the company was controlled by the state-owned company which owned 33.74%, where additionally a staff of Ningbo city electric industry bureau took a position of chief director. As a result, the Daihua Bodao Technological Development Company as the founder has 33% of the whole capital and its control position became weaker than before. In the globally competitive international market, Chinese economic policy shifted from the privatization of state-owned enterprises to the reorganization of private and state-owned enterprises, which resulted in internationally competitive enterprises in terms of innovation as well as cost advantage. New state-owned companies which were reorganized under stock system and the absorption of social public capitals make the most of the communist party and government idea (synthetic strategy) and the synthetic power to aim at the world hegemony in markets. The Chinese government is presently actively promoting the strengthening of autonomous innovation competence of private firms for "going abroad" (Hashida 2008). Against this backdrop, the third wave of management system could, quite conceivably, be born in China. Figure 11.4 just shows a process in which a township enterprise incorporated by individuals and town government was transformed into a state-owned corporation with large social capitals.

With strong governmental funding, the reorganized enterprises will be able to execute the same policy as Huawei's global and integrated strategy of combination (world marketing strategy and module system). Chinese enterprises will, therefore, be able to shift from the old dictatorial type of management to the new combined type in which the best combination of international technologies and management methods is integrated by the harnessing of world markets. If other countries take for granted their use of Chinese labor and other resources to expand their share in the Chinese market, before they know it, their best technologies and parts will be exhausted and their markets already taken by Chinese big enterprises. We should all take more notice of the relationship between this new phenomenon emerging from China and the formation of a global third wave of management system.

Innovation of Business Management and Uncertainty in 'New Normality'

At present, the formation of global enterprises in China, which this chapter has so far inquired into through examining the reorganization process of enterprises and the separation process between large companies and small and medium companies, keeps step with national strategy toward the establishment of mighty position in the international economy, or 'going global' strategy. The two sides of socialism (government and leadership) and market economy are going to strengthen globalization. As a result, Chinese enterprises as well as capitalist ones are deeply influenced by the international environment of uncertainty. The global financial crisis in 2008 also had a serious effect in Chinese economy, in which the traditional economic strategy of high economic growth based on continually expansive investment and export should be reconsidered. When fix asset investment and domestic demand began to reduce as overseas trade and foreign currency decrease, the government strongly supported financial backing for stimulating the economy. However, it led to overinvestment and excess production capacity in some heavy industries, excess debts in companies, and nonperforming debts in banks (see Song 2016). Under such condition, the former economic policy based on continual 10% economic growth must be changed to the 'new normality' policy which focuses on product quality (function), not low-cost product, high effectiveness, and environmental consciousness on the basis of stable economic growth. Therefore, business management must also be redesigned to realize this 'new normality' which aims at shifting economy from high growth to stable growth and lessening the strains of vigorous economic growth on the national economy.

Professor Song (2016) gives an objective recognition of the 'new normality' as its 'high uncertainty' not 'stable situation', because of the unstable recovery of international economy and trade demand, although he is fundamentally confident of the rightfulness and the possibility of its realization. Shao (2015) also points out some problems by which Chinese multinational enterprises may be confronted in the near future: increase in domestic production cost, intensification of competition in domestic markets, and difficult acquisition of domestic human resources. Professor Song (2016) gives "adjustment", "innovation", and "fast holding of reform and open policy" as important subjects to realize the "new normality" and refers to the roles of business management in relation to the adjustment as follows: "Under 'adjustment', enterprises must further take priority of wrestling with the improvement of effectiveness through modernization of enterprise governance in business management and advancement of product quality and function through their improvement." At the same time, some academic circles advocate the establishment of Chinese type of management theories and practical methods (Pen et al. 2017).

Li and Wan (2016) point out the contemporary challenge for innovating business management as follows:

> As globalized knowledge economy and network technologies develop, environments for existence of organizations display more complicated, fast changeable, vague, and uncertain features. These features have profoundly an important effect on contemporary management practices and stimulates their innovation. Environment of high uncertainty gradually becomes 'normal'. Existing organizations must face this 'normality' or a challenge to the whole business management. It is necessary for organizations to establish new business management models to cope with the new challenge.

They just clarify that the "new normality" policy must be implemented under uncertainty environment and business management theory and practice should be innovated.

As stated above, the innovation and specialization of management theory and practice are now discussed in China from the viewpoints of institution, culture, social responsibility, and environmental protection (see Pen et al. 2017). However, what influence uncertainty exerts on business management and how it changes the essence and form of management are critical subjects to be discussed in the 'new normality'. Therefore, we will examine the present situations and problems of Chinese enterprise risk management in the next chapter, which may symbolize the control of uncertainty. This examination may further the understanding of special and general relation of management and management accounting with uncertainty that we have arranged in terms of capitalist market economy in Chaps. 1–9.

11.7 Conclusion

This chapter has examined recent trends in the transformation of Chinese enterprises and the relationship of such transformation with management system, pointing out the possibility of a new wave of management system emerging from China, although we cannot yet witness its concrete form. Although only the general framework of present management system in China is examined, it makes available some symptomatic evidence for the possibility of this new wave, from the viewpoints of the economic situation and business management.

In cooperation with one of Toyota-affiliated firms, some Japanese researchers, impressed with the remarkable growth of Chinese competitive power, proposed 'Product Management Accounting' related to 'Sustainable

Business Enterprise' in which module idea is applied to product-oriented management system (Kawada 2003). The integration of the world marketing strategy and module management system will be developed in various forms of management system in order to aim at speed and global marketing. The management system in Dell Inc. gives us a fundamental idea of the new wave, since this company does not design and produce its own parts and only assemble them on the basis of direct sales and 'Build to Order's system' (system of orders-received production) (Negoro 2008). This idea may be the original form of the Chinese module system. Chinese firms actualized it in the cellular phone handsets production and connected it with the world marketing strategy. The integration of global marketing and module management system will become the mainstream of international management and accounting as a result of Chinese management development.

The global development of Chinese enterprises leads to generalization, practicability, and a cross-science approach in management system, and there is a fair opportunity for a Chinese type of management system to gain general currency in the international market. The behavior of Chinese enterprises provides suggestions as to the future development of international management system; enterprises worldwide would be wise to learn from the Chinese example, developing and creating the most advanced technologies and management methods in the context of intense international competition while at the same time combining foreign advanced outcomes with its own technologies and methods to create a new type of management system which is superior in cost and quality.

The global development of Chinese enterprises will serve to further intensify international competition and 'the law of the jungle' in the international market. Simultaneously, management system will be regulated by this law. In order to realize a globally peaceful and stable society, we should move toward a true third wave of international management system which is based on sustainable growth of the global economy and environmental and ecological preservation. All researchers on management and accounting should assume responsibility for making clear the relationship between economic competition and social stability. Therefore, they should more eagerly study management system from the viewpoint of enterprise social responsibility and governance, and more deeply clarify its relationship with management system from the scientific viewpoint. At present, management system cannot be described independently of enterprise governance since the former is not separable from the latter in present practices.

Furthermore, in China where innovative management theories and practices are newly groped for to realize 'new normality' policy, the third wave of business management should also be investigated from the viewpoint of uncertainty in the same way as Western business scholars and managers take a strong interest in the control of uncertainty and enterprise risk management. Today, all enterprises could do nothing but to ensure business sustainability and stability by using a new proactive type of management model based on enterprise risk management and global socio responsibility. Next chapter will clarify the structures and features of a government-based enterprise risk management in China, compared with Western enterprise risk management in order to recognize the commonality and peculiarity of relation between management, management accounting, and uncertainty.

Notes

1. Data for each cellular phone manufacturer are quoted from their financial reports and edited for the purpose of this article: http://www.chinabird.com/zh-cn/about/; http://money.finance.sina.com.cn/corp/go.ghp/vFD_FinancialGuideLine/stocid/600057/displaytype/4.pthml; http://www.cinafo.com.cn/gszx/gszx000100.html; http://www.cinifo.com.cn/gszx/gszx6000057.html; http://share.jrj.com.cn/cominfo/ggdetail_2008-06-07_600,057_648490_stock.htm: ZTE Corporation Annual Report, 2007 and its Summary; Xiaxin Electronic Joint-Stock Company Annual Report 2005, Annual Report Summary 2006 and Annual Report 2007: Huawei Technologies Co., Ltd. Annual Report 2004, 2006 and 2007.
2. TCL refers to the TCL group which was established in 1980 by a local government in Guangdong Province, which became TCL Communication Facilities Corporation, Ltd. in 1985 (Hashida 2008).
3. Bodao is officially Fenghua Bodao Company, which was established in 1992 by four private capitalists and local government. It rapidly grew in the domestic of cellular phone production market, passing top Western manufacturers (Nokia and Motorola) in market share in 2003.
4. Huawei Technologies Co., Ltd. was established as a private science and technology company in 1988 by Ren Zhengfei, who was discharged from military service. It is well known for its rapid growth in mobile communication and information machinery marketing (Hashida 2008).
5. ZTE is Zhongxing Communication Stock Co., Ltd. established in 1985 in Shenzhen. It is one of the two most successful companies in Chinese communication facilities production (Li 2007).
6. Xiaxin is officially Xiaxin Electronic Co., Ltd. and is in the same situation as Bodao.

Bibliography

Ai, X. (2008). *The Tragedy of Firms with the Wrong Strategy*, http://www.adfaith.com/cn/newscontent.asp?InfoID=1421. Accessed 10 Aug 2008.

Cheng, D., & Liu, L. (2008). *The Truth of Huawei*. http://blog.chinaunix.net/u.304/showart_201971.html. Accessed 2 Sept 2008.

Hashida, T. (2008). *High Technology Industry in China (in Japanese)*. Tokyo: Hakuto Publishing Company.

Huang, L. (2006). An Essay on Chinese Enterprise Business System. *Journal of National Economy, 194*(1), 1–14.

Kawada, M. (2003). Reconsideration on Product Management Accounting. *Meijo Review, 3*(4), 169–186.

Kawamura, K. (2008). *The Growth and Problems of Cellular Phone Terminal Units Manufacturers in China*, http://www.jotsugakkaior.jp/doc/2006-6-25/25-E-Kawamura.pdf. Accessed 7 July 2008.

Kimura, K. (2010). Mobile Phone Handset Industry: Rapid Growth and Groping of Major Chinese Mobile Phone Manufacturers. In T. Marukawa & M. Yasumoto (Eds.), *The Evolution of Mobile Phone Industry: Why Japan Has Been Isolated in the World* (pp. 173–195). Tokyo: Yuhikaku Publisher.

Li, C. (2007). Internationalization Strategy and International Standards in Chinese Communication and Information Firms. In S. Kawai (Ed.), *International Research on Interface and Institutional Innovation of Chinese Internationalization.*, Report of Japan Society for the Promotion of Science (pp. 17–60). Nagoya: Aichi University.

Li Peng-fei, & Wang Lei. (2016, January). New Challenges for Management in New Normality: Review of 2015 Annual Conference of Management in China (8th). *Chinese Journal of Management, 13*(1), 33–39.

Marukawa, T. (2009). Why Japanese Multinationals Failed in the Chinese Mobile Phone Market: A Comparative Study of New Product Development in Japan and China. *Asian Pacific Business Review, 15*(3), 411–431.

National Bureau of Statistic of China. (2007). *China Statistical Year Book 2007*. http://www.stats.gov.cn/tjsj/2007/indexch.htm.

Negoro, T. (2008). University and Peculiarity. http://www.waseda.jp/negoro/SupplyChain/Dell_model.html.

Nishimura, A. (2003). *Management Accounting in Asia: feed forward and Asian perspectives*. Hampshire: Palgrave Macmillan.

Pen Da-long, Ge Jiang, & Wang Lei. (2017, June). Management Theory Innovation in the New Competition Environment: Review on 2016 Annual Conference on Management in China (9th). *Chinese Journal of Management, 14*(6), 806–813.

Sakamoto, H. (2007). China, Recent Trends and Prospects for Major Asian Economics. *East Asian Economic Perspectives, 18*(1), 27–38. February (Special Issue).

Shao Yong Yu. (2015). Present Situations and Prospects of Expanding Chinese Overseas Direct Investments, *Mizuho China Monthly*, May, pp. 3–5.

Song Li Shui. (2016). How Do We Grasp Chinese Economy in the New Normality? *The Meiji-Gakuin Review: The Papers and Proceedings of Economics, 151*, 13–28.

Xu J, & Imai, K. (2007). Market Size and Industrial Heightening: The Case of Local Cellular Phone Industry. In K. Imai & K. Ting (Eds.), *Tide of Heightening in China: Changes of Industry and Enterprise* (pp. 7–44). Tokyo: Asian Economic Research Institute.

ZTE Corporation (2004, 2006, 2007, 2008, 2010, 2012, 2014). *Annual Report*: http://www.zte.com.cn/global/about/investorrelations/corporate_report/annual_report

CHAPTER 12

Examination of Chinese Enterprise Risk Management from the Perspective of the Integrated Management of Profit Opportunity and Risk

12.1 Structure and Meanings of Government-Based Enterprise Risk Management

Regulations and Meanings

In China today, enterprise risk management is still in its infancy in state-owned enterprises, many of which play a leading role in business management (Wang 2010). Chinese government organizations and enterprises have become concerned about risk management after seeing the economic impact of events such as the accounting scandals at Enron in 2001 and the WorldCom group in 2002 as well as the global financial crisis of 2008. In such situations, the central government began to grapple with the regularization of enterprise risk management, as well as to strengthen internal control systems. The State-Owned Assets Supervision and Administration Commission (SASAC), as a special organization under direct control of the State Council, issued 'Guidelines for Comprehensive Risk Management in Central Enterprises' in 2006[1] (hereinafter referred to as 2006 guidelines). In accordance with these guidelines, the Ministry of Finance also circulated 'Enterprise Internal Control Standards: Fundamental Standards and 17 Special Standards' in 2007 (hereinafter referred to as 2007 standards). Under the new standard, the 'Internal Accounting Control Standards, 2001' were more systemized and the relationship between internal

A. Nishimura, *Management, Uncertainty, and Accounting*,
https://doi.org/10.1007/978-981-10-8989-3_12

controls and risk management were clearly indicated. Since that time, on the basis of the above guidelines, SASAC has also put forth "the notification related to the comprehensive enterprise risk management report in central enterprises of 2010" and "the notification of related matters for central enterprises to comprehensively develop risk management activities of 2013".[2] These notifications call for the inspection of firms' actual enterprise risk management practices and promote the systemization and standardization of risk management activity, based on the 2006 guidelines.

The 2006 guidelines and 2007 standards have given enterprise risk management a regulatory framework. The 2007 standards were enacted for listed companies under national laws and rules such as the 'Company Law' and 'Interim Regulations for the Administration and Supervision of State-Owned Assets of Enterprises'. Their purpose is to strengthen and standardize enterprise internal controls, enhance the level of enterprise business management and *the defensive capacity against risks*, promote the sustainable development of the enterprises, maintain order in the socialistic market economy, and protect the social public interest[3] Therefore, SASAC, as stockholders and the national supervisor of central enterprises, directed listed central companies to develop comprehensive risk management practices, strengthen their competitive power, increase returns on investment and promote sustainable, sound, and stable development (Art. 1 of the Guidelines of 2006). As shown above, central enterprises, particularly listed central companies, are compelled toward enterprise risk management as a result of the incorporation of risk management into the internal control regulations for the protection and strengthening of state-owned assets. Enterprise risk management practices seem to have further spread to other types of enterprises via the state-owned enterprises. As Meng (2010) stated, "Internal auditing is an important component of contemporary enterprise system, a key link between enterprise internal control and risk management, and *a self-immunity system* in enterprise economic movement."

It is quite obvious from the abovementioned relationship between the 2006 guidelines and the 2007 standards that enterprise risk management is deeply subsumed within internal control systems (particularly, internal auditing) and has taken root as part of the governmental administration of enterprises, given that the 2007 standards are governmental regulations for the supervision and auditing of listed central companies as state-owned assets and provide clear direction for risk management for this purpose. Under the 2007 standards, firms must divide risks into internal risk (risks related to human resources, business- and safety environment, independent innovation and finance) and external risk (risks related to the economy, law, society, science/technology, and natural environment). Firms are tasked with recognizing risks, correctly evaluating internal and external risks that are closely related to the achievement of a control target, and determining the recipient degree of risk clearly. The control target aims at producing maximum enterprise value with minimum risk. This form of enterprise risk management involves both enterprise self-management and the governmental administration of its management, where the stratified control structure includes the board of directors, superintendents and the internal auditing department under the authority of SASAC, and external auditors from a certificated public accountant office. Each of these layers plays an important part in administrating risk management activities.

The Company Law and the Financial Instruments and Trading Law in Japan also require large companies and their allied companies to exercise internal control. Under these laws, such companies must be punished with a fine when they inflict serious damage or loss on interested parties and society without appropriate compliance with internal control regulation. Moreover, companies bear their own responsibility for failed risk management in the form of bankruptcy or lower social reputation. However, the government-based enterprise risk management in China is more rigorous and takes a more strongly preventive and precautionary approach since the enterprise risks are directly identified with governmental risks. At the same time, both governments and enterprises must cover all risks, even if they result in a governmental burden eventually.

From this discussion, we can say that state-owned enterprises were the first in China to establish internal control systems for risk management. In developing these systems, state-owned enterprises referred to American-style systems and worked to keep step with governmental regulations. The close relationship between internal control systems and governmental administration distinguishes Chinese enterprise risk management from Western systems that focus on the development of original enterprise strategies and the use of transparency and disclosures in risk management. In contrast with the Chinese system, Western risk management and corporate governance is treated as self-responsibility. The dual type of enterprise risk management in China leads to a pyramid type of risk management inside and outside an enterprise group, particularly between parent and subsidiary companies and between original contractors and suppliers, as will be discussed in the following section where practical risk management in a group company and supply chain is examined.

The Structure of the Dual Type of Risk Management

Although the process extending from risk evaluation, control, information and communication, and countermeasure against risks to superintendence is a fundamental and universal series of actions in risk management for every business organization, its precise form and meanings vary greatly according to the social system in which they arise. How each enterprise controls risks related to uncertainty is influenced by the specific type of social system and the place of the enterprise in the system. The decisive difference between the dual type of risk management and enterprise-own risk management based on social responsibility is especially noteworthy in our coming discussion.

Figure 12.1 shows the dual structure in which not only risks are managed by an enterprise but their management activities are also administrated by governments through an internal control system and other mechanisms. The flow of risk management consists of the following five parts: the collection of incipient information on risks, *the assessment of these risks*, the decision on countermeasures against the risks, the proposal and implementation of settlement methods, and *the supervision and improvement of risk management*. Of these five parts, the second and the fifth,

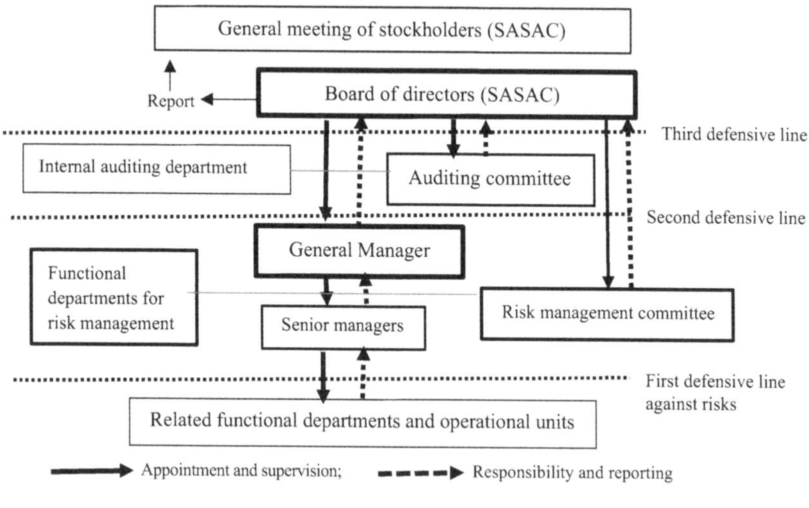

Fig. 12.1 Relation between administrative control and risk management in Chinese central enterprises

italicized above, are strongly related to internal control and auditing. This risk management is carried out under three defensive lines against risks. At the first line, each functional department or operational unit carries out daily operational activities in risk management for which the general manager and senior managers, as his or her designees, are ultimately responsible. At the same time, the general manager and senior managers assume all responsibility when the organization drafts a structural and functional plan for enterprise risk management. All functional departments must report about risk management activities to the managers. At the second line, the risk management committee and functional departments related to risk management are responsible for the *effectiveness* of comprehensive risk management and the general manger assumes responsibility to the board of directors for achieving this *effectiveness*. At the third line, the internal auditing department and auditing committee assigned by the board have responsibility to audit the *effectiveness* of risk management and the board assumes the responsibility to all stockholders for effectively implementing comprehensive risk management. Thus, SASAC, as the stockholders of state-owned companies, plays a critical role in carrying out enterprise risk management comprehensively through auditing and risk management committees and the general manager. In this case, internal auditing and the auditing committee play an important role in this system. Article 40 of the 2006 guidelines requires that the internal auditing department in the enterprise supervises the process through which related functional departments and operational units carry out risk management activities effectively according to prescribed rules and must evaluate the process at least once per year. The internal auditing department should directly send the report on this supervision and evaluation to the board of directors, the risk management committee and the auditing committee. This work can be conducted as part of annual auditing, regular auditing, or special auditing work.

Enterprise risk management has been institutionally established under governmental leadership in China. State-owned enterprises then began to build up systems of internal control and risk management. Thus, enterprise risk management is still in a relatively early phase of development. As Wang (2010) notes, "[s]tate-owned enterprise is still at the early stage of comprehensive risk management because related functional departments and posts, and their duties are by no means arranged rationally. In some enterprises, internal auditing department concentrically handles a course of risk management activities and its responsibility becomes too heavy"

(p. 56). According to Wang (2010), comprehensive risk management is at an early stage and has not yet fully developed in 76.1% of investigated enterprises. In 57.13% of the enterprises, internal auditing department bear primary responsibility for activities related to enterprise risks. Wang found that, for a long time, internal auditing was not viewed as a significant activity in some enterprises, and in terms of occupational preparedness, some internal auditors was not sufficiently trained, despite the fact that new professional knowledge was required for risk management auditing (Wang 2010). We should more deeply elucidate the practical characteristics of enterprise risk management in order to clarify the features of the dual type of risk management and the key issues it faces.

12.2 Governmental Economic Policy and Enterprise Risk Management

Enterprise risk management has jointly permeated state-owned enterprises along with internal control systems that play an important role in governmental administration of enterprises. As another impetus for risk management, the shift in governmental economic policy from an 'absorbing foreign power' strategy to a 'going global' strategy has enhanced enterprises' risk consciousness in regards to enterprise strategic management since large enterprises began to enter into global competition in the international markets that was unlike their prior experience in the domestic markets. In this new environment, enterprises began to shift their business objective from "becoming large" to "becoming strong" (Zhang 2004).

In the early 2000s, enterprises began to focus on the modernization of business management, which aimed at strengthening production capacity to earn foreign currency through exports by means of improving product quality and reducing energy consumption and costs. At this time, business reform and change was viewed as a "business opportunity" (Pan 2000) and risk consciousness, in contrast, was relatively weak because the better-positioned state-owned enterprises had the survivable scale in competitive domestic markets, given their stronger connection with government, as we examined in a previous chapter (Chap. 10; see also Nishimura 2008).

Under the 12th Five-Year Plan (2006–2010),[4] enterprises that accumulated foreign exchange through exports could start on the path of 'going global' to search for larger profit opportunities in globally competitive markets. In this strategic transformation, "Chinese multinational companies are also confronted with many kinds of risks and threats" (Xu et al. 2009, 142).

These firms are exposed to internationalized risks by pursing global profit opportunities and must establish strategic management. Although enterprises' strategies and risks do not always align with governmental strategy, they are required to obey governmental external economic and political strategy. According to the governmental plan, in internationally competitive markets, enterprises "should take their right courses and strengthen management on the authority of governmental laws and policies to protect national interest".[5]" The following commentary by Wang highlights some of the tensions between governmental planning and market competition, which also holds true for enterprises pursing a 'going global' strategy:

> There is a Governor's will when government establishes five- or ten-year plan. Enterprises should attain abnormal development speed irrespective of their internal conditions and business environment in order to accomplish the Governor's economic development target. Such long-range economic planning management is always inherently an obstacle to the connection between enterprise long- and short-range plans. Yearly plan under market environment is very difficult to align with long-range plan. This situation is surely represented by the following phrase afloat in business circles: "Guihua (規劃: planning) is Guihua (鬼話: fiction)". (Wang 2002, p. 44)

However, enterprises that make inroads into global markets in pursuit for greater opportunity are always supported in the face of dangerous risks by governments. As Cha et al. (2013) point out, the Chinese government is the most reliable supporter when Chinese enterprises are confronted with political risk events overseas. These enterprises are inseparably connected in their risk and strategic management with governmental supports. In this sense, "Chinese entrepreneurs should be an analyst of not only political situations but also economic conditions. Therefore, enterprise leaders should earnestly study governmental documents and leaders' lecturers and be good at seizing opportunities in crisis" (Liu 2011).

Although Chinese enterprise risk management also seems to generally follow a management process of forecasting opportunities and risks and planning for and controlling business activity through profit management, even if this is not yet done systematically, governmental and political opportunities or risks are intricately entangled in this process, and accounting income in a company by no means results only from the profit opportunities and risks of enterprise's own business activity, but is more deeply connected to political factors. Because business uncertainty is strongly influenced by the relationship of the enterprise to the global economy and governmental foreign strategy, enterprise risk management also takes the dual system of governmental and enterprise risk managements. Thus, this type of risk management moves far beyond the micro level of enterprise risk management in the Western sense.

Risk management in large Chinese companies was established through alignment with governmental regulations. For example, Chinese Oil and Natural Gas Group Company, as a large international enterprise group, started to establish an internal control system following the COSO framework of internal control in 2003. The company implemented risk control through financial reporting and established standardized and regulatory control procedures of risk management after having experienced risk control related to the monitoring, analyzing, and evaluating of important risk points. Then in 2006, the company formally started establishing an internal control system and has steadily moved toward the establishment of a comprehensive risk management system that stressed the protection against risks and their control as part of its fundamental governance and process controls, and the firm now attempts to rebuild and optimize their flow diagram. The company constantly expands risk control and management from an internal and external viewpoint and is now working to perfect these measures (Gong 2008). Recently, the company has joined risk management with the implementation process of enterprise strategy and has worked to continually improve enterprise risk management as a part of strategic management system (Bo and Lu 2013).

Risk consciousness in enterprises has also changed along with the shift in governmental economic policy from 'absorbing foreign power' to 'going global', or from risk management as part of an internal control system to strategic risk management for the establishment of an internationally strong and competitive enterprise.

Wang (2014) examined the risk consciousness of 69 central enterprises in China. Together, these firms held 78% of total central enterprise assets, 83% of operational revenues, and 83% of profits. In this analysis, Wang contends that these enterprises attached too much importance to investment risk and health safety and environmental protection risk. In these research findings, Wang finds that enterprises ranked investment risk as being of greatest concern out of 526 risk items, over the period from 2008 to 2010. In 2011, enterprises ranked health safety and environmental protection risks as the most important risk. Cash flow risk, policy risk,

Table 12.1 Risk items of greatest concern to Chinese central enterprises

Risk item	*2011*	*2010*	*2009*	*2008*
Risk of health, safety, and environmental protection	◎	○	○	○
Investment risk	○	◎	◎	◎
Cash flow risk	○	○	○	○
Policy risk	○	○	○	○
Human resources risk	○	○	○	○
Competition risk	○	○	○	○
Price risk	○	○	○	○
Strategy management risk	○	○	○	
Internationalized business risk	○	○		
Project risk	○			

○ indicates items ranked among the top ten risks, ◎ indicates the top-rated item

Source: Wang (2014)

human resources risk, competition risk, and price risk were also among the top ten risks from 2008 to 2011. These results are summarized in Table 12.1. We find from these facts that when pursing an 'absorbing foreign power' strategy, routine and operational internal risks had maintained a prime position in enterprise risk consciousness.

The enterprises began to devote greater attention to strategic management risk beginning in 2009 and internationalized business risk from 2010. This can likely be attributed to alignment with the recent governmental overseas expansion policy (Wang 2014, p. 38). Even in the central enterprises, strategic risk did not originally form the foundation of its risk management, but recently has begun to be accepted as a risk item in relation to governmental international strategy. At present, health safety and environmental protection risk and investment risk still take the more critical position in enterprise risk management compared with internationalized business risk and strategic risk. The enterprises tend to take a more serious view of operational and routine risks than Western enterprises. Moreover, it is very interesting that market demand risk, corporate governance risk, macroeconomic risk, and exchange and interest rate risk are left out from the top ten in 2011, despite ranking in the top ten in some of the previous three years. These different trends in risk consciousness compared with Western companies may reflect the special feature of Chinese enterprise risk management under governmental protection and the strong control of foreign exchange and interest rates.

Wang et al. (2012) looked at risk recognition by a coal mine acting as a cost center of a group (a certain coal industry limited liability company) that produces raw coal and clean coal. It is natural that, as a cost center, operational risks are a point of emphasis in risk evaluation rather than other items such as market, law, and finance risks. Among 260 listed risk items highlighted by the firm, key items of concern included internal control (22) and operational risks such as healthy safety and environmental risk (29), production management risk (28), safety management risk (27), and equipment and facilities risk (23) (Wang et al. 2012). Risk management is carried out by a risk management office in the finance section. It is important to note that in this case risks are recognized as a financial matter despite the fact that the mine is strongly focused on physical production and the internal control system has a great impact on risk management. Wang et al. (2012) find that enterprise risk management succeeds due to the connection of risk management with this internal control (p. 95). Except for multinational companies, most enterprises, even those pursing a 'going global' strategy, still seems to focus on internal and operational risk management in the same way when pursuing an 'absorbing foreign power' strategy (see Sun 2003).

12.3 Practical Risk Management Problems in a Group Company and Supply Chain

Risk Management of a Finance Company in a Group Company

Recently, state-owned enterprises have expanded to different businesses outside of their own industry through mergers, acquisitions, and reorganizations and have grown into group companies[6] by incorporating affiliated enterprises as stock companies (Chap. 10; see also Nishimura 2008). Finance *company* is a common subsidiary in many of these group companies. As business and capital scale grows, the group company establishes the finance company to effectively use and adjust funding and cut down capital costs. Although the finance company focuses mainly on the management of internal funds (deposits from the affiliated companies, internal loans, settlement of accounts, and loans to external companies), it may seem obvious that companies will seek to extend their international financial business in step with the strategic shift from 'absorbing foreign power' to 'going global'. However, at the early stage, the financial *department* in the group company controlled virtually all important financial affairs, particularly international finance, and finance company's business affairs were limited (see Yuan and Zhang 2011, 2015). On the global financial stage, it remains an unsettled question on how to decentralize the centralized functions of a financial department into a finance company. This question is closely related to enterprise risk management in a group company.

As Yuan and Zhang (2011) show on the basis of interview research, the finance company is actually controlled in voting power by the group (parent) company as the leading shareholder. This equity control influences the state of risk management in the finance company, since the boards of directors of both the parent company and the finance company are jointly responsible for risk management (pp. 66–67). From this fact, even though the finance company has a board of directors, its independence is doubtful, since there is little room for the finance company to independently direct strategic risk management. For this reason, enterprise risk management in the group company can be viewed as having a pyramid-type structure.

Yuan and Zhang also examine the situation where the board director of the finance company establishes a risk management committee. Even though the establishment of such a committee indicates that the general manager of the group company is paying more attention to risk, the role and function of the committee in risk management is actually weakened because the committee is not permanent and its regular scope of work is not fixed (Yuan and Zhang 2011, pp. 67–68). Only two out of ten group companies researched placed risk evaluation in an operating division and only five established an evaluation standard or mechanism. However, one of these five group companies, an electric power company, viewed its actual execution as being 'very elastic'. In another group company, the evaluation standards and mechanisms were not used, despite the fact that such standards and mechanisms were formally established (Yuan and Zhang 2011, pp. 69–70).

In another paper, Yuan and Zhang (2015) describe how a finance company, as a subsidiary company, depends upon the overall development strategy and business targets of the group company. In addition, the finance company works under the internal supervision and control of the group company and the external supervisory and administration of China Bank Regulatory Commission. The finance company is a unique business operation compared with other operational units in the group company, given the dual supervision from both the company and external organizations. They arrive at the following conclusion:

> The model, with which the group indirectly supervises and controls the finance company and depends upon the autonomy of the finance company in risk management, takes a comparatively large ratio in the investigated companies. The group is not only lacking in the management control of external funds, but also risks derived from expanded business works (particularly credit risk, liquidity risk, and market risk) tend to increase daily inside the group. These problems show not only the limited controllability of the group, uncompleted management method and the deficient meticulousness and professionalization of risk management, but also that the group is short of attaching importance to the risks of the finance company and serious emergent accidents. (Yuan and Zhang 2015, p. 41)

The division of affairs in risk management is not yet established among companies in the group. Comparatively low awareness of foreign exchange and interest risks, to which strong importance ought to be attached in contemporary financial society, may be due to this situation.

This state of affairs is problematic when the finance company grows into an international finance company or leaves as an internal finance organization at the 'going global' stage. Problems also arise due to the state of enterprise risk management in China specifically. In a pyramid-type risk, management structure with the group (parent) company at the apex, key problems to address are who is responsible for recognizing and controlling market risks (i.e., the financial department or the finance company) in international competitive markets. Regardless, profit opportunity seems to secure due to government protection and the pyramid type of management system. However, the intention of the governor may change and may even occasionally be cut off from the realities of a constantly changing global market. How can enterprises absorb this political risk in their risk management system? The relationship between the concentration and decentralization of responsibilities in risk management appears to be unsettled in Chinese state-owned group companies. Next, turning from risk management inside the group company, we will look into enterprise risk management in the supply chain.

Risk Management in the Supply Chain: The Case of Shen Long Automobile Company

The supply chain of Shen Long Automobile Company is organized in a pyramid-type structure for risk management (Shen Long Automobile-Limited Liability Company 2015, p. 55). The structure is made up of three levels. At the first level, the corporate auditing and risk management committee determines corporate risk management targets and countermeasures against risks and discusses critical risk items and other important matters of risk management. At the second level, risk management committee in each department is responsible for planning, organizing, and cooperating on risk management matters within its department and among related departments. At the third level, each section is responsible for the daily operational work of risk management (p. 56). This company asks all companies within its supply chain to carry out risk management using this three-level structure. The company spreads this pyramid-type organizational structure for risk management to its suppliers and logistical and distribution providers. The company oversees the whole organizational structure chart and maintains a list of names and liaison methods, while each enterprise (supplier) carries out risk management and holds a stratified connection to the vehicle manufacturers (p. 56).

Both the automobile company itself and its supply chain fundamentally implement risk management according to the plan–do–check–act (PDCA) method. However, management of each risk type is vertically organized through the whole supply chain, taking the automobile company as the leader. This is an intensification of government-based enterprise risk management. This vertical and unified risk management structure seeks to secure safe and uninterrupted production throughout the whole organization rather than each company's exploitation of new profit opportunity, because profit opportunity can only be exploited and actualized with the strong leadership of the original contractor, given the governmental economic strategy that aims at establishing an internationally competitive automobile group. In the case of Shen Long group, uninterrupted production in the supply chain is viewed as being of utmost importance. For example, a production interruption of more than eight hours is the most dangerous risk, an interruption between four and eight hours is a dangerous risk, an interruption between one and four hours is a moderate risk, and interruption of less than one hour is a low risk (Shen Long Automobile-Limited Liability Company 2015, p. 56). Each supplier must endeavor to comply with the contractor's demand for risk-free operation before everything else. As the company's report points out, an effective method for strengthening enterprise competitive power is to establish a supply chain risk management system under the leadership of the automobile manufacturer as the key company, since such a system is able to adjust to the needs of the automobile industry and the globalization of supply chain and results in enhancement of the risk management ability of supply chain. In this sense, operational risk takes a dominant position for suppliers (p. 55).

We must note, in passing, that supply chains also face supply risk for both raw and processed materials. Properly speaking, it is impossible that this risk occurs in China since companies cannot supply materials and automobile parts to areas outside those prescribed by local governments. However, 'outside competitors' are not subject to this constraint and may seek supplies outside of this orderly system, which can intensify supply competition. Therefore, this risk can be considered not only as materials supply risk but also as a public relations risk that enterprises would not face if the government effectively intervenes on their behalf (PricewaterhouseCoopers 2014a, b). Another potential risk occurs when regulations are not properly enforced. Therefore, the stratified and united risk management of supply chain first fulfills its function when closely aligned with the appropriate enforcement of governmental regulations. If this is not the case, negligence in implementation of regulation creates new risks for enterprises as well as governments.

In the supply chain, even if a pyramid-type structure of risk management with the main contractor (assembling company) in the lead was successful in securing continuous and stable production when government strategy focused on 'absorbing foreign power', it remains a point for further investigation as to whether this type of management serves as an internationally competitive strategy for the whole supply chain and the competitive autonomy of each supplier at the 'going global' stage. How does a globally oriented strategy affect the organic relationship between the total risk management of the whole supply chain and each supplier's autonomous risk management? In the supply chain, as well as in the relationship between a parent company and the finance company, the pyramid-type structure of risk management was advantageous, given the government-oriented and top-down, or heteronomous, risk management. However, in the global economy where the market environment and competitive conditions are always changing, flexible and autonomous risk management is necessary for sustainable growth of an enterprise. It remains an unsettled and interesting question as to how risk management is concentrated and decentralized between the government, parent company (main contractor), and subsidiary companies (suppliers) when pursing the shift from an 'absorbing foreign power' strategy to a 'going global' strategy.

12.4 Profitability and Enterprise Risk Management

Profitability of Top 500 Enterprises by Revenue: Background on Risk Management

Chinese enterprise risk management, as discussed thus far in this chapter, should also be reexamined through the lens of the actual profitability of Chinese enterprises to further elucidate its meaning and key areas of concern. As discussed in the previous chapters (Chaps. 7, 8, 9, and 10), risk cannot be estimated and controlled in contemporary management separately from profit opportunity because the two concepts are related and are the result of the same business strategy. This book has focused on the close relationship between enterprise risk and profit opportunity in order to develop a modern comprehensive risk management proactively and synthetically. Unfortunately, little is known about the integrated management of enterprise risk and profit opportunity from the perspective of opportunity and lost opportunity. Just as the real income in each enterprise results from the proactive management of profit opportunity and enterprise risk, Chinese enterprise risk management must also be seen through the retrospective examination of actual income and the clarification of the relationship between risk management and its effects on income.

We use financial data[7] on the top 500 enterprises in China by revenue in 2011, 2015, and 2016 to analyze the characteristics of firm profitability and the trends in profitability by industry in the 'going global' period. We then judge the fundamental trend in profit opportunity and enterprise risk by using this retrospective information.

Table 12.2 provides statistical data on the profitability of the top 500 companies by revenue in the three fiscal years and their changes from 2011 to 2016. Profitability is calculated by the ratio of net profit to revenue (RPR).

Table 12.2 Profitability of the top 500 companies by revenue in the three financial years

Year	*Range*	*Maximum*	*Minimum*	*Average*	*Standard deviation*	*Variance*
2011	0.83	0.58	−0.25	0.0944	0.11057	0.012
2015	0.7	0.48	−0.23	0.0713	0.10028	0.010
2016	1.3	0.73	−0.57	0.0717	0.12563	0.016

Table 12.2 indicates that 2016 had the largest range of profitability in the years examined in terms of the total difference between the maximum and the minimum profitability levels. This large range also results in 2016 having the largest standard deviation and variance. In 2016, profitability ranged from a high of 73% to a low of −57%. In contrast, the narrowest range was observed in 2015. Over the time period, average profitability decreased from 9.4% in 2011 to 7.2% in 2016. This decline in the average ratio is another noteworthy point. As the decline had occurred by 2015, the pattern for 2016 seems to be a contemporary indication. Table 12.3 shows the total variance in the top 500 companies' profitability in the three years in detail. The range in 2015 is mostly similar to that in 2011, but the average is the same as in 2016. The average profitability in 2015 dropped down to about 7%, which is almost the same as in 2016, but the range in 2015 was narrower than that in 2016. However, in actuality, the fundamental trends in the RPR in 2015 are almost as same as in 2016. We can understand the present situation of profitability, as measured by RPR, through the basic changes observed from 2011 to 2015 and 2016.

As shown in Table 12.3, although the RPR of firms is concentrated in 2015 as it is in 2011, the concentration of companies with a low level of profitability (from 0% to 1%) in 2011 disperse into the two poles of higher and lower profitability in 2015, with the lower pole including many with a negative RPR value. This general pattern also holds for 2016 when the distribution of the two poles is the most remarkable. The number of firms with a higher level of profitability (between 40% and 60%) increased from 17 (3.4%) in 2011 to 30 (5%) in 2015, while the lower-ranking firms (i.e., negative ratio) also increased from 8 (1.8%) in 2011 to 24 (5.6%) in 2015. Despite the low variance and standard deviation, the gap between the most and least profitable companies widened. Thus, the situation in 2015 is closer to that in 2016 than in 2011, and 2015 exhibits many of the same features as 2016. In 2016, 47 companies (9.4%) had a negative RPR (i.e., deficit operations), whereas 32 companies (42%) can be classified as a having high RPR levels (between 40% and 90%), including 13 (2.6%) that had more than a 50% RPR.

The next question that we must consider is which industrial sectors are represented by companies in the two poles of best and worst RPR and how the situation of these two poles relates to enterprise risk management. Next, we concretely investigate the movement and changes of the companies in the two poles and clarify the contemporary problems of Chinese enterprise risk management.

Table 12.3 Distribution of the top 500 companies by RPR in 2011, 2015, and 2016

	Number of companies			*Each and cumulative percentages*					
	2011	*2015*	*2016*	*2011*		*2015*		*2016*	
Below 0.8			**1**					**0.2**	0.2
0.7			**1**					**0.2**	0.4
0.6			**1**					**0.2**	0.6
0.5	**2**	7	**10**	**0.4**	0.4	**1.4**	1.4	**2**	2.6
0.4	**15**	**23**	**19**	**3**	3.4	**4.6**	6	**3.8**	6.4
0.3	**18**	14	24	3.6	7	2.8	8.8	4.8	11.2
0.2	**35**	81	82	7	14	16.2	25	16.4	27.6
0.1	81	263	243	**16.2**	**30.2**	**52.6**	**77.6**	**48.6**	**76.2**
0.01	293	81	66	**58.6**	**88.8**	**16.2**	**93.8**	**13.2**	**89.4**
0	*48*	7	4	*9.6*	98.4	1.4	95.2	0.8	90.2
−0.01		*19*	*31*			**3.8**	99	**6.2**	96.4
−0.1	*7*	*4*	*13*	*1.4*	99.8	**0.8**	99.8	**2.6**	99
−0.2-		*1*	*3*			**0.2**	**100**	**0.6**	99.6
−0.3	*1*			*0.2*	**100**				
−0.4									
−0.5			*2*					**0.4**	**100**
Total	500	500	500	100	100				

Table 12.4 indicates in which industrial sectors the top 50 companies in terms of RPR are located in 2011 and the overall trend in sector representation in the top 50 in 2011, 2015, and 2016. It is clear from Table 12.4 that although companies in various industrial sectors ranked in the top 50 in each year, firms in certain sectors are more highly represented, including those in the banking, securities, electric power, information technology and networking, real estate, and liquor and beer sectors. In particular, firms in the banking and securities sectors are well represented among the most profitable firms, which has been the case since 2011. Table 12.5 provides additional detail on the distribution of firms by sector and level of profitability in 2016 (and 2015). In 2016, as compared with 2015, companies in the banking, securities, and information technology and networking sectors not only were well represented in the high profitability range (with RPR from 40% to 80%) but also increased their numbers and level of profitability.

In 2016, companies with higher RPRs were concentrated in the financial and information technology sectors, although companies in the liquor and beer sectors have traditionally had the highest profitability in China.

Table 12.4 Top 50 companies by industrial sector and RPR (2011) and trends (2011, 2015, 2016)

Number of companies in each industrial sector	*Below 0.6*	*0.5*	*0.4*	*0.3*	*Number of companies ranked in top 50 in RPR*		
					2011	*2015*	*2016*
Banking and investment		5	12	1	18	18	21
Securities		3	3		6	7	10
Electric power			1		1	2	4
Information technology and networking		3		1	4	3	4
Real estate	1	1		3	5	4	2
Transportation		1	2	2	5	4	3
Liquor and beer		2		3	5	3	3
Oil and gas development				2	2	3	
Coal mining				2	2		
Agriculture	1				1		
Motor vehicle parts				1	1		
Other						6	3
Total	2	15	18	15	50	50	50

Note: 60%~70% means more than 60% and less than 70%

Having looked at the most profitable companies, we must now look at the other side of the 500 largest companies, namely those with the lowest RPR, to clarify the overall state of profitability of Chinese companies.

Interestingly, the situation of the bottom 50 companies is quite analogous to the top 50 companies in 2015 and 2016 (see Table 12.6). Although the bottom companies in terms of RPR belong to a variety of industrial sectors in 2011, they tend to be concentrated in certain industrial sectors such as the steel, coal mining, nonferrous metal, trade and commerce, building materials, and chemistry sectors in each of the years examined. In the coal mining sector, in which many medium and small firms are scattered over the whole country, a number of profitable companies have fallen into lower and negative profitability over this period. Table 12.7 shows the serious profitability situation facing the bottom 50 companies among top 500 companies in 2015 and 2016.

In 2016, more companies fell into negative RPR and the level of unprofitability was greater than in 2015. Companies that had a focus on manufactures related to environmental protection (e.g., solar power generation) and those with traditionally strong profitability (liquor and

Table 12.5 Top 50 companies by industrial sector and profitability in 2016 (2015 in parentheses)

Number of companies in each industrial sector	*80%~90%*	*70%~80%*	*60%~70%*	*50%~60%*	*40%~50%*	*30%~40%*	*20%~30%*
Banking and finance				3 (3)	14 (13)	4 (1)	(1)
Securities		1		5 (2)	3 (5)	1	
Liquor and beer				1 (1)	1 (1)	1 (1)	
Electric power				1 (1)		3	(1)
Real estate and developer					(1)	2 (3)	
Information technology and networking	1		1		(2)	2 (1)	
Oil and gas development						(2)	(1)
Transportation						3 (4)	
Other					1 (1)	2 (2)	(3)
Total (out of 50)	1	1	1	10 (7)	19 (23)	18 (14)	(6)
Percentage	2	2	2	20 (14)	38 (46)	36 (28)	(12)

Note: Numbers in parentheses represent the values in 2015. 80%~90% means more than 80% and less than 90%

Table 12.6 Bottom 50 companies by industrial sector and the ratio of net profit to revenue (2011) and trends (2011, 2015, and 2016)

Number of companies in each industrial sector	*−0.3*	*−0.1*	*0*	*0.01*	*Number of companies ranked in the bottom 50*		
					2011	*2015*	*2016*
Steel		2	1	9	12	13	17
Coal mining and related chemistry				1	1	5	7
Nonferrous metal		1	1	2	4	4	5
Science and technology department	1	1		3	5	1	
Electric power		1		4	5	4	2
Trade and commerce				5	5	6	6
Electric machine				4	4	3	2
Liquor and beer							2
Food and daily necessities						4	
Information and network				2	2	3	1
Chemistry				1	1	5	
Oil and gas development				1	1		2
Tire				2	2		
Medicine		1	1		2		
Building material				1	1		3
Bay				1	1		
Heavy industry		1			1		
Motor car				1	1		
Construction				1	1		
Spinning				1	1		
Others						2	3
Total	1	7	3	39	50	50	50

electric machine) had a difficult time, as did traditionally deficit-facing companies (steel, coal mining, nonferrous metal, and cement), given the rapid deceleration in the macroeconomic growth rate. Among the bottom 50 firms, the traditionally deficit-facing companies fell into a more serious situation. Some of them continue to exist but depend on loans from banks or other governmental supports and are seen by many as propped-up zombie companies. These firms are confronted with limited options including reorganization, merger, or discontinuance of the business in order to rearrange their operations and reduce their excess capacity (Matsumoto and Nakagawa 2016; Matsumoto and Fujisawa 2016).

The reform of state-owned enterprises has been a subject of discussion for many years in order to resolve their inefficiency resulting from excessive capacity and overemployment (Nishimura 2008). However, the shift

Table 12.7 Bottom 50 companies by industrial sector and profitability in 2016 (2015 in parentheses)

Number of companies in each industrial sector	*−0.5*	*−0.2*	*−0.1*	*−0.05*	*−0.01*	*0(−0.001)*	*0(0.0001)*	*0.01*
Steel		2 (1)	7 (1)	5 (2)	3 (3)		(2)	(4)
Coal and gas			1	2	4 (3)	(1)		(1)
Chemistry					(3)			(2)
Nonferrous metal			(1)	2	2 (1)	1 (1)		(1)
Information technology and networking				(1)	1 (1)		(1)	
Cement and building materials	1		1		1			
Oil			1		1			
Food and daily necessities			1		(1)	(3)		
Liquor			1					
Electric machine				1	1 (1)	(2)		
Electric power	1	1	(1)		(1)		(1)	(1)
Trade and commerce			1 (1)	1	4 (1)		(2)	2
Science and technology department					(1)			
Other					3		(1)	(1)
Total (out of 50)	2	3 (1)	13 (4)	11 (3)	20 (16)	1 (7)	(7)	(12)
Percentage	4%	6 (2)	26% (8%)	22% (6%)	40 (32)	2% (14%)	(14%)	(24%)

Note: Numbers in parentheses represent values in 2015. 'Other' in 2016 includes companies related to shipbuilding, transportation, and investment, while 'Other' in 2015 includes shipbuilding company and real estate dealer

in foreign policy focus to the 'going global' strategy for Chinese business and the governmental countermeasure of reflation during the global financial crisis in 2008 gave an incentive for fixed capital investment by enterprises for a time. As a result, overproduction capacity again reappeared in some industries when global market and demand scaled down. Therefore, at present, every enterprise should steadily pay attention to risk management to dissolve overproduction capacity so as not to turn into a zombie firm.

Present Problems Facing High-Profit and Deficit Enterprises

Although companies with the highest profitability seem unrelated to firms with negative RPR and debt-ridden enterprises, a more global perspective and deeper discernment may offer a key to understanding some not-so-visible aspects of their close relationship.

State-owned enterprises in key industrial sectors such as steel, coal, and cement, which have tended to face a deceleration in profitability, could continue to carry on business by virtue of governmental supports and social systems unique to the Chinese environment (e.g., no bankruptcy system in the securities market) (Huang et al. 2008). In particular, after the economic downturn precipitated by the Lehman Brothers bankruptcy in 2008, the central government paid about 4 trillion yuan as part of a reflation policy and product capacity was rapidly developed in real estate and iron/steel (Kurosawa 2016). Against the backdrop of weakened global and domestic demand, overproduction, excess inventory, and excess capacity rapidly developed in the iron and steel, cement, and non-ferrous metal industries. It is now reported that excess production capacity for iron and steel is now between 400 million and 500 million tons per year and the central government currently has targeted a reduction in production of crude steel between 100 million and 150 million tons per year (Matsumoto and Nakagawa 2016). At the same time, banks and financial organizations have continued to actively furnish funds to these enterprises in key industrial sectors, which means that they are assuming serious potential risks.

At the end of 2015, the value of outstanding loans increased by 14.3% compared with the prior year and the value of new loans issued swelled to 2.5 trillion yuan, an increase of 70.7% compared to 2014. The balance of bad debts among all financial organizations amounted to 1.2744 trillion yuan, an increase of 51.2% compared with the previous year, and the ratio of nonperforming loans increased to 1.7% (Seki 2016).

As shown in Tables 12.6 and 12.7, steel companies with low or negative RPR may seem to have nothing to do with high RPR banks, which is indicated in Tables 12.4 and 12.5, both steel companies and banks have received strong governmental supports, and steel companies have actually given profit opportunities to banks, despite the actual level of risks or potential for future loss, though these risks also seem to be opportunities for these companies to keep business. Banks have taken risks that are substantial and long term in nature.[8] Because of banks' focus on immediate risks and looking for short-term profit opportunity, invisible risks in the past manifest themselves as visible risks (e.g., overproduction, excess capacity, zombie enterprises) in the long run. The opposite ends of the RPR spectrum are different expressions of the same root cause.

Such a phenomenon is related to Chinese enterprise risk management. As risk management in steel companies is almost the same structure as that described previously in Sects. 12.1, 12.2, 12.3 and 12.4, here risk management in banks is touched upon for its peculiarity. The profitability of Chinese banks mainly relies on exploiting the margin in interest rates between their debts and credits. Given the stable and inflexible interest rate in China, banks seek to increase their returns resulting from this margin in interest rates by expanding loan volumes, rather than other strategies such as asset securitization (Baradwaj et al. 2014). Due to such monotypic profitability, Chinese banks lack "asset quality control and effective risk management" and do not use "effective screening and monitoring to evaluate borrowers' creditability" (Tan and Floros 2014, p. 47). The outcome of banks' loans has become more closely bound up with the increase in credit risks (Tan and Floros 2014, 40). In this sense, the increase of credit risks in Chinese banks, which has been veiled behind high short-term profitability, has stayed in step with the deficit operation and lower profitability of companies in the steel, coal, and cement industries as representative borrowers (see Jia Jin-jing 2016; Liu Bao-xing 2016).

12.5 Chinese Enterprise Risk Management and the Comprehensive Opportunity and Lost Opportunity Control Model[9]

It may be recognized from the above examination of the top 500 companies by revenue, which consists of Chinese representative and big enterprises, that the top 50 companies by RPR exhibits a striking contrast to the bottom 50 companies, and the both sides in 2016 are poles apart in profitability. If this phenomenon is considered from the viewpoint of risk management based on profit opportunity and enterprise risk, 'profit opportunity' in financial business organizations would connect closely to 'risk' in steel companies. Even though manufacturing companies suffer a deficit, they afford 'profit opportunity' to banks so much as they can pay interest on borrowed money and as they, particularly in listed companies, can continually keep business through the safeguards of governments (too low tax rate and safeguard from bankruptcy)

(Huang et al. 2008). Even in 2006, as Huang, Ning, and Yu (2008) pointed out, "Based on the 2006 annual reports, 65 of 1501 listed companies carry on business under the situation in which assets cannot cover debits, their capitals are negative, and they are always on the verge of bankruptcy. --- --- Such companies would not be considered to keep business in markets just as it was without local government safeguards" (pp. 7–8). In microeconomic base, true profit opportunity as well as enterprise risk becomes invisible, and much less to investors. Therefore, the veiled profit opportunity and enterprise risk behind the microeconomic structure (market mechanism) and the macroeconomic policy (strong safeguards for the stabilization of employment, contribution to governmental finance, and technological development) dilute the comprehensive and synthetic development of risk management in individual company despite the serious situation of the top and bottom companies that have been definitely examined in detail by the previous RPR analysis. When a company as a borrower is a central and listed company even though its operation is red, banks may give credit to the company as a sign of profit opportunity. The company also believes this insolvent loan not as risk but profit opportunity, since an entrepreneur expects to recover business while continuing to maintain business by means of governmental supports.

Wang (2010) fairly points out that there exist three risks in state-owned enterprises. The largest risk is the two weaknesses of key management and core competitive power, since their ability of 'becoming strong' related to strong key management and core competitive power is far behind the ability of 'becoming large' that is easy to enlarge through reorganization and integration of assets. The second risk is the weakness of the resource integration ability that leads to its effective arrangement and maximum efficacy. The third risk is related to corporate governance. As for this risk, Wang indicates as follows: "On the basis of agency theory, in the state-owned enterprises, superintendence department and enterprise auditing committee need to evaluate the unsound and ineffective situations of corporate governance" (p. 57).

Under the governmental safeguards, favorable income tax rate, and the inexistence of effective bankruptcy system in securities markets (Huang et al. 2008, p. 7), profit opportunity and enterprise risk that should be considered of most significance in Western risk management would be more invisible to listed companies and central enterprises with the speedy progression of market economy, although the two sides of the top profitable and the bottom deficit enterprises are brought closer together in strategic risk management. Due to this invisibility, enterprises focus not on the comprehensive and integrated management based on profit opportunity and enterprise risk, but mainly on immediate and visible risks, or operational and routine risks and internal control system

With regard to risk management in Western enterprises, the structure and meanings of the integrated profit opportunity and enterprise risk management were inquired into from the viewpoint of the comprehensive opportunity lost opportunity control (COLC) model in the previous chapters. Profit opportunity stands in parallel with enterprise risk on the common basis of enterprise strategy and cannot be exploited without taking risk. As shown in Table 12.2, the COLC model grasps profit opportunity and enterprise risk synthetically and proactively as both sides of strategy by connecting this information to management processes and to accounting profit or loss at settlement of accounts. These actions aim at establishing an optimal profit plan and efficiently and effectively controlling business activities toward the plan through continuous variance analyses and improvements. At the same time, all performances are evaluated from the angle of actualized opportunity and lost opportunity (opportunity cost) to clarify optimal planning and improvements in the next period. As a result, proactive information on profit opportunity and enterprise risk ends in accounting profit or loss through the interim analyses and various improvements. The COLC model systematically captures the essence of contemporary risk management and accounting in Western enterprises. The question that we must consider next is whether or not the COLC model is applicable to risk management in Chinese enterprises, particularly state-owned enterprises (Nishimura 2015a, b, 2016) (Fig. 12.2).

In China, the profit opportunity of an enterprise is basically influenced by governmental economic strategy and the adherence of the enterprise to this strategy. As long as enterprises search for strategies involving profit opportunity within this range, they need not suffer large loss involving this risk for a while when this strategy is unsuccessful, because the government is fundamentally responsible for the strategic decision-making and associated risks. Even if the enterprise bears responsibility for its failure, its burden is limited to a part of the whole, as far as it does not extend beyond the governmental strategy. Therefore, the governmental and political factors dominate enterprise economic activities in profit opportunities and risks control in these situations. Not every enterprise can execute profit opportunity and enterprise risk management independently of governmental

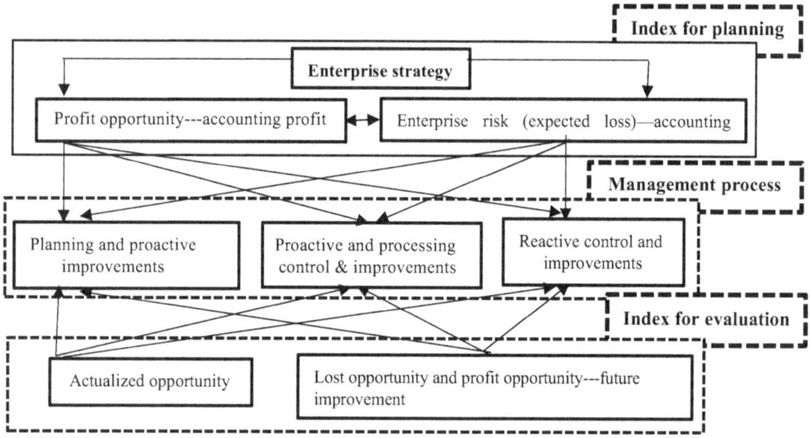

Fig. 12.2 Planning, control, and evaluation in the COLC model

policy, even though it can exploit new profit opportunities. However, as the national economy advances into the global economy, each enterprise also must bear self-responsibility for business. Although until now central enterprises in key industrial sectors have been sensible of their responsibility for imminent profitability and risk under internal control and governmental safeguards, under stagnant global economy, they as well as governments would begin to recognize the macro economic integration of profit opportunity and enterprise risk, as indicated in the problems of zombie enterprises and overproduction capacity.

From these observations, we can recognize that it may be hard to directly apply the COLC model to Chinese enterprise risk management, since their enterprise strategy and profit opportunity are strongly influenced by governmental economic strategy and political opportunity and risk. In this sense, the strong, political connection with administrative authorities has a decisive importance for Chinese enterprises to actualize and measure profit opportunity. Their strategic risk is completely different from that of Western enterprises. Correspondently, Chinese enterprises may be confronted with a unique 'connection' risk when the failure of administrative economic strategy results in lost opportunity. In comparison with the Western case, enterprise risk management in China seems to have traditionally focused on routine and operational risks, especially in state-owned enterprises that must devote themselves to stable and effective production under the protection of governmental economic policy. At the internationally competitive stage, how do they change the traditional strategic stance and risk management system to compete with foreign competitors? This successful change may result from the subjectivity and autonomy of the enterprise in strategic risk management in globally changeable competition and from cooperativeness with governmental foreign policy. At the same time, this change may force enterprises to conform to international management rules and accounting standards, while they also take part in making these regulations.

No country or enterprise can escape uncertainty or risks in today's globally finance-oriented economy. Compared with Western enterprises, *at present* Chinese enterprise pursue government-based enterprise risk management and risk responsibility. China can cope with uncertainty or risks by means of more unified and concentrated countermeasures, whereas in Western countries each enterprise must do so by using dispersed and various counteractions. Thus, the Western enterprises must always communicate with society through disclosure (transparency) and corporate governance (internal control) to mitigate risks socially and transform uncertainty to stability. However, the Chinese government must proactively absorb information on the total risks and uncertainty for the whole country and enterprises should also synthetically decide a strategic risk direction in order to avoid complete social uncertainty. We should now first recognize that even though every enterprise must cope with uncertainty to move toward greater stability, a governmentally administered economy is fundamentally different in system and form from an economy based on enterprise self-responsibility.

When applying the COLC model to enterprise risk management in China, we know its limitation in the place where governments and enterprises jointly cope with uncertainty and enterprise risks. Even if new methods for macro and micro risk management are identified, there are complicated and difficult problems to confront before implementing them because government must first establish a model that can recognize and measure uncertainty from a social perspective and control it from the political and macro viewpoint. Then enterprises must build up a micro model based on the above model. Besides the overall subjectivity of politics, enterprise must cope with the specific political reality in which they operate and manage the ambiguous boundary between opportunity and risk related to politics and enterprise opportunity and risk related to the business. However, this ambiguity makes it difficult to calculate the probabilities of various outcomes arising therefrom. It is impossible to methodically discuss profit opportunity and enterprise risk unless the related probabilities can be estimated. Even though it is very difficult to estimate the probability of profit opportunity or enterprise risk involving *economic phenomena*, statistics or objective experiences can be used to make reasonable assumptions. However, it may be beyond our ability to make assumptions about the probability of *subjective and political phenomena.* Moreover, such political factors must be converted into proactively measurable information in the micro model to be useful for enterprise planning and control through accounting information and evaluation.

Even though their factors are reflectively calculated as accounting income, it may take much time and trouble to assemble a new type of enterprise risk management accounting model that can proactively forecast political and economic opportunities and risks and control for them through variance analyses based on macro information since most companies in China are still unaccustomed to controlling risks from an accounting perspective (see Yin Chong 2015). At present it may be difficult to forecast information on political and macroeconomic opportunity and risk and tie these together with accounting information. However, this endeavor to establish such a model will certainly lead toward greater stability out of the current uncertainty, even if it treads a thorny path. In both a state-planning society and a freely competitive society, no enterprise can carry on business with utter disregard of uncertainty or risks in the contemporary age. Despite the continuous development of harmonized and advanced management and information systems, uncertainty has increasingly become a difficult matter for businesses to contend with. Therefore, everyone should always make efforts to move toward greater stability and harmony beyond the chaos of uncertainty. We all should always continue to develop management and accounting systems to take steps forward toward a more stabilized harmony. Therefore, Chinese enterprises and researchers should also continue to make efforts for development of a new model that integrates systems of enterprise risk management with governmental risk management policy.

12.6 Conclusion

Chinese state-owned enterprises have begun to introduce risk management, following the example of Western businesses, as they seek to increase their market share in an internationally competitive finance-based economy. At first Chinese enterprise risk management was government based and strongly regulatory in its use of internal control systems to secure state property and continually ensure stable production for exporting cheaper and higher-quality products and gaining foreign currency. With the shift away from an 'absorbing foreign power' strategy to a 'going global' strategy, risk management systems in these enterprises will have to become more strategic and autonomous. In this sense, Chinese enterprises must wrestle with numerous complicated issues to establish a new model in which micro risk management is organically integrated with macro risk management.

In today's finance-oriented global economy when every enterprise employs global strategic management, the comprehensibility of risk management is very important to proactively and synthetically control profit opportunity and enterprise risk from the strategic viewpoint. In Chinese enterprise risk management, profit opportunity and enterprise risk have been veiled behind various governmental safeguards and supports and become invisible to individual enterprise and bank. Probably, profit opportunity and enterprise risk should first be visualized to build a comprehensive enterprise risk management in China. On this basis, the integrated management of profit opportunity and enterprise risk and the control model based on opportunity and lost opportunity (opportunity cost) will organically be systemized together with effective risk management accounting.

In this chapter, risk management has also been discussed from the perspective of the COLC model on the basis of the expectation that Chinese enterprises will establish a unique risk management model that differs from the COLC model, working together with governments to do so. However, this effective model may be based on the common concepts of proactive and preventive control and information systems as understood in the COLC model. At its core, the COLC model involves feed-forward management accounting in which future-oriented accounting information is closely integrated with a proactive and preventive management system. As learned from Western bitter experiences, haphazard and unfair management and nonsystematic and inaccurate accounting information may mislead managers and other persons into continually underestimating the actual progress achieved in trying to manage uncertainty. In this sense, the COLC is useful for comprehensive risk management. As Chinese enterprises develop their business more broadly in the globally competitive economy and inevitably face greater uncertainty, they will be required to take additional steps to improve risk management by building an effective control model.

Notes

1. Central (national) enterprises are state-owned enterprises under supervision of SASAC and the administration sections of the State Council. Furthermore, state-owned enterprises primarily consist of the above central enterprises and nonfinancial state-owned and state-holding enterprises under supervision of 36 provincial governments. Though the number of the state-owned enterprises accounts only for very low percentage of total number of enterprises (about 2%), their role in national economy is tremendous. They occupy over half of total national sales in nine key industries such as resources, energy-related business, electric power, gas, iron and steel, and others, with governmental guardianship acting as a regulatory barrier to entry. Their added value accounts for about 20% of the national GDP, their fixed assets investment for 19% of total social fixed assets investment, and their taxes paid for 34.6% of the national financial revenue annually from 2007 to 2013. The number of *central enterprises* that are counted among the Fortune 500 increases every year. As for the listed central companies under supervision of SASAC, the converted ratio of assets into securities amounts to 50% of the total assets and governmental stockholders' equity is overwhelmingly high in comparison with minority stockholders' equity (20%). (See Yang and Song 2014, pp. 23–26.)
2. For further details on recent regulations affecting risk management, see SASAC General Office (2009), and SASAC General Office (2012).
3. For further details on national laws and regulations involving internal control systems and enterprise risk management, see SASAC's document (2006), and Ministry of Finance (2008): mof.gov.cn/zhengwuxinxi/caizhengwengao/caizhengbuwengao2008/caizhengbuwengao200810/t20081030_86252.html.
4. For further details of the plan, see Ninth Five-year Plan of National Economic and Social Development in the People's Republic of China and Outline for Long-range Goal till 2010, *Chinese Communist Party's Papers and Documents/Data*, 1996: available online at: <cpc.people.com.cn/GB/64184/64186/4494253.html#>.
5. Regarding governmental documents, see Important Strategic Mission (1986), *Enterprise Management*, No. 5, pp. 24–25; Outlines for the Modernization of Enterprise Management (1986), *Enterprise Management*, No. 6, pp. 43–47.
6. This chapter discusses 'group companies' on the basis of findings of Yuan and Zhang (2011) and Yuan and Zhang (2015). In the former paper, eight of the ten researched companies were state-owned enterprises and two companies were private enterprises; while in the latter, eight of the ten researched companies were state-owned enterprises, one was a local government–owned enterprise and the other was a private enterprise.

7. The data is obtained from the following sources: Strong 500 Ranking in China (List of Companies Names), *FORTUNEChina.com*, 2011, 2015 and 2016: fortunechina.com/fortune500/c/2016-07/13/content_266415.htm, 2015-07/08/content_242835.htm and 2011-07/13/content_62684.htm.
8. See Questions and Answers: Nobel Laureate Robert Engle on systemic risk and financial volatility in China, *ARCH-economist*, 19 December 2014: Chinaeconomicreview.com/ARCHeconomist.
9. This model analysis is part of the stream of inquiry into the relationship between uncertainty and management accounting. Particularly, the COLC model contributes much to the systemization and conciseness of comprehensive enterprise risk management (see the following papers: Nishimura 2006a, b, 2016).

Bibliography

Baradwaj, B. G., Flaherty, S. M. V., & Shao, Y. Y. (2014). The Impact of Lending Growth on the Risks of Chinese Banks. *The Chinese Economy, 47*(5–8), 29–49.

Bo Qi-liang, & Lu Ru-quan. (2013). Structuring and Implementation of Multinational Business Strategic Management. *Enterprise Management, 3*, 90–93.

Cha Jin-cai, Cao Tao, & Luo Ji. (2013). Overseas Political Risk and Proactive Control. *Enterprise Management, 12*, 89–91.

Gong Hua-Zhang. (2008). Risk Management in Chinese Oil Company: Recognition and Practices. *Enterprise Management, 1*, 68.

Huang Jian-ping, Ning Jinng-bian, & Yu Ying-hua. (2008). Empirical Study on the Decision-making of Risk Management in Chinese Listed Companies. *Economic Management, 30*(12), 4–9.

Jia Jin-jing. (2016, June 6). Background of Zombie Enterprises: What Is True Causes, *Chinese Reform Forum*. http://Chinareform.org.cn/economy/Enterprise/Practice/201606/t201606_250397.htm.

Kurosawa, H. (2016, April 12). The Prolongation of Zombie Enterprises Due to Speculative Buying Even After President Li's Expression of Overproduction Capacity Curtailment, *Economist* (Japan), *94*(16), 34–35. Mainich Shinbun Publishing Inc.

Liu-Bao-xing. (2016). Over 3 Trillion Liabilities in Steel Industry: Some Listed Companies to Make Choice of Withdrawal from Markets, *Securities Time*, 20 October. http://www.Stcn.com/2016/0120/12554759shtml.

Liu Ji-shen. (2011). Enterprise Strategic Risk Management Under New Competitive Condition, 28 September, *Baidu Wenku*. www.wenku.baidu.com/view/b64f2290daofSef/baiBd3cba.html?frw=search&isbta=###.

Matsumoto, A., & Fujisawa, T. (2016, September 13). Structural Reform as Pie in the Sky: Ten Industrial Sectors of Resolving New Overcapacity. *Economist* (Japan), *94*(34), 18–21. Mainich Shinbun Publishing Inc.

Matsumoto, A., & Nakagawa, M. (2016, April 12). Limitation of Arbitrary Reform: Outliving Zombie Enterprises. *Economist* (Japan), *94*(16), 18–21. Mainich Shinbun Publishing Inc.

Meng Jian-ming. (2010). *Speech in the Working Conference of Central Enterprises Internal Auditing*. xxgk.sasac.gov.cn/gdnps/content.jsp?id=1260973.

Ministry of Finance. (2008). *Circular Related to the Printing and Distribution of "Fundamental Standards of Enterprise Internal Control"*. http://www.mof.gov.cn/zhenwuxinxi/caizhengwengao/caizhengbuwengao200810/t20081030_86252.html.

Nishimura, A. (2006a). Enterprise Governance and Management Accounting from the Viewpoint of Feed Forward Control. *Asian-Pacific Management Accounting Journal, 1*(1), 1–17. Public Knowledge Project (Open Journal System). http://arionline.uitm.edu.my/ojs/index.php/APMAJ/issue/view/20.

Nishimura, A. (2006b). Analysis of Industrial Structure and Profitable Structure in China; Recent Development and Problems Chinese State-owned Enterprises: Structures of Industry and Deficit. *Business Administration and Management Accounting in Asia* (pp. 257–279 and 311–334), Tokyo: Chuou Keizai Publisher.

Nishimura, A. (2006c). *Business Management and Management Accounting in Asia (Japanese)*. Tokyo: Chuokeizai Publisher.

Nishimura, A. (2008). Effect of Management System on Management Accounting: The Case of Chinese Cellular Phone Terminal Unit Manufacturers. *Asian-Pacific Management Accounting Journal, 3*(1), 87–105. Public Knowledge Project (Open Journal System). http://arionline.uitm.edu.my/ojs/index.php/APMAJ/issue/view/18.

Nishimura, A. (2015a). Comprehensive Opportunity and Lost Opportunity Control Model and Enterprise Risk Management. *International Journal of Business and Management, 10*(8), 73–87. https://doi.org/10.5539/ijbm.v10n8p73.

Nishimura, A. (2015b). Strategic Management Accounting and Feed-forward Management: With Reference to the Unified Management of Profit Opportunity and Risk, *Global Management, 3 & 4 (combined)*, 1–19.

Nishimura, A. (2016). Foreign Exchange Risk and Profit Improvement in the Comprehensive Profit Opportunity and Lost Opportunity Control Model. *International Journal of Business and Management, 11*(4), 1–13.

Pan, C.-L. (2000). Carefully Prepared Plan for Enterprise Future. *Enterprise management, 2*, 5–6.

PricewaterhouseCoopers. (2014a). Big Four Blind Points of Enterprises Risk Management to Effectively Avoid Risks, *Chief Finance Officer*, 19 November.

PricewaterhouseCoopers. (2014b). Four Mistakes for Effective Evasion of Risk Management, *Chief Finance Office*, 11 November. http://topcfo.net/index.php/news/index/id/38752.html.

SASAC's document. (2006). *Circular Related to the Printing and Distribution of Guidelines of Comprehensive Risk Management for Central Enterprises.* http://www.xxgk.sasac.gov.cn/gdnps/content.jsp?id=1319184.

SASAC General Office. (2009). *Notifications Related to the 2010's Comprehensive Enterprise Risk Management Report in Central Enterprises.* http://www.xxgk.sasac.gov.cn/gdnps/content.jsp?id=1262589.

SASAC General Office. (2012). *Notification of Related Matters for Central Enterprises to Comprehensively Develop Risk Management Activities in 2013.* http://www.xxgk.sasac.gov.cn/gdnps/content.jsp?id=1261301.

Seki, S. (2016, April 12). The Rapid Increase of Bad Debits: Ten Trillion Yuan Including the Bad Debits of Shadow Banks and Anxious Forbearance Lending to State-owned Enterprises. *Economist* (Japan), *94*(16), 32–33. Mainich Shinbun Publishing Inc.

Shen Long Automobile Limited Liability Company (Dongfeng Peugeot/Citroen Company Ltd.). (2015). Enterprise Risk Management in Supply Chain. *Enterprise Management, 6*, 55–59.

Sun Chang-qi. (2003). Four Blind Areas of Strategic Management. *Enterprise Management, 9*, 25–28.

Tan, Y., & Floros, C. (2014). Risk, Profitability, and Competition: Evidence from the Chinese banking Industry. *Journal of Developing Areas, 48*(3, Summer), 303–319.

Wang Jing-Feng, Li Dong-Mei, & Zhang Tong-Quan. (2012). Study on Enterprise Practices of Risk Assessment: Based on Experiences of A Coal Mine in a Certain Coal Industry Limited Liability Company. *Auditing Research, 4*, 89–96.

Wang Min. (2014). Strategic Thinking on the Information Orientation of Risk Control Management Implemented by Central Enterprises. *Contemporary Economic Management, 36*(2), 36–39.

Wang Xiao-xia. (2010). Responsibility and Target Structure of State-owned Enterprise Risk Management Auditing, *Auditing Research, Third issue*, pp. 54–58.

Wang Yi. (2002). Present Situation and Future Analysis of Chinese Enterprise Strategic Management Development. *Global Management Research, 11*, 43–46.

Xu Hui, Zou Hui-min, & Wang Jian-Ming. (2009). Risk Classification and Cognition of Multinational Companies under Globalized Strategic Transformation. *Economic Management Journal, 30*(9), 142–150.

Yang Hao-Hui, & Song Zhi-Cai. (2014). Research Study on the Business Situations of State-owned Enterprises. *New Wisdom, 9*, 23–26.

Yin Chong. (2015). Rising and Development of Dynamic Risk Management Accounting. *The Chinese Certificated Public Accountant Journal, 4*, 57–60.

Yuan Lin & Zhang Hong-liang. (2011). Board of Directors' Governance and the Risk Management of Finance company. *Accounting Research, 5*, 65–71.

Yuan Lin & Zhang Wei-hua. (2015). Management Control of Group Company and the Risk Management of Finance Company. *Accounting Research, 5*, 35–41.

Zhang Jian-she. (2004). Missed Strategy or Lost Management? *Enterprise Management, 11*, 28–30.

Bibliography

Abe, T., Yoshikawa, K., & Hasegawa, H. (2000). Risk Management in IT Business Age. *Nikkei Information Strategy*, December, Nikkei Business Publications, 37.

Abrams, C., von Känel, J., Mäller, S., Pfitzmann, B., & Ruschka-Taylor, S. (2007). Optimized Enterprise Risk Management. *IBM System Journal, 46*(2), 219–234.

Ai, X. (2008). *The Tragedy of Firms with the Wrong Strategy*, http://www.adfaith.com/cn/newscontent.asp?InfoID=1421. Accessed 10 Aug 2008.

American Accounting Association. (1966). *A Statement of Basic Accounting Theory*. Evanston: AAA.

Anthony, R. N. (1965). *Planning and Control Systems: A Framework for Analysis*. Boston: Division of Research, Graduate School of Business Administration, Harvard University.

Appleyard, T., & Pallet, S. (2004). *Successful Foreign Acquisitions* (pp. 16–17). Burlington: CIMA publishing.

Arena, M., Arnaboldi, M., & Azzone, G. (2010). The Organizational Dynamics of Enterprise Risk Management. *Accounting, Organizations and Society, 35*(7), 659–675.

Arnold, V., Benford, T., Canada, J., & Sutton, S. G. (2011). The Role of Strategic Enterprise Risk Management and Organizational Flexibility in Easing New Regulatory Compliance. *International Journal of Accounting Information Systems, 12*, 171–188.

Atkinson, A. A., Banker, R. D., Kaplan, R. S., & Yong, S. M. (2001). *Management Accounting*. Upper Saddle River: Prentice Hall.

Baldwin, H. (2015, June 9–15). The Rapidly Changing Role of the CIO, *Computer Weekly*, pp. 15–16.

Banks, E. (2004). *Corporate Governance: Financial Responsibility, Controls and Ethics* (pp. 26–27). Basingstoke: Palgrave Macmillan.

A. Nishimura, *Management, Uncertainty, and Accounting*,
https://doi.org/10.1007/978-981-10-8989-3

Baradwaj, B. G., Flaherty, S. M. V., & Shao, Y. Y. (2014). The Impact of Lending Growth on the Risks of Chinese Banks. *The Chinese Economy, 47*(5–8), 29–49.

Belkoui, A. (1983). *Cost Accounting: A Multidimensional Emphasis*. Chicago: The Dryden Press.

Bell, H. W. (1925). *Accountants' Report* (2nd ed.). New York: The Ronald Press.

Beppu, Y. (2005). Environmental Management and Business Strategy: The Case Studies of Japanese Companies in Oceania (3). *The Teikyo University Economic Review, 38*(2), 25–73.

Berle, A. A., & Means, G. C. (1932). *Modern Corporation and Private Property*. New York: Macmillan.

Bhimani, A. (1995, June). Target Excellence: Target Cost Management at Toyota in the UK. *Management Accounting, 73*(6), 42–45.

Bhimani, A. (2009). Risk Management, Corporate Governance and Management Accounting: Emergence Interdependences. *Management Accounting Research, 20*(1), 2–5. https://doi.org/10.1016/j.mar.2008/11.002.

Bhimani, A., & Langfield-Smith, K. (2007). Structure, Formality and the Importance of Financial and Non-financial Information in Strategy Development and Implementation. *Management Accounting Research, 18*(1), 3–31.

Birkinshaw, J., Bouquet, C., & Barsoux, J-L. (2011). The 5 Myths of Innovation, *MIT Sloan Management Review* (MIT Sloan Management Review, Sloan-select collection, winter, 1–8).

Bo Qi-liang, & Lu Ru-quan. (2013). Structuring and Implementation of Multinational Business Strategic Management. *Enterprise Management, 3*, 90–93.

Borge, D. (2001). *The Book of Risk*. New York: Wiley.

Borison, A., & Hamm, G. (2010). How to Manage Risk (After Risk Management Has Failed). *MIT Sloan Management Review, 52*(Fall), 51–57.

Bouch, W. G. (2006). FedEx Freight-Putting: People First. In H. D. Edward & K. K. Cameron (Eds.). *Leading with Values: Positivity, Virtue and High Performance* (pp. 29–54). Cambridge/New York: Cambridge University Press.

Boudreau, K. J., & Lakhani, K. R. (2009). How to Manage Outside Innovation, *MIT Sloan Management Review*, Summer (MIT Sloan, *Management Review*, Sloan-select Collection, Winter 2011, 50–57).

Brecht, H. D., & Martin, M. P. (1996). Accounting Information Systems: The Challenge of Extending Their Scope to Business and Information Strategy. *Accounting Horizons, 10*(4), 16–22.

Buffet, W. (2002). *Warren Buffett's Letters to Berkshire Shareholders*. Omaha: Berkshire Hathaway, Inc. http://www.berkshirehathaway.com/letters/2002.html.

Burnham, J. (1941). *The Managerial Revolution: What Is happening in the World*. New York: John Day.

Calderon, G. T., Cheh, J. J., & Kim, I. (2003). How Large Corporations Use Data Mining to Create Value. *Management Accounting Quarterly, 4*(2), 1–11.

Cant, S. (2006, April). Value-based Management. *Financial Management*, pp. 33–34.

Cha Jin-cai, Cao Tao, & Luo Ji. (2013). Overseas Political Risk and Proactive Control. *Enterprise Management, 12*, 89–91.

Chandler, A. D., Jr. (1977). *The Visible Hand: The Managerial Revolution in American Business.* Cambridge, MA: Belknap Press of Harvard University Press.

Cheng, D., & Liu, L. (2008). *The Truth of Huawei.* http://blog.chinaunix.net/u.304/showart_201971.html. Accessed 2 Sept 2008.

Cheng, T. C. E., Yip, F. K., & Yeung, A. C. L. (2012). Supply Risk Management Via *Guanxi* in the Chinese Business Context: The buyer's Perspective. *International Journal of Production Economics, 139*, 3–13.

Chesbrough, H. W. (2003). The Era of Open Innovation, *MIT Sloan Management Review*, Spring (ibid., 35–41).

Chesbrough, H. W. (2007). Why Companies Should Have Open Business Models, *MIT Sloan Management Review*, Winter (ibid., 68–74).

Christensen, C. M., Anthony, S. D., Berstell, G., & Nitterhouse, D. (2007). Finding the Right Job for Your Project, *MIT Sloan Management Review*, Spring (ibid., 58–67).

Christopher, M. (2000). The Agile Supply Chain: Competing in Volatile Markets. *Industrial Marketing Management, 29*, 37–44.

Christopher, M., & Denis, T. (2001). An Integrated Model for the Design of Agile Supply Chains. *International Journal of Physical Distribution & Logistics Management, 31*(4), 235–246.

Clarke, C. J., & Varma, S. (1999). Strategic Risk Management: The New Competitive Edge. *Long Range Planning, 32*(4), 414–424.

Collier, P. M., & Berry, A. J. (2002). Risk in the Process of Budgeting. *Management Accounting Research, 13*, 273–297.

Collin, J., & Lorenzin, D. (2006). Plan for Supply Chain Agility at Nokia: Lessons from the Mobile Infrastructure Industry. *International Journal of Physical Distribution & Logistics Management, 36*(6), 418–430.

Collins, J. (2009). *How the Mighty Fall and Why Some Companies Never Give in.* New York: HarperCollins Publishers Inc.

Committee of Sponsoring Organizations of the Treadway Commission (COSO). (2004). *Enterprise Risk Management: Integrated Framework*, COSO, September, 13.

Connell, B. (2004, April). Perspective on Enterprise Governance, Presented to the *CMAC Management Accounting Conference*, Kuala Lumpur.

Cooper, R., & Slagmulder, R. (1997). *Target Costing and Value Engineering*, New jersey: Institute of Management Accounants & Portland: Productivity Press.

Cooper, R., & Slagmulder, R. (1999). Develop Profitable New Products with Target Costing. *MIT Sloan Management Review, 40*(Summer), 23–33.

Cooper, R., & Slagmulder, R. (2004). Achieving Full-Cycle Cost Management. *MIT Sloan Management Review, 46*(Fall), 45–52.

COSO. (2004, September). *Enterprise Risk Management-Integrated Framework: Executive Summary Framework*, The Committee of Sponsoring Organizations of the Treadway, NJ (US).

Cowell, F. (2006, November). Risk Management for Derivatives. *Derivatives Use, Trading & Regulation, 12*(3), 228–243.

Culp, C. (2001). *The Risk Management Process: Business Strategy and Tactics.* New York: Wiley.

Cushing, B. E. (1968, October). Some Observations on Demski's Ex Post Accounting System. *The Accounting Review, 43*(4), 668–671.

Demski, J. S. (1967, October). An Accounting System Structures on a Linear Programming Model. *Accounting Review, 42*(4), 701–712.

Demski, J. S. (1968, October). Some Observations on Demski's Ex Post Accounting System: A Reply. *The Accounting Review, 43*(4), 672–674.

Demski, J. S. (1969, October). Decision-Performance Control. *Accounting Review, 44*(4), 669–713.

Demski, J. S. (1977). Analyzing the Effectiveness of the Traditional Standard Cost Variance Model. In G. J. Benston (Ed.), *Contemporary Cost Accounting and Control* (2nd ed., pp. 222–236). Boston: CBI publishing Co. Inc.

Denso Corporation. (2010). *Supplier CSR Guidance*, April, 6.

Denso Corporation. (2014). *Product-Environmental Management*.http://www.denso.co.jp/ja/csr/environment_report/management/product/index.html/. Accessed 9 Apr 2014.

Dickinson, G. (2000). Risk Role Grows to Enterprise Scale: Enterprise Risk Management Provides Control Over Disparate Risks in the Business Environment. Gerry Dickinson Explains How: [Surveys ed.], *Financial Times*, London (UK), 13 November; 8.

Dietl, H. M. (1998). *Capital Markets and Corporate Governance in Japan, Germany, and the United States* (pp. 23–44). London: Routledge.

Dressler, S. (2002). Management Accounting Master: Closing the Gap Between Managerial Accounting and External Reporting. *Journal of Cost Management, 16*(January/February), 18–29.

Drnevich, P. L., & Croson, D. C. (2013). Information Technology and Business-level Strategy: Toward an Integrated Theoretical Perspective. *MIS Quarterly, 37*(2), 483–509.

Drori, G. S. (2006). Governed by Governance: The New Prism for Organizational Change. In G. S. Drori, J. W. Meyer, & H. Hwang (Eds.), *Globalization and Organization: World Society and Organizational Change* (pp. 91–118). New York: Oxford University Press.

Drury, C. (2001). *Management Accounting for Business Decisions.* Bedford: Thomson London.

EDINET (Electronic Disclosure for investors 'NET-work.: http://disclosure.edinet.fs.go.jp and 'kabupro.jp': http://www.kabupro.jp: *Concerning Annual Securities Reports* (fiscal year 2005 and fiscal year 2013) of the Japanese 100 companies.

Elkins, D. A., Huang, N. J., & Alden, J. M. (2004). Agile Manufacturing Systems in the Automobile Industry. *International Journal of Production Economics, 91*, 201–214.

Ellram, L. M. (2000). Purchasing and Supply Management's Participation in the Target Costing Process. *The Journal of Supply Chain Management, 36*(Spring), 39–51.

Ellram, L. M. (2006). The Implementation of Target Costing in the United States: Theory Versus Practice. *The Journal of Supply Chain Management, 42*(Winter), 13–26.

Emerson, H. (1909). *Efficiency as a Basis for Operation and Wages*, New York: The Engineering Magazine, 131.

Enterprise Bankruptcy in Japan. (2003). http://www.tdb.co.jp/tosan/syukei/03nen.html.

Falta, M., Gallagher, L., & Willett, R. (2006). Modeling 'Hard-To-Measure' Costs in Environment Management Accounting. *Asia-Pacific Management Accounting Journal, 1*(1), 127–125.

Florricel, S., & Ibanescu, M. (2008). Using R&D Portfolio Management to Deal with Dynamic Risk. *R&D Management, 38*(5), 452–467.

Frestad, D., & Beisland, L. A. (2015). Hedge Effectiveness Testing as a Screening Mechanism for Hedge Accounting: Does it Work? *Journal of Accounting, Auditing & Finance, 30*(*1*), 35–56.

Fujita, K. (2003). Effectiveness and Limitation of Hedging Accounting. *Ritsumeikan Keieigaku, 42*(*2*), 1–18.

Gabriel, M., Tschandl, M., & Posh, A. (2014). Sustainability-Oriented Lifecycle Costing. *International Journal of Engineering, 12*(1), 33–40.

GADSL. (2011). *Global Automotive Declarable Substance List: Guidance Document, 2011–2012.* http://plastics.americanchemistry.com/Stand-Alone-Content/Global-Automotive-Declarabble-Substance=Document/. Accessed 14 Mar 2014.

Gates, S., Nicolas, J. L., & Walker, P. L. (2012). Enterprise Risk Management: A Process for Enhanced Management and Improved Performance. *Management Accounting Quarterly, 13*(3), 28–38.

Geissler, C., Ikeda, R., & Cook, A. (2006, July). Corporate Germany Must Change? *Diamond Harvard Business Review* (Japanese version), pp. 44–56.

Gibson, M. S. (2007). Credit Derivatives and Risk Management, *Economic Review, Fourth Quarter*, pp. 25–40.

Glynn, M., & Jamerson, H. (2006). Principled Leadership: A Framework for Action. In D. E. Hess & S. K. Cameron (Eds.), *Leadership with Values: Positivity, Virtue, and High Performance*. Cambridge, NY: Cambridge University Press.

Goldbach, M. (2010). Organizational Settings in Supply Chain Costing. In S. Seuring & M. Goldbach (Eds.), *Cost Management in Supply Chains* (pp. 89–108). Heidelberg: Physica-Verlag.

Gong Hua-Zhang. (2008). Risk Management in Chinese Oil Company: Recognition and Practices. *Enterprise Management, 1*, 68.

Govindarajan, V., & Trimble, C. (2004). Strategic Innovation and the Science of Learning, *MIT Sloan Management Review*, Winter (ibid., 19–27).

Grégoire, D. A., Barr, P. S., & Shepherd, D. A. (2010, March–April). Cognitive Processes of Opportunity Recognition: The Role of Structural Alignment. *Organization Science, 21*(2), 413–431.

Grigore, S. D. (2007). Supply Chain Flexibility. *Romanian Economic and Business Review, 2*(1), 66–70.

Grote, G. (2014). Promoting Safety by Increasing Uncertainty-Implications for Risk Management. *Safety Science*. https://doi.org/10.10176/j.ssci.1014.02.010.

Gruber, M. M., Ian, C., & Thompson, J. D. (2008, September). Look before You Leap: Market Opportunity Identification in Emerging Technology Firms. *Management Science, 54*(9), 1652–1665.

Guilding, C., Cravens, K. S., & Tayles, M. (2000). An International Comparison of Strategic Management Accounting Practices. *Management Accounting Research, 11*(1), 128.

Gungor, A., & Gupta, S. M. (1999). Issues in Environmentally Conscious Manufacturing and Product Recovery: A Survey. *Computers & Industrial Engineering, 36*, 811–853.

Harrison, G. C. (1918a, October). Cost Accounting to Aid Production-1, Application of Scientific Management Principles, *Industrial Management, 56*(2), pp. 278–281.

Harrison, G. C. (1918b, November). Cost Accounting to Aid Production-II, Standards and Standard Costs, *Industrial Management, 56*(4), pp. 391–398.

Harrison, G. C. (1918c, December). Cost Accounting to Aid Production-III, The Universal Law of System, *Industrial Management, 56*(5), pp. 456–461.

Harrison, G. C. (1919a, April). Cost Accounting to Aid Production-VII, Extension of Application of Scientific Management Principles, *Industrial Management, 57*(4), pp. 314–321.

Harrison, G. C. (1919b, June). Cost Accounting to Aid Production-IX, Conclusion and the Future of Cost Accounting, *Industrial Management, 57*(6), pp. 314–321.

Harrison, G. C. (1920, March). Basis for Cost Accounting, *Industrial Management, 59*(3), pp. 237–242.

Hashida, T. (2008). *High Technology Industry in China (in Japanese).* Tokyo: Hakuto Publishing Company.

Haynie, M. J., Shepherd, D. A., & McMullen, J. S. (2009, May). An Opportunity for Me? The Role of Resources in Opportunity Evaluation Decision. *Journal of Management Studies, 46*(3), 337–360.

Heath, R. L., Lee, J., & Ni, L. (2009). Crisis and Risk Approaches to Emergency Management Planning and Communication: The Role of Similarity and Sensitivity. *Journal of Public Relations Research, 21*(2), 123–141.

Henri, J.-F., & Joumeault, M. (2010). Eco-control: The Influence of Management Control Systems on Environmental and Economic Performance. *Accounting, Organizations, and Society, 35*(1), 63–80.

Hewlett Packard. (2014). *International Material Data System to Automotive Industry.* http://h50146.www5.hp.com/solutions/industry/manufacture/sol/imds/. Accessed 14 Mar 2014.

Hilton, W. R. (2005). *Managerial Accounting: Creating Value in a Dynamic Business Environment* (6th ed.). New York: McGraw-Hill.

Hino Motors Ltd. (2015). *Annual Securities Report.* http://www.kabupro.jp/mark/2015622/S10050CE.h.

Hitachi Manufacturing Company Ltd. (2015). *Annual Securities Report.* http://www.kabupro.jp/edp/20150625/S10055M4.htm (2014). *EDINET.*

Holmquist, E. (2012). Risk Management and Business Strategy. *The RMA Journal, 94*(10), 40–45.

Hopkins, M. S. (2010). The Four Ways IT Is Revolutionizing Innovation (Interview), *MIT Sloan Management Review*, Spring (ibid., 75–80).

Horváth, P., & Berlin, S. (2012). Green Target Costing; Getting Ready for the Green Challenge! *Cost Management, 26*(3), 25–36.

Huang, L. (2006). An Essay on Chinese Enterprise Business System. *Journal of National Economy, 194*(1), 1–14.

Huang Jian-ping, Ning Jinng-bian, & Yu Ying-hua. (2008). Empirical Study on the Decision-making of Risk Management in Chinese Listed Companies. *Economic Management, 30*(*12*), 4–9.

Hunkeler, D., Lichtenvort, K., & Rebitzer, G. (Eds.). (2008). *Environmental Life Cycle Costing,* Florida: CRC Press, Taylor & Francis Group and SETAC.

IASB (International Accounting Standard Board). (2014, July). *IFRS 9 Financial Instruments.* http://www.iasplus.com/en-gb/standards/ifrs-en-gb/ifrs9.

IBM Japan. (1999). *Environment & Well-being Progress Report 1999.* Environment & Safety/Sanitation/Health, 10–11.

IBM Japan. (2000). *Environment & Well-being Progress Report 2000*, 16–17.

IBM Japan. (2001). *Environment & Well-being Progress Report 2001*, 24–25; As for the Relation Between Product Development and ECP Based on Integrated

Product Development Plan, and Green Supply Chain, See the Released Documents on Green Supply Chain: IBM Environmental Conscious Product Design (Green PLM). http://www-06.ibm.com/services/bcs/jp/solutions/sc/menu/green_plm.html. Accessed 17 Feb 2014.

IFA. (2004). *Enterprise Governance: Getting the Balance Right*, booklet prepared by the Professional Accountants in Business Committee (PAIB). New York/UK: International Federation of Accountants (IFA)/CIMA.

Ilgin, M. A., & Gupta, S. M. (2010). Environmentally Conscious Manufacturing and Product Recovery (ECMPRO): A Review of the State of the Art. *Journal of Environmental Management, 91*, 563–591.

IMA. (1994). Implementing Target Costing. *Statements on Management Accounting*, Institute of Management Accountants (Canada).

Imai, N. (2010). Proposal of Dual Mode Management Accounting Model: With a View to Dissolve "Accounting Lag". *Meijo Journal, 10*(4), 61–87.

Imai, N. (2014). Concept of Proactive Slack: A Study on Essence on Toyota's Performance Accounting. *Journal of Japan Management Diagnosis Association, 14*, 41–46.

Imoto, S. (1999, June). What Distinguishes Nakauchi (Chairman of Daiei) from Ito (Honor Chairman of Ito-Yokado Co Ltd)? *Nikkei Venture*, pp. 82–6.

Ingrassia, P. (2011). *Crash Course: The American Automobile Industry's Road to Bankruptcy and Bailout—And Beyond*. New York: Random House Inc.

Ishikawa, A., & Smith, C. H. (1972). A Feed Forward Control System for Organizational Planning and Control. *ABACUS, 8*(2), 163–180.

Ishiyama, S., Kimura, Y., & Kumagaya, T. (2006, July). German Business Report. *Diamond Harvard Business Review* (Japanese version), pp. 68–174.

Itami, H. (2000). *Japanese Corporate Governance*. Tokyo: Nihon Kezai Sinbun.

Ito, Y. (2006). Subjects of Environmentally Conscious Cost Design. *Accounting, 170*(4), 485–499.

Ito, Y. (2007, May). *Investigation and Research on Environmentally Conscious Cost Design*, Report to Japan Society for Promotion of Science, pp. 37–40.

Ito, T., Koibuch, S., Sato, K., & Shimizu, J. (2013, April). Exchange Rate Exposure and Exchange Rate Risk Management: The Case of Japanese Exporting Firms, *The Research Institute of Economy, Trade, and Industry, Discussion Paper Series, 13-E-025*. http://www.rieti.go.jp/en/.

Jaafari, A. (2001). Management of Risks, Uncertainties and Opportunities on Projects: Time for a Fundamental Shift. *International Journal of Project Management, 19*, 89–101.

JAMS. (2005). *The Situation and Subjects of Cost Design in Japanese Leading Companies*, Research Report to Japan Society for Promotion of Science, 2004–2005: Japanese Association of Management Researchers (JAMS).

JAMS. (2009). *The Situation and Subjects of Cost Design in Japanese Leading Companies*, 2008–9's Survey by JAMS.

Japan Environmental Management Association for Industry (2014). II B Environmental Management Accounting Text in Environmental Management Practical Course: http://www.meti.go.jp/policy/recycle/main/3r_policy/pdf/text_2.2.b.pdf.

Japan Times. (2004). Scandal-wracked Mitsubishi Motors Struggling to Survive, *Japan Times*, August 22.

Jia Jin-jing. (2016, June 6). Background of Zombie Enterprises: What Is True Causes, *Chinese Reform Forum*. http://Chinareform.org.cn/economy/Enterprise/Practice/201606/t201606_250397.htm.

Johnson, H. T. and Kaplan, R. S. (1987). *Relevance Lost; the Rise and Fall of Management*. Boston: Harvard Business School Press.

Johnson, L. T., Bullen, H. G., & Kern, V. W. (1994, January). Hedge Accounting: Is Deferral the Only Option? *Journal Accountancy, 177*(1), 53–58.

Kajihara, T., Park, K. Y., & Kato, Y. (2009). Environmentally Conscious Design and Cost Design: Preparatory Investigation on Survey Research. *Kokumin-Keizai Zasshi (Journal of National Economy), 199*(6), 11–28. Kobe University.

Kajüter, P. (2002). Proactive Cost Management in Supply Chains. In S. Seuring & M. Goldbach (Eds.) (ibid., 31–51).

Kaplan, R. S. (1984). The Evolution of Management Accounting. *The Accounting Review, 59*(3), 390–418.

Kaplan, R. S., & Cooper, R. (1998). *Cost and Effects: Using Integrated Cost Systems to Drive Profitability and Performance*. Boston: Harvard Business School Press.

Kaplan, R. S., & Norton, D. P. (1996). *The Balanced Scorecard: Translating Strategy into Action*. Boston: Harvard Business School Press.

Karame, M. (2004, May). Leading a Value-Based Management Implementation. *The Trusted Professional, 7*(8). http://www.nysscpa.org/trustedprof/504/tp15.htm.

Kato, Y. (1993a). Target Costing Support Systems: Lessons from Leading Japanese Companies. *Management Accounting Research, 4*, 37–47.

Kato, Y (1993b). *Cost Design: Strategic Cost Management*, Nikkei Newspaper Office.

Kato, N. (2010). Discussion on Impoverished Problems of Suppliers in Cost Design. *Oita University Economic Review, 62*(1), 23–49.

Kato, Y., Böer, G., & Chow, C. W. (1995). Target costing: An Integrative Management Process. *Journal of Cost Management, 9*(Spring), 39–51.

Kawada, M. (2003). Reconsideration on Product Management Accounting. *Meijo Review, 3*(4), 169–186.

Kawada, M. (2009). From *Profit* to *Profit Potential*: Redesign the Performance Indicator to Support Toyota Production System, *Contemporary Issues of Management and Accounting in the World Financial Crisis*. Proceedings of the 5th Asia-Pacific Management Forum in Japan, the Asia-Pacific Management Accounting Association.

Kawaller, I. G. (2002, September/October). Hedge Effectiveness Testing: Using Regression Analysis, *AFP Exchange, 22*(5), 62–68.

Kawaller, I. G. (2004, May/June). Ways to Test Hedge Effectiveness: Reconsidering Regression Analysis, *AFP Exchange, 24*(3), 62–63.

Kawaller, I. G., & Koch, P. D. (2013). Hedge Effectiveness Testing Revisited. *Journal of Derivatives, 21*(1, Fall), 83–94.

Kawamura, K. (2008). *The Growth and Problems of Cellular Phone Terminal Units Manufacturers in China*, http://www.jotsugakkaior.jp/doc/2006-6-25/25-E-Kawamura.pdf. Accessed 7 July 2008.

Kelly, L. (2013). CIOs Should Be Prepared for Broader Role in the Future, *Computer Weekly*, 30 July–5 August, pp. 22–25.

Kikukawa, T. (2007). Importance of Continual Public Relation Activities. *Business Research, 1*, 14–18.

Kim, K. S. (1995). *Chaebol and Corporate Governance in Korea* (pp. 47–49). Arbor: UMI Dissertation Services, a Bell & Howell Company.

Kim, S., & Collier, R. (2013). Risk and Risk Management in Management Accounting and Control. *Management Accounting Research, 24*(2), 82–87. https://doi.org/10.1016/j.mar.2013.04.003.

Kimura, K. (2010). Mobile Phone Handset Industry: Rapid Growth and Groping of Major Chinese Mobile Phone Manufacturers. In T. Marukawa & M. Yasumoto (Eds.), *The Evolution of Mobile Phone Industry: Why Japan Has Been Isolated in the World* (pp. 173–195). Japan: Yuhikaku Publisher.

Klovienė, L., & Gimžauskienė, E. (2014). Development of Accounting System According to the Information Technology. *Review Of Economic Studies and Research Virgil Madgearu, 2*, 59–74.

Knight, F. H. (1921). *Risk, Uncertainty and Profit*. Chicago: University of Chicago Press. Reprint version: Cosimo Classic, New York, 2005.

Kobayashi, T. (1993). *Current Costing Theory-Approach to Strategic Cost Management (in Japanese)*. Tokyo: Chuo Keizai Publisher.

Kobayashi, T. (1996). Life Cycle Cost and Cost Design. *Kokumin-Keizai Zasshi (Journal of National Economy), 173*(3), 1–13. Kobe University.

Kokubu, K., & Nakashima, M. (2003). Environmental Accounting in Ricoh Company. *Kokumin-Keizai Zasshi (Journal of National Economy), 188*(3), 41–56. Kobe University.

Konno, J., Yashima, K., & Mizunaga, K. (2008). Environmental Improvement Activities in Semiconductor Factories. *FUJITSU, 52*(2), 185–189.

Kornish, L. J., & Ulrich, K. T. (2011, January). Opportunity Spaces in Innovation: Empirical Analysis of Large Samples of Ideas. *Management Science, 57*(1), 107–128.

Kreuze, J. G., & Newell, G. E. (1994, February). ABC and Life-Cycle Costing for Environmental Expenditures. *Management Accounting, 75*(8), 38–42.

Kuita, T. (2009, June). 'Business Enterprise' and 'Businessmen's Viewpoint' in Veblen's Theory of Business Enterprise. *Artes Liberales, 84*, 103–125. Iwate University.

Kumarasinghe, S., & Willett, R. (2010). What Can Management Accounting Practitioners and Academics to Improve Risk Measurement and Foreworn Impending Financial Crises? *Asia-Pacific Management Accounting Journal, 5*(2), 1–10.

Kurogi, Ryo. (2001). Frank Knight's Conception of Entrepreneur and the Competitive Economic Order: The Significance of Risk, Uncertainty, and Profit (Japanese), *Annals of the Society for the History of Economic Thought*, The Japanese Society for the History of Economic Thought, *40*(November), 43–55.

Kurogi, Ryo. (2002). Homogeneities and Divergences between Veblen and Knight: On Their Theories of the Entrepreneur, *Annals of the Society for the History of Economic Though*, The Japanese Society for the History of Economic Thought, *42*(November), 71–83.

Kurosawa, H. (2016, April 12). The Prolongation of Zombie Enterprises Due to Speculative Buying Even After President Li's Expression of Overproduction Capacity Curtailment, *Economist* (Japan), *94*(16), 34–35. Mainich Shinbun Publishing Inc.

Kyosera. (2014, March). Annual Securities Report. *EDINET.*

Langlois, R. N. (2003). The Vanishing Hand: The Changing Dynamics of Industrial Capitalism. *Industrial and Corporate Change, 12*(2), 351–385.

Laurie, L. D., Doz, Y. L., & Sheer, C. P. (2006, May). Creating New Growth Platform. *Harvard Business Review*, pp. 80–90.

Lavastre, O., Gunasekaran, A., & Spalanzani, A. (2012). Supply Chain Risk Management in French Companies. *Decision Support Systems and Electronic Commerce, 52*, 828–838.

Leung, F., & Isaacs, F. (2008). Risk Management in Public Sector Research: Approach and Lessons Learned at a National Research Organization. *R&D Management, 38*(5), 510–519.

Li, C. (2007). Internationalization Strategy and International Standards in Chinese Communication and Information Firms. In S. Kawai (Ed.), *International Research on Interface and Institutional Innovation of Chinese Internationalization.*, Report of Japan Society for the Promotion of Science (pp. 17–60). Nagoya: Aichi University.

Li Peng-fei, & Wang Lei. (2016, January). New Challenges for Management in New Normality: Review of 2015 Annual Conference of Management in China (8th). *Chinese Journal of Management, 13*(1), 33–39.

Lichtenvort, K., Rebitzer, G., Huppes, G., Ciroth, A., Seuring, S., Schmidt, W-P., Günther, E., Hoppe, H., Swarr, T., & Hunkeler, D. (2008). History of Life Cycle Costing, Its Categorization, and Its Basic Framework, In D. Hunkeler, K. Lichtenvort & G. Rebitzer (ibid.)

Lim, M. (2011). Full Cost Accounting in Solid Waste Management: The Gap in the Literature on Newly Industrialized Countries. *Journal of Applied Management Accounting Research, 9*(1), 21–36.

Liu-Bao-xing. (2016). Over 3 Trillion Liabilities in Steel Industry: Some Listed Companies to Make Choice of Withdrawal from Markets, *Securities Time*, 20 October. http://www.Stcn.com/2016/0120/12554759shtml.

Liu Ji-shen. (2011). Enterprise Strategic Risk Management Under New Competitive Condition, 28 September, *Baidu Wenku*. www.wenku.baidu.com/view/b64f2290daofSef/baiBd3cba.html?frw=search&isbta=###.

Lockamy, A., & Smith, W. (2000). Target Costing for Supply Chain Management: Criteria And Selection. *Industrial Management+Data Systems, 100*(5), 210–218.

Lombardi, L. J. (2010). Monitoring Changes in Capital and Hedge Effectiveness Under Fair Value Accounting Principles. *North American Actuarial Journal, 14*(*1*), 1–15.

Malmi, T., & Ikäheimo, S. (2003). Value Based Management Practices – Some Evidence from the Field. *Management Accounting Research, 14*(3), 235–254.

March, J. G. (1991, February). Exploration and Exploitation in Organizational Learning. *Organizational Science, 2*(1), 71–87.

Marple, R. P. (1936). *Capital Surplus and Corporate Net Worth* (p. 7). New York: The Ronald Press.

Marukawa, T. (2009). Why Japanese Multinationals Failed in the Chinese Mobile Phone Market: A Comparative Study of New Product Development in Japan and China. *Asian Pacific Business Review, 15*(3), 411–431.

Marx, K. (1867). *Capital: A Critical Analysis of Capitalist Production, Volume 1.* Moscow: Foreign Language Publishing House.

Marx, K. (1965). *Das Kapital: Kritik de politischen Ökonomie*, Erster Band, Dietz Verlag Berlin (*Capital: A Critical Analysis of Capitalist Production*, Volume 1, Moscow: Foreign Languages Publishing House).

Matsumoto, A., & Fujisawa, T. (2016, September 13). Structural Reform as Pie in the Sky: Ten Industrial Sectors of Resolving New Overcapacity. *Economist* (Japan), *94*(34), 18–21. Mainich Shinbun Publishing Inc.

Matsumoto, A., & Nakagawa, M. (2016, April 12). Limitation of Arbitrary Reform: Outliving Zombie Enterprises. *Economist* (Japan), *94*(16), 18–21. Mainich Shinbun Publishing Inc.

McCarrol, J., & Khatri, G. R. (2014, April). Aligning Hedge Accounting with Risk Management. *Accounting Ireland, 46*(*2*), 36–38.

McKinsey, J. O. (1922). *Budgetary Control.* New York: The Ronald Press Company.

McKinsey, J. O. (1924). *Managerial Accounting.* Chicago: University of Chicago Press.

Mcmillan, C. J. (1984). Cost Information and Competitive Strategy: Lessons from Japan. In L. C. Rosen (Ed.), *Topics in Management Accounting* (3rd ed.), New Yorl: McGraw-Hill Ryerson.

Meng Jian-ming. (2010). *Speech in the Working Conference of Central Enterprises Internal Auditing*. xxgk.sasac.gov.cn/gdnps/content.jsp?id=1260973

Mercy, S. (2006). Failures Continue Evaluating Hedge Effectiveness, SEC Official Says. *Accounting Policy & Practice Report, 2*(25), 1–2.

METI. (2002). *Environmental Management Accounting (EMA) Workbook*. Tokyo: Japanese Ministry of Economy, Trade and Industry.

METI. (2008, June). *White Paper on Manufacturing Industry (Monotsukuri) in 2007*. Joint Project with Ministry of Health, Labor, and Welfare, and Ministry of Education, Culture, Sports, Science and Technology, pp. 18–45.

Metzger, L. (2009). Measuring Hedging Effectiveness for Derivatives. *The Journal of Government Financial Management, 58*(4, Winter), 48–53.

Mikes, A. (2011). From Counting Risk to Making Risk Count: Boundary-work in Risk Management. *Accounting, Organization and Society, 36*(4–5), 226–245.

Ministry of the Environment (1998). Law concerning the promotion of the measures to cope with warming: http://www.env.jo.jp/en/laws/global/warming.html.

Ministry of Finance (2008). Circular related to the Printing and Distribution of "Fundamental Standards of Enterprise Internal Control": http://www.mof.gov.cn/zhenwuxinxi/caizhengwengao/caizhenbuwengao2008/caizhenbuwengao200810/t20081030_86252.html.

Mitsubishi Electric Corporation. (2002). *Environmental Sustainability Report*.

Mitsubishi Electric Corporation. (2010). *Corporate Social Responsibility Environmental Report*.

Mitsuoka, S. (1981). *Opportunity Cost and Management Accounting (Japanese)*. Chuo-ku: Chikura Publisher.

Mizuho ISD. (2014). How Do We Consider Weak Yen' s Influences? *Mizuho Short Industry Focus, Oct. 120*, Industrial Survey Division (ISD) of Mizuho Corporate Bank, 1–5. http://www.mizuhobank.co.jp/corporate/bizinfo/industry/pdf/msif_120.pdf.

Mochizuki, K. (1995). Preface: Project Objective, In David H. Kaufman (Ed.), *Japanese Corporate Governance: A Comparative Study of Systems in Japan and the United States* (pp. ix, 15). New York: The Asian Institute.

Möller, K., & Svahm, S. (2006, July). Role of Knowledge in Value Creation in Business Nets. *Journal Management Studies, 43*(5), 994–989.

Molloy, S., & Schwenk, G. (1995). The Effects of Information Technology on Strategic Decision Making. *Journal of Management Studies, 32*(3), 284–311.

Monden, Y. (1994). *Toyota Production System: An Integrated Approach to Just-In-Time* (2nd ed.), Chapman and Hall, Foreword, London.

Monden, Y. (1999). Cost Design Schedule of Automobile Industry. In Y. Monden, K. Hamada, & K. Lee, (Ed.), *Japanese Cost Management* (pp. 115–127), in Japanese, Dobunkan Publisher.

Monden, Y. (2006). Business Value, Human Assets and Organizational Restructuring. In Y. Monden, K. Miyamoto, K. Hamad, G. Lee, & T. Asada (Eds.), *Value-Based Management of the Rising Sun* (pp. 3–4). Singapore: World Scientific Publishing.

Monden, Y., & Hamada, K. (1991). Target Costing and Kaizen Costing in Japanese Automobile Companies. *Journal of Management Accounting Research, 3*(Fall), 16–34.

Morgan, M. (1992). Feed Forward Control for Competitive Advantage: The Japanese Approach. *Journal of General Management, 17*(Summer), 41–52.

Morris, D. (2005). A New Tool for Strategy Analysis: The Opportunity Model. *Journal of Business Strategy, 25*(3), 50–56.

Murthy, U. S. (2016). Researching at the Intersection of Accounting and Information Technology: A Call for Action. *Journal of Information Systems, 30*(2), 159–167.

Nabeyama, T. (2011, September). Examination of Supply Chain Reconstruction after the Great East Japan Earthquake, *Joyo ARC*, AREA Research Center, pp. 6–11.

Nagaike, K. (2010, October). Rising Global Horizontal Integration Business Network Systems in Electronics Industry and Reorganization Strategies of Japanese Electronics Companies. *Journal of Strategic Management Studies, 2*(1), 29–37.

Nakajima, H. (2004). Treatment of Life Cycle Costs in Target Costing; A Review of Past Research and Examination of Unsettled Subjects. *Study of Business Management, 21*, 119–139.

Nakajima, H. (2011). *Life Cycle Costing: Development in UK*, Souse Publisher National Bureau of Statistic of China (2007), *China Statistical Year Book, 2007*, http://www.stats.gov.cn/tjsjlndsj/2007/indexeh.htm. Accessed 10 Aug 2008.

National Bureau of Statistic of China (2007). *China Statistical Year Book 2007*: http://www.stats.gov.cn/tjsj/2007/indexch.htm.

Naylor, B. J., Naim, M. M., & Berry, D. (1999). Legality: Integrating the Lean and Agile Manufacturing Paradigms in the Total Supply Chain. *International Journal of Production Economics, 62*, 107–118.

NEC. (2012). *Environmental Activity. Report, 2012*: http://www.nec.com/en/global/eco/product/eco_pro/index.html/. Accessed 19 Feb 2014.

NEC (Nippon Elctronic Corporation) (2017). *Annual Environmental Report*: http://www.nec.com/en/globa/eco/annual/index.html; *Environmental Accounting*: http://www.nec.com/en/global/eco/announce/accounting/calculate.html.

Negoro, T. (2008). *Universality and Speciality*. http://www.waseda.jp/negoro/SupplyChain/Dell_model.html.

Nikkei (Nihon Economic Newspaper). (2011a). *Japanese and Korean Cooperation for Development of Smartphone Semiconductors*, September 13.

Nikkei (Nihon Economic Newspaper). (2011b). *Komats Searches for Its Course* (1), September 13.

Nikkei (Nihon Economic Newspaper). (2011c). *Why Is Ink-jet Expensive?* December 12, 2011.

Nikkan Kogyo Shinbun. (2014, February 11). *Recall of the Two Types of Cars in Honda: Fit Hybrid Cars*, Daily Industry Newspaper, Ltd. http://www.nikkan.co.jp/. Accessed 22 Feb 2014.

Nikkei Venture. (2001). *Study on Bankruptcy*. Tokyo: Nikkei BP.

Nishimura, A. (1996). New Development of Japanese Management Accounting: From Cost Design to Strategic Cost Design. *Journal of Political Economy, 62(1–6)*, 241–251.

Nishimura, A. (2000). *Accounting Control and Management Accounting*, Dobunkan: Tokyo.

Nishimura, A. (2001). Feed Forward Cost Accounting and Strategic Management, *International Journal of Accounting Literature, 1*(2, 3 and 4), 117–136.

Nishimura, A. (2003). *Management Accounting in Asia: feed forward and Asian perspectives*. Hampshire: Palgrave Macmillan.

Nishimura, A. (2005). Strategic Management and Contemporary Management Accounting. In A. Nishimura & R. Willett (Eds.), *Management Accounting in Asia* (pp. 1–8). Singapore: Thomson Learning. (A division of Thomson Asia Pte Ltd.).

Nishimura, A. (2006a). Enterprise Governance and Management Accounting from the Viewpoint of Feed Forward Control. *Asian-Pacific Management Accounting Journal, 1*(1), 1–17. Public Knowledge Project (Open Journal System). http://arionline.uitm.edu.my/ojs/index.php/APMAJ/issue/view/20.

Nishimura, A. (2006b). Analysis of Industrial Structure and Profitable Structure in China; Recent Development and Problems Chinese State-owned Enterprises: Structures of Industry and Deficit. *Business Administration and Management Accounting in Asia* (pp. 257–279 and 311–334), Tokyo: Chuou Keizai Publisher.

Nishimura, A. (2006c). *Business Management and Management Accounting in Asia (Japanese)*. Tokyo: Chuokeizai Publisher.

Nishimura, A. (2007). Conceptual Analysis of Value-based Management and Accounting: with Reference to Japanese Practices. *Asian-Pacific Management Accounting Journal, 2*(1), 71–87. Public Knowledge Project (Open Journal System). http://arionline.uitm.edu.my/ojs/index.php/APMAJ/issue/view/54.

Nishimura, A. (2008). Effect of Management System on Management Accounting: The Case of Chinese Cellular Phone Terminal Unit Manufacturers. *Asian-Pacific Management Accounting Journal, 3*(1), 87–105. Public Knowledge Project (Open Journal System). http://arionline.uitm.edu.my/ojs/index.php/APMAJ/issue/view/18.

Nishimura, A. (2011). Uncertainty and Management Accounting: Opportunity, Profit Opportunity and Profit. *Asia-Pacific Management Accounting Journal, 6*(1), 81–101. Public Knowledge Project (Open Journal System). http://arionline.uitm.edu.my/ojs/index.php/APMAJ/issue/view/13.

Nishimura, A. (2012). Profit Opportunity, Feed Forward Innovation, and Management Accounting. *Asian-Pacific Management Accounting Journal, 7*(2), 65–98. Public Knowledge Project (Open Journal System). http://arionline.uitm.edu.my/ojs/index.php/APMAJ/issue/view/12.

Nishimura, A. (2014). Transforming Cost Design Into Environmentally Conscious Cost Design in Japan: Likelihood and Problems for Further Development. *Journal of Management Control, 25*(*1*), 55–75. https://doi.org/10.1007/s00187-014-0190-x.

Nishimura, A. (2015a). Comprehensive Opportunity and Lost Opportunity Control Model and Enterprise Risk Management. *International Journal of Business and Management, 10*(*8*), 73–87. https://doi.org/10.5539/ijbm.v10n8p73.

Nishimura, A. (2015b). Strategic Management Accounting and Feed-forward Management: With Reference to the Unified Management of Profit Opportunity and Risk, *Global Management, 3 & 4 (combined)*, 1–19

Nishimura, A. (2016). Foreign Exchange Risk and Profit Improvement in the Comprehensive Profit Opportunity and Lost Opportunity Control Model. *International Journal of Business and Management, 11*(*4*), 1–13.

Nishimura, A., & Hirai, K. (1983, December). New Development of Profit Variance Analysis on a Linear Programming Model. *Business Accounting, 35*(3), 113–127.

Nishimura, A., & Willett, R. (1997). Structures and Features of Japanese Accounting. In N. Baydoun, A. Nishimura, & R. Willett (Eds.), *Accounting in the Asia-Pacific Region*. Singapore: John Wiley & Sons (Asia) Pte Ltd.

Nishimura, A., & Willett, R. (Eds.). (2005). *Management Accounting in Asia*. Malaysia: Thomson Learning. (A division of Thomson Asia Pte Ltd.).

Niyama, Y. (2001). *Dispute on Corporate Governance. Study Meeting of Business and Law Affairs*. Japan: Tokyo.

Olsen, E. (2002). Rethinking Value-Based Management. *Handbook of Business Strategy*. http://w.w.w.bcg.com/publications/files/Rethinking-Value-Based-Mgmt-Sept-02pdf.

Orita, Y. (2012). The Whole Company's Improvement Process of Cost Management, Reexamination of Management Accounting for Manufacturing, *Report in the Third Forum* (December 8, Tokyo), Japanese Association of Management Accounting.

Oshita, J. (2012, December). Paradox of Control and Management Accounting. *Annual Report of Economics Science, Kyushu Association of Economic Science, 50*, 19–31.

Otsuka, T., & Ichikawa, Y. (2011). How Is Japanese Supply Chain Judged? *Mizuho Research Institute Review, 3*, 1–9.

PAIB. (2004). *Enterprise Governance: Getting the Balance Rights*. New York/ London: IFAC/CIMA.

Pan Cheng-lie. (2000). Carefully Prepared Plan for Enterprise Future. *Enterprise management, 2*, 5–6.

Panasonic Corporation. (2014). *Sustainability Report, 2014*, 20–25. http://www.panasonic.com.jp/corporate/sustainability/downloads/back_number/pdf/2014/sr2014j.pdf.

Panasonic Corporation. (2015). *Annual Securities Report*. http://www.kabupro.jp/mark/2015626/S100562ZF.htm.

Panasonic Corporation. (2017). *Sustainability Data Book 2017*: http://www.panasonic.com/global/corporate/sustainability/pdf/sdb2017e-2.pdf.

Papa, V. T., & Peters, S. J. (2011). User Perspectives on Financial Instruments Risk Disclosure under International Financial Reporting Standards (IFRS): http://www.cfainstitute.org/ethics/Documents/financial_instruments_risk_disclosure_report_volume_1.pdf.

Park, K. P. (2007, March). Subjects on Environmental Conscious Development. *Economic Review, 79*(4), 87–108. Kagawa University.

Park, K. P. (2009). Fact Finding of Environmental Conscious Product Issues. *Research Report, 49*, 73–93.

Parker, L. D. (2000). Green Strategy Costing: Early Days. *Australian Accounting Review, 10*(1), 46–55.

PC3R Promotion Association. (2014). Guideline of PC3R Promotion Association. http://www.pc3r.jp/association/index.html/. Accessed 14 Mar 2014.

Pen Da-long, Ge Jiang, & Wang Lei. (2017, June). Management Theory Innovation in the New Competition Environment: Review on 2016 Annual Conference on Management in China (9th). *Chinese Journal of Management, 14*(6), 806–813.

Phillips, S. M. (1995). Derivatives and Risk Management: Challenges and Opportunities. *Northwestern Journal of International Law & Business, 15*(2), 239–247.

Pondeville, S., Swan, V., & Rongé, Y. D. (2012). Environmental Management Control Systems: The Role of Contextual and Strategic Factors. *Management Accounting Research, 24*(4), 317–332.

Porter, M. E. (1985). *Competitive Advantage, Creating and Sustaining Superior Performance*. New York: Free Press, a Division of Simon and Schuster, Inc.

Porter, M. E. (1998). *On Competition, Harvard Business Review Book Series*. Boston: Harvard Business School.

Porter, M. E., & Kramer, R. M. (2007). Strategy & Society: The Link Between Competitive Advantage and Corporate Social Responsibility. *Harvard Business Review*, January, *84*(12), 78–92.

Powely, H. E., & Taylor, N. S. (2006). Values and Leadership in Organizational Crisis. In H. D. Edward & K. S. Cameron (Eds.), *Leading with Values.* New York: Cambridge University Press.

Power, M. (2007). *Organized Uncertainty: Designing a World of Risk Management.* New York: Oxford University, Press.

PricewaterhouseCoopers. (2014a). Big Four Blind Points of Enterprises Risk Management to Effectively Avoid Risks, *Chief Finance Officer*, 19 November.

PricewaterhouseCoopers. (2014b). Four Mistakes for Effective Evasion of Risk Management, *Chief Finance Office*, 11 November. http://topcfo.net/index.php/news/index/id/38752.html.

Prickett, R. (2004, March). Up the Right Tree. *Financial Management, 33*(1), 12.

Rappaport, A. (2006, September). Ways to Create Shareholder Value. *Harvard Business Review*, pp. 67–77.

Rasid, S. Z., Isa, C. R., & Ismail, W. K. W. (2014). Management Accounting Systems, Enterprise Risk Management and Organizational Performance in Financial Institutions. *Asian Review of Accounting, 22*(2), 128–144. https://doi.org/10.1108/ARA-03-2013-0022.

Rebitzer, G. (2010). Integrating Life Cycle Costing and Life Cycle Assessment for Manufacturing Costs and Environmental Impacts in Supply Chains. In S. Seuring, & M. Goldbach (Eds.) (ibid., 127–146).

Reuer, J. J., & Tong, T. W. (2010, January–February). Discovering Valuable Growth, Opportunities: An Analysis of Equity Alliances with IPO Firms. *Organization Science, 21*(1), 201–215.

Richardson, J. G. (2009). Uncertainty, the Critical Basis of Risk Management. *Foresight, 11*(6), 42–56.

Richardson, J. G. (2010). The Certainty of Uncertainty: Risk Management Revisited. *Foresight, 12*(4), 49–64.

Rimienè, K. (2011). Supply Chain Agility Concept Evolution (1990–2010). *Economics and Management, 16*, 892–899.

Road Transport Bureau. (2013). *The Analyzed Results of Contents Notified as Recall of Cars*, Road Transport Bureau, Japanese Ministry of Land, Infrastructure, Transportation and Tourism, April 19.

Russell-Jones, M. (2014, March). Financial Risk Management: Derivatives. *Governance Directions, 33*(1), 81–84.

Sakai, Y. (2012). The Economic Thought of Frank Knight: With Special Reference to Risk and Uncertainty, *CRR Discussion Paper*, Shiga University, No. J-19, 1–26. http://hdl.handle.net/10441/9743.

Sakamaki, H. (2007). Digging Out Profit Through Elimination of Waste. *Business Research, 1*, 33–40.

Sakamoto, H. (2007). China, Recent Trends and Prospects for Major Asian Economics. *East Asian Economic Perspectives, 18*(1), 27–38. February (Special Issue).

Sakata, J. (2016). Analytical Study on Strategic Use of Information System and the Depth of Chief Information Officer's Competence. *The Journal of J.F. Oberlin University Business Management Review, 7*, 23–47.

Sakurai, M. (1989). Target Costing and How to Use It. *Journal of Cost Management*, (Summer), *2*, 39–50.

Sakurai, M. (1991). *Change in Business Environment and Management Accounting*. Tokyo: Dobunkan Publisher.

Samuels, J. M. (1965). Opportunity Costing. *Journal of Accounting Research, 3*(2), 182–191.

Sarkis, J. (1995). Manufacturing Strategy and Environmental Consciousness. *Technovation, 15*(2), 79–97.

SASAC Document (2006). Circular related to the Printing and Distribution of Guidlines of Comprehensive Risk Management for Central Enterprises: http://www.xxgk.sasac.gov.cn/gdnps/content.jsp?id=1319184.

SASAC General Office (2009). Notification related to the 2010's Comprehensive Enterprise Risk Management Report in Central Enterprises: http://www.xxgk.sasac.gov.cn/gdnps/content.jsp?id=1262589.

SASAC General Office (2012). Notification of related Matters for Central Enterprises to Comprehensively Develop Risk Management Activities in 2013: http://www.xxgk.sasac.gov.cn/gdnps/content.jsp?id=1261301.

Sato, Y. (2009). The Soul of Cost Design (1): *Nikkei Monotsukuri (Manufacturing)*, September, 113–116.

Sawhney, M., Wolcott, R. C., & Arroniz, I. (2006). The 12 Different Ways for Companies to Innovate, *MIT Sloan Management Review*, Winter (ibid., 28–34).

Scapens, R. W. (1991). *Management Accounting: A Review of Contemporary Developments* (2nd ed.). London: Macmillan Education Ltd.

Scapens, W. R. (2006). Changing Times: Management Accounting Research and Practices from a UK Perspective. In A. Bhimani (Ed.), *Contemporary Issues in Management Accounting* (pp. 329–354). Oxford: Oxford University Press.

Schneier, R., & Miccolis, J. (1998). Enterprise Risk Management. *Strategy & Leadership, 26*(2), 10–16.

Scholes, M. S. (2000). Crisis and Risk Management (the Near Crash of 1998). *The American Economic Review, 90*(2), 17–21.

Seal, W. (2006a). Management Accounting and Corporate Governance: An Institutional Interpretation of the Agency Theory. *Management Accounting Research, 17*(4), 389–408.

Seal, W. (2006b). Management Accounting and Corporate Governance: An Institutional Interpretation of the Agency Theory. *Management Accounting Research, 17*(4), 389–408.

Seiko-Epson Corporation. (2012), *Annual Securities Report*. www.epson.jp/IR/library/yuho/yuho-bbn.htm.

Seki, S. (2016, April 12). The Rapid Increase of Bad Debits: Ten Trillion Yuan Including the Bad Debits of Shadow Banks and Anxious Forbearance Lending to State-owned Enterprises. *Economist* (Japan), *94*(16), 32–33. Mainich Shinbun Publishing Inc.

Seuring, S. (2004). Industrial Ecology, Life Cycles, Supply Chains: Differences and Interrelations. *Business Strategy and the Environment, 13*, 306–319.

Seuring, S. (2010). Supply Chain Target Costing: An Apparel Industry Case Study. In S. Seuring & M. Goldbach, (Eds.) (ibid., 111–125).

Shane, S. (2000, July–August). Prior Knowledge and the Discovery of Entrepreneurial Opportunities. *Organization Science, 11*(4), 448–469.

Shank, J. K., & Fisher, J. (1999). Case Study Target Costing as a Strategic Tool. *MIT Sloan Management Review, 41*(Fall), 73–82.

Shank, J. K., & Govindarajan, V. (1993). *Strategic Cost Management: The New Tool for Competitive Advantage*. New York: Free Press, A Division Simon and Schuster, Inc.

Shank, J. K., & Miguel, J. G. (2009, January/February). Merging Financial and Managerial Accounting, Strategic Cost Management and Enterprise Risk Assessment Under SOX, *The Journal of Corporate Accounting & Finance, 20*, 83–99.

Shao Yong Yu. (2015). Present Situations and Prospects of Expanding Chinese Overseas Direct Investments, *Mizuho China Monthly*, May, pp. 3–5.

Sharp Corporation (2011). *Environmental and Social Report*: http://www.Sharp.world.com/eco/report/backnumber/pdf/esr2011e.pdf.

Sharif, H., & Zhang, Z. (1999). A Methodology for Achieving Agility in Manufacturing Organizations: An Introduction. *International Journal of Production Economics, 62*, 7–22.

Shen Long Automobile Limited Liability Company (Dongfeng Peugeot/Citroen Company Ltd.) (2015). Enterprise Risk Management in Supply Chain, *Enterprise Management*, No. 6, 55–59.

Siegel, J. G., & Skim, J. K. (2000). *Dictionary of Accounting Terms* (3rd ed.). Hauppauge: Barron's Educational Series, Inc.

Simanis, E., & Hart, S. (2009). Innovation from the Inside Out, *MIT Sloan Management Review*, Summer (ibid., 9–18)

Simon, H. A. (1969). *The New Science of Management Decision*. New York/Evanston: Herper & Row, Publishers.

Simons, R. (1995). *Levers of Control: How Managers Use Innovative Control Systems to Drive Strategic Renewal*. Boston: Harvard Business School Press.

Sipko, J. (2011). Derivatives and the Real Economy. *Creative and Knowledge Society/Industrial Specific Journal, 1*(*1*), 33–43. https://doi.org/10.2478/10212-011-0003-7.

Smistad, R., & Pustylnick, J. (2012). Hedging, Hedge Accounting and Speculation: Evidence from Canadian Oil and gas Companies. *Global Journal of Business Research, 6*(*3*), 49–62.

Smith, A. (1776). *An Inquiry into the Nature and Causes of the Wealth of Nations,* The Modern Library (reprinted in 1937), 423, New York.

Smith, P. G., & Merritt, G. M. (2002). *Proactive Risk Management: Controlling Uncertainty in Product Management.* New York. Productivity Press.

Society for Study of Risk Management and Internal Control. (2003). *Internal Control in the New Age of Risks.* Tokyo: The Japanese Ministry of Economy and Industry.

Solomon, J., & Solomon, A. (2004). *Corporate Governance and Accountability* (pp. 169, 177, 179 and 181). West Sussex: John Wileys and Sons.

Sommer, S. C., & Loch, C. H. (2004, October). Selectionism and Learning in Projects with Complexity and Unforeseeable Uncertainty. *Management Science, 50*(10), 1334–1347.

Sommer, S. C., Loch, C. H., & Dong, J. (2009, January–February). Managing Complexity and Unforeseeable Uncertainty in Startup Companies: An Empirical Study. *Organization Science, 20*(1), 118–133.

Song Li Shui. (2016). How Do We Grasp Chinese Economy in the New Normality? *The Meiji-Gakuin Review: The Papers and Proceedings of Economics, 151*, 13–28.

Sony Corporation. (2001). *Environmental Report 2001: Entertaining the World, Caring for the Future.* http://www.sony.co.jp//SonyInfo/csr_report//2001/qfhh7c00000d76pv_att/copy_of_2001_all.pdf. Accessed 15 Aug 2013.

Sony Corporation. (2014). *Annual Securities Report*, June, EDINET.

Sony Corporation. (2017). *Sony CSR Report.* Retrieved from Sony.co.jp/SonyInfo/csr-report/issues.

Special Article. (2000, December). Risk Management in the New Day of Information Technology. *Nikkei Strategy*, 26–46.

Special Issue. (2007). Work Visualization and Workshop Improvement. *Nikkei Research, 4*, 19–47.

Special Report. (2003). The Leadership: Challenge 2003, *Strategys+Business*, pp. 49–50.

Steen, B. (2005). Environmental Costs and Benefits in Life Cycle Costing. *Management of Environment Quality, 16*(2), 107–118.

Stockstrom, C., & Herstatt, C. (2008). Planning and Uncertainty in New Product Development. *R&D Management, 38*(5), 480–490.

Stuart, I., & Stuart, B. (2004). *Ethics in the Post-Enron Age.* Cincinnati: Thomson South-Western College Pub.

Sumida Group. (2012). *Guideline for Green Procurement*, July, Sumida Corporation.

Sun Chang-qi. (2003). Four Blind Areas of Strategic Management. *Enterprise Management, 9*, 25–28.

Swarr, T., & Hunkeler, D. (2008). Life Cycle Costing in Life Cycle Management. In D. Hunkeler, K. Lichtenvort & G. Rebitzer (Eds.) (Ibid., pp. 77–90).

Taka, T. (2005). Veblen's Theory of Evolution and the Instinct of Workmanship: An Ethological and Biological Reinterpretation. *The History of Economic*

Thought, 47(2), 32–44. The Society for the History of Economic Thought, Japan.

Tan, Y., & Floros, C. (2014). Risk, Profitability, and Competition: Evidence from the Chinese banking Industry. *Journal of Developing Areas, 48*(3, Summer), 303–319.

Tanaka, M. (1985, July/August). New Approach to the Function Evaluation System in Value Engineering, *International Journal of Production Research, 23*(4), 625–638.

Tanaka, T. (Ed.). (1991). *Contemporary Management Accounting System*. Japan: Chuou-keizaisha.

Tanaka, T. (1992). *Field-Study: Contemporary Management Accounting System*. Tokyo: Chuo-keizaisha Publisher, Co.

Tanaka, T. (1993). Target Costing at Toyota, *Journal of Cost Management*, Spring, 4–11.

Tanaka, M. (1995). *Theory and Practices of Cost Design*. Tokyo: Chuo-keizaisha Publisher, Co.

Tanaka, M. (2002). *Profit Strategy and Value Engineering: How to Implement Practical Cost Design*. Tokyo: Sangyo Noritu University Publisher.

Tanaka, M. (2008). Report on Practical Improvement of Accounting for Manufacturing: Practices of J Cost Theory, *MMRC Discussion Paper*, No. 208, Manufacturing Management Research Center, Tokyo University.

Tanaka, M. (2009). *Accounting of Toyota Type of Improvement (Kaizen)*. Tokyo: Chukei Publisher.

Tanaka, M. (Ed.). (2015). *Cost Design and the Development Strategy of Purchasing*. Tokyo: Chuokeizai Publisher.

Tanaka, M., Ishizaki, T., & Harada, N., eds. (2006). *Accounting for Performance Evaluation: The Development of Plural and Various Evaluations*, Chou-Keizaisha, 22–29.

Tang, O., Matsukawa, H., & Nakashima, K. (2012). Supply Chain Risk Management. *International Journal of production Economics, 139*(1), 1–2.

Tani, T. (1994). Interactive Control in Cost Design: Significance. *The Kokumin-Keizai Zasshi (Journal of National Economy), 169*(4), 19–38. Kobe University.

Tani, T. (1995). Interactive Control in Target Cost Management. *Management Accounting Research, 6*, 399–414.

Tani, T., Okano, H., Shimizu, N., Iwabuch, Y., Fukuda, J., & Cooray, S. (1994). Target Costing Management in Japanese Companies: Current State of the Art. *Management Accounting Research, 5*, 67–81.

Taylor, F. W. (1911). *The Principles of Scientific Management*. New York/London: Harper & Brothers Publishers. (Reprinted version: Martino Publishing, Mansfield Centre, CT, 2014).

The Nikkei. (2014, February 12). Recall of 1.9 Million Hybrid Cars in Toyota in Japan and Abroad, *Nihon Keizai Shinbun* (Japan Economy Newspaper) Inc.

http://www.nikkei.com/article/DGXNASDG1203y_SaA210CR8000/. Accessed 22 Feb 2014.

The Wall Street Journal (2010, March 5). Japanese Version. http://jp.wsj.com/layout/set/print/Business-companies/Autos/node_26986.

Thun, J., & Hoenig, D. (2011). An Empirical Analysis of Supply Chain Risk Management in the German Automotive Industry. *International Journal of Production Economics, 131*, 242–249.

Toshiba Group. (2013). *2013 Environmental Report.* http://www.toshiba.com/csr/docs/env_report13_all.pdf. Accessed 10 Jun 2014.

Toyota Industries Corporation. (2015). *Annul Securities Report.* http://www.kabupro.jp/mark/20150611/S1004VXD.htm.

Toyota Motor Co. (2016). Toyota, Acceleration of "Connected Technologies", *Toyota Global News*, 4 January, http://newsroom.toyota.co.jp/jp/detail/10140379/.

Toyota Motor Corporation. (2011). *Toyota Green Purchasing Guidelines*, December.

Toyota Motor Corporation. (2013). *Report for the Planet: Toyota's Environmental Initiatives*, 22–23.

Toyota Motor Corporation. (2015). *Annual Securities Report.* http://www.kabupro.jp/mark/20150624/S1005156.htm.

TRC. (2004). *The Definitive and Digestible Book on Risk Management: The Newest Version.* Tokyo: Tokio Marine Risk Consulting, Co. Ltd.

Ueno, S. (2007). *Management Accounting for Value Creation*, 3rd ed. Zeimukeirikyoukai.

Ueno, T., & Aoyama, S. (2011). Influences of Strong Yen on Enterprise Management: Findings of Questionnaire Research by Nissay Co. in January, *NLI Research Institute Report*, April, 16–21.

Veblen, T. (1898, September). The Instinct of Workmanship and the Irksomeness of Labor. *American Journal of Sociology, 4*(2), 187–201.

Veblen, T. (1904). *The Theory of Business Enterprise.* New York: Charles Scribner's Sons. (Reprinted Version: Martino Publishing, Mansfield Centre, CT, 2013).

Wang Jing-Feng, Li Dong-Mei, & Zhang Tong-Quan. (2012). Study on Enterprise Practices of Risk Assessment: Based on Experiences of A Coal Mine in a Certain Coal Industry Limited Liability Company. *Auditing Research, 4*, 89–96.

Wang Min. (2014). Strategic Thinking on the Information Orientation of Risk Control Management Implemented by Central Enterprises. *Contemporary Economic Management, 36*(2), 36–39.

Wang Xiao-xia. (2010). Responsibility and Target Structure of State-owned Enterprise Risk Management Auditing, *Auditing Research, Third issue*, pp. 54–58.

Wang Yi. (2002). Present Situation and Future Analysis of Chinese Enterprise Strategic Management Development. *Global Management Research, 11*, 43–46.

Weick, E. K. (2006). The role of values in high-risk organizations, In H. D. Edward & K. S. Cameron (Eds.). *Leading with Values: Positivity, Virtue and High Performance*, 55–67, Cambridge/New York: Cambridge University press.

Woods, M. (2008). Linking Risk Management to Strategic Controls: A Case Study of Tesco plc. *International Journal of Risk Assessment & Management, 7*(*8*), 1074–1088.

Worline, M., & Boik, S. (2006). Leadership Lessons from Sarah: Values-Based Leadership as Everyday Practice. In D. Edward & K. S. Cameron (Eds.) (ibid., 108–131).

Xu J, & Imai, K. (2007). Market Size and Industrial Heightening: The Case of Local Cellular Phone Industry. In K. Imai & K. Ting (Eds.), *Tide of Heightening in China: Changes of Industry and Enterprise* (pp. 7–44). Tokyo: Asian Economic Research Institute.

Xu Hui, Zou Hui-min, & Wang Jian-Ming. (2009). Risk Classification and Cognition of Multinational Companies under Globalized Strategic Transformation. *Economic Management Journal, 30*(*9*), 142–150.

Yamaha Motor Co. Ltd. (2015). *Annual Securities Report*. http://www.kabupro.jp/mark/2015327/S1004DPT.htm.

Yamamoto, K., & Kokubu, K. (2001). *Environmental Management in IBM*. Tokyo: Toyo Keizai Inc.

Yang Hao-Hui, & Song Zhi-Cai. (2014). Research Study on the Business Situations of State-owned Enterprises. *New Wisdom, 9*, 23–26.

Yagi, K., Araki, H., and Akiyama, K. (2009). Support Systems for Front Loading of Target Cost Management, *Panasoni Work's Technical Report*, September, 57(3), 76ff.

Yin Chong. (2015). Rising and Development of Dynamic Risk Management Accounting. *The Chinese Certificated Public Accountant Journal, 4*, 57–60.

Yoshida, E., Fukushima, K., & Senoo, T. (2012). *Studies of Japanese Management Accounting*, Chuo Keizaisha.

Yoshikawa, T. (1994). Some Aspects of the Japanese Approach to Management Accounting. *Management Accounting Research, 5*, 279–287.

Yuan Lin & Zhang Hong-liang. (2011). Board of Directors' Governance and the Risk Management of Finance company. *Accounting Research, 5*, 65–71.

Yuan Lin & Zhang Wei-hua. (2015). Management Control of Group Company and the Risk Management of Finance Company. *Accounting Research, 5*, 35–41.

Zhang Jian-she. (2004). Missed Strategy or Lost Management? *Enterprise Management, 11*, 28–30.

ZTE Corporation Annual Report. (2004, 2006, 2007, 2008, 2010, 2012, 2014). http://zte.com.cn/global/about/investorrelations/corporate_report/Annual_report.

Index[1]

[1] Note: Page numbers followed by 'n' refer to notes.

A. Nishimura, *Management, Uncertainty, and Accounting*,
https://doi.org/10.1007/978-981-10-8989-3

FSC
www.fsc.org
MIX
Papier | Fördert
gute Waldnutzung
FSC® C083411

Kolibri 360 GmbH
Ferdinand-Jühlke-Straße 7
99095 Erfurt, Deutschland
produktsicherheit@kolibri360.de